OUTRAGEOUS FORTUNES

OUTRAGEOUS FORTUNES

MEDIA BILLIONAIRES AND HOW THEY CHANGE WORLD CULTURE

BY ROD AND ALMA HOLMGREN

JACKSON PRESS

For information write:
Jackson Press
3398 Taylor Road
Carmel, California 93923

Book Design by Tim Sachak, Hartmann Design Group, Carmel, CA

Cataloguing-in-Publication Data

Holmgren, Rod.

Outrageous fortunes: media billionaires and how they
change world culture / Rod Holmgren, Alma Holmgren; -Carmel, CA
: Jackson Press, 2001.

p. ; cm.

ISBN: 0-971 3929-0-0

1. Mass media and culture; 2. Mass media-Social aspects;

3. Mass media-influence, 4. Billionaires, I. Holmgren, Alma. II. Title.

P94.6.H65 2001 2001094782

302.2308 -dc21 CIP

First Edition

10 9 8 7 6 5 4 3 2 1

ACKNOWLEDGMENTS

We are indebted to the many friends and family members who cheered us on our way to create this book. We are especially indebted to Ben Bagdikian, Karlyn Barker, Roberta Bialek, Ed Bishop of the St. Louis Journalism Review, Pierre Denain, William Dorman, Connie Eckert, Riane Eisler and David Loye, Sam Feldman, Mildred Hamilton, Alice McGhee, Frank McGovern, Maggie Murphy, Paul D. and Katie Oberst, Mark Pinsky, Margaret Ralston, Elliot Roberts, Jerry and Pat Werthimer, Robert H. Wood, and the librarians at the Monterey Institute of International Studies, the Monterey City Library, Seaside Library, and the University of California-Berkeley Library.

CONTENTS

INTRODUCTION

One way to visualize the meaning of "billionaire" is to place two stacks of $1,000 bills side by side. One, eight inches tall, is $1 million.

The other, $1 billion, rises 555 feet, as tall as the Washington Monument!

In the late twentieth century, ownership in the media was an open door to huge fortunes, just as control of the oil and steel industries was in the late nineteenth century. As he neared retirement from the presidency in 1959, Dwight Eisenhower warned the country about the dangers of "the military-industrial complex." Today we face the information-entertainment complex. The ninth largest American industry is communications, and it is the fourth fastest growing industry in the country, growing at 10 percent a year.

As the media have played a larger and larger role in our economy, their owners' hunger for profit has led to increased emphasis on advertising and marketing, almost always at the expense of quality content. This emphasis eclipses that of the press lords in the first half of the 20th century, partly because many of the moguls have come from fields other than the media. Two major networks -- NBC and CBS -- were owned in the late 20th century by the power companies General Electric and Westinghouse, respectively. Michael Armstrong of AT&T controlled the country's biggest cable network, TCI; and John Malone, who had been in charge of TCI, was called "Pa Bell" because he owned a huge chunk of AT&T stock.

Earlier press lords thought of their occupation as public service; today's moguls think of their occupation as business, and business is good. Not only have the moguls developed extremely effective methods of marketing and advertising, but where Hearst and Scripps operated inside America's borders, today's titans -- AOL-Time Warner, Viacom-Paramount-CBS, News Corporation, and now Vivendi-Universal-PolyGram -- all have global reach. The media's share of America's GNP (gross national product) has risen dramatically since World War II.

Billionaires, specifically multi-media billionaires, are the subject of this book. As key shapers of American society and culture, even world culture, these multi-media moguls — the 31 American and 17 foreign billionaires, including the billionaire families, profiled here — control enormous, highly diversified conglomerates, some of them started many years ago and some created by multi-billion dollar mergers and buyouts starting as recently as 1985.

These transactions included the merger of American Broadcasting Company (ABC) with the Capital Cities newspaper chain in 1985; the buyout of Columbia Broadcasting System (CBS) by theater-chain owner Lawrence Tisch, also in 1985; the purchase of 20th Century-Fox Studios by Rupert Murdoch; and — at the end of the decade — the merger of the *Time* empire with Warner Studios to form Time-Warner, the largest media colossus in the world. Throughout the decade, John Malone of Telecommunications Inc. (TCI) was buying one cable network after another.

The merger frenzy accelerated in the mid-'90s, with Time-Warner buying the Ted Turner empire to form Time-Warner-Turner; Westinghouse buying CBS from Tisch; Sumner Redstone's Viacom buying Paramount Studios; Disney Studios taking over ABC; and AT&T buying TCI. To round out the decade in 1999, Redstone bought the CBS Network to add to his already-huge Viacom Blockbuster-Paramount empire.

"Combine or die is the theory now driving the media business," Max Frankel commented in a *New York Times Magazine* article.[1] To that journalism professor Leo Bogart added, "Entertainment increasingly overshadows information, blurring the difference between what is real and what is not."[2]

As the new century began, a new kind of merger came when America Online's Steve Case embraced Time Warner's Gerald Levin to celebrate the January 11 marriage of the world's largest "new media" company with the world's largest "old media" conglomerate. Case, pictured on covers of four major news-magazines, instantly joined the company of multi-media billionaires. That event was followed six months later, when French conglomerate Vivendi merged with Edgar Bronfman Jr.'s Seagram-Universal-Polygram to form another immense international combination.

Among the best-known American media billionaires are Rupert Murdoch, Sumner Redstone, Ted Turner, John Malone, Warren Buffett, Edgar Bronfman Jr., Steven Spielberg and his DreamWorks partner David Geffen, animation genius George Lucas, Michael Bloomberg, and the Newhouse brothers, Simon and Donald. However, two of those who run giant empires, Gerald Levin of Time Warner and Michael Eisner of Disney-ABC, haven't joined billionaire ranks yet. But a Disney-ABC magnate who has just joined those ranks is Roy E. Disney, nephew of founder Walt, who runs the huge animation operations of Disney Studios.

Equally famous are those listed by the *Forbes 400* under "families": Hearst, Cox, Pulitzer, Chandler, Graham, McGraw, and E.W. Scripps. Almost all members of these families clip coupons, and some of the younger ones work in fields other than media. Only the Graham, Cox, Pulitzer and McGraw families still have members in the management of their empires. The CEOs who run the family conglomerates know the bottom line is what counts to members of the owner families.

Probably the best known billionaire of all is the country's richest man, cybernerd Bill Gates, who has started a round-the-clock news operation — MSNBC — and an Internet magazine, *Slate*. His vast Microsoft empire is clearly part of the media since it brings both information and entertainment to a huge, rapidly growing audience.

Paul Allen, who co-founded Microsoft and still has a major stake in it, has added $660 million to the DreamWorks war chest of Spielberg, Katzenberg and Geffen; has invested in some 140 media companies; and owns the fourth largest number of cable channels in the U.S.   Another cybernerd in the billionaire group is Patrick McGovern, who publishes magazines and the popular books "for dummies."

McGovern is not well-known, nor are John Werner Kluge, who owns TV and radio stations and movie studios; Edward Gaylord, who presides over newspaper and entertainment properties; Kirk Kerkorian, who owns MGM Studios; Mortimer Zuckerman, with a newspaper and a big name magazine; the Cox sisters, whose media empire is centered in Atlanta; and Lowry Mays, whose radio and TV stations stretch around the world.

All over the world, the number of media billionaires grows. In Europe, England has Richard Branson and Lord Rothermere; France has Jean Luc Lagardere; Italy, Silvio Berlusconi; and Germany: Dieter Holtzbrinck,   Reinhard Mohn and Leo Kirch. In the Western Hemisphere we find Kenneth Thomson and Israel Asper in Canada, Emilio Ascarraga Jean in Mexico and Roberto Marinho in Brazil. Elsewhere in the world, there are media billionaires in Japan, Masayoshi Son and the family of the late Akio Morito; in Malaysia, Robert Kuok; in Saudi Arabia, Prince Alwaleed; and in Australia, Kerry Packer.

The American magnates are far from shy about buying and operating media properties abroad. Rupert Murdoch is best known for his global media spread, which includes holdings in New Zealand, Australia, England, Germany, Japan, Southeast Asia, Latin America and — on a big scale — the United States. Murdoch pioneered in satellite broadcasting in England and Asia, then joined a satellite broadcasting group in Latin America, and is now involved in an American satellite operation. He operates in nine different media on six continents.

AOL-Time-Warner-Turner has joint broadcasting ventures in Europe, New Zealand and Asia. And Ted Turner brought to Time-Warner his own global con-glomerate with TV channels around the world and joint broadcasting ventures on five continents. The Disney-ABC empire includes Eurosport network, a German cable channel, and more channels in Austria, Hungary and Finland. Redstone's Viacom is also spread out, with MTV and six other cable channels reaching almost everywhere. All the chieftains — Murdoch, Eisner, Turner and Redstone — have expressed determination to spread even further globally. Satellite and broadcast technology have so blotted out national boundaries that American movies blanket four-fifths of foreign screens, and just under half of overseas TV programming comes from American studios. The American slice of the world media pie is huge and grows almost daily.

Of course, some of the foreign media billionaires also capture wealth from American readers, viewers and listeners. Canada's richest man, Lord Kenneth Thomson, was selling a long list of daily and weekly papers in the United States in 2000, in order to concentrate on electronic reference material for lawyers, educators and scientists in the U.S. and abroad. A major share of Gruner & Jahr, in turn, is owned by Reinhard Mohn, who controls Bertelsmann AG, which owns RCA and Arista Records, and in 1998 bought the prestigious American publisher Random

House. Almost a third of Mohn's company's $7.9 billion annual revenue comes from American buyers. France's Jean Luc Lagardere publishes *Americana Encyclopedia* and his Hachette SLA publishes a number of American magazines including *George,* edited before his tragic death by John E. Kennedy, Jr., son of the late President. At the end of the 20th century, the media empires were indeed global.

When Pulitzer Prize-winner Ben Bagdikian wrote the first edition of *The Media Monopoly* in 1983, he found that 50 companies dominated most of America's media — newspapers, magazines, books, films, radio, television, cable and music. By the sixth edition in 2000, he was able to reduce that number to six. "Each is a subsidiary of a larger parent firm," he wrote, adding, "The six parent firms are General Electric, Viacom, Disney, Bertelsmann, Time Warner, and Murdoch's News Corp."[3] And he called attention to the fact that News Corp. is Australian and Bertelsmann, German.

Murdoch and Redstone were jubilant when they learned about the rising profits from history's most expensive movie, *Titanic.* Murdoch's 20th Century Fox and Redstone's Paramount had both helped produce the blockbuster, which by early fall 1998 was sending them $700 million to share. Their jubilation underscored the importance of movie studio ownership. Six of the billionaires can claim that. Operation of a studio means television program production, and TV reaches 99 percent of American homes daily. It also means movies, of course, but film is not as reliable a profit source as television.

The Disney Studios is now married to the powerful ABC network. Warner Brother Studios is tied to the three-year-old WB Network and to all the cable broadcast properties brought to the merger by Ted Turner. Universal Studios, owned by the Bronfmans until the merger with Vivendi in 2000, produces films and — since forming an alliance with NBC — television programs. And when the Bronfmans bought PolyGram in 1997, they doubled the reach of Universal, since PolyGram has a Hollywood studio plus a wealth of music recording subsidiaries. Redstone's Paramount Studios produces both movies and TV programs, as does Murdoch's 20th Century Fox. The other major studio — Columbia — is owned by Sony's billionaire family of the late Akio Morita, the only foreigner to invade Hollywood successfully. In addition to its film and TV studios, Sony now has record labels Columbia and Epic. Metro-Goldwyn-Mayer, owned for the third time by Kirk Kerkorian, is today a secondary player on the Hollywood scene. Movies produced by Big Six studios show up as re-runs on TV networks and stations as well as cable outlets, making for continuing sources of profit. Still more profit comes from video rentals. The studios now share a big chunk of box office income with theater owners, and the number of movie screens has multiplied in recent years.

Because TV is the nation's most popular medium, with more than 200 million American viewers spending an average of four hours a day with it, the media moguls are eager to control as much as they can.[4] Until 1985, we had three networks — NBC, CBS and ABC. Then Murdoch bought 20th Century Fox studios and at the same time a cluster of TV stations from media billionaire John Kluge, and Fox became the fourth network. Eight years later, Time-Warner joined the Tribune Company to start the WB Network. After Sumner Redstone took over Paramount Studios, he formed UPN, United Paramount Network, in a 50-50 alliance with

Chris-Craft. As this is written, Murdoch has UPN in his gunsight. The WB group reaches almost two-thirds of American homes, while UPN brings the sex-soaked *Melrose Place* and *Beverly Hills 90210* to nine-tenths of American homes via its 152 stations. So quite apart from the proliferating cable channels, we now have six commercial TV networks — NBC, ABC, CBS, Fox, UPN and WB.

In addition to their film studios, TV networks and cable channels, the media moguls have large holdings in radio, a highly profitable area itself. The 1996 Telecommunications Act made it possible for an owner to have eight radio stations in a community, rather than two, and the change led to a frenzy of station purchases across the country. When the dust settled, a few big corporations owned most of the country's radio stations. Example: Clear Channel Communications, owned by Lowry Mays, has more than 1,000 radio stations in the U.S..

Some of the moguls also publish books, between them controlling most of the U.S. publishing industry. They include Murdoch's Harper Collins; AOL-Time-Warner's Time Life Books; Disney's Hyperion and Chilton; Redstone's Simon & Schuster; and the McGraw family's control of the world's largest textbook empire, McGraw-Hill. Bertelsmann's purchase of Random House from the Newhouse brothers in 1998 was a major invasion of America's book industry.

These titans also control a great many newspapers and magazines. Murdoch's name pops up again, for he owns 132 newspapers spread across Australia, England and the United States. In this country, he owns 25 magazines, including 19 percent of *TV Guide*. While AOL-Time-Warner-Turner doesn't have newspapers, it has 24 magazines in a list topped by *Time, Fortune, People,* and *Sports Illustrated.*

All the Big Six are involved in cable operations. Here the best-known mogul is John Malone, who in 1998 sold the huge Telecommunications Inc (TCI) to AT&T for $40 billion. But he still controls Liberty Media with its operation of cable *content* providers such as Fox Sports, QVC, and United Video Satellite. He also has TCI International with cable properties in England, Japan and Chile. When AT&T became the largest cable provider after its deal with Malone, Time-Warner-Turner remained second with an empire that includes HBO, the largest pay channel in the world.

Disney operates three major cable channels that circle the globe — the Disney Channel, ESPN and ESPN2 — and has holdings in Eurosport Network and cable channels in Germany, Austria, Hungary and Finland. Under Sumner Redstone, Viacom has a major interest in the USA cable network, which serves the largest American cable audience, and also USA Network Latin America. Redstone's MTV cable channel reaches a large and growing world audience, as does his Nickelodeon. And now he owns the Columbia Broadcasting System network. But Turner and Murdoch are the most truly global media magnates. Together with his partner Time-Warner, Turner has TV channels around the world and joint operations on five continents. After the AOL-Time Warner merger, Turner's management of those channels became limited.. Murdoch has satellite services in both Asia and England, and stakes in such services in both Latin America and the U.S. The National Broadcasting Company (NBC), owned by General Electric, has a global outreach, too: its Super Channel uses the Sky satellite in Europe. NBC's Canaldo Noticias and Azteca TV cover most of Central and South America.

Congress and a succession of presidents starting in the 1970s have been quite friendly to the media giants. The giants in turn have poured funds of all permissible kinds into campaign coffers of both parties and maintain batteries of lobbyists in Washington who know which buttons to push in the House, the Senate and the White House. After a run of deregulation decisions in the 1970s, the Reagan administration presided over more far-reaching attacks on media regulation, especially broadcasting. For example, the number of TV and radio stations that could be owned by a network was raised to twelve. Then, early in 1996, Congress passed and President Clinton signed into law the Telecommunications Act, which had been titled the Telecommunications *Deregulation* Bill while it was still in committee. Some broadcast lobbyists were even allowed into committee offices to help shape the bill. Passage had been confidently anticipated by those who arranged the gigantic mergers of 1995. And the signing was quickly followed by waves of mergers and buyouts of local radio and TV stations around the country.

The new law mandated that ownership of radio and TV stations could no longer be limited by *number* but by *audience coverage*. Any network can now own stations -- TV or radio -- reaching as much as 35 percent of the national audience. The act also makes it possible for a single company to own both a TV and a radio station in any local market, or to own both a television network and a cable network. The FCC was ordered to explore abolition of restrictions which had historically barred ownership of more than one TV station in a local market. The Act's national policy clause called for "diversity of media voices," but its other features worked in the opposite direction, *against* diversity. As Dean Alger comments in his book, *Megamedia*, "The provisions giving away the broadcast spectrum and other provisions seem to work against such diversity."[5] The Center for Responsive Politics said, "Contributions from communications and electronic sources to federal candidates in the 1995-6 election cycle totaled $53,179,278, divided almost equally between Republicans and Democrats."[6] George Gerbner, media scholar who started the Cultural Indicators Project in the 1960s, called it "truly one of the most corrupt pieces of legislation in American history (which) basically hands over all communications to a few conglomerates."[7] Conservative columnist William Safire wrote that "the ripoff is on a scale vaster than dreamed by yesterday's robber barons."[8] The value of the "giveaway" was put at $70 billion by an article in *Brill's Content*.[9] Almost none of these comments or the behind-the-scenes work of media lobbyists, was reported in daily papers or on TV newscasts.

What does all this concentration of the media in a handful of mega-conglomerates mean for the cultures and life-styles of the countries of the world? That's a serious question. We'll explore the effects of the multi-media empires on cultures everywhere after we have told the stories of the media billionaires, both American and foreign To underscore the significance of the wealth of these billionaires, we'll discuss the major differences between rich and poor. Then, in our concluding chapter, we'll consider what we, as ordinary citizens can do about the situation.

BILL GATES–THE RICHEST,
AND PAUL ALLEN–THIRD RICHEST, IN THE COUNTRY

1

Only in their forties, Bill Gates is the richest man in the world and Paul Allen is the third richest. Because of federal court decisions in the still-running Justice Department anti-trust case against Microsoft, and because of drops in the stock market, the Gates fortune fell from $85 billion to $58.7 billion in the *Forbes* for July, 2001, and Allen's from $40 billion to $30.4 billion, but they remain the richest and third richest. Gates was only 31 when he reached his first billion in 1986.

Why are these computer nerds listed among America's "Multi Media Moguls"? Microsoft is itself a major electronic media institution, with its magazine *Slate* and round-the-clock news on the MSNBC channel, run jointly with the National Broadcasting Company. When *New York Times* publisher Arthur Sulzberger Jr. introduced Gates at a newspaper publishers convention in 1997, he said, "Microsoft increasingly competes against almost everyone in this room for readers' time and advertising dollars. If you don't consider it a competitor today, in this increasingly digital world in which we live, all I can say is 'Wait'."[1] By the fall of that year, MSNBC reached 38 million American homes and had three million viewers daily; its goal was 56 million homes by the end of the year 2000.

Gates and Microsoft are exploiting the Internet not only for *Slate* and MSNBC, but also through their big stake in the major cable operator Comcast and their Web site *Sidewalk*, providing entertainment listings, restaurant reviews, travel advice, movie tips, book reviews — in short, many of the services traditionally associated with newspapers. By late 1997, 300 journalists worked for Microsoft's media trio — *Slate, Sidewalk,* and MSNBC. Gates clearly intends eventually to charge for use of his media products, even though he withdrew his announced charges for *New york times* in 1999. He has also become a cable mogul with his huge investment in Comcast, which offers both information and entertainment.

Moreover, whether its software is Microsoft or Lotus, the desktop computer is an ultra-modern vehicle of both information and entertainment. Microsoft is one of many vehicles running on former Vice President Al Gore's "communications superhighway." A *New York Times* 1995 story characterized Microsoft as "a software company with the broadest possible understanding of SOFTWARE: not just computer code but books, news services, music, movies, paintings, maps and directories of people and businesses. It believes you can buy all of these on line, and intends to deliver them."[2] Indeed, Microsoft even delivers an encyclopedia, *Encarta*. Microsoft "now calls itself a media company."[3]

Paul Allen is even more clearly a media mogul, quite apart from his 9.5 percent stake in Microsoft and its media offerings. He speaks often of what he calls the "wired world." As early as 1995, he invested $500 million in the new DreamWorks launched by Steven Spielberg, Jeffrey Katzenberg and David Geffen. Then he set up Vulcan Ventures as a venture capital company; by 1999, it had bought a variety of Internet and cable companies with a total value of $25 billion. His Charter Communications is the fourth largest cable company in the country. One reason for his big investments in cable properties is that he's "hoping that a shift to digital will enable them to sell a bundle of video, Internet and phone services, raising revenues per subscriber to an average of $100 a month from $40."[4] By Christmas, 2000, one million subscribers had signed up for his digital cable services. But he's also involved in the non-wired world. He has a 49 percent stake in Metricon, a wireless network, one of 100 or more non-cable companies, valued at $5 billion, which he owns wholly or in part. Many of them provide Internet content, e-commerce, music or portal sites.

Gates, born in 1955, was only 12 and Allen, born in 1953, 14, when they persuaded the Mothers' Club at Lakeside School in Seattle to let them use the Club's computer time to set up class schedules. In addition to earning $4,200 for the summer's work, Gates scheduled himself into classes with the prettiest Lakeside girls.

Next the pair worked out an electricity grid as employees of the Bonneville Power Administration and at 15, Gates and 17-year-old Allen started Traf-O-Data to examine traffic patterns in and around Seattle. When Bonneville administrators learned how young their employees were, the two were fired. Then they got jobs at a Vancouver, Washington, software company, TRW, to work on software development. For that Gates arranged a temporary leave of absence from high school but returned in time to finish the senior year and graduate.

Gates was 18 when he entered Harvard. Allen drove cross-country, also to enter Harvard and work in Gates' Boston neighborhood. Two years later, Allen learned about a new computer, the first desktop, called the Altair 8080, being made in Albuquerque by MITS (Micro Instrumentation and Telemetry Systems). The pair went to work in their rooms at Harvard on a program language for Altair, even though they didn't have an Altair. After two months, they called MITS head Ed Roberts to say they had developed a program that would run on Altair, called BASIC (Beginners' All-purpose Symbolic Construction Code). When Roberts invited them to come and show it to him, Allen was the one chosen to fly to Albuquerque. He tried BASIC on the Altair, and it worked — the first time! After

Allen came back to Boston, the two refined the operations of BASIC. Then Allen was invited to return to Albuquerque to work for MITS, and he readily agreed and dropped out of Harvard. Gates joined him in Albuquerque to work on more BASIC improvements, dropping out of college after his junior year.

Microsoft was born in Albuquerque in 1975 when Gates and Allen signed an agreement for the licensing of BASIC. During their year and a half there, the two young nerds worked up programs for both Apple and Commodore. Then came a disagreement with MITS management over who owned BASIC. The case went to arbitration and the young pair won, after which they decided to leave New Mexico. Before long, Microsoft was in business in Bellevue, Washington. Two years later, an IBM official told the pair that his company was planning to market a desktop computer and invited them to work up a program for it. They did. The product was the Microsoft Disc Operating System — MS-DOS. Before long MS-DOS was being used all over the country on IBM's early personal computers. By early 1984, more than two million copies of MS-DOS were in use — made by Microsoft. Then Gates and Allen responded to requests of the makers of Apple computers for software to be used on their machines. Shortly thereafter Radio Shack knocked on the door. Even Japanese electronic companies invited Microsoft to develop software for their infant computer industry.

Microsoft's explosive early growth sprang from the 1980 linkup with IBM. In 1990, a *Fortune* feature said, "Since 1982, the first full year after the deal with IBM, Microsoft has grown nearly 50-fold without a blip."[5] A major player in that growth was Steve Ballmer, who has been a "friend of Bill" since they studied, gambled and played together at Harvard. Even before 1980, Gates realized that he urgently needed someone to manage the growing company's business. Ballmer had won two internships for the coming summer, having graduated from Harvard, but Gates persuaded him to come to Microsoft as assistant to the president at $50,000 a year — more than most staff members were making. Ballmer was soon a player in the negotiations with IBM for a contract, which was signed two days before the November, 1980 elections. He negotiated the creation of Microsoft as a Washington State corporation in mid-l981, with Gates getting 53 percent of the stock, Allen 31 percent and Ballmer eight percent. He led the early round of hiring that brought dozens of smart young employees to Microsoft's rapidly growing campus in the early '80s. As the launching of the first Windows was delayed repeatedly, Ballmer was key to pushing for completion and marketing. He clearly matches the competitiveness of his best friend, Bill Gates.[6] After Gates resigned as CEO during the anti-trust trial, Ballmer took on the key Microsoft job, in effect running the company.

In September 1982, while on a European speaking tour, Allen noticed lumps in his throat. He flew home, where doctors told him he had Hodgkins' Disease -- lymphoma. He immediately started the first of two five-week courses in X-ray therapy, continuing to work at Microsoft half-time. But in March, 1983, feeling much better, he resigned from Microsoft and started to travel to Europe "to think about the kind of things I wanted to do."[7] He didn't return to Microsoft until 1990, when he joined the company's board of directors. Two years later, he started IRC (Interval Research Company) in Palo Alto, California, on the edge of Silicon Valley, to explore high bandwidth communication by satellite. Meantime he had become part owner of the Portland Trail Blazers of the National Basketball Association, and later he bought the Seattle Seahawks football team, pushing plans for a new Seahawk stadium. His interests are widespread, as indicated by his launch of Asymetrix, a software tools company, later renamed Click2learn. He also bought a controlling interest in Ticketmaster, a computerized system for selling tickets of all kinds. And he bought shares of other software companies, including CD-Roms, sports data services, TV programming and wireless paging. In March, 2000, he paid $1.79 billion to AT&T for cable systems in four states.

While Allen was away, Gates began introducing Microsoft to overseas markets, beginning in 1983. By 1990, Microsoft sales abroad topped MS-DOS sales at home. Microsoft went to Wall Street in 1986, when its shares sold at $7. Their price had jumped 500 percent by 1990.

The growing dominance of Microsoft reflected the way the staff was organized and worked, first in Bellevue, and then in its new campus-like setting in Redmond, also a Seattle suburb. The still-growing staff works in units, often made up of only 30 members. Each unit works on a software type, seeking improvements or alternatives for an existing program. Gates stays in touch with each unit, trying to give same-day response to the dozens of e-mail messages he gets. Microsoft workers, who by 1995 numbered 18,000, don't seem to object to working as many as 75 hours a week; after all, Gates himself puts in that many hours. Some 2,000 of them have become millionaires. Many are multi-millionaires. Steve Ballmer, now titled executive vice president, was listed at $17 billion in 2000 -- the seventh richest man in the country..

Working on what is sometimes called the "magic carpet to the future," Microsoft leaders seek to produce new programs frequently because they want to continue dominating the still-growing software industry. After MS-DOS in 1980 and OS/2 in 1987, versions of Windows 3.0 came in 1985, l986 and 1988, and Windows 3.1 in 1992 In 1995, a gigantic festival atmosphere prevailed at the unveiling of Windows 95 in Redmond. Explorer 3.0 arrived in December 1996 to make access to the Internet easier. Windows 98 was delayed when the Justice Department opened anti-trust proceedings against Microsoft, but the new software program was released in July as scheduled. Windows 2000, originally due in 1999, was delayed until February 2000, and Windows XP was to be launched late in 2001.

By the mid-1990s, Gates realized the importance of the Internet. In his book, *The Road Ahead,* he wrote "The popularity of the Internet is the most important single development in the world of computing since the IBM PC was introduced in 1981."[8] Microsoft's MSN (Microsoft Network) is competing fiercely with AOL (America OnLine) for users of the Internet who want entertainment, bill paying, communications, and/or shopping.

Gates was 35 years old when he began dating Melinda French, who worked as a product manager at Microsoft, in 1988. It was an on-and-off relationship that picked up intensity in the early 1990s. They became engaged in April, 1993, and she joined him in planning his huge new house overlooking Lake Washington. They married on New Year's Day in 1994 in Hawaii, with Willie Nelson furnishing the music. In summer 1995, Melinda organized a lengthy vacation trip to China, with seven couples floating down the Yangtse River, visiting the Great Wall and of course the Forbidden City in Beijing. The couples included another multi-media mogul, Warren Buffett and his wife Susan, and there were endless games involving math puzzles. Gates took advantage of the days in Beijing to meet with President Jiang Zemin, who then announced that Microsoft's Windows was to be China's software standard.

While the enormous, 48,000 square foot, $113 million Lake Washington mansion was in its third year of construction, Melinda gave birth to Jennifer in April, 1996 By then she had left her Microsoft job and become active in charitable work, just as Bill's mother had. Their second child, Rory John, was born in the spring of 1999.

Both friends and enemies use the word "competitive" when they talk or write about Bill Gates. He is always looking for ways to guarantee that Microsoft products will win, even dominate, in the marketplace. "At bottom, he was a businessman," wrote the authors of a Gates biography, adding, "a mere businessman, a Thomas Crown, a Thomas Watson -- an entrepreneur, not a scientist. He was more a Henry Ford than a Thomas Edison."[9] That assessment was underscored in 1999 when Microsoft became part of the Dow Jones Industrial Average.

Gates and those who work with him constantly seek new ways to court computer users, and to overwhelm rivals. A *New York Times* writer commented in 1995, "Microsoft stumbles, but less often than its competitors, and when its competitors make mistakes, Microsoft historically has managed to take advantage. It has cultivated an aura of inevitability. It has failed so far to overcome some rivals, but it has never lost an important franchise once gained."[10]

Paul Allen's character is very different from Gates's. He's much more relaxed. His work week is far more normal than the Gates 75-hour week. During his evenings and days off, he parties, watches basketball and football, listens to music. Still single, he has been dating Jerry Hall, a fashion model and former wife of Mick Jagger. He has homes in southern France, London, Long Island and Seattle. He plays guitar occasionally with a rock band, the Threads. His interest in music led him to plan a big London recording studio, at the suggestion of his British rock musician friend, Dave Stewart of the Eurythmics. Even more impressive, he spent $250 million to build a rock music museum in Seattle, titled Experience Music and designed by famed architect Frank Gehry. He likes to party and to give parties. In 1997, he flew a number of American guests to Cannes for the annual film festival, then flew them to Venice for a masked ball. A year later, some 400 friends were guests on a chartered cruise to Alaska

When he goes to his Vulcan Ventures office, Allen surveys the field of possibilities for investment. A long *Los Angeles Times* article in September, 1999, gave a sampling of what it called his "scattershot" approach to investing. "He owns stakes in Web merchants . . . enabling technology firms. . . 20 percent of DreamWorks SKG, $100 million worth of Oxygen Media, a ballyhooed new women's-entertainment firm that counts Oprah Winfrey as an investor; and leading technology-oriented Web site Cnet (CNET). The value of most of these companies has mushroomed since the companies completed their IPOs."[11] Vulcan Ventures has funded a Web site, POP.com, which offers comic video segments and live Internet broadcasts. The Web site is operated by DreamWorks and Imagine Entertainment. He now owns about 140 companies. Allen's wide-ranging interests have also led him to put many millions into SETI - the Search for Extra-Terrestrial Intelligence Institute. Vulcan also recently bought ZDTV, the cable channel serving all-computers-all-the-time, headquartered in San Francisco. He already owned 27 percent of RCN, a fiber builder. To boost its sports holdings, Vulcan Ventures bought One-On-One Sports Inc., a sports radio network with stations in Chicago, Los Angeles, Boston and New York. The November, 2000, buy was followed by a name change to Sporting News Radio Network. By then, Allen had bought *Sporting News* magazine from the Times-Mirror Co. To help fund purchases like these, Allen occasionally sells some of his Microsoft stock. In 2000, he sold $8.5 billion worth. In the fall of 2000, he resigned from the Microsoft board of directors, but still advises Gates.

Gates became tenser than usual when the U. S. Justice Department and 19 state attorneys general brought anti-trust charges against Microsoft in 1997. After an 18 month trial, Federal District Judge Thomas P. Jackson released his 200-plus page findings in 1999, concluding that Microsoft was indeed a monopoly. Jackson commented, "I think (Gates) has a Napoleonic concept of himself and his company, an arrogance which derives from power and unalloyed success, with no leavening hard experiences, no reverses."[12] Then federal appeals judge Richard A. Posner tried for months to mediate an agreement. *New Yorker's* Ken Auletta believes that news stories reporting Judge Posner's failure to broker an agreement "didn't capture how eager Microsoft had been to settle — so eager that Bill Gates had been willing to abandon endlessly touted principles to achieve an armistice."[13] After mediation failed, the Justice Department went to the Supreme Court, which refused to hear the case and sent it to an appeals court.

Even as the court case dragged on, Gates set up the Bill and Melinda Gates Foundation, initially funded at $17 billion, then raised until it was up to $21 billion by the year 2001. It gave away $1.4 billion in 2000. Melinda helps oversee the grants, which go mainly to health care and improvement of education for children all over the world, including minority scholarships in the U.S. The Foundation "outspent the U.S. government last year (2000) by nearly $300 million, to battle global health threats, such as AIDS, malaria and tuberculosis."[14] The Foundation chairman is William H. Gates Sr., who in 2001 led the campaign by many wealthy people, including Warren Buffett and George Soros, against repeal of the estate tax.

In Microsoft's early years, both Gates and Allen were often quoted as putting "a computer on every desk in every home" as their objective. Gates has added a phrase, so it now reads,"A computer on every desk in every home, *all running on Microsoft software.*"

Gates told a *Time* editor in 1997 that he intended to stay as Microsoft's head another ten years, which would be until 2007. Then, he said, he will start to give most of his money away. The $21 billion foundation provides a good start on that. But his retirement is six years off. Meantime the Gates battle with the Justice Department continues — and Microsoft continues to churn out its products. While Bill Gates's fortune has dropped $26 billion, he's still the richest man in the world, and his old pal Paul Allen is third richest.

WARREN BUFFETT—THE ORACLE OF OMAHA

2

Warren Buffett of Omaha, Nebraska, is the second richest man in America, worth $32.3 billion in the *Forbes* for July 9, 2001. His wife, Susan, is listed at $2.3 billion. Most of his wealth has come from his skill at watching stocks listed on Wall Street, and buying those that he is convinced have a strong future, then holding on and selling when he thinks they have peaked.

Numerous biographies of him have been published in recent years, all emphasizing his ability to use investment strategies that work. For example, in 1965, when he took over control of Berkshire Hathaway, a failing textile company, he knew it had subsidiaries that could be used as venues for buying stocks in other companies. By 1996, its stock had risen from $18 a share to $31,700 a share. At that point, Buffett announced a Class B stock, "more affordable" at $1,000 a share. Five of the other investors in Berkshire Hathaway have become billionaires. By January, 2000, Berkshire Hathaway class A stock was up 300,000 percent over its 1965 price. By February, 2001, a single share was worth $70,000. Such successes have earned him the sobriquets "wizard," "Midas," and "Oracle of Omaha."

Early in his investment career, he became interested in media stocks. Starting in 1973, after checking newspapers around the country, he bought stock in the *Washington Post* at about the same time as Katharine Graham took over. Some years ago he and Mrs. Graham became good friends and he visits her whenever he's in Washington. He now owns 17 percent of the Post Company's stock, worth about $1 billion, and sits on its board of directors. He says he especially enjoys ownership in stock of newspapers and other media.

Not long after his first purchase of *Post* stock, Buffett bought the *Buffalo Evening News* for $33 million, about a third of his personal fortune at the time. He quickly ordered plans for a Sunday edition. The opposition paper, *Courier Express*, whose

Sunday paper was by far its most profitable venture, sued, arguing that Buffett intended to drive it out of business. The judge supported the argument and set limits on what Buffett's Sunday paper could do. But two years later the U. S. Court of Appeals reversed the judge. After a few years, the *Courier Express*, losing $3 million a year, closed its doors. Buffett's *Evening News* quickly became the morning *Buffalo News*, which now earns $40 million a year, serving Buffalo citizens with a widely praised paper.

Buffett was born August 30, 1930, in Omaha, the son of a local stockbroker, Howard Buffett. When his father was elected to Congress, the family moved to Fredericksburg, Virginia, and then to Spring Valley in northwest Washington, where, at age 13, Warren took over two paper routes, delivering the *Washington Post* and the *Times-Herald*. His father's congressional terms lasted from 1942 to 1948, and then from 1950 to 1952.

The paper routes started his use of investment strategies. With the money earned from newspaper delivery, he and a classmate bought remodeled pinball machines and persuaded local barbers to put the machines in their shops. The seven machines gave them a weekly income of $50.[1] When he graduated from high school at sixteen, Buffett had $6,000 in the bank. At his father's insistence, he went on to two years at the Wharton School of Finance in Pennsylvania, then concluded his college education at the University of Nebraska in Lincoln. There he read *The Intelligent Investor*, by Benjamin Graham. He was excited by the central thesis of the book — buy stocks only after thoroughly investigating the company, then hold onto them until they have reached what you think is their highest point. So he moved to New York to enroll in the Columbia Graduate Business School, where Graham was then teaching. They became good friends, and during the two years from 1954 to 1956, Buffett worked at the Graham-Newman Corporation.

Having mastered Graham's theory, Buffett went back to Omaha at age 25, and immediately sought the support of family and friends to form his first investment firm, Buffett Associates Ltd., capitalized at $105,000. After forming ten such partnerships, he merged them to form Buffett Partnership Ltd. During its sixteen years of operation, the Partnership investments rose at the rate of 295 percent a year, even during the five years in which the stock market declined. While the Partnership continued to thrive, some members joined him in investments in Berkshire Hathaway, a New England company with several textile mills. Once Buffett was in control, he began to use it to buy into, or even take over, other companies with no relation to textiles. In 1969, four years after taking over Berkshire Hathaway, Buffett dissolved the Partnership which had enjoyed a 30-fold payoff in the value of the original investment. He still occupies the office in downtown Omaha which he opened when the Partnership was formed.

From the late 1960s to the '90s, Berkshire Hathaway invested in the National Indemnity and National Fire and National Marine insurance companies, the *Buffalo News*, Blue Chip Stamps, See's Candies, Nebraska Furniture Mart and Borsheim's Jewelry in Omaha, Fechheimer Brothers (uniform maker), Scott & Fetzer Company (Kirby Vacuums), *World Book Encyclopedias*, Wayne furnace burners, Campbell Hausfield, and two shoe companies -- H. H. Brown in 1991 and Dexter Shoes in

1993. When in July 1995, *Forbes* reported that in the preceding year, his net worth had jumped from $7.9 billion to $10.7 billion, it was partly because he had bought huge chunks of Coca Cola, Gillette and GEICO (Government Employee Insurance Company). When he bought the Gillette stock, he remarked, "It's pleasant to go to bed every night knowing there are 2.5 billion males in the world who have to shave in the morning."[2] In the early '90s, he had also bought more than ten percent of American Express.

Buffett was visiting Washington one day in February, 1985, when he got a call from Tom Murphy, chairman of Capital Cities, a newspaper and broadcasting company. He had known Murphy since he bought Capital Cities stock in 1977. He had later sold the stock and regretted it. Now Murphy told him that Cap Cities was buying the ABC-TV network, but needed help in the financing. Buffett's $500 million commitment turned out to be the difference that made it possible for Cap Cities to close the deal. He soon went on the ABC-Cap Cities board of directors, giving up his *Washington Post* board position in accordance with anti-trust regulations.

Ten years later Buffett's friendship with Murphy again helped in the megamerger of ABC-Cap Cities with Disney Studios, forming one of the six biggest media conglomerates in the world. The 1995 merger sprang from the annual conference of media magnates in Sun Valley, Idaho. There, Disney's Michael Eisner fell into conversation with Buffett, who by then was regularly invited to the conferences. In the transaction, approved a year later by the Federal Trade Commission, Berkshire Hathaway took only stock in the new Disney-ABC, 20 million shares, or three percent of the conglomerate. Buffett thus continued to be an investor in major media. And he was free to return to the *Washington Post* board of directors.

Charles Munger is Buffett's "not so silent" partner, who lives in Los Angeles but talks with Buffett almost daily. He has been vice chair of Berkshire Hathaway since 1978. He was the one who changed Buffett's investment strategy, which had been based on the Graham principles of buy cheap, hold for a long time, sell only when the stock is very high. Munger persuaded him that even if a stock is high, if the company has a good record and continues to show solid promise, it's worthwhile to buy it and hold for a long time.[3] On that basis, Buffett made many of his major purchases, including Geico and Coca Cola. Before 2000, Munger was mentioned as Buffett's possible successor. He lives in Los Angeles and in addition to his Berkshire Hathaway stock, owns the Daily Journal Corp., which publishes 19 newspapers, most of which are legal sheets. He graduated from Harvard Law School.

In the early 1990s, the Oracle of Omaha was caught up in a bizarre series of events involving one of the country's preeminent Wall Street firms, Salomon Brothers. The story begins in the fall of 1987, when Salomon's CEO, John Gutfreund, asked Buffett to ward off a takeover attempt by Ronald Perelman. By buying $700 million of Salomon stock, Buffett sent Perelman packing. But the real crisis came four years later when it developed that two of Salomon's security traders had repeatedly violated Treasury rules during 1990 and 1991, and that the company's top officials had failed to report it. Buffett was called in when the company finally got ready to tell Federal Reserve Bank President Gerald Corrigan the story. But then it turned out that CEO Gutfreund had failed to tell Salomon some important facts, including a threatening letter he had received from Corrigan. There was a run on Salomon securities, at which point Salomon stopped trading in its own securities.

On Sunday morning, August 18, 1991, the Treasury notified Salomon's office that it was about to announce a ban on Salomon trading in its auctions -- for itself or its customers. Working feverishly to stop the ban announcement, Buffett reached Treasury Secretary Nicholas Brady in Saratoga Springs. Brady finally agreed to lift the ban on Salomon's trading at auctions. Before the day was over, the board had elected Buffett as interim chair and fired Gutfreund. Then Buffett was paid $1 for staying nine months in the Salomon office, bringing its affairs back to normal. By May, 1992, Salomon's stock had risen dramatically and Buffett was replaced by a permanent chairman.

Later in the decade, Buffett's Berkshire Hathaway paid an average of $5 an ounce for silver bullion and in time held 37 percent of the world supply. His purchases pushed the market price to above $7. As the price fell from the March 1997 high of $7.27, Buffett gradually sold off all of Berkshire Hathaway's silver holdings.

Easily the biggest single investment ever made by Buffett was his 1998 takeover of General Re Corporation, an insurer of insurance companies, for $22 billion. He had invested years earlier in National Indemnity, also a re-insurance company that protects insurers against natural catastrophes such as earthquakes and floods. Berkshire Hathaway is also very heavily invested in Geico, America's seventh biggest auto insurer. Because the investment in General Re was so big, Buffett called a special meeting of Berkshire stockholders, who gave their approval. It should be noted that the insurance business provides about half of Berkshire Hathaway's profits. The next year, even though Berkshire Hathaway was doing poorly, he made a $9 billion investment in MidAmerica Energy, a regional utility holding company based in Houston.

The year 1999 was called Buffett's "annus horribilis" in a story in *U.S. News & World Report*.[4] Berkshire Hathaway stock fell 19.8 percent during the year, mostly reflecting poor performances by Coca Cola, Gillette and Walt Disney Co. Taking the blame himself in his report to shareholders, Buffett said, "Even Inspector Clouseau would find last year's guilty party: your Chairman."[5] The stocks that were rising dramatically all through the nineties were mostly in high tech and new media, and Buffett had shunned them all, and in 1998-99, the older stocks didn't do so well, either. Buffett and Munger told shareholders what was being done to correct the problems.

And the problems were, indeed, cleared up, so that by the end of December, 2000, BH stocks had risen 24 percent, while Nasdaq dropped 30 percent. Net profits had gone up 114 percent over 1999, giving a value of $70,000 for each Berkshire Hathaway share. During the year, Berkshire invested in Tricon (Pizza Hut, Taco Bell and KFC), and "agreed to buy Johns Manville Corp. For $2.2 billion in cash and assumed debt . . .Buffett had already agreed to spend $3.6 billion this year to buy Dalton-based carpet-maker Shaw Industries Inc., paint manufacturer Benjamin Moore & Co., and brick maker Justin Industries Inc."[6]

Buffett is usually responsive to reporters, but not much information is available about his private life, other than the fact that he lives simply. The Omaha house he bought for $31,500 in 1958 is a three-story Dutch colonial in which he still lives.

His biographers and reporters all agree on his "simple, straightforward, forthright" personality, which combines "sophisticated dry wit and cornball humor."[7] He spends five or six hours a day reading, and a lot of time on the phone. He's a registered Democrat, having switched from the Republican Party in the early 1960s. Indeed, he gave money to Hilary Clinton's campaign for the U.S. Senate, spoke for her at Columbia University, and co-hosted fund-raisers in Manhattan and Omaha.

He is an investor, not a journalist. His major writings appear in the densely-written annual reports to Berkshire Hathaway stockholders, which biographer Robert Hagstrom says run to 60 or 70 pages with "no pictures, no graphics, no charts," but a "healthy dose of financial acumen, folksy humor, and unabashed honesty,"[8] As many as 14,000 shareholders attend Berkshire Hathaway annual meetings, held in a huge hall in Omaha, and at the one in May, 2000, Buffett and Charles Munger answered questions for six hours.

Buffett's wife, Susan, from whom he separated in 1977 after 25 years of marriage and three children, remains a very good friend. Even though she lives in San Francisco, 1,500 miles away, Susan accompanies Buffett on most of his trips, and they see each other at least once a month, talking on the phone even more often. Several years ago, Susan and Warren joined Bill Gates and his new wife in a long trip to China. The evening before every Berkshire Hathaway annual meeting, Susan, Astrid Menks -- Buffett's housekeeper/companion, selected by Susan -- and Warren go to a party at Borsheim's Jewelry store.

Susan, their oldest offspring, called "Susie," is a director of the Buffett Foundation, which her ex-husband, Allen Greenberg, runs. Their son Howard, now 46, is a farmer in Decatur, Illinois, and also chairman of the GSI Group, which makes grain storage bins. He lives on his 700-acre farm with his wife, Devon, a son, also named Howard, and one of four stepdaughters. Before moving to Decatur, Howard was a corporate vice president and assistant to the chairman of Archer Daniels Midlands, the big midwest grain company. The other son, Peter, is described as "a successful musician/businessman in Milwaukee . . . recording commercial jingles for companies like DuPont, Infiniti, CNN and Levi Strauss."[9] He also sits on the Foundation board.

For some years, Buffett traveled in a privately-owned plane he called "the Indefensible." But in 1998 he had Berkshire Hathaway pay $500 million for NetJet, a corporate aircraft company. In March, 2001, he flew in a NetJet plane to Europe for a three-day tour to promote the company. A London paper commented, "Timeshare on aircraft is becoming more popular as companies dispose of their own fleets because of uncertain economic conditions."[10]

After Buffett underwent surgery in July, 2000, for removal of non-cancerous polyps on his colon, he hinted to a *New York Times* reporter that his son Howard, the farmer, will succeed him as chairman of Berkshire Hathaway. Howard already sits on the Berkshire Hathaway board. "The elder Mr. Buffett has arranged matters . so that, although his son will not run the company himself, he will provide crucial oversight."[11] Others mentioned as possible high level managers are Lou Simpson and Tony Nicely, both high officials at Geico. At the same time, Buffett assured the reporter that his health is good.

Buffett has indicated that he is backing away from his plan to leave only a little of his wealth to his children. Speculation has suggested the two or three million dollars figures — for each. He calls inherited wealth "food stamps for the rich."[12] The major beneficiaries of Buffett Foundation charities so far have been in the nuclear disarmament and population control causes: family planning, sex education, birth control and abortion rights. But the amounts going to those causes have been fly-specks when measured against his wealth.

In the end the Buffett Foundation will have enormous wealth to distribute. Where? Buffett says he's sure society will still face serious problems, and since he will leave more money than he has now, society will enjoy greater benefit. But Buffett's legacy may be his own unique story, the story of a capitalist with superb financial skills matched with a high social conscience.

SUMNER REDSTONE–KING OF EMPIRE NUMBER THREE

3

Sumner Redstone, at 78, has transformed a small chain of drive-in movies into one of the biggest multimedia conglomerates in the world. He says "We're in the midst of a global revolution in entertainment, and it's escalating,[1]" and the escalator carried him to a *Forbes* listing at $12.8 billion in July, 2001.

His National Amusements and Viacom became America's third-largest media empire in September, 1999, when he completed a $37.3 billion merger with CBS Corp. Viacom was already a major player in every media field — production of both movies and TV programs, music production on cable TV, children's TV programs, and pay TV, even a five-year-old television network — UPN. Viacom also operates the biggest chain of video stores — 6,400 in 27 countries, and the biggest chain of music stores — 500 plus — in the world, each named Blockbuster. It has six theme parks, located in Australia, Canada, North Carolina, California, Virginia and Ohio, to say nothing of 19 television stations. Less than a year after he bought CBS, he bought Infinity Broadcasting, to raise the number of Viacom's radio stations from 14 to 184. There's also the hugely profitable cable systems, plus the 150,000 collection of TV programs, which includes a large number of movies. Another subsidiary is Spelling Entertainment, which produces TV sitcoms and movies. National Amusements, the small chain of drive-in movies with which Redstone's family started it all, has more than 1,200 movie theaters around the world.

When the FCC approved the CBS merger, it ordered the sale of some TV stations, since the CBS-Viacom combination exceeded the limit of 35 percent of the national audience set by the 1996 Telecommunications Act.

CBS brought the most profitable TV network to the merger, along with its 15 television stations and the country's largest group of radio stations. It's buying the money-making billboard giant Outdoor Systems Inc, which will give Redstone another huge venue for advertising. Total CBS revenue for 1998 came to $6.8 billion, while Viacom took in $18.9 billion. The two companies have a total stock market value of $72 billion, compared with Time Warner's $80.5 billion. At the time of the merger, Viacom had 90,000 employees, while CBS had 12,000.[2] A year after the merger, *Vanity Fair* reported that Viacom's price per share has climbed more or less steadily since the CBS deal was announced."[3]

Magazine articles often use such words as "competitive," "hypermotivated," and "aggressive" to describe Redstone. He "works all the time, and operates in only one mode: relentless."[4] For years, his normal work day stretched over 18 hours.

He was born into the middle class family of Michael and Belle Rothstein in Boston, May 27, 1923. When he was still a child, they changed their name to Redstone. His father sold linoleum and liquor, and in the 1930s began to acquire drive-in movie theaters. Young Redstone enrolled at Boston Latin School, where, when he graduated in 1940, he had not only won a series of academic prizes but had the highest grade point average in the school's long history. He went immediately to Harvard, where he majored in foreign languages, learning not only French and German, but Japanese. He was not yet 20 when he graduated from Harvard, earning a bachelor's degree in two and a half years. By now, the United States was fully engaged in World War II, and Redstone was invited by Edwin Reischauer, a Japanese scholar at Harvard, to join a special corps of cryptographers to break Japanese military and diplomatic codes. He excelled at this task, winning two army commendations and promotion to first lieutenant.

The war over, Redstone quickly enrolled at Harvard Law School and gained his law degree by 1947. While working on his law degree, "he used his GI discount to buy large quantities of surplus military merchandise, including office supplies and tools, which he sold for a hefty profit at local department stores."[5] He also somehow found time to court Phyllis Rafael, "a petite, vivacious girl who had been known as the best dancer in her sorority."[6] Married in 1947, they had two children, Shari, now 46, and Brent, now 50. Once he had the law degree, he worked briefly as a clerk in the federal appellate court in San Francisco, at the same time teaching a course in law and labor management at the University of San Francisco. Then he went to Washington to serve for three years as a special assistant to Attorney General Tom Clark, working on tax cases. From that job he moved to a private law firm, also in Washington, staying three years, long enough to learn the intricacies of business law. When he decided to join the world of business, he and his family returned to Dedham, Massachusetts, where his father and brother were operating a small chain of drive-in theaters scattered around New England states.

During the next two decades, the Redstones added more and more drive-ins, so that by 1974, they owned 125. Despite his family's success, Sumner Redstone saw that drive-in theaters were becoming outdated. He hit upon the idea of converting the drive-ins to large indoor theaters housing multiple screens. For them he invented the trade name "multiplexes." They are now the standard for most movie theaters in the country; by 1994 the Redstones owned 855 of them.

Traveling for the family company, Sumner was staying at Boston's Copley Plaza in March, 1979, when he was trapped by a fire. The fire spread so quickly that he was forced to climb out of his third floor window and cling to the ledge, waiting to be rescued. More than 40 percent of his body was severely burned; it took more than a year for him to recover. After many skin grafts, his main reminder of the fire is in his right hand, which has no tendons. Although the injury forces him to strap his tennis racket to a glove, he still plays an aggressive tennis game, often winning because of his fierce focus on every play. "He screams and argues about every point," according to Robert Evans, who used to head Paramount Studios.[7]

Not many years after he brought his family back to Dedham, he started to search for a new enterprise because National Amusements had become so predictable that he found it dull. In 1977, he began investing in movie stocks; he realized a $20 million profit from 20th Century Fox; $25 million from Columbia Pictures; and $15 million from MGM/UA stock.

By now he had decided that *company* ownership was better than *stock* ownership. With his stock market profits, he began to invest in Viacom International Inc., which owned a number of TV and radio stations, as well as cable systems and above all the MTV, VH-1, Nickelodeon, Showtime and Movie cable channels. Coincidentally, it also owned Madison Square Garden and two big league teams, the Knicks and the Rangers. A year later he began what became a six-month campaign to take over Viacom. Opposing his 1987 campaign, some of Viacom's executives tried unsuccessfully to make the company private. Redstone finally won 83 percent of Viacom, after hiking his offer three times. The cost came to $3.4 billion, most of which he borrowed.

Realizing that Viacom was a far more complicated enterprise than a movie chain, he turned over management of National Amusements to Ira A. Korff, husband of his daughter Shari. Then he brought in Frank Biondi as president and CEO to help him run the Viacom conglomerate. He began to spend four days a week in Viacom's office on Times Square, and to travel much more than in the past. Over a few years he added TV and radio stations in five states to the Viacom stable. But he focused especially on Viacom's cable channels. Although he found MTV's music distasteful, he saw that it already had a good audience with tremendous potential for growth. By 1998, MTV had moved overseas and was being heard in 298 million homes in 82 countries, including India, China and Korea. "From the British dance floor to Moscow's Red Square, where 200,000 Russian youths gathered recently for an MTV concert, on to the Philippines, where it is the number two cable channel, MTV rules. The outfit that all but invented the rock video is now the premiere platform for marketers aiming to woo the young and acquisitive overseas."[8] Redstone credited MTV as an important part in the 600 percent increase on Viacom stock value from 1987 to 1993, his first six years in control.

As MTV's audience grew around the world, Redstone was also pleased by VH-1, a cable channel with music targeting 25-to-34-year-olds , and Nickelodeon, a cable channel with videos for children between two and 15. Now, said a *Forbes* article in 1994, "Viacom has it all figured out. Children age 2 to 15 are targeted by Nickelodeon, 12 to 25 by MTV, and over 25 by VH-1, and Nick at Nite after nightfall. (Nick at Nite recycles such shows as *Get Smart* and *Mr. Ed*). The idea is to hook viewers at an early age and build enough brand awareness to keep them for life."[9]

Both Nickelodeon and MTV are widely criticized. With its enormous audience all over the world, "MTV has at least one occurrence of violence in more than 50 percent of its videos," according to *We the Media*.[10] There's violence in both its rap music and film videos. "Music videos glamorize violence and weapons, and MTV is the main culprit," according to a study published in the *Journal* of the American Medical Association.[11] The MTV Music Video Awards are handed out at Radio City Music Hall, and in September, 2000, the "foul-mouthed rapper Eminem performed" and "then walked away with top honors."[12] There's also a lot of violence in *Beavis and Butthead*, launched in 1992 on MTV, and vulgarity on *South Park*, carried on Comedy Central.[13] In addition, Nick at Nite felt obliged to warn listeners when it started reruns of *All in the Family*, giving it a PG (Parental Guidance) rating because "it contains bigoted remarks, racial epithets and adult subject matter."[14] Moreover, Viacom's Showtime, a pay TV channel, has been found to carry almost twice as much violence as the regular broadcast networks. Commenting on the effects of the Viacom-CBS merger, Mark Crispin Miller, director of the Project on Media Ownership, wrote, "The corporation that gives us Butthead, Howard Stern and the WWF's *Smackdown* (wrestling) may be disinclined to welcome tough inquiries into the effects of such fare on the young."[15]

Redstone responds to these attacks. In a June, 1999, comment on criticism of sex and violence in the media, he said, "I have nothing to be ashamed of."[16] He added, "Let's distinguish between sex and violence. Sex is good, violence is bad." Moreover, in that same year, the Academy of Television Arts and Sciences gave awards to six Nickelodeon shows for "promoting racial understanding" — *Doug, Nick News, Hey Arnold, Sports Theater, Mystery Files of Shelby Woo,* and *Secret World of Alex Mack.* [17]

However, politicians in Washington continued to bash the entertainment industry, and in the fall of 2000, four of the eight major film studios made sharp cuts in the number of commercials for R-rated movies on programs aimed at youngsters. That was expected to cause a drop in MTV Networks' income.

In addition to MTV and MTV1, there is MTV2, which reaches 30 million homes, having "taken over the Box, an interactive all-request video music cable channel."[18]

Even as his TV and cable programs drew increased press attention, Redstone kept looking for ways to pare down the enormous debt tied to the Viacom purchase. One was to sell the syndication rights to *The Cosby Show,* which netted $55 million for Viacom in 1988. And in December 1990 Time Warner agreed to merge the HBO Comedy channel with Viacom's Ha! Channel to form Comedy Central, now owned jointly by the two giants.

But Redstone, whose early wealth had come from the *exhibition* of movies, now wanted to control the *making* of movies. In Paramount Studios he saw the company he wanted. It didn't come easily or cheaply. The first step seemed easy — a friendly merger announced by Redstone and Martin Davis, the Paramount CEO, in September, 1993. A week later, Barry Diller challenged the merger with a higher bid, which was supported by TCI's John Malone and Conde Nast's Si Newhouse. But Redstone made a stock swap merger with the Blockbuster video and music store chain, and walked off with Paramount for $10 billion.

To pay for his huge buy, he sold Viacom's cable systems to TCI; his half of USA

Networks to Edgar Bronfman Jr.; Madison Square Garden, the New York Knicks (basketball) and New York Rangers (hockey); and the education section of book publisher Simon & Schuster to England's Pearson media group. To Kirch, the German media group, he sold the *use* of Paramount's film library in Germany over 10 years for $2 billion. He kept Paramount's studios, its film library and enormous TV program library as well as its TV stations and theme parks.

Now in control of Paramount, he ordered the studio to limit its production to 15 films a year rather than the 25 or more it had been producing. During the year of acquisition, 1994, the studio finished *Forrest Gump* and *Clear and Present Danger,* both with high box office returns.. He also worked out co-production deals with other studios to cut risks. Thus, he shared the costs and profits of *Saving Private Ryan* with DreamWorks, Steven Spielberg's company, and of *Titanic* with Disney Studios. By 1999, the money magazines were calling Paramount the most profitable of Hollywood studios. Released in 2000 were *Mission Impossible II* and *Shaft.* Scheduled for 2001 were *Along Came a Spider, The General's Daughter,* and *Rules of Engagement.* A *Los Angeles Times* critic commented that "Paramount isn't shy about selling two key story elements that TV can't offer enough of: nail-biting suspense and steamy sex."[19]

With Paramount in hand, he was able to join Chris-Craft in launching a new TV network, UPN (United Paramount Network) which so far is still operating in the red, overshadowed by the Big Four - NBC, CBS, ABC, and Fox. By 2001, Redstone had all of UPN, and also won FCC approval for ownership of two networks by a single company. Redstone's other network, of course, is CBS.

In the same year, Viacom bought BET (Black Entertainment Television) for $2.3 billion. It is the country's biggest cable channel serving blacks, and it also owns a jazz music cable channel, publishes books and makes movies. But the transaction had its critics. Both the Reverend Jesse Jackson and NAACP President Kweisi Mfume expressed anger at Viacom's takeover. An article in *Progressive* magazine said, "Nielsen ratings indicate that BET's prime time shows garner around 1 percent of the black population."[20] The author added, "From sexually explicit music videos, featuring epic levels of misogyny and violence, to near endless comedy showcases and celebrity infotainment, BET has never lived up to the promise that people believed was inherent in its charter."

Doubt about the freedom of CBS reporters in coverage of Viacom's vast holdings was expressed in the *Columbia Journalism Review.* Redstone had commented that journalists shouldn't be "unnecessarily offensive in countries in which you operate" In CJR, Mark Crispin Miller commented, "With Nickelodeon in Turkey and Indonesia, MTV in India, Russia, and Colombia as well as China, Viacom has a vested interest in maintaining editorial tact in places where 'offensiveness' may be the proper course."[21]

As he looked closely at all Viacom operations, including Paramount, he became dissatisfied with CEO Biondi's management methods and decisions. Two years after the Paramount takeover, he asked the Viacom board's permission to dismiss Biondi, who got a handsome severance package as Redstone took over completely. Mel Karmazin, who had been running CBS, became chief operating officer, and

Redstone has indicated that the 56-year old Karmazin will ultimately succeed him.

Concerned about Blockbuster's low profits, Redstone went to the Dallas headquarters of the huge chain and found that Blockbuster was paying the studios as much as $65 for a single video. After months of negotiations, he worked out a series of partnerships with the studios under which Blockbuster now pays between $3 and $8 for each video and gives 40 percent of the rentals back to the studios. Result: Blockbuster profits zoomed more than 90 percent in the year ending in March, 1999, with "all major divisions of Viacom stronger and more profitable today than they were under Biondi."[22]

But Blockbuster's new success came at the expense of independent video store owners, some 2,500 of whom went out of business in the two years after 1998. So early in 2001, 200 independent video store owners filed a suit against Blockbuster, arguing that the company is using illegal business methods. They say Blockbuster's purchasing agreements with the movie studios are illegal.

Needless to say, Redstone has paid attention to the computer's Internet. Viacom has numerous sites, including cbs.sportsline.com, cbs.marketwatch.com, mtv.com, vhi.com, and iWon.com, CBS's new portal. Probably the most visited sites are in the MTVi Group of 14 web properties worldwide, including MTV.com, VH1.com and SoniNet.com in the United States. In July, 2000, Blockbuster signed a 20-year contract to partner with Enron Corp. in delivery of video on demand over Enron's high speed Internet access. Blockbuster had already set up a Web site to list new movies.

In recent years, Redstone's intense focus on his huge, scattered properties has caused major trouble for his marriage. Less than a fortnight after he slapped hands with Karmazin over the merger announcement, he was handed a multi-billion dollar divorce claim -- half of his wealth -- by his wife, Phyllis. After 52 years of marriage, she charged "adultery and cruel and abusive treatment."[23] Before the merger announcement, "Sumner had been seen in the company of Christine Peters, the ex-wife of Hollywood producer Jon Peters," a news story said.[24] Mrs. Redstone had filed three earlier divorce suits, including one soon after Viacom's purchase of Paramount, but they were all withdrawn. This one apparently will not be withdrawn. A Viacom spokesman said, "He wishes her well and continues to do everything possible to make the divorce settlement reasonable."[25]

While he and Phyllis had lived in "a modest three-bedroom home in Newton Center, Massachusetts (which) he bought in the 1950s,"[26] he has spent much — or most — of his time over the years in New York hotels, first the Carlisle and now a rented suite in the Pierre.

Politically, he remains a liberal. Indeed, a *New Yorker* article called him "a lifelong liberal Democrat, who worked with the Truman administration and has raised money for the Kennedys and Clinton."[27] But Viacom was among the top 50 contributors to Republican John McCain's presidential campaign in 1999. Reason: McCain's Senate bill to allow networks to own stations reaching 50 percent of U.S. households, rather than the 35 percent set by the 1996 Telecom Act. When the primaries were over, Viacom gave more than $95,000 to the Gore campaign, and a *Nation* article said, "Now that Viacom has merged with CBS, the media giant's clout in Washington is only growing."[28]

He has set up handsome trusts for his daughter Shari, vice president of National Amusements, and son Brent, a Denver attorney, who is a director of both Viacom and National Amusements. He serves on many boards and has received a long list of awards.

A Passion to Win is the title of Redstone's autobiography, which was published in June, 2001. His own Simon & Schuster is the publisher. The first chapter begins with the line, "Viacom is me."

At 78, he is physically fit, jogs every day and eats carefully, often consuming a bowl of hot Irish cornmeal for lunch. He remains both owner and CEO of the third largest media conglomerate in the world. Two *Business Week* reporters paid tribute to him when they wrote, "With his tirelessness, his passionate enthusiasm, and his laser beam intellect, Redstone has long been Viacom's greatest asset."[29] His own assets jumped from $6.4 billion in 1998 to $12.8 billion in 2001, doubling in just three years. Clearly, Sumner Redstone is still riding the escalator of entertainment — and wealth.

THE COX SISTERS–THE RICHEST WOMEN IN AMERICA

4

They are called "the richest women in America" by *Forbes*. The two sisters, Anne Cox Chambers and Barbara Cox Anthony, inherited 98 percent of Cox Enterprises and in 2001 were worth $23.4 billion — $11.7 billion each.

Now in their seventies, they are the children of James Cox, who started his journalistic ventures with the *Dayton Daily News*, which he bought in 1898 for $26,000. The Dayton paper became his springboard to three terms as Ohio governor. He ran unsuccessfully for president in 1920, with Franklin D. Roosevelt as his running mate.

But Cox left politics and turned his full attention to newspapering with the 1939 purchase of the *Atlanta Journal*, followed eleven years later by the *Atlanta Constitution*. The evening *Journal* and morning *Constitution* were merged to become the flagship of Cox Enterprises, which now operates dailies, weeklies, broadcast stations and cable networks scattered around the country. Cox Enterprises is easily the outstanding media company in the southeast.[1] "We cover Dixie like the dew" is the slogan, but the empire reaches other parts of the country, too.

When James Cox died in 1957, his son James Jr. took control of Cox Enterprises and before long began to buy cable companies. Regulatory problems led to a spin-off of the cable system into Cox Communications, which until 1990 was publicly traded.

James Jr. survived his father by only seventeen years, dying in 1974. That left the empire to his two sisters, Barbara and Anne. Barbara's husband, Garner Anthony, was given control of Cox Enterprises from 1974 to 1987, when Barbara's son by an earlier marriage took over. The son, James Cox Kennedy, assumed control when he was only 40, and he quickly showed his determination to improve the quality of both the *Journal* and *Constitution*, indeed to make them world class papers. He hired Bill Kovach, a veteran *New York Times* reporter with an outstanding reputation as the *Times* bureau chief in Washington. Kovach discovered that there were serious problems including scant coverage by both papers of Atlanta's large black population. The record had been good in the 1950s and '60s, when Ralph McGill was editor. McGill was ardently anti-segregationist, and the papers scrupulously reported events of those turbulent decades. But in the 15 years after McGill's death, the papers see-sawed on the main racial issues, sharply critical of some local black leaders part of the time, then leaning over backwards to be favorable at other times.[2]

Kovach replaced Jim Minter as editor in 1986. Minter had held back on at least two stories on African-Americans and whites in Atlanta. James Bond, the famous civil rights leader, claimed the papers had made a number of attacks on him, including "red baiting" because of his opposition to the Vietnam war. Then he led the Atlanta NAACP chapter in petitioning the FCC to investigate possible anti-trust violations by both the Cox newspapers and the local cable company. The NAACP action resulted in reorganization of the cable business into Cox Communications Inc. as a separate enterprise. All this was part of the papers' history that left an image Kovach was determined to change.

The Kovach period lasted only two years. During his earlier career as a reporter, he had covered the Nashville race riots, and he considered himself a liberal. But he made the powerful Atlanta business community unhappy. The papers began to cover the Atlanta gay community in much the same way as San Francisco papers do. They covered both local and national political stories vigorously. And they looked closely at operations of Coca Cola Company and Atlanta Power, both major employers in Atlanta.[3] But the biggest Kovach period story gave readers evidence that Atlanta banks had been refusing to make home loans to black applicants.

While the business community was clearly angered by Kovach, both papers thrived financially. But there were disagreements between Kovach and his boss, Kennedy, over the papers' aggressiveness. The climax came in a row over the Washington bureau of the Cox papers. The resident editors complained that Kovach was trying to take control; he replied that he was merely calling for more aggressive coverage of capitol events. Afterward, Kennedy would only say that the disagreement had resulted from "poor communications." Kovach's story was heavily featured in a PBS documentary, "Fear and Favor in the Newsroom." Even though the *Atlanta Constitution* was nominated for five Pulitzer prizes within a year after Kovach's arrival — a national record — he resigned after only two years in the Georgia capitol. Explaining the departure, Kennedy said only that "Kovach's vision and our vision were different." The papers "had regressed to familiar territory within days of Kovach's departure," according to Nicholas Coleridge in his book, *Paper Tigers*.[4] Criticism has also come from a former *Journal* and *Constitution* reporter, Kevin Sack, who now works for the *New York Times*. He wrote, "It's hard to pick up (the *Journal* and *Constitution*) and get a clear feel for what's significant."[5]

The two papers are today the home of an empire that is growing rapidly. Sunday circulation was 686,000 and daily circulation 511,000 in 1995. Cox Enterprises also holds 14 smaller dailies in Florida, Texas, Ohio, Colorado and North Carolina, 15 weeklies, 15 TV and 14 radio stations, 23 profitable cable companies, and 26 car auction businesses.[6] In July, 2000, it bought a group of newspapers in southwest Ohio from the Canadian Thomson Corp.. Manheim Auctions is the name of the car auction business — the biggest used car company in the country. Manheim has 97 sites in North America, Europe and Australia. It expanded in the fall of 2000 when it paid $1 billion for ADT Automotive from Tyco International. The buy added 28 auto auction sites in the U.S. AutoTrader, which lists used cars online, has about five million visitors a month.

Cox Enterprises is the largest company in Georgia, with one-third of its 37,000 employees working in the state. Kennedy, now 54, is powerful in both city and state. Apart from his intense interest in the Cox media empire, he is what many would call a "health nut." He swims a mile every day and then works out in a gym for an hour. He likes to play tennis, to canoe and to windsurf. Several years ago, he led a bicycle team in a race from Irvine, California, to Savannah, Georgia — 2,900 miles, winning in five days, ten hours. Before taking over in Atlanta, he learned about newspapering by working in three key departments — press, news and advertising. Then he went to Grand Junction, Colorado, where he took on the title of publisher for the local Cox paper. His two children were born in Colorado, where Kennedy became an environmentalist, serving on the state's wildlife commission.

The papers defer to the business community in which they operate, but Kennedy insists that local editors decide editorial policy alone. He emphasizes local autonomy. Local editors decide on which presidential candidates to support. The editor of the *Atlanta Constitution's* editorial page is an African-American, Cynthia Tucker, whose columns are syndicated and who appears regularly on the PBS *Lehrer News Hour*. Since Kennedy took over in 1988, Cox revenues have quadrupled from $1.7 billion to almost $8 billion annually. Looking toward his ultimate retirement, Kennedy named G. Dennis Berry as president and chief operating officer in 2000.

The Atlanta papers are among 1,200 in the country now offering 900 telephone numbers to provide the latest weather, sports and stock market news. The service gets 1.5 million calls a month.[7] In the fall of 2000, Cox Enterprises bought a 25 percent interest in Creative Living, an alternative newsweekly chain. The parent company, Cox Enterprises, moved into new media with a subsidiary, Cox Digital TV and a small holding in the Primestar satellite company, but it sold its digital wireless telephone network in 1999. Then in May, 2000, Trader Publishing Co, half of which is owned by Cox Enterprises, paid $520 million for 300 free distribution classified advertising magazines. The sprawling Cox Enterprises also owns Val-Pak, a direct mail company that uses colored envelopes to mail coupons for national and regional advertisers to more than 70 million homes several times a year.

Cox Enterprises doesn't always win. In June of 2000, it bought 3.5 million shares of MP3.com, an online music company, for $27 a share. After MP3.com ran into copyright problems with Universal Music, Cox sold 500,000 shares in August and a million shares in October.

Anne Cox Chambers, Kennedy's aunt, is at 79 the older of the two Cox sisters. She is a long-time supporter of the Democratic Party, and a good friend of former President Jimmy Carter. Indeed, Carter appointed her as U.S. Ambassador to Belgium, a post she held four years. She has engaged in fund-raising for Carter, Michael Dukakis, Bill Clinton, and late in 1999, Bill Bradley. In 1993, President Francois Mitterand awarded her the medal of the French Legion of Honor. Her nephew, James Cox Kennedy, is also involved in liberal causes, campaigning for the rights of Jews and African-Americans. He is described as involved in "all the right charities."[8] Incidentally, while Mrs. Chambers is chairman of the Atlanta papers, she seems to have no influence on which presidential candidates get their support. Both the *Journal* and *Constitution* endorse Republican candidates more often than Democratic.

This multi-media billionairess has lovely homes in several places — La Petit Fontanille villa in Provence, France; Rosewood, a large estate in Atlanta; and a 12,000- acre plantation in South Carolina. In France her neighbors include Stephen Spender, John Malkovich and Monaco's Princess Caroline. Spender says, "She has a great gift for friendship." She flies in a Gulfstream jet to Washington, New York or Paris as she likes, but always appears at quarterly board meetings. Twice divorced, she has three children, Margaretha Johnson Taylor, Katherine Anne Johnson and James Cox Chambers. Calling her "the first lady of Atlanta," a *Vanity Fair* reporter wrote that she did "innumerable good works all the way from funding a literacy program for inner city youth to donating paintings to the local museum."[9] She seems untroubled by the fact that most of her friends are Republicans while she is an active Democrat. "I just don't discuss politics with my friends," she says. "No use having fights."[10]

The younger sister, Barbara Cox Anthony, has a villa in Honolulu and a ranch in Australia. She serves as chair of the company's Dayton, Ohio, holdings, and attends quarterly board meetings. At 76, she has been divorced, then widowed after a second marriage, and then married a third time. She has two children, Blair Parry-Okeden and James Cox Kennedy, who runs the Atlanta papers and Cox Enterprises. She is a very private person.

The two sisters leave the day-to-day management of the empire — newspapers, radio, TV and cable — to Kennedy. Although Cox Enterprises is family owned, he and other Cox managers make decisions in much the same way as managers of Gannett, Knight-Ridder or any other media company with stock on Wall Street. Their eyes are always on the bottom line. The current Atlanta editor is Ron Martin, who finds plenty of news in the explosive growth of Atlanta and its surrounding suburbs.

When Barry Diller was eagerly trying to buy Paramount Communications in the fall of 1993, Cox Enterprises joined the Newhouse family in supporting the bid with a promise of $1 billion, $500 million each. Diller's bid failed. The following year Cox Enterprises paid $2.3 billion to Times Mirror Corporation for its cable operations. The purchase brought Cox cable customers to more than three million. Then in May, 1999, Cox Communications paid $3.26 billion for TCA Cable TV, becoming the fourth largest cable company in the country, behind Time Warner, AT&T and Comcast. The Cox family received the Distinguished Service Award from the National Association of Broadcasters the same year. In the mid-nineties, Cox Communications had joined Times Mirror Company in creating two new cable sports channels — Outdoor Life and Speedvision race car network. The Outdoor Life channel relies on the Times Mirror magazine of the same name, as well as *Field and Stream* and *Skiing* magazines.

In 1987 and 1990, the Cox grandchildren sold their shares in Cox Enterprises for $1.26 billion. The transactions took the empire off the stock market and back entirely into family hands. The moves had two purposes: to protect Cox Communications from a raid by a company hungry for its $2 billion annual income, and to reduce taxes for many years because of the substantial debt.[11]

When the Olympic Games began in Atlanta in July, 1996, the *Constitution* and the *Journal* assigned about 300 reporters and photographers to coverage. Special sections which had been started a year earlier were enlarged and published during the Games. But the *Constitution*'s coverage of the Olympic Park bombing during the Games led to a major court case when Richard Jewell sued the paper for libel in its stories about the police hunt for the bomber. Sources for the stories were not given. Jewell's suit was filed a year after the bombing.

The huge Cox empire marches on, the twelfth largest media conglomerate in the U.S. It reaches from Atlanta to most parts of the country. Its profits rise continually. In October, 1990, *Forbes* 400 credited the sisters with joint wealth of $5.2 billion. By 2001, that figure had jumped to $23.4 billion.

JOHN KLUGE–THE MEDIA MOGUL
WHO ALSO OWNS RESTAURANTS

5

John Werner Kluge's last name means "clever" in German, and he's been proving that he deserves it since he came to America as an eight-year-old in 1922. For three years in a row — 1989, 1990 and 1991 — *Forbes* called him America's richest man. In 1989 he was worth $5.9 billion; as of 2001, $10.3 billion.

The *Forbes 400* describes his empire as an "international telecommunications/entertainment/media company." He owns Metromedia Company, a huge media conglomerate with TV and radio stations, cellular communications, a fiber network, and two movie studios — Samuel Goldwyn Company and Motion Pictures Corporation. In recent years, he has reached overseas to form Metromedia International, which is constructing wireless cable TV and telephone networks in key cities in Russia, Eastern Europe and China. Over the years he has gobbled up the Steak and Ale, Bennigan's, Bonanza, and Ponderosa restaurant chains, some franchised, with more than 1,500 locations, all specializing in low-price meals. In 1999, Bonanza and Ponderosa were brought into Metromedia Family Steakhouses, with 45,000 employees. The next year, Bennigan's officials announced plans for 65 more restaurants across the country.

Illustrating the wide diversity of Kluge's empire, his Metromedia Company, based in East Rutherford, New Jersey, has 25 subsidiaries operating all over the U.S. and abroad, as well as 50 joint ventures in some 24 countries. His Morven Partners, headquartered in Edenton, North Carolina, sells peanuts, pecans and almonds under the label Chock Full 'O Nuts. His lawn mower company makes Snapper. The Kluge-owned Cogent Light Technologies, working from Los Angeles, makes high intensity lights for surgery; his Axon Systems makes sensing equipment to help surgeons monitor the brain activity of their patients. And his Metromedia Technologies has a machine that prints billboard scenes on vinyl, eliminating the need for either paint or paper. He didn't invent these processes, but was clever enough to see their commercial possibilities.

Born in 1914 in Chemnitz, Germany, Kluge came to the United States with his mother after his engineer father died in 1922. Living in Detroit, he worked on an automobile assembly line before going to Wayne State University, and then Columbia University. While at Columbia on a scholarship, he played poker regularly and had accumulated $7,000 in winnings when he graduated. In 1946, a year after he left the U.S. Army as a captain in the intelligence branch, Kluge came up with $15,000 to buy KWAY, a radio station in Silver Springs, Maryland. In the 15 years after the war, other enterprises included wholesale food and investment companies in both Washington, D.C., and Ft. Worth, Texas.

His media interests became stronger in 1959 when he bought control of Metropolitan Broadcasting Corporation, which had been the DuMont network. The corporation owned TV stations in New York and Washington and a radio station in Cleveland. In the next few years he changed the name to Metromedia and bought radio and TV stations all over the country in such key cities as Boston and Los Angeles. He briefly owned World Wide Broadcasting, a shortwave world news station, but found that it wasn't profitable enough, so he sold it to the Mormon Church after two years, at a $1 million profit.[1]

In 1960, a year after Kluge took over Metromedia, he bought three outdoor advertising companies, and within four years he owned 35,000 billboards. His TV stations carried re-runs of such programs as *Father Knows Best* aimed at a new generation of viewers. To provide for new programs, he bought Wolper Productions, which made movies, documentaries and TV specials, such as those of Jaques Cousteau and National Geographic.

Most of his ventures turned out well, so that by 1983 he was able to buy all Metromedia stock, taking the company wholly private. For this he borrowed $1.2 billion, which Wall Street experts called highly risky. "Then he enraged former shareholders by selling off pieces for $8 billion."[2] The "pieces" included seven TV and seven radio stations, the billboard companies, the Harlem Globetrotters and the IceCapades, plus the cellular telephone and paging services he had bought in 1982. The billboard empire went to Patrick Media, which became the country's biggest owner of outdoor advertising. But Kluge retained Metromedia Technologies, which simplifies production of whatever goes on billboards. Rupert Murdoch was the buyer of the TV stations, which became the basis for the Fox Network. The price was $2 billion. By the fall of 1988, Kluge's debt had been turned into a $2.2 billion surplus. The sale of the cellular telephone and paging businesses brought $1.3 billion on what had been a $300 million investment only four years earlier.

The name Metromedia has been used over and over for his companies as he bought and sold properties — Metromedia Inc., Metromedia Company, Metromedia Technologies, Metromedia Long Distance, Metromedia ITT Long Distance, Metromedia Communications Corporation, and Metromedia Steakhouses Inc.. Metromedia has a "grab bag of services, which range from wireless cable TV and telephone to paging," a *New York Times* profile said in early 1997.[3] The reporter listed Orion Pictures (since sold) and included among Kluge's "personal holdings" the Ponderosa and Bonanza restaurant chains; two Manhattan hotels, the Barbizon and Radisson Empire; and even a professional soccer team, the MetroStars. Not mentioned were Kluge's 130 laundromats, Chock Full 'O Nuts, meat processing plants, feed lots, lawn mowers, the Fiber Network and Big City Radio with stations in New York, Los Angeles and Chicago.

In the last few years, Kluge's Metromedia Fiber Network, listed on Wall Street, has been laying fiber optic lines covering 51 American cities, including New York, Boston, Philadelphia and Washington, and 16 European cities. A deal with Bell Atlantic early in 1999 leases fiber for Bell to build its own network between New York and White Plains. Later in 1999, Bell Atlantic paid $1.68 billion for 19 percent of Metromedia Fiber Networks and as a result, Metromedia was expected to double the number of fiber optic networks it's building in major U.S. cities. Bell, in turn, got access to lines that cover more than 7,000 miles in U.S. and eight major European cities. At almost the same time, Kluge's Fiber Network paid $1.33 billion for AboveNet, which runs server forms for Internet customers, such as RealNetworks Inc. and WebMD Inc.[4] They, in turn, provide high speed Internet connections. Then the Fiber Network paid $1.23 billion in October, 2000, to buy the year-old SiteSmith Inc., which helps design and build companies' Internet operations. "With SiteSmith, Metromedia hopes to sell customers more Internet services, which have wider profit margins than just carrying the traffic, said Vic Grover, a Kaufman Brothers analyst."[5] Metromedia Fiber also began to build fiber networks in Germany and Great Britain.

Kluge's main focus now is on expansion of Metromedia International Group's operations overseas. He foresees his wireless telephone and wireless cable TV reaching as many as 100 million customers in Russia, Ukraine, Georgia, Latvia and Kazakstan. Metromedia International has also been buying up radio and TV stations in some of the same cities. On the cable and the TV stations, program directors draw from Kluge's film libraries for such golden oldies as *Guys and Dolls* and *Pride of the Yankees*. In late 1999, Metromedia International Group took over PLD, a leading telecom company in Russia. Because Kluge's friend Rupert Murdoch owned a big stake in PLD, the new deal gave him 10 percent of Metromedia International. The buy brought to 72 the number of Metromedia companies in Russia and eastern Europe. And the same Metromedia company is part of a joint venture in such Chinese cities as Tianjin and Nanning. He sees telephone as riding a wave of the future in places where phones have been unthinkable in the past. He knows that more than half of the world's people have never made a phone call. "Communication is not a luxury in emerging markets; it is a necessity," the astute Kluge says.[6]

One successful example of Metromedia's wireless cable operations is in Riga, Latvia, where for the local equivalent of $9 a month, subscribers get six channels. They include MTV, with the Russian language dubbed in; ESPN's Eurosport; CineRus, which provides movies dubbed in Russian; and a local Latvian channel with news and music. Kluge found a studio in Moscow where he can have films dubbed not only into Russian but nine other languages. The movies include such blockbusters as *Platoon* and *RoboCop*. The signals for these wireless cable operations are sent from a microwave tower to dishes fixed to rooftops. The same system can be used for wireless telephone, which helps to explain the astute Kluge's double-barreled entry into both Chinese and Eastern European markets. By mid-June, 1999, Kluge's company had "nearly 50 joint ventures in some two dozen countries; it is in everything from paging and cable to radio and cellular telephony."[7] The cable broadcasts offer local TV channels in the same way that wired cable companies do in America, and add such standbys as CNN, BBC, and the Discovery channel with golden oldies like TV's *Flipper* and *Gentle Ben*.

The main value of Kluge's movie studios — Samuel Goldwyn and Motion Pictures Corporation — has been their film libraries with both movies and TV programs. With the Goldwyn Company, he has 850 film and TV titles, as well as the Landmark Theater Group which operates 150 screens in 52 theaters showing art and other specialized films.

Kluge, now 87, has been married three times. His first marriage was to Theodora Thomson in 1949; his second, to Yolanda Zucco in 1969, produced two children, Samantha and Joseph. Then his nine-year marriage to Patricia Rose Gay resulted in adoption of a son, John W. Kluge, Jr. He divorced Patricia in 1990; her settlement reportedly gives her $80 million a year. The only daughter, Samantha, became beauty editor of Hearst's *Cosmopolitan* magazine in 1998, and is rumored to be Kluge's possible successor.

Like most other billionaires, he has homes in several places. The most valuable is Morven Farm, which cost $250 million and covers 10,000 acres not far from Charlottesville, Virginia. On Morven Farm is Albemarle House, a 50-room residence beside a golf course designed by Arnold Palmer. Patricia still lives in Albemarle House, while Kluge spends part of his time at Morven House at the other end of the huge acreage. It contains the only thing he brought with him when he came from Germany as an eight-year-old — a Dresden china horse.

He had a castle on 80,000 acres in Scotland, but sold it in 1995 to a preservation group. He spends most of his time in New York. The lavish penthouse apartment where he had lived on East 67th Street was taken over in 1999 by Rupert Murdoch for a Fox TV channel office. Kluge moved to a midtown apartment. He also has a $30 million home in Palm Beach, and when he chooses to visit Florida by sea, he sails on his 206-foot yacht.

Because he got his bachelor's degree at Columbia University, Kluge has donated more than $125 million to the university, most of it for minority scholarships. He has also contributed to medical causes, and gave more than $5 million to a digital collection at the Library of Congress. Then his October, 2000, gift of $60 million to the Library of Congress was earmarked for an annual $1 million prize in human sciences.

With his fiber networks growing in America and his wireless and broadcast networks growing in Russia, Ukraine, Georgia, Latvia, Kazakhstan and eastern China, far-sighted John Kluge is still showing that he knows when to buy and most of all, when and where to expand. At 86, he's still showing that "kluge" means clever.

TED TURNER–CAPTAIN OUTRAGEOUS

6

Multi-billionaire Ted Turner arrived on the national scene just about 20 years ago, but he has regularly made headlines ever since. One sensational story came in 1995 with the merger of the Time Warner empire with his, putting Turner second in command of the super-conglomerate. Even more sensational was the merger early in 2000 of America Online (AOL) with Time-Warner-Turner, which brought him stock and options worth about $10 billion.

Between the two mergers, he made headlines with announcement of a $1 billion gift to the United Nations. Then in December, 2000, he offered another gift of $34 million to make up for a shortfall in U.S. dues to the UN. And less than a month after that, he set up a $250 million non-profit organization to reduce the global threat from nuclear arms and other weapons of mass destruction, with former Senator Sam Nunn in charge.[1]

Other Turner highlights: he started the country's first super-station in 1976; won the America's Cup in 1977; started CNN and its round-the-clock news broadcasts in 1980, followed by Headline News in 1982; bought the huge MGM film library in 1986; and began to put the old movies on a new cable channel, TNT, in 1988.

By the end of the century, his empire had reached global dimensions with CNN listener-viewers all over the world. In 1985 he founded the Better World Society to encourage peace and friendly relations among nations; spent $26 million to sponsor the Goodwill Games in Moscow the next year; and repeated that five years later with the Seattle Goodwill Games, losing $44 million in the process.

After two earlier wives who bore his five children, he married super-star Jane Fonda in December, 1991, and she brought her own multi-layered achievements as well as considerable wealth to the altar. Even before the wedding, she had sold her property in Santa Barbara and brought her horses to his 300,000-acre ranch near

Bozeman, Montana. There Turner has torn down all fences so that a herd of buffalo can roam freely in what *Time* magazine has called "a private national park."[2]

His name is so closely associated with CNN and Atlanta that few people know he was born in Cincinnati, Ohio, on November 19, 1938. His father, Ed Turner, had come from his birthplace in Mississippi when the family farm was forfeited during the Great Depression. His mother's family owned a Cincinnati grocery chain.

Ted went to a Cincinnati public school until he was nine. Then his father moved the family to Savannah, Georgia, where he bought two billboard poster companies. Son Ted was sent to Georgia Military Academy, near Atlanta, and then the McCallie School in Chattanooga, Tennessee, where he was a member of a team that won the state's high school debating championship. After McCallie he went to Brown University in Providence, Rhode Island, where he resumed debating activities and also a long-time interest in sailing.

During summers, the young student worked, at Ed Turner's insistence, at his father's business headquarters in Savannah. On his return to Brown for his sophomore year, Turner joined some classmates in an evening of heavy drinking, climaxed by a noisy visit to a nearby women's college, for which he was suspended. As a result, his father ordered him to join the Coast Guard Reserves, and he spent six months on active duty. Soon after his return to Brown, he was caught with a young lady in his room and was expelled for good. During his less than three years in college, his major accomplishment was election as co-captain of the sailing team which won the Schell Trophy, the top award in New England college racing.

Returning home in 1960, young Ted Turner was made general manager of his father's branch in Macon, Georgia. In June of that year, he married the beautiful Judy Nye, a Northwestern University graduate he'd met while yachting for Brown. Their daughter, Laura Lee, was born a year later. They had been married only two years when Judy, disgusted by Turner's constant womanizing and alcoholism, secured a divorce. She moved to Florida, but soon realized that she was pregnant again. When Ted Turner learned this, he drove to Florida and persuaded her to return to Macon with him. However, even though she wanted to remarry, he put her off. Robert Edward Turner, IV, was born in May, 1963 and a year later Ted and Judy separated permanently.

Meantime, Ted's father was continuing to expand his profitable billboard business and to buy large properties — plantations — in South Carolina and Georgia. To accomplish this, he sold his Savannah company and moved to Atlanta, the main base for his new holdings spread over Georgia and Virginia. When his debts became too great for him to handle, Ed Turner began to plan a sale of his holdings, and checked briefly in at Silver Hill, an alcohol recovery center. Ted learned about the plans to sell and objected strenuously, urging his father in a long telephone conversation to hang on. But Ed Turner felt trapped ; one day, only six months after he had made his big purchase, he shot himself in the head.

Ted quickly arranged to revoke the contract his father had signed to sell the new holdings. To do this, he had to come up with $200,000. For a start, he sold the family plantations, and then got a concession to pay off the rest of the debt over five years. Now Ted was in charge of his father's company, with plants in Atlanta,

Augusta, Macon, Columbus, Charleston, Richmond, Roanoke and Covington. Soon after he took over, business flourished. He began to buy new billboard companies. In 1964, it was the Tennessee Advertising Company, followed by the Knoxville Post Company in 1965. By then, he owned the largest billboard firm in the eight Southern states.

During this time he continued to race yachts. In August, he and Judy entered, and won, the Y-Flying Class race — a national championship. Less than a year later, in June, 1964, Ted Turner married Jane Smith who was pregnant with his child. Their first child was named Rhett. Jane bore two more children, Beauregard and Jennie, in just a few years. Meantime, Judy had also married again, and her second husband was extremely abusive to Ted's older children. When Ted heard about this, he arranged for her to send both children to Atlanta. In the end, Ted and Jane, or "Janie," raised a household of five children.

By the late 1960s, Ted was getting bored with billboards.[3] He bought a radio station in Chattanooga, and then stations in Jacksonville and Charleston. In 1970 he heard of a money-losing station in Atlanta — WJRJ/Channel 17. He bought it, changing its call letters to WTCG, an acronym for Turner Communications Group. An ultra-high frequency station with a tiny audience, it didn't show up on many screens and had frequent technical problems. His purchase of WJRJ launched what was ultimately to become a worldwide empire. He gradually built the station's local audience, using live broadcasts of sports, re-runs of movies and old TV situation comedies. In the first five years, losses mounted to $2 million, all covered by billboard profits during the early '70s. By then Turner was a multi-millionaire.

In 1975, the Federal Communications Commission loosened its restrictions on cable TV. In the same year, RCA launched its first satellite, SATCOM I. By hooking up to SATCOM I at the end of 1976, Turner's WTCG was suddenly heard and seen in two million homes, and its audience increased rapidly. He had bought the Atlanta Braves baseball team in 1975 and he could broadcast the games easily; before 1976 was over, he also owned the Atlanta Hawks basketball team

While buying baseball and basketball teams, Turner continued to follow his passion for yachting. His forays under sail climaxed with capture of the America's Cup in 1977. As a result, he was named Yachtsman of the Year for the third time, the first person to be so honored.

In the meantime, he had continued to build his film library to 2,700 movies. By now Turner was calling WTCG a "super station." It has been re-named again to WTBS, a key anchor of the Turner Broadcasting System. Once the satellite hookup had been made, Turner's fortunes rose rapidly. But he and the managers on his staff considered news a secondary feature of the super station's programming. The idea of round-the-clock programming didn't emerge until 1979, and by then the station was carrying not only sports and movies, but also special events, children's programs, adult programs in prime time — and news.

As early as 1978, Turner had begun to sound out associates and friends about the idea of a 24-hour news program, broadcast to cable viewers. His staff warned him that it would be extremely costly, reminding him that all his broadcast properties in the past had shown contempt for news. He met with Reese Schonfeld, who operated the Independent Television News Association. Schonfeld assured him that the 24-hour news idea was workable, but also warned about start-up costs — as much as $100 million. Then Turner revealed that he had already decided on a name — CNN, Cable News Network. The high start-up costs for CNN meant selling the Charlotte station, and ultimately the Westinghouse Group bought it for $20 million. Daniel Schorr, who had been a correspondent for CBS and more recently for ITNA, was invited to be CNN bureau chief in Washington.

Turner and Schonfeld found a two-story building near Georgia Tech that could house studios and offices of both CNN and WTBS. At a May, 1979, press conference in Las Vegas during a cable industry meeting, Turner announced that CNN would debut in November, but it didn't happen until June, 1980. CNN's opening day was bumpy, with technical problems and reporters having trouble finding enough stories to fill the time. The problems continued for months. A more serious concern for Turner was that CNN was reaching only 1.7 million homes instead of the expected 3.5 million. He pushed constantly for more subscribers and more advertisers, but for the first two years, the money crisis was continuous. In late 1980, Group W of Westinghouse joined with ABC in announcing not one but two cable channels offering round-the-clock news. Turner's response was to announce CNNII, which became Headline News. The cable audience for CNN, which had been disappointing at the start, gradually grew to some 10 million by December, 1981.

In the years since the 1980 launch, CNN has covered all the major world events. During the first few of those years, Turner's behavior was noisy, hyperactive, pugnacious and disagreeable, both at home with his wife Janie and their children, and in the office with associates. At Janie's insistence, he began to visit Dr. Frank Pittman, an Atlanta psychiatrist, in 1983, 23 years after his father's suicide. The doctor suggested that he start taking lithium, a drug for those with manic depression. J.J.Ebaugh, the woman with whom he began to live the following year, said the lithium led to "an enormous change in his behavior."[4] Turner was 47 years old; his explosively growing CNN had been operating five years.

Now he began to build an overseas empire. Reacting to the linkup of ABC with BBC, Turner created Cable News Network International — CNNI. In 1991 he set up bureaus in Amman, Rio de Janiero and New Delhi, and a year later in Bangkok. In 1992, he joined several former communist administrators to form the first independent television channel in Russia. He also ordered two hours a day of news summaries in Spanish fed to 19 countries in Central and South America. As CNNI got into the '90s, the broadcasts included segments in Russian, German, French, Japanese and Chinese. By mid-1993, CNN and CNNI were "reaching 200 countries and more than 16 percent of the world's 800 million homes."[5]

As his empire continued to grow in the 1980s, Turner hankered for a larger film library, and in 1985, he bought MGM/UA from Kirk Kerkorian for $1.5 billion, reportedly overpaying by $300 million, with rights to the historic but aging MGM studios and a library of 3,500 MGM films. However, when he found it impossible to raise enough money, in March, 1986, Turner had to return the MGM/UA studio to Kerkorian, keeping only the film library. But he still had a heavy debt for the film library and sought help from TCI's John Malone. At a meeting of both Time and

Warner cable subsidiaries, Malone cobbled together the $562.5 million which Turner still owed. In return, TCI and the other cable operators got 22.5 percent of TBS and seats on Turner's board went to Malone as well as Time and Warner. Three years later, Time and Warner merged to become Time-Warner.

Even while the frantic negotiations were going on, Turner went to Moscow for the Goodwill Games, the "un-Olympics" which he arranged and financed. Here athletes from a wide assortment of nations in the West and in the Soviet orbit competed in 18 sporting events. Soviet athletes had not been invited to compete since the 1976 Olympics in Montreal. As the main sponsor of the Games, Turner lost $26 million. His Goodwill Games in Seattle in 1990 drew a more favorable public response, worldwide, than the earlier games, but here Turner's loss was $44 million.

Demonstrating his passion for both peace and the environment, Turner launched the Better World Society in 1985. In public comments he spoke of Mahatma Ghandi and Martin Luther King as his heroes. He added Jacques Cousteau as an environmental icon after joining him for a sailing trip on the Amazon. Turner then gave Cousteau $4 million to produce environmental documentaries for TBS, and this led him to fund the Audubon Society's production of nature programs to be broadcast on Turner networks.

After closing the MGM library purchase, Turner started another cable network — TNT, Turner Network Television. TNT was launched in October, 1988, with the classic *Gone With the Wind*, Turner's favorite movie, shown on opening night. The new network also became home to sporting events, especially those featuring the Atlanta Braves and Hawks. The starting audience for TNT was 17 million, rising to 50 million in just one year. Almost immediately, Turner ordered colorization of the old classics, despite strong objections by some of the living stars. In response to those who didn't like the color, he said the original black and white prints were still available.[6]

In 1989 Turner met Jane Fonda. She had broken up with California politician Tom Hayden after 16 years of marriage. She and Turner met at a political fund-raising event in Hollywood that summer. When he learned that her brother Paul had a ranch near his Flying D in Montana, he invited them over to spend a day. Turner then began to bombard her with phone calls and escorted her to the 1990 Academy Awards. By then Jane Fonda had become famous for her aerobics classes and videos, for such Hollywood movies as *Coming Home* and *Fun With Dick and Jane*, and for her "Hanoi Jane" trip to Vietnam. The relationship grew, highlighted by an Aegean Sea cruise. In *Citizen Turner*, Robert and Gerald Jay Goldberg characterize the courtship this way: "The growing romance with Jane dovetailed neatly with Turner's increasing activism. Given their parallel ideologies and similar wide-eyed sincerity, proselytizing around the planet to rescue the trees, the wetlands, the indigenous peoples, anything that needed saving. Ted's credo was: Think globally, act locally. . . . and especially, talk globally. Their mission: Save the earth."[7] They were married in December, 1991, at Avalon, Turner's property in Tennessee.

On both his TV networks and his land properties, Turner has demonstrated his increasingly sophisticated interest in the environment. On WTBS and TNT, he has devoted thousands of hours to documentaries and programs with environmental content. On his two huge ranches in Montana and New Mexico, he has worked with the Nature Conservancy to create "conservation easements," legal dedication of the land as permanent open space. The ranches cover some 600,000 acres, more area than the entire state of Rhode Island. In late spring, 1999, he added 34,000 acres to his Nebraska holdings to give his buffalo more room.[8] Altogether, he owns at least 1.5 million acres. But the conservation easement policy apparently is flexible. When he bought the 578,000-acre Vernejo Park Ranch in New Mexico in 1996, he announced that the land would be preserved as open space. But three years later, Pennzoil announced plans to drill hundreds of oil wells on the ranch. Turner had agreed to the oil exploration in return for a three percent royalty.[9]

CNN continued to grow and become more profitable. With 20 international bureaus scattered around the world, it raked in greater profits from 1991 to 1995 than the Columbia Broadcasting System, not just the CBS News Division. CNN was now reaching 45 million homes around the world.

Even before the Turner-Fonda wedding, he had begun to gather awards. Honorary doctorates came from Lehigh, Tufts, the University of North Carolina, and his alma mater — Brown University. At the Emmy Awards affair in 1992, he got a Lifetime Achievement Award. The Committee to Protect Journalists gave him the Burton Benjamin Memorial Award in 1993 and he also has the Horatio Alger Award. Most newsworthy was the "Man of the Year" cover story in *Time* magazine on January 6, 1992. Summarizing his life story, with emphasis on CNN's accomplishments, *Time* called Turner the "Prince of the Global Village."

During 1991, he organized the Turner Family Foundation to make semi-annual contributions to his favorite causes — population control and sustainable growth. His biggest, most dramatic contribution was made in September, 1997, when he announced to 500 diners at a United Nations Association gathering in New York a gift of $1 billion to the United Nations. It was the biggest charitable contribution ever made to any organization. To administer the foundation which gives the money — $100 million a year for 10 years — he named former Colorado Senator Tim Wirth, who in the first year distributed funds for women's issues, children's health, land mine clearing, drug control, environmental protection and climate change. After that, Turner became an evangelist for greater charitable contributions by the wealthy. In recent years, he's also made grants totaling $75 million to Brown University, the Citadel and his favorite McCallie School. His Turner Foundation continues to dispense at least $7 million a year for a variety of causes. Joining him in running the Foundation are his five children.

Always looking for new business possibilities, Turner started the Cartoon Network in late 1991, stocking it with films from Hanna Barbera Productions, which he bought for $320 million. The new network quickly started to pay off its cost. Thinking and acting globally, he soon had both TNT and the Cartoon Network in Europe and Asia and the Cartoon Network in Latin America. He also comes up frequently with ideas for specials or series such as the 25-part documentary, *Cold War*, which ran on TNT in late 1998 and early 1999. Another indication of his close attention to programming was his 1998 order banning use of R-rated (Restricted) films on the Turner Classic Movie channel.

After he had been forced to return MGM's movie production studios to Kerkorian, Turner still hankered for a film-making company. In August 1993 he paid $572 million to buy Castle Rock and New Line studios. Castle Rock made such well-known films as *A Few Good Men* and *In the Line of Fire*. With New Line, Turner got worldwide distribution ability plus the producer of such films as *Teen Age Mutant Ninja Turtles* and *Nightmare on Elm Street*. In April, 1993, he launched TCM, Turner Classic Movies, to show oldies-but-goodies from his vast MGM library, competing with the already-established AMC, American Movie Classics.

His discussions with Time Warner's Gerald Levin about a possible deal ran from 1993 to the summer of 1995, when Turner and Levin smacked each other's hands at a press conference announcing a merger of their giant empires. The deal left Turner $2 billion richer, second in command at the merged conglomerate, with 10 percent of Time Warner Turner stock.

Several months before the merger with Time Warner, Turner had launched a financial news network, CNN fn, in December 1995. At its start-up, it had only 5.5 million subscribers, compared to the 56 million subscribers for General Electric's CNBC. And the financial news network was still struggling in 2000. In February, 1996, TBS announced a sports network, CNN/SI, to be started later in the year. The channel was scheduled to provide sports news rather than event coverage. It was to rely on staffs of both CNN and Time Warner's *Sports Illustrated* magazine.

While he welcomed and embraced the merger, Turner recognized the danger Ben Bagdikian, retired *journal*ism dean at University of California in Berkeley, had predicted in his several editions of *The Media Monopoly*, the likelihood that the 50 corporations that owned and operated most of America's media in 1983 would be reduced to five or six by the end of the century. Speaking at a cable executives' conference three months after the merger was finalized, Turner said, "It would be a very, very sad day if we just had four or five big companies controlling all the programming and all the pipelines in the country. It would be bad for our country and bad for the world."[10]

But that was a theme he had apparently forgotten by January, 2000, when America Online and Time-Warner-Turner merged. He was no longer Number 2 in the leadership, but was expected at first to hold major power in both the film and music divisions. That expectation was dashed in May when AOL-Time Warner completed a "restructuring" that left Turner sharing the title of vice chairman with Kenneth J. Novak. He also became a "senior adviser" but no longer has operational control of the TBS-CNN segment of the vast empire. The *New York Times* said, "Turner has relinquished control of his baby."[11]

"Egotist, risk-taker, showman, non-stop talker, environmentalist, visionary of lost causes, extremist" are among the terms used most often to describe Ted Turner. Despite the fact that five biographies of Turner have been published, none has kept pace with his frenetic personal and business life. He seems always on the move.

Biographers Robert and Gerald Jay Goldberg make one kind of summary: "Through years of therapy, reading and intensive study, he has worked hard to remake himself from a self-centered, parochial Southern skirt-and-money chaser to a slightly less self-centered father, husband, and global citizen-magnate of the

1990s."[12]   That summary was published in 1995.   In November, 1998, Turner revealed that he and Jane Fonda were meeting with a marriage counselor.   And by the time of the AOL-Time Warner merger early in 2000, they had separated.   Their divorce was finalized in May, 2001.   This coincided with a variety of signs that Ted Turner had been sidelined at CNN and all the other properties he had launched.   He was no longer running his empire.

In addition to owning a large chunk of the world's biggest media empire and being listed at $8.8 billion in the *Forbes* for July 8, 2001, a jump of $5 billion in two years, Turner is the world's largest landowner with 1.7 million acres, including ranches, plantations and estates; has a great variety of friends, many of whom are celebrities; and enjoys his children and his newborn first grandchild.   At age 62, the Mouth of the South, also known as Captain Outrageous, is still regularly making headlines.

RUPERT MURDOCH–THE GLOBAL MEDIA EMPEROR

He's been called buccaneer, tycoon, octopus, gambler, union scourge and pirate. The subject of numerous biographies as well as countless magazine profiles, he's in the news frequently, almost as often as his rival Ted Turner. His media empire is the most truly global of all — major newspaper and broadcast holdings in Asia, Australia, New Zealand, Great Britain, Europe and United States, and satellite services that reach three-fourths of the world's population. He heads one of the six largest media conglomerates in the world, in the same league as AOL-Time Warner, Disney-ABC, Viacom-CBS, General Electric-NBC, and Bertelsmann AG.

Worth $7.8 billion in 2001, Rupert Murdoch, a native Australian, became an American citizen at age 54 in 1985 when he found that ownership of a U.S. broadcast network was forbidden for foreigners. Australia has a similar ban on foreign ownership of its TV stations. Once he became an American citizen, Murdoch had to find a way to get around that Australian law, so he put control of his Down Under properties in a trust with voting control in the hands of family members who still kept their Australian citizenship.

Murdoch was born March 11, 1931, in Melbourne, where his father, Keith, was chief executive of the *Herald* newspaper group. The elder Murdoch, in recognition of the power and holdings of his group, was knighted in 1933 by King George V and his wife became Dame Elisabeth.

The young Rupert and his three sisters grew up on Cruden Farm, a country home near Melbourne, with nannies making sure all went well. In 1941, he was sent to Geelong Grammar boarding school, southwest of Melbourne. He started at Oxford ten years later after spending the summer of 1950 working at the *Birmingham Gazette*. Before long he claimed to be a socialist, displaying a bust of Lenin in his room. When his father died in 1952, his mother sold the family shares in both the

Melbourne Herald and *Brisbane Courier-Mail* to pay taxes, leaving only the *Adelaide News* in family hands.

During the following summer he worked on Lord Beaverbrook's *London Daily Express*. When he returned home to take over the reins in Adelaide in September 1953, he was 22. Five years later he bought an Adelaide TV station and the *Sunday Times* in Perth. He quickly made the red ink Perth paper profitable. Murdoch continued to consider himself left wing.

Three years after taking over his late father's *Adelaide News*, he married Patricia Booker, a former airline hostess. Their daughter Prudence was born in 1959 but the marriage began to fall apart in the early '60s. Then Rupert met Anna Torv, a young reporter on the staff of his newly bought *Sydney Mirror*. After an unpleasant divorce which gave custody of Prudence to her father, Murdoch married Torv in 1967. At 18 she was half his age. From that marriage came three children, Lachlan, James and Elisabeth. Anna, an ardent Catholic, became a novelist.

After taking over the *Sydney Mirror*, Murdoch bought a TV station in Wollengong, a suburb of Sydney. Then he bought a 25 percent interest in TV stations in both Sydney and Melbourne. By now he was regularly scanning the horizon for properties to buy. " 'Expand or die' was already his watchword," according to one biographer.[1] In 1964 he launched a national paper, the *Australian*, a very big gamble. Headquartered in Sydney, the *Australian* is today profitable after years of losses — and is far more conservative than in its early years, as is Murdoch, who became more and more conservative as his properties and wealth grew.

By 1968, Murdoch was ready to move into the British newspaper market, which he had dreamed about since his years at Oxford. He learned about the availability of the *News of the World*, a Sunday paper in London with six million circulation, controlled by the family of Sir William Carr. He made two key promises to the Carr family: first, that Carr would continue as chairman; second, that the paper's content would stay the same. Not long after the Carr family let Murdoch become managing editor, he moved not only to buy more shares but asked Carr to resign as chairman. It was the first of many promises he has broken over the years.

Once in control of *News of the World*, he ordered the editor to buy the memoirs of Christine Keeler, the prostitute whose trysts with the Macmillan war minister, John Profumo, had led to the government's downfall. When publication of the memoirs was widely criticized, Murdoch was quoted as saying, "People can sneer as much as they like, but I'll take the hundred and fifty thousand extra copies we're going to sell."[2]

Then he moved to capture more British media properties. The daily *Sun* came under his wing in 1969 and he quickly applied the methods he had been using in Australia and at *News of the World*. One feature was a picture of a bare-breasted woman on page three, a feature that continues today, more than 30 years later. The *Sun*'s success pushed other London dailies down-market, with increasing emphasis on sex, celebrity and sensation. By the year 2000, *Sun* circulation had 10 million readers. With the *Sun*, Murdoch became a full-throttle capitalist and ardent defender of conservative Margaret Thatcher.

Early in 1981 he bought the *London Times* and *Sunday Times* from the family of Lord Roy Thomson. Murdoch thought he knew why the Thomson papers had been losing money: the Fleet Street unions. He found his solution outside Fleet Street, in Wapping, a highly industrial suburb on London's edge. He secretly bought a substantial piece of land and began to build a complete newspaper plant with the most up-to-date technology, at a cost of $140 million. When the unions heard about it, he told them that he planned another paper and needed overflow printing facilities. When the unions demanded the same rights in Wapping they had on Fleet Street, Murdoch in effect thumbed his nose. In January, 1986, he announced that all his Fleet Street operations were being moved to the well-guarded plant in Wapping. The unions struck. He promptly closed the struck plants and announced the dismissal of 5,000 workers. Within weeks, the four papers --*Sun, News of the World*, Sunday *Times* and *Times* were being published in Wapping and distributed all over the empire. Murdoch had won — and saved himself labor and production costs of at least $85 million a year.

Having won strong toeholds in both Australia and England, Murdoch turned to the United States. In l973, after a quick look at the newspaper horizon, he bought three San Antonio papers, the morning *Express,* evening *News* and *Sunday Express-News.* He quickly applied his tried-and-true tabloid formulas, with big headlines touting celebrities, sex and violence, supported by heavy promotion. He also started the *National Star* to compete with such checkout counter tabloids as the *National Enquirer.* By l98l, the *Star's* circulation had climbed to 3.5 million.

Looking for a New York City daily, he met Dorothy Schiff, owner of the liberal afternoon *Post.* She was a good friend of Clay Felker, founder and editor of *New York* magazine. Felker helped him purchase the money-losing *Post* for $30 million. Murdoch quickly began to make the *Post* more down-market. The highly respected *Columbia Journalism Review* ran an article calling the *Post* not only a "journalistic problem" but "a social problem — a force for evil."[3] Meanwhile, Murdoch bought *New York* and then maneuvered Felker out. In protest, 40 members of *New York*'s staff resigned. With *New York*, Murdoch also got *Village Voice*. He tried to oust Marianne Partridge as *Voice* editor, but when he found that the whole staff supported her, he let her stay until her contract expired three years later.

Now Murdoch bobbed back to Australia, where he had a chance to take over Sydney's Channel l0 TV station. To get the approval of the Australian Broadcasting Tribunal, he solemnly promised to make no change in management. The Tribunal gave him its blessing, and two weeks later, the station's general manager was replaced. It was Murdoch true to form. Over the years, Murdoch had made small investments in Australia's Ansett Airlines, and by early l980, he controlled both a national Australian TV network and an Australian airline..

As l982 ended, Murdoch's biographer, Michael Leapman, wrote, "The chances are that he will continue to live dangerously, bidding for almost anything that is going and buying some of it; hiring, firing, cajoling, telephoning, browbeating employees and politicians alike, living out of a suitcase and flying by the seat of his pants."[4] Even as Leapman's book was being published in 1983, Murdoch bought the *Boston Herald-American*, a paper already as down-market as the *New York Post*. Not long after that, he bought the *Chicago Sun-Times* from the Marshall Field family, which had owned it since its founding in 1941. This brought vigorous protests throughout the Chicago community, as well as the resignation of Mike Royko, easily the city's most popular columnist. "No self-respecting dead fish would want to be wrapped in a Murdoch paper," Royko commented.[5] Soon the *Sun-Times* looked much like the *New York Post* and *Boston Herald-American*. After two years Murdoch sold the *Sun-Times* to a staff consortium for $145 million; his profit, $55 million.

Early in 1985, Murdoch bought a 50 percent share in 20th Century Fox, the movie studio. Much more dramatic was the buyout of his friend John Kluge's Metromedia TV stations, all seven of them in major cities, for $2 billion. Owning 50 percent of 20th Century Fox was not enough for Rupert; he wanted complete control. After months of argument with Marvin Davis, the investor who owned the other half, he bought out Davis for $325 million. Now he owned a movie studio and enough television stations to form a network.

Suddenly he faced two major problems. First, to own an American network, he would have to become an American citizen. Second, to meet legal requirements which forbid ownership of a newspaper and a broadcast station in the same city, he would have to shed the New York and Boston papers. After completing the necessary paperwork, he was sworn in as an American citizen in September 1985. Then he persuaded the FCC to give him temporary waivers on the sale of the *Post*, but Senator Edward Kennedy got legislation through Congress that forced the sale. The buyer was Peter Kalikow, a real estate operator. That left Boston, where Murdoch owned both a TV station and a newspaper. To get around that problem, he placed the TV station in a trust, which the FCC allowed.

With the Metromedia and Fox combination, Murdoch entered the playing field which had been dominated for decades by CBS, NBC and ABC. He had a movie studio and a TV network which included a well-stocked film library. To complete these transactions, he had assumed $2.9 billion in debt. To cut that figure, he sold one of the seven Metromedia stations - WCVB in Boston - for $430 million.

While he waited for final settlement of the Metromedia deal, he bought Salem House, a small book publisher. He had been interested in book publishing even before he left Australia for England. He owned Angus and Robertson in Australia, and by 1981 he owned 41.7 percent of William Collins, one of Britain's most prestigious publishers. He also had control of two seats on the Collins board. In 1987, Murdoch bought Harper & Row in the U.S. for $300 million, and then sold half of the U.S. publishing house to Collins for $150 million, thereby creating HarperCollins. In effect, Murdoch had — and still has -- control of a major U.S-British book publisher. Recently, he bought Avon Books and William Morrow & Co. from the Hearst Corp., which made his book publishing empire the second largest in the United States.

His eyes always scanning the horizon, Murdoch again looked to Europe, where first steps were being taken to allow commercial television. He worked out an agreement with the large Belgian company Groupe Bruxelles Lambert, which owned CLT (Compagnie Luxembourgeoise de Teledeffusion), a radio-and-TV operation covering France, Germany and Belgium from Luxembourg. But the prized commercial TV license that he and CLT wanted in France didn't go to CLT, mainly because the left-wing Mitterand government knew a lot about Murdoch's conservative politics and his support for Margaret Thatcher in England and Ronald Reagan in the U.S.

Rupert continued to seek satellite channels and ownership of all or most of each satellite himself. Beginning in 1983, he launched Sky Television, which merged with BskyB eight months later -- with Murdoch in control. The satellite venture operated four years before it reported any profits, with 3.25 million subscribers, about 15 percent of the potential number. In addition, cable networks in Britain now distribute BskyB programs to their subscribers.

By now, the annual interest on News Corporation debts had risen to $400 million. It was due to go still higher. The total Murdoch debt topped $4 billion. But in mid-1988, Murdoch again startled Wall Street and the media world with the $3 billion purchase of Triangle Publications from Walter Annenberg. The package included *TV Guide*, with the largest circulation of any magazine in the country, as well as *Seventeen, Daily Racing Form,* and a magazine distribution company. John Malone of Liberty Media also bought a big interest in *TV Guide*, but with its takeover by Gemstar in 2000, the Malone and Murdoch shares dropped to 19 percent each.

TV Guide and *Seventeen* were not Murdoch's first American magazines. He had joined France's Hachette SA in 1985 in the startup of a fashion magazine, *Elle*. And in 1989 he was to launch *Mirabella*, another fashion magazine named for its first editor, Grace Mirabella, who had been fired as a *Vogue* editor.

Bothered by the enormous size of his debt, Murdoch sold his Ziff-Davis travel and hotel publications, which he had bought in 1984, for $825 million, which meant a profit of $400 million. Now Murdoch's American properties were worth considerably more than those in either Australia or Britain. But his debts had risen to $7.6 billion. As most of these debts were about to come due in the fall of 1990, Murdoch faced a crisis -- a money crisis. On the eve of the Gulf War, with America's economy suffering a recession, money markets in Australia were suddenly frozen. A major fraction of Murdoch's total debt, $2.3 billion, was in short term notes because he had been hoping for a reduction in interest rates. But all rates, both short and long term, were higher. Suddenly it became clear that Murdoch owned not one or a dozen companies, but more than a hundred. The debt was huge and extremely complicated, with loans at 145 banks all over the world. Young Ann Lane, vice president at Citibank, where Murdoch's debt was largest, took on the job of making new long-term loans. She worked with Murdoch's staff well into 1991 restructuring the finances. On February 1, 1991, the last of $7.6 billion in new loans, most of them long term, was signed.

To pay off some of his debts in time, Murdoch engaged in a selling spree. For $650 million he sold a magazine stable - *New York, New Woman, Seventeen, European Travel, Life* and *Soap Opera Weekly* Still needing more money, he cut his family's Cruden Trust holdings to 39.5 per cent, enough to leave the Murdoch family in control.

Early in 1992, the man who had run the Fox Network from its beginnings under Murdoch in the mid -'80s, Barry Diller, announced his resignation and got a $34 million settlement. With Diller gone, Murdoch now paid more attention to his network and film studio. The Fox audience was increasing dramatically, responding to the tabloid program content. *Married ... With Children, Studs,* and *A Current Affair* were among the highest rated. *Cops, America's Most Wanted, Melrose Place, Beverly Hills 90210, Ally McBeal* and *Baywatch* joined the down-market lineup. Many Fox programs, such as *The X-Files* and a string of "shockumentaries," include heavy doses of violence. Columnists and critics frequently comment on the high rates of violence and foul language on Fox network programs. The low program quality continued in 1999, with the debut of *Action,* in which "a prostitute holds the high moral ground," a TV critic commented in the *San Francisco Chronicle.*[6] In 2000, syndicated columnist Cynthia Tucker characterized *Who Wants to Marry a Multimillionaire* as "a new low, even for the bottom-feeding Fox network."[7]

Murdoch's major focus in this period was on buying exclusive rights to broadcast sports events on Fox stations, on his BskyB satellite in western Europe and on the Star-TV satellite in Asia. Here he was again ready to lay out staggering sums. In 1993 he paid $1.6 billion for the right to carry National Football League games on Fox for four years and the championship games at the end of each season. He also paid $400 million for broadcast rights to four years of soccer in the British Premier League. The games are broadcast by Sky Sports, an all-sports channel on BskyB, his satellite TV service. In 1994 he came up with $155 million to broadcast games of the National Hockey League in the U.S. for five years, and lost money every year. Then came 1995 and a $575 million deal to broadcast baseball and in 1997 payment of $350 million to buy the Los Angeles Dodgers and their ballpark. Fox Entertainment now owns 19 of the 23 regional sports networks on U.S. cable. While sports broadcasting is usually profitable, the Fox Network lost money on the National Hockey League five years in a row.

Murdoch was also reaching for sports audiences in Australia and Asia. He launched his own Super League for rugby competition in his birth country. In 1994 his Star satellite TV outfit won exclusive rights to broadcast badminton to Asian viewers for 10 years. Star TV, broadcasting in English, in 1995 reached 42 million homes in 54 Asian countries. In the fall of 1995, News Corp joined TCI (Telecommunications Inc) in creating what it called a global sports network, exploiting Murdoch's satellite outlets in Europe, Asia and the United States. The Sports Net is now competing vigorously against Disney's ESPN, which since the 1980s had controlled most sports coverage. The TCI connection gave Murdoch audiences in the 10 regional sports networks of Liberty Media. In April, 1999, John Malone's Liberty traded its half-share in Fox/Liberty Sports for 51 million shares of News Corp., making Malone's eight percent stake well below that of the Murdoch family in control of News Corp. Obviously, Murdoch sees sports broadcasting as extremely profitable.

While he continued to scan the global horizon, the old problem of whether his American citizenship made Fox a U.S.-owned network came up again. This time both NBC and the NAACP filed objections, arguing that the network was really owned by News Corp., an Australian enterprise. The FCC, however, decided unanimously in May 1995 that even though News Corp remained the majority owner of Fox stations, the "public interest" would best be served if Murdoch continued to control the network. In the same month, News Corp got a $2 billion infusion from MCI Communications Corporation, the worldwide long distance company. MCI bought a 13.5 percent stake in News Corp., and Murdoch committed to MCI the use of any and all of Fox film and TV entertainment. The telephone company thus has the potential to send an enormous amount of information and entertainment to its customers. Murdoch expected that MCI would increase the number of subscribers using his Delphi service on the Internet. He had bought the Delphi program in October 1993. And in spring 1995 he launched Delphi in the United Kingdom.

In July, 1996, Murdoch took over New World Communications for $2.5 billion, increasing the number of Fox Network television stations to 22, and adding *Premiere* to his stable of magazines. The newly acquired stations brought Fox coverage of the nation's viewer-listeners to a shade under the 35 percent limit set by the 1996 Telecommunications Act. That coverage compares with the recently-merged Viacom-CBS at 41 percent, NBC at 24.65 percent and Disney/ABC at 24 percent. The buy brought to Fox Network every top market in the U.S. except San Francisco, where independent stations are affiliated to Fox.

Less than a year later (March 1997) Murdoch's News Corp bought Heritage Media Corporation. The Dallas company owned six TV stations and 24 radio stations, but Murdoch made clear his intention to sell both the TV and radio stations immediately. The main Heritage properties coveted by Murdoch were coupon dispensers for supermarkets and drug stores and a direct mail marketing company.

After a year of preparation, Fox Network launched a 24-hour news channel to compete with CNN and MSNBC. Chosen to head the new program was Roger Ailes, who had been media advisor to Presidents Richard Nixon, Ronald Reagan, and George Bush and then executive producer of Rush Limbaugh's short-lived TV show. As of November 1999, the all-news channel had paid $400 million, at $10 per subscriber, to cable operators to carry it to 43 million viewers, and suffered $281 million in operating losses.[8] Murdoch gets only 10 cents a month from cable subscribers. But Fox News gives Murdoch non-financial rewards. A *Nation* article commented on "the blatant partiality of Fox's regular staff, contributors and guests," which "combines to create a calculated mouthpiece for the right."[9] When Fox News began, Murdoch announced a new magazine, the *Weekly Standard*, with right-wing commentator William Kristol as editor.

Occasionally, Murdoch's horizon-scanning goes south of the border. He joined two of the most powerful Central and South American media magnates in formation of a program to start satellite broadcasting, even though only 15 percent of the TV owners subscribed to cable. The Latino magnates were Emilio Azcarraga Jean with his Grupo Televisa in Mexico and Roberto Marinho with his Organizacoes Globo in Brazil. John Malone's TCI bought a 10 percent slice of the enterprise. The four groups launched Sky Latin America in May 1995. By the fall of 1998, Sky Latin America had signed up 400,000 customers in Brazil, Mexico and Colombia.

Consistent with the conservative politics of the *Weekly Standard* and the *New York Post*, Murdoch bought the Family Channel from Pat Robertson in 1997. The price: $1.2 billion, which meant another loan. The channel enjoys the tenth largest audience in the country -- 67 million homes -- with such programs as *The Waltons, Mary Tyler Moore*, and Robertson's own weeknight *700 Club*.

At the start of 1996, Murdoch and MCI together bought into AskyB, the American broadcasting satellite, for $680 million. But AskyB was unable to compete with DirecTV, which had most of America's satellite subscribers. "Mr. Murdoch ended up by selling to Charlie Ergen, for which he got 37 percent of Mr. Ergen's Echostar . . .Mr. Ergen keeps control."[10] With Echostar out of the picture for Murdoch, in late 2000 he was "scrambling to raise $8 billion to sweeten his cash and stock offering to buy DirecTV . . . the No. 1 satellite broadcaster."[11] John Malone had offered to help in the purchase of DirecTV with $500 million. To strengthen its hold in Europe, in late 1999, BskyB bought a 24 percent interest in Kirch Pay TV, a subsidiary of Leo Kirch's media empire in Germany, for $520 million. In Asia, News Corp. owns Star TV, a satellite service based in Hong Kong. With DirecTV still a possibility, Murdoch's satellite holdings were entertaining more than 85 million views in May, 2001.

Thinking it was sensible for Star TV headquarters to remain in Hong Kong, Murdoch made conciliatory gestures to Beijing. He withdrew BBC programs from the Star TV schedule, and he arranged for news from his services to go to the English-language *China Daily*. He also arranged for Harper/Collins to publish a flattering biography of Deng Xiaoping and he ordered cancellation of a biography of Chris Patton, the former Hong Kong governor. But Star TV, which cost $900 million to start, is still losing $100 million a year. It doesn't collect any fees from Chinese viewers and it carries few commercials. Murdoch's son James, who heads News Corp's Asian division, spoke critically about Falun Gong, the Chinese religious group, at a business meeting in Los Angeles in March, 2001, and he "criticized Western news organizations for portraying China in a harsh light."[12] He call Falun Gong "dangerous" and an "apocalyptic cult."

After a long delay, "News Corp. seems to have awakened to the Web's possibilities," *Business Week* reported in July, 1999, adding, "In Australia, it's launching career and auction sites; in Britain, it's rolling out a free Internet service provider, called CurrantBuns, linked to the racy *Sun* tabloid."[13] The article added that "News Corp. and Softbank are forming e-ventures, a $50 million partnership to launch versions of U. S. Web businesses in Australia, Britain, India, and New Zealand." In December, 1999, News Corp. paid $1 billion for a 10.8 percent stake in Healtheon WebMD, an Internet media company providing online healthcare information.

While this media magnate still has a multi-billion dollar debt, he long ago devised means to avoid taxes. For example, when he paid $350 million for Ziff-Davis publications in 1984, he arranged to have one of News Corp's many divisions -- the one based in the Netherlands Antilles -- front the purchase. There are almost no taxes in the Antilles, where most of his newspaper and magazine publishing profits are sent. As a result, when the Ziff-Davis properties were sold for a $325 million profit, there were almost no capital gains taxes.[14] A long *Nation* magazine article in 1998 spelled out more about the off-island arrangements. "In 1996 News Corporation earned $1.32 billion in operating profits, but by utilizing a variety of loopholes and accounting tricks, it paid just $103 million in worldwide taxes, for a rate of about eight percent. That's about $350 million less than Murdoch would have paid at the standard U.S. corporate income tax rate of 35 percent."[15] Moreover, because his interests are so global, his financial staff people borrow on worldwide markets -- wherever interest rates are lowest. In 1986, News Corp earned $60 million simply by trading in currencies. A *Fortune* reporter pointed out in 1999 that "News Corp.'s tax rate has averaged 5.7 percent in the 1990s, while Walt Disney's, Time Warner's, and Viacom's averaged between 27 percent and 32 percent."[16] Incidentally, News Corp. now has some 800 subsidiaries, and enjoys a total annual income of $14 billion.

When he reached 66 in 1997, Murdoch began to talk to reporters about his successors, at the same time announcing that he intends to stay in charge for at least another 10 years. So far he has made it clear that while his children will ultimately take over, the likeliest early successor is Peter Chernin, CEO of the Fox Group, who oversees such TV programs as *Ally McBeal, Dharma & Greg* and other highly rated Fox prime time series, and who had a hand in six of the 10 top grossing films of all time, including *Titanic, Star Wars: The Phantom Menace* and *Independence Day.*

Murdoch's oldest daughter, Prudence, no longer works for News Corp. She has launched her own company, Shine Television, to produce movies for television. Lachlan, 27 in 1999, lives in New York and is senior vice president of News Corp., running both Australian operations and the U.S.-based Harper/Collins publishing house, the *New York Post* and News America Marketing, a newspaper insert, in-store advertising and marketing business. He is now Number Three in the empire, with Peter Chernin as Number Two. James, the second son, was named chairman and CEO of Star TV in May, 2000. He was given "the task of turning around the troubled pan-Asian media group, which has had losses of $30 million a year since takeover and has suffered a series of setbacks including cultural clashes with various governments."[17] Star TV operates 20 channels in 50 countries across Asia.

In April, 2000, Murdoch was diagnosed with prostate cancer, with no public indication of how serious the illness was. The revelation came less than two years after he divorced Anna, his wife for 32 years, and married Wendi Deng, age 32. Born in China, his new bride had gone to U.S. colleges, including Yale, where she got an MBA. They met when she worked at Star TV in Hong Kong. After the marriage aboard Murdoch's yacht in New York harbor and a Mediterranean cruise, the two moved into a new apartment in SoHo, New York. They spend much of their time in a big Beverly Hills villa. Murdoch also has a ski lodge in Aspen, a fashionable house near St. James Square in London, a house in Melbourne and the family's Cruden ranch near Canberra. Murdoch makes quarterly visits of 10 days each to every division of his global empire. That calls for a lot of traveling on his private plane.

When he reached 70 in March, 2001, his wife arranged a dinner party for him with close friends and immediate family in their downtown Manhattan apartment. The *London Independent* ran a long story quoting a close insider, "He (Murdoch) seems incredibly perky. He is incredibly focused on five million different things and gets each of them done."[18]

He has created a family foundation, which gives to the education needs of inner city children in New York, Los Angeles and Australia.[19] He doesn't like to talk about his philanthropy. The amount of the foundation's funding is not made public.

As a boss, as a competitor and as a media mogul, Murdoch has been the subject of sharp criticism. Harold Evans, who resigned as editor of the *London Times* a year after Murdoch bought the paper, said, "He's a good businessman and a lousy journalist, and he doesn't keep his promises, he's a liar, he's incontinent in breach of promises, and also he's a very treacherous person, it has to be said."[20] Even harsher was the "assessment" by David Plotz on *Slate* magazine, who said, "It is universally acknowledged that Rupert Murdoch is scum. The media tycoon has built his global empire on schlock and sleaze, used heavy-handed tactics and legal chicanery to expand his domain" and "made mockery of the grand traditions of Australian/British/American journalism."[21] Murdoch's most exhaustive biographer, William Shawcross, says, "He is accused by some critics, especially in Britain, of having lowered the standards of both television and the press, of coarsening everything he touches."[22] In her biography of Simon Newhouse, Carol Felsenthal writes, "Murdoch is not so much interested in imposing his conservative politics on government as in influencing presidents, prime ministers and politicians at all levels to give him the breaks he needs to expand, to make the next deal, to gamble and to win."[23] Ken Auletta, media columnist for the *New Yorker*, says, "Murdoch is a pirate; he will cunningly circumvent rules, and sometimes principles, to get his way."[24] And Auletta adds, "He has built a world-wide company, but he has rarely elevated taste or journalism."

The Murdoch story is not over. His name is in headlines almost daily. He owns quantities of newspapers on four continents; many magazines; two television networks (one in U.S., the other in Australia); many TV stations in both Australia and U.S.; a major book publishing house with affiliated imprints; and a Hollywood movie studio. He has major interests in satellite TV operations in Europe, Asia, South America and the United States. The stock of his News Corp. went up 34 percent in 1999. American critics call attention to the fact that 72 percent of New Corp's income comes from the U.S.

Even at 70, the eyes of this buccaneer, tycoon, octopus, gambler, union scourge and pirate still scan the horizon. When biographer William Shawcross in mid-1999 asked him about the future of his empire, Murdoch said, "It's still a work in progress. And always will be."[25]

HEARST FAMILY–MOSTLY THEY CLIP COUPONS

8

The Hearst family, heirs to an empire left by William Randolph Hearst, share a $7.3 billion fortune. Each of the five branches of the family owns one-fifth of the estate.

Most older media families turn over management of their properties to business professionals. That was underscored when William Randolph Hearst III, "Will" to his family and friends, resigned as publisher of the *San Francisco Examiner* in January, 1995. Without explaining why he was leaving the paper that had founded his family's empire, the 45-year-old grandson of "Citizen Hearst" announced that he was joining management of a new high tech company in Silicon Valley, home of the computer revolution, near San Jose. Two years later he was CEO of "Excite@Home," a national high speed data service, and sat on the boards of Com21, Viewpoint and DataLabs. In 1999, he wrote an op-ed piece in the *San Francisco Chronicle*, arguing against local regulation of Internet services, not mentioning his connection to "Excite@Home," an Internet service, partly owned by the Hearst empire. By then he was no longer working at Excite@Home, but remained on its board of directors. With Will's departure from the *Examiner*, only two family members were still working in the empire. One, Austin Hearst, Will's brother, whose share of the Hearst fortune is $900 million, is vice president of Hearst Entertainment and Syndication. The other, Stephen Hearst, runs the real estate operations.

Will's management, however, had been local, confined to a single paper. The top manager for the enormous Hearst Corporation, based in New York, is Frank Bennack, Jr., 63, who has been president and chief operating officer for 20 years. Under his direction, the conglomerate has quadrupled in size and now includes more than 100 separate businesses — almost all in the media -- with a payroll of more than 15,000. Bennack has worked in Hearst operations since he started at the *San Antonio Light* more than 40 years ago. Significantly, he is also a director of Chase Manhattan Bank, American Home Products Corp. and Ralph Lauren Corp.

When the deYoung family of San Francisco announced in mid-1999 that its whole media empire was up for sale, the Hearst Company quickly bought the *San Francisco Chronicle*, the main rival of its afternoon paper, with about five times the *Examiner's* circulation. Less than a year later, the corporation sold its founding paper, the *San Francisco Examiner*, to Ted Fang, who said he would continue publishing his *San Francisco Independent*, a three-times-a-week giveaway. Hearst officials confirmed that they would subsidize Fang's *Examiner* operation with $66 million over three years. When the deal with Fang closed four months later, with Justice Department approval, the *Examiner's* long-lasting Joint Operating Agreement with the *Chronicle* expired. A federal judge approved the purchase of the *Chronicle* by Hearst interests in late July, 2000. The judge's ruling came in a case brought by Clint Reilly, multi-millionaire defeated San Francisco mayoral candidate, whose suit had claimed violation of anti-trust laws.

While many members of the Hearst family still live in the San Francisco Bay area, management of the far-flung conglomerate remains in New York. It embraces 12 newspapers spread across the country; 16 wholly-owned TV stations plus a joint ownership of the Hearst Argyle chain of 14 stations and three satellites; seven radio stations; six book publishing houses; a news service; a feature syndicate; interests in 14 cable networks; nine new media companies; and, of course, lots of real estate. The Hearst Corporation is the world's largest publisher of monthly magazines, with 16 of them, including *Cosmopolitan, Esquire, Redbook, Good Housekeeping,* and *Popular Mechanics.* In 1998 it joined Miramax in publication of Tina Brown's *Talk* magazine, and in 1999 it launched *Cosmogirl*, aimed at 12-to-17-year-olds. Its 15 trade magazines include *Official Used Car Guide* and *Official Guide to Disneyland.* In 1998, Hearst revenues came to $3.3 billion.

In remaining private (except for Hearst-Argyle, which went public in 1998) the Hearst enterprise differs from many other media companies which have their stock on Wall Street. But it's clear that Bennack and the others running the company are just as focused on the bottom line as are managers of any Wall Street company.

Though W. R. Hearst III resigned as *San Francisco Examiner* publisher, he remains on the Hearst Corporation board, where the chairman was his uncle, Randolph A. Hearst, who died at 85 in December, 2000. Randolph was one of the twin sons of empire builder William Randolph and Phoebe Apperson Hearst. *Forbes* listed his wealth at $1.8 billion in October, 2000. He had three wives and five daughters, including the famous Patty Hearst, whose kidnapping made headlines in 1974. Patty has now become a movie actress, and in 2000 was appearing in her fourth film, *Cecil B. Demented*, playing the mother of a terrorist who kidnaps a Hollywood actress, played by Melanie Griffith.[1] Patricia was one of 140 Americans pardoned by President Clinton during his last day at the White House..

Bennack and two other Hearst Corporation managers were targets of a 1997 lawsuit filed by William Randolph Hearst II and his sisters Joanne Hearst Castro and Debra Hearst Gay. The court suit alleged that the heirs had been denied access to information about the company. The three wanted to know how much corporation executives are paid, details of the 1997 corporate reorganization which they claim raised taxes for all the heirs, and what parts of the corporation provide income for the heirs. Corporation executives responded by calling attention to the provision in Hearst's will which says that any heir challenging the estate or its management risks disinheritance. The judge threw out their case and an appeals court upheld his decision. W. R. Hearst II and his sisters are among 11 family members who now get between $3.1 million and $12.6 million a year from the estate.[2]

When Randolph Hearst died in December 2000, his will gave $100,000 each to his four daughters, including Patricia, the one who had been kidnapped. The will called for the money to be spent within a year on "something special, such as a trip or purchase which such child would not otherwise make."[3] The heirs range in age from 45 to 6l.

News of the unusual gifts coincided with reports that a famed London architect, Norman Foster, had been hired to design an addition to the six-story Hearst Magazine Building on Columbus Circle. Built it 1926, it now houses the *Good Housekeeping* staff.

The Hearst media empire was founded in San Francisco when gold mining magnate George Hearst bought the daily *Examiner* in 1880. When in 1887 his son William Randolph was expelled from Harvard for low grades and painting professors' names in chamber pots, George, then a U.S. Senator, gave him the paper. Overnight, young Hearst brought sensationalism to his new toy — bigger headlines, comic strips and more photographs. Only eight years later, he moved to New York and brought the same sensational style to the *New York Journal* after he bought it for $180,000, a piddling sum to the young Hearst, who got a $7.5 million gift from his mother the same year.

Focusing on his new property, Hearst hired cartoonist Dick Outcault away from Pulitzer's *New York World* to produce his famous "Yellow Kid" strip for the *Journal*. That led ultimately to characterization of Hearst's sensational practices as "yellow journalism." Today we call the style "tabloid," with heavy emphasis on sex, violence and crime. But the paper also contained the kind of editorial liberalism, in some cases radicalism, which Hearst would ultimately reject entirely. The liberalism included frequent attacks on "criminal trusts," support for trade unions, and development of public schools.

Both Pulitzer's *World* and Hearst's paper campaigned for and then vigorously supported the 1898 war with Spain. Indeed, even before the American battleship Maine blew up in Havana harbor, Hearst cabled his photographer, Frederick Remington, "You furnish the pictures and I'll furnish the war." By the end of the war, *Journal* circulation had jumped to 1,600,000. Referring to the *Journal*'s sensational, nationalistic content, Mark Twain called the paper "the calamity of calamities."[4]

When the war ended, Hearst began building what became his press empire. He started another paper in New York, two in Chicago and one in Boston. He also entered Democratic Party politics and in 1902 was elected to Congress, where he answered roll calls only nine times in two years. Then he ran unsuccessfully for both New York governor and New York City mayor. When Al Smith refused to run on the same presidential ticket with him in 1922, he gave up politics for good.

But he continued to manage his papers, especially the editorial pages. When World War I began in Europe, Hearst papers strenuously opposed American intervention. Many readers considered his papers more friendly to Germany than the Allies, and clearly anti-British. Before the U.S. entered World War II, his papers ran columns by both Hitler and Mussolini. When America finally entered the war, his papers gave only lukewarm support to the Allies.

Hearst prospered through the 1920s, so that by the end of the decade his wealth was reputed to be $150 million. He went on a great buying splurge, buying more newspapers, magazines and radio stations, as well as art objects of all kinds. In Europe, Egypt and Mexico, he bought Crusaders' armor, tapestries, choir stalls, whatever caught his eye, filling warehouses in New York. Also during the '20s he oversaw construction of San Simeon, which ultimately cost $40 million, with its four huge buildings, a private zoo, even an air field. But as his wealth grew, he became more and more conservative, and so did his papers. Once an advocate of the graduated income tax and a supporter of unions, he now opposed both. Once a hero to progressive Americans, Hearst was now looked upon as an enemy, especially when he made a 180 degree turnabout after supporting Franklin D. Roosevelt in the 1932 campaign, then opposing every Roosevelt program, including the National Recovery Act (NRA).

His empire's expansion and his personal spending spree couldn't last. When the Great Depression started in 1929, the company owed $126 million. Not until large chunks of the empire, including seven newspapers and seven radio stations, had been sold by 1945 did the balance sheet return to the black. Hearst himself spent his last years in relative seclusion at the home of his long time companion, Marion Davies, dying in 1951.

At the end of his biography of *Citizen Hearst*, W. A. Swanberg wrote, "Hearst's influence on journalism was mostly bad," and added, "As a politician, his chief contribution was probably a negative one . . . his crippling weakness was instability, vacillation, his inability to anchor his thinking to a few basic rocklike truths."[5] In *The Powers That Be*, David Halberstam concluded his review of Hearst with the comment, "No newspaper corporation in the country was as poorly run in the postwar years as the Hearst empire, the narrowness and shallowness of the political view exceeded only by the corporate side."[6] In *The Chief*, the latest biography of Hearst, David Nasaw writes, "Hearst had changed the rules, in politics as well as in publishing. He had demonstrated decisively, over the course of a half century, that 'by using money as a heavy club,' an individual could, with the mass media as a loudspeaker, make his voice heard in every corner of the nation."[7]

However, it seems clear that the papers' quality has improved somewhat since the 1970s. They are much less sensational, and more willing to report both sides of controversial issues. The conglomerate has now spread overseas with a magazine publishing house in England operating six titles published in 10 languages and distributed to 70 countries. The British magazine *Harpers* and *Queen* carries as many as 400 pages in a single issue. In Los Angeles, the Hearsts made an unfortunate deal with the Chandlers which guaranteed the *Los Angeles Times* monopoly readership early in the Age of TV. In 1962, the Hearsts agreed to kill their morning paper and the Chandlers agreed to kill the *Evening Mirror*, on which they had been losing millions.[8]

When William Randolph Hearst died in 1951, his trust was written to control the estate through the next two generations, until the death of the last of his eight grandchildren. That could be 30 to 50 years from now, according to the 1991 prediction of W. R. Hearst Jr..[9] Meantime, business professionals, led by Frank Bennack, continue to manage the corporation's affairs. The five branches of the Hearst family have reason to be happy, despite the pending suit by one branch. Their combined wealth jumped from $4.5 billion in 1995 to $7.3 billion in 2000.

KIRK KERKORIAN–HE OWNS MGM
AND MUCH OF LOS VAGAS

9

Four years after he bought Hollywood's most famous studio, MGM, for the third time, octogenarian Kirk Kerkorian was listed by *Forbes* in 2001 as worth $6.4 billion. His Hollywood MGM, which he apparently intends to keep this time, produces movies and has a rich film and TV library with an estimated 5,000 titles -- more than half of all films produced in Hollywood since 1948. He also owns one of the biggest hotels in Las Vegas, the MGM Grand, with more than 5,000 rooms, where he stays when he visits the casino city.

He expanded his Las Vegas empire in March, 2000, with the $6.4 billion purchase of Mirage Resorts Inc. The buy meant that Kerkorian's MGM Grand owns 14 casinos, including its own MGM Grand hotel, New York-New York, Mirage, Treasure Island and Bellagio, for a total of more than 18,000 rooms along the Las Vegas Strip. Kerkorian also owns casinos in other Nevada cities as well as in Mississippi, Detroit and Australia. Unreported in the mainstream press was a point made in a *Columbia Journalism Review* article about the Mirage buyout. It said the stories failed to tell "what the deal held for labor where the notoriously anti-labor MGM is now the state's (Nevada's) largest employer."[1]

Kerkorian made headlines in November, 2000, when his company, Tracinda, sued the DaimlerChrysler auto company for $8 billion. Tracinda claimed that Kerkorian and other Chrysler board members would not have voted for the $34 billion deal if it had been billed as a German takeover rather than the "merger of equals" pitched by Daimler chairman Juergen Schrempp and Chrysler chairman Robert Eaton. Two months later, Kerkorian sold 10 million shares of Daimler Chrysler, keeping 23 million shares.

He's not so much a media mogul as an investor — in gambling casinos and hotels, in an airline, even in a giant auto company. In his first two MGM studio ventures, starting in 1969, he added $1.5 billion to his wealth. The first purchase squeezed out Edgar Bronfman Sr., of Seagram's, who had bought 15 percent of MGM during the '60s and was even its board chairman. Kerkorian's 1969 buy ushered in an era of drastic cost-cutting and the sell-off of historic property, including a *Ben Hur* chariot and the slippers worn by Judy Garland in *The Wizard of Oz*. The studio continued to lose money, even after Kerkorian bought United Artists in 1981 and renamed the company MGM/UA. He made a mistake when he put David Begelman, who had run Columbia Pictures, in charge. That lasted only a year because while Begelman was a big spender, his pictures all flopped.

Seeking a way out, Kerkorian sold the combined MGM/UA studios to Ted Turner. But Turner wasn't able to pay the agreed price of $1.5 billion. Kerkorian then paid Turner $780 million to let him buy back all of the studios except the prize Turner especially wanted to keep -- the pre-1948 MGM film library, which included the classics *Gone With the Wind, Mutiny on the Bounty, The Thin Man, An American in Paris* and *Singing in the Rain*.

Turner's withdrawal from the studio didn't solve MGM/UA's problems. So Kerkorian made his second sale, this time to an Italian company, which defaulted to a bank, from which Kerkorian made his third purchase. This time, he didn't buy alone, but was joined by Seven Networks of Australia. Then Kerkorian bought Goldwyn Entertainment and Orion Pictures from John Kluge's Metromedia.

So he now has the post-1948 MGM film library as well as the UA, Orion and Goldwyn film libraries. Among TV programs in the MGM/UA portfolios are *LAPD, In the Heat of the Night* (now in syndication), and *Thirtysomething*. But in mid-1998, MGM was at the bottom of major Hollywood studios, with less than 3.5 percent of market share. Most of its income that year came from *The Man in the Iron Mask*, with $150 million worldwide, and the latest James Bond film, *Tomorrow Never Dies*, which grossed $450 million globally.

The studio was clearly in trouble again. There was speculation that Kerkorian might seek, or was already seeking, a partner to share the risks of the movie studio. In spite of United Artists and its other partners, MGM doesn't enjoy income sources such as theme parks, cable, record music companies, or TV stations. Disney, Warner Brothers, 20th Century Fox and Universal Studios all reap such benefits. *Business Week* reported that Jerome York, who runs Tracinda, the Kerkorian holding company, had held talks with both Time Warner and News Corp. "about supplying cash infusions in exchange for the use of MGM's hefty film and TV library."[2]

But Kerkorian made a series of moves in 1999 that demonstrated determination to bring MGM out of the red. Early in the year, he paid $235 million for 1,300 films from the PolyGram library, adding to the Orion, United Artists and MGM titles he already had. The buy was interpreted as proof that he wants to exploit his valuable film library for such new venues as the Internet and digital delivery movies. A *San Francisco Chronicle* story reported "plans to create an MGM cable or satellite TV network."[3]

In late April he replaced Frank Mancuso, who had run MGM/UA for six years, with Alex Yemenidjian, who had been running MGM Grand in Las Vegas but had no movie experience. At the same time, Chris McGurk, who had been Universal Pictures President, came aboard to manage the studio. In the fall, Kerkorian announced a $720 million rights offering, making it possible for shareholders to buy more MGM stock for $14.50 a share, $3 below the market price, which quickly rose to $22.50. And in November he put $721 million of his own money into the company. The funds from both moves helped pay off MGM debt and finance new films. It seemed clear that Kerkorian intended to keep MGM.

Among the 10 movies released in 1999 was another .007 thriller, *The World is Not Enough,* which carried the MGM label, rather than United Artists, which had been credited with the first 18 Bond thrillers. Other MGM movies released during the year with good box office returns were *The Thomas Crown Affair, Stigmata, Flawless,* and *Tea With Mussolini.*

Meantime, Yemenidjian had made a deal with Miramax, the Disney subsidiary, to co-produce eight films on a 50-50 basis, sharing both costs and profits. Also in July, Yemenidjian arranged for Murdoch's Fox Filmed Entertainment to handle international distribution of all MGM movies as well as cassette and DVD releases. Planned co-productions with Fox include *Cold Mountain* and *Harvey.* Kerkorian and Yemenidjian expected the new Bond film, *The World is Not Enough,* to do as well as *Tomorrow Never Dies.* They also want continued success for MGM productions on television, such as *Stargate SG-1* and *The Outer Limits.* Yemenidjian also revealed plans to release MGM movies on digital movie discs and the Internet, commenting, "We inherited a company with the best content and the weakest distribution." In June, 2000, he offered a ground-breaking plan to get television networks to advance production costs on five films, in return for the right to broadcast the movies when they are made. The list included *Hannibal, Outlaws, Windtalkers, Dragonfly,* and a remake of *Rollerball.* Scheduled for release on HBO in March 2001 was *Things You Can Tell Just By Looking At Her.* Sigourney Weaver starred in *Heartbreakers,* released the same month.

The MGM ventures, spread over 30 years, are only part of the Kerkorian story. Born June 6, 1917, in Fresno, in California's San Joaquin Valley, he is the grandson of Armenian immigrants who settled in the farm region. He later told a reporter that because his father changed jobs often, the family moved twenty times as he grew up, finally settling in Los Angeles. He dropped out of high school to join the Civilian Conservation Corps, faking his age, and worked six months in Sequoia National Park. Then he worked at cleaning and selling used cars, installing furnaces, and at 20 took up amateur boxing. After winning all but four of 33 matches, he realized that he preferred piloting airplanes. A friend had taken him up in a Piper Cub, and when he landed, he immediately sought out an instructor. In exchange for lessons, he milked cows and shoveled manure on the ranch of his instructor. He entered World War ll as a civilian pilot in the British Royal Air Force Transport Command, ferrying bombers from Canada to England, Scotland, and even India and Africa's Gold Coast. In 1942 he married Hilda Schmidt, an American, a match which lasted until 1951.

After the war ended, he bought and converted surplus military planes and sold them to commercial airlines at a sizeable profit. Then he started his own airline charter service, flying passengers from Los Angeles to Las Vegas. During his layovers in Las Vegas, he became interested in gambling. He also married a showgirl, Jean Hardee in 1954, and they had two daughters, Tracy and Linda. Before that marriage, which ended in a 1963 divorce, he had started a second air charter service, Trans International Airlines (TIA), which he sold 15 years later for his first million. He used the money to buy 40 acres of land near the Flamingo Hotel. Within three years he had bought TIA back. When he offered public stock in the airline, it was bought up by Armenian-Americans who by then were familiar with his name. Ultimately, he sold the airline to Transamerica for $85 million in stock.

When Caesar's Palace opened in 1966, it was on land owned by Kerkorian; the operators paid him $4 million a year in rent. The Palace owners bought the land after two years, handing Kerkorian a $12 million profit. By then he had bought land elsewhere in Las Vegas and had begun to build the International Hotel, which opened in 1967. But his biggest hotel property, the MGM Grand, was a prize he spun off during his first purchase of the Hollywood studio. Built at a cost of $1.1 billion, it has 5,005 rooms, some of them two-floor suites, and its casino alone brings him an income of $200 million a year. Now he also has the newly-purchased Mirage Resorts, and the New York-New York casino-hotel, also in Las Vegas, which is a 50 percent subsidiary of MGM Grand.

His friends and business associates were startled when, in the fall of 1990, Kerkorian bought a 9.8 percent stake in the auto giant Chrysler Corp. The move opened a contentious period, during which he bought still more Chrysler stock, and in April, 1995, he offered to take over the whole company for $22.8 billion. Only a month later, he had to withdraw the offer because he couldn't borrow enough money to finance it. But in the end, his venture paid off handsomely when Germany's Daimler-Benz bought Chrysler in 1998, giving Kerkorian a $3.5 billion profit on his $1.5 billion of investments, and leaving him with four percent of the stock in the new DaimlerChrysler company.

That four percent, and what had been Kerkorian's seat on the Chrysler board, led to the suit in November, 2000, filed by his Tracinda Corp. By then the "merger of equals" was exactly two years old, and by then Daimler's Schrempp had told the *Financial Times* that he had intended from the start to make Chrysler a division of Daimler-Benz. During the two years, many top Chrysler officials had quit or been fired, the company's stock had plunged 55 percent and Chrysler had suffered heavy losses. Tracinda's suit emphasized that Kerkorian and other Chrysler board members would not have voted favorably if they had not been told it was a "merger of equals." An AP story said, "Kerkorian is seeking more than $2 billion in actual damages, including compensation for the drop in the value of DaimlerChrysler shares since the merger and punitive damages of at least $6 billion."[4]

Meantime, his MGM Studios appear to have turned a corner in 1999. The strong showing at the box office caused a 50 percent gain for MGM stock for the year. Yemenidjian seems to have provided the magic needed for MGM success. In January, 2001, he got an estimated $30 million from the ABC Network for use of 13 James Bond films for a year and a half. A month later, a *New York Daily News* story said, "MGM, the *Hannibal* studio, is looking to devour the box office with the most ambitious slate of films in the history of the studio."[5] "The once-given-up-for-dead studio," it added, "wants to reclaim its lost stature by releasing 20 star-studded, high-profile films this year." The releases were to include *Heartbreakers, What's the Worst That Could Happen?*, and the World War 11 drama *Hart's War*.

Moreover, studio heads had "plans to turn MGM into a global entertainment company with broadcast outlets and cable and satellite channels," a long *Forbes* article reported.[6] "MGM already holds stakes in 14 foreign TV channels," the story added. It also owned one-fifth of the Rainbow cable networks , which include Bravo, Women's Entertainment and American Movie Classics, bought for at $825 million.

Kerkorian cherishes his privacy and rarely talks to reporters. He is described as "an intensely shy man who hates small talk."[7] He seldom attends shareholders meetings of his companies. He doesn't go to Hollywood screenings, even of MGM films. His friends and associates often wonder how he makes decisions. "According to industry analysts," a profile says, "his decisions seem to be primarily the result of intuition. He also draws on the counsel of a coterie of trusted aides and his own wealth of experience."[8]

Unlike many of his fellow billionaires, Kerkorian is quite generous. A lengthy *Forbes* profile in 1997 said, "Quietly and without any fanfare, Kerkorian has also given away millions to Armenian causes and more than 20 percent of his net worth to charities in general."[9]

The 83-year-old was sued for divorce in September, 1999, by his wife of three weeks, Lisa Border, age 30-plus, who asked for custody of their 18-month old daughter, Kira. They had been living together in his Beverly Hills home when the child was born.

Now he's paying close attention to his MGM investment and its many properties. He's still active at 84. But while he's in Hollywood, he knows that most of his wealth comes from Las Vegas and Detroit. In 1999, he found time to open his new $750 million casino in Detroit, where there's much less competition for gambling customers. Whether it's looking in the direction of Hollywood, Las Vegas, or Detroit, Kirk Kerkorian's eye for investment remains sharp.

SI AND DON NEWHOUSE–
THEIR GIANT EMPIRE IS PRIVATELY OWNED

10

The fortune shared by Si and Donald Newhouse -- reported in 2001 at $10 billion — had its origins in the purchase made by their father, Samuel I. Newhouse I, of a little newspaper on Staten Island — the *Advance* — in 1922. By the time he died in 1979, the elder Newhouse — whose father was from Russia and mother from Austria -- owned 42 newspapers, many of which he merged after buying them. Circulation of his papers topped 3,200,000 daily and his magazines sold more than 27 million copies. His empire also included radio and TV stations in Birmingham, Alabama; TV stations in Elmira, N.Y. and St. Louis, Missouri; and radio and TV stations in Syracuse, N.Y., Portland, Oregon, and Harrisburg, Pennsylvania.

Newhouse closed his evening papers in order to build circulation — and profitability — of his morning papers. His gaze seldom left the bottom line, and the quality of his papers suffered for it: in the 1970s a critical journalism review listed three of his papers in the top 10 worst big- circulation dailies in the country. He fought unions wherever they showed up. He cut the staffs of his papers to the bone. Biographer Richard Meeker quotes one of his editors as saying, "If S. I. Newhouse owned a national football team, he would play with ten men."[1]

In 1959, Sam heard that the Conde Nast chain of slick magazines was losing $500,000 a year and was for sale. He quickly bought it for $5 million. The Conde Nast group then included *Vogue, Glamour, Mademoiselle,* and *House and Garden.* Another magazine chain, Street & Smith, appeared on the market at the same time, and Newhouse snapped it up too. He quickly merged Street & Smith's *Charm* into *Glamour,* and *Living for Young Homemakers* into *House and Garden.* To give his magazines good positions on newsstands, Sam Newhouse relied on his old friend Henry Garfinkle, who controlled half of all magazines sales in the country through operation of distribution centers.[2] Seventeen years after he bought Conde Nast and Street

& Smith, Newhouse paid $305 million to buy eight Booth newspapers in Michigan and another magazine, *Parade*. With the weekly *Parade*, he got a publication loaded with national advertising and soft features by or about celebrities, inserted into many of the country's metropolitan Sunday editions.

Toward the end of his lengthy buying career, he sought respectability for his name and his properties by large gifts to Syracuse University. The gifts led to creation of the Newhouse Communications Center for teaching and research in newspapers, magazines, radio and television. Newhouse looked upon it as "a way to legitimize his massive communication holdings in the eyes of the rest of the world."[3] It also helped make up for his son's ejection, some years earlier, from what was then Syracuse's Department of Journalism. Sam Newhouse's money was also responsible for putting the name Mitzi Newhouse on a theater that is part of New York's famous Lincoln Center. But his gifts failed to stop the critics. After he bought two papers in New Orleans, both *Business Week* and *Time* were harsh. "This solid gold pyramid (the *Advance* chain) was erected by a man who knows nothing about the editorial end of journalism and cares even less," said *Time*.[4]

His two sons, Si and Donald, were groomed from birth to take over the empire. The oldest son, Samuel I. Newhouse Jr. (Si), was born in November, 1927; his brother Donald, in August, 1929. Si went to the Horace Mann private school in the Bronx, where his record was undistinguished. But it was here that he met Roy Cohn, with whom he remained friends even after Cohn achieved notoriety as a close McCarthy ally, was disbarred for a variety of tax dodges, and revealed his homosexuality as he was dying of AIDS.

From Horace Mann, Si went to Syracuse University in upstate New York, a city where his father owned not only morning and evening dailies, but also radio and TV stations. By then his father was a millionaire and he wanted desperately to succeed in college as his father expected. But he was shy and had trouble making friends. He was ejected from the university's journalism department because of poor grades. He left the university in his junior year. His record was repeated several years later by his brother Donald, who also dropped out of Syracuse in the junior year.

Before he left Syracuse, Si met Jane Franke, who stayed and got her bachelor's degree in fine arts. After dropping out, Si worked at his father's *Long Island Press*, then signed up in the U.S. Air Force. He was still in the Air Force in March 1951 when he and Jane were married in a Waldorf-Astoria Hotel ceremony. The marriage produced three children — Samuel, Wynn and Pamela. Si worked in a series of company properties, including a Portland radio station and the *Long Island Press*. But five years after the marriage, Si and Jane were divorced in a friendly separation. The children stayed with their mother, who later remarried.

Si was still working unenthusiastically at the *Long Island Press* and *Newark Star-Ledger* when his father bought the Conde Nast and Street & Smith magazine chains. Sam Newhouse touted the Conde Nast purchase as a 35th wedding anniversary gift to his wife. Indeed, Mitzi Greenhouse loved the fashion magazines, especially *Vogue*, and she now began annual expeditions to Paris fashion shows. She also began arranging social affairs for *Vogue* editors and some of the celebrities they wrote about.

A few months after the Conde Nast purchase, Si left the newspapers for *Vogue*, where his father named him publisher. At last Si had found his niche. He settled in to learn the business of slick magazines thoroughly. As time went on, he appeared more self-assured to friends and associates. His chief mentor was Alexander Liberman, *Vogue* art director, who became editorial director of all Conde Nast magazines only two years after Sam Newhouse bought them. Liberman was a Russian refugee who had migrated from France when the Germans invaded, and was now a painter much sought after by New York socialites. Liberman began to take Si with him to a variety of social affairs.

With Newhouse's approval, Liberman persuaded Diana Vreeland to leave *Harper's Bazaar* to become editor of *Vogue*, and photographer Richard Avedon also joined the *Vogue* staff. Through the '60s, the magazines, especially *Vogue*, enjoyed a large circulation. But as the '70s began, the circulation — and income — slipped, and Si Newhouse abruptly asked Vreeland to retire. She was replaced by Grace Mirabella.

The abrupt dismissal of employees turned out to be a common practice for Si Newhouse. Margaret Case, who had worked at *Vogue* for 40 years, many as society editor, was fired without notice in 1971. She committed suicide, jumping from a window of her apartment. The abruptly dismissed included not only Vreeland and Case, but William Shawn, editor of the *New Yorker*; Anthea Disney, editor of *Self*; Robert Bernstein, Random House chairman; Andre Schiffrin, publisher of Pantheon Books; Louis Gropp, editor of *House and Garden*, and Robert Gottlieb, Shawn's successor at the *New Yorker*. Indeed, "the head shots of the beheaded looked like a Who's Who of New York's literary world," wrote Thomas Maier in his Newhouse biography.[5]

By now it was clear that Si had learned all he wanted to know about magazine publishing. Conde Nast contracted with a research company to study readers' reactions to various articles and pictures. "Using these tools, the Newhouse organization marketed their magazines as any other consumer item — like toothpaste, perfume or dog food is researched — in a way that greatly influenced the rest of the media."[6]

Seventeen years after his divorce, Si married Victoria di Ramel in April, 1973. She shared his sophisticated liking for art, and had edited art and architecture books in France. With her, he settled down to a quieter life than he had led in the long period after his divorce, during which he dated a number of women. Victoria brought social and intellectual polish to Si. She enjoyed entertaining, and her mastery of several languages, especially French, helped to draw a wide variety of guests. Taller and 10 years younger than Si, the brainy "Victoria was linked, from her first marriage (to a French count) and from her manners, to a time of elegance and culture."[7] She drew the job of overseeing their house, with its valuable art collection.

Si was named chairman of Conde Nast publications in 1975. He began to emulate his father's interest in taking on new enterprises, but rather than buy them, he started them. In 1979, *Self* was launched to give health and fitness advice. Four years later, *Vanity Fair* was re-born. All this was based on market research, which some Conde Nast editors scorned. But the magazines flourished. Where Conde Nast publications had been losing money before the Newhouse takeover, they enjoyed rising profits in the '70s and '80s.

Twenty years after Si Newhouse began at Conde Nast, his father suffered a stroke, followed by clear signs of senility. For two years he behaved like a child, using crayons to write simple words like "cat." The family isolated him from public view. A second stroke led to his death in August, 1979.

Then came one of the most complicated inheritance tax cases ever handled by the Internal Revenue Service. It wasn't settled until 1989 — ten years later. The difference came from contrasting interpretations of what the deceased owned. Starting in 1936, Sam Newhouse had amended the Advance Publications charter at least four times. The IRS argued that he owned $962 million that was taxable. Family lawyers argued that ownership — and decision-making — had been shared by many members of the family, and that only a part of the empire had been Sam's. A federal judge finally ruled that Sam Newhouse had owned only a thousand shares of common stock in the company, worth $176 million of the $1.5 billion value of the Advance conglomerate. He set the inheritance taxes at $48 million, one million less than the family had offered ten years earlier. But the inheritance tax problem remains. After they paid the $48 million, Si and Donald signed an agreement with the IRS providing that when they die, the full value of the properties will be taxed at normal rates.

After two decades running Conde Nast, Si Newhouse was secure enough in operation of the magazine empire to look into book publishing. Early in 1980, he bought Random House from RCA Corporation for $70 million. Press accounts assured the public that Newhouse would run the book publisher as his father had run his newspapers, keeping hands off editorial decisions and leaving content up to management. *Time* magazine wrote of what it called the Newhouse "hands off" approach. Robert Bernstein, who had been managing Random House for 15 years, felt reassured. The Random House group included Alfred A Knopf, Ballantine, Pantheon, and Modern Library. Not long after the Random House purchase, Newhouse bought Fawcett Books, a paperback publisher, from CBS. From 1980 to 1990, Random House's income jumped from less than $200 million to almost $900 million. During the same period, Villard Books joined the stable, as did the *Times* Books imprint of the *New York Times*. The exploding profits of Random House and its subsidiaries were fueled in part by the new practice of making both authors and editors into celebrities. The buildup of authors in the mainstream press was now being pushed by public relations experts at Random House and all the other big houses. Si Newhouse's approach was to offer almost any price for a book by or about a celebrity — a blockbuster. Bernstein felt that this practice was at the expense of the publisher's ability to buy what he called "quality" books, those not likely to sell huge numbers.

In late 1988, despite Bernstein's misgivings, Si bought Crown Publishing Group for $200 million. It turned out to be a money-losing deal. But Bernstein did his best to iron out the serious financial problems. Nevertheless, in late 1988, Si announced what he called Bernstein's retirement. For replacement, he chose Albert Vitale, who had been managing Bantam Doubleday Bell. Vitale brought the simmering unhappiness of some Random House editors to a head when he forced

Andre Schiffrin to resign as head of Pantheon Books. The house had been losing money, but it had published a number of outstanding books, some by liberal-to-left authors. Vitale ordered Schiffrin to cut his new titles by two-thirds. When Schiffrin resigned, Pantheon writers staged a demonstration, with more than 300 setting up a picket line outside the Random House building. Many sent press releases expressing their outrage to New York papers and network newsrooms, bitterly attacking Vitale. Some Pantheon editors resigned. Schiffrin supporters pointed out that while Pantheon had lost money on its new books the year before, it had made $3 million in profits on its backlist — books published in earlier years. Schiffrin soon launched his own publishing house, The New Press, and many of the former Pantheon writers, such as Studs Terkel, began to submit their manuscripts to him.

In Si Newhouse's book publishing domain, mass marketing and promotional hype became the way to sell books, regardless of their content. The prestigious Random House and Knopf hyped sexy as well as intellectually serious books — especially big books, those that were sure to achieve positions on the *New York Times* best seller list. One editor commented that while Random House had once had the reputation of publishing *good* books, it was now known for its *big* books - the blockbusters.

Si brought *Vanity Fair* back to publication in 1983, 47 years after it had been suspended during the Great Depression. He had been urged to do so by Liberman, who had started at *Vogue* in 1941, and who wanted *Vanity Fair* to focus on popular culture and politics. Liberman master-minded the selection of the first two short-lived editors, and he controlled their products, which got lots of criticism and little praise. Then came Tina Brown, an English-born editor who had breathed life into the dying *Tatler* during the Thatcher era. She had married Harold Evans in 1981, when he was editor of Rupert Murdoch's *London Times*. A year later, Si Newhouse had bought the *Tatler*, and when she left it, Tina Brown moved to America and became a consultant to *Vanity Fair*. Late in 1983, Si offered her the job of editing *Vanity Fair*. After making clear that she would have to be entirely in charge, she quickly rejuvenated the magazine with profiles of celebrities and wealthy Americans.

Two years after he bought the *New Yorker*, Si fired William Shawn, the highly venerated 79-year-old who had edited the magazine for 35 years. Before Newhouse bought the magazine, he had repeatedly promised *not* to fire Shawn. Now he went to Shawn's office, told him that Robert Gottlieb would replace him, and handed him a note saying that Shawn would retire two months later. When more than 150 famous writers signed a letter of protest, Si extended Shawn's departure date by a few months. Gottlieb had been editor at Knopf for many years. He tried hard to continue Shawn's traditions at the *New Yorker*. But circulation and advertising went into decline. Ad lineage in 1991 dropped to a third of its levels during the peak of Shawn's reign. The *New Yorker* was clearly losing money. But Si allowed Gottlieb to run the magazine for five years. By then Tina Brown had edited *Vanity Fair* eight years. When Newhouse asked her to move to the *New Yorker* in late 1991, she accepted the invitation and quickly moved to change the magazine.. One change lowered the iron wall which had separated the editorial from the advertising department ever since the magazine was edited by the legendary Harold Ross. Tina Brown even began to host parties at which advertisers were the main guests.

Eric Utne, writing in the *Columbia Journalism Review* 15 months after Tina Brown took over, quoted an unnamed staff writer as commenting on Brown's "unflagging preoccupation with being hot, snappy and of-the-moment."[8] The result, said the writer, is that some editorial decisions were made so close to deadline that the fact-checking was inadequate. Utne, who publishes the *Utne Reader: the Best of the Alternative Press*, summarized Brown's early changes: fewer long articles, fewer articles about foreign affairs, more color cartoons, ads for such products as blue jeans and underwear, some new regular writers, and black-and-white photos. Utne concluded that "Brown has transformed the *New Yorker* and especially 'Talk of the Town' with a kind of weekly epistle for America's new orthodoxy — the cult of personality. She rules as its high priestess." Despite the criticism, both circulation and advertising for the magazine went up.

Now editors and other staff leaders at Conde Nast magazines agreed that Si Newhouse was very much in charge. They also knew quite well about his style of sudden dismissals, and of encouraging competition between editors. But while his magazines capitalize on celebrities, Newhouse himself remains in the shadows. Biographer Thomas Maier comments, "Almost always, Si Newhouse has managed to escape public scrutiny. Only the insiders seem to know the power and fear inside the Newhouse kingdom. Sometimes they even laugh about it — nervously."[9]

While the glamorous part of the Newhouse empire is Conde Nast magazines, the more profitable parts are the newspaper chain and broadcast cable holdings. The newspapers and cable companies are worth at least $10 billion. The captain of both these enterprises is Si's younger brother, Donald, who inherited the job at his father's death and who is described by Maier as "a thoughtful, amiable man" who "resembles his father, Sam, with a more genial-looking face, straight dark hair, and equally short stature."[10] He operates one of the country's largest newspaper chains as an absentee landlord, paying attention to editorial content only when it affects the bottom line. Each paper or group of papers has an overseer, a member of the Newhouse family. Donald commutes by limousine from his Park Avenue home to Advance Publications headquarters in Newark, New Jersey. The papers are no longer as universally mediocre as they were when Sam Newhouse ran them. Under Sam, Newhouse papers in the South, notably the *New Orleans Times-Picayune* and the *Birmingham News*, failed to join the racial equality movement in the 1960s. In the 1980s, they were far behind other papers, North and South, in reporting on speeches and actions of neo-Nazi David Duke. The *Portland Oregonian* staff had knowledge of complaints by women of sexual harassment by Senator Bob Packwood, but they held the story until Packwood was re-elected in 1992 and the *Washington Post* made a major issue of the charges. Similarly, the *Newark Star-Ledger* gave its readers no hint of the tensions in the 1960s which led to serious race riots.

All that has dramatically changed in recent years. A *Columbia Journalism Review* article early in 2000 said, "sometime in the last decade or so, the Newhouses decided profitable newspapers weren't enough."[11] Perhaps the most outstanding of the chain is the *Portland Oregonian*, which in 1999 won a Pulitzer Prize for explanatory journalism, and was ranked the 12th best paper in the country in a *Columbia*

Journalism Review poll.

Empire builder Sam Newhouse had usually sought papers with a monopoly in their communities. Where there was no monopoly, he would buy — and then kill — the other paper. Donald Newhouse followed his father's example in Cleveland and New Orleans. And when the Newhouse paper in St. Louis failed to compete successfully with the Pulitzer family's *Post-Dispatch*, Don stopped publication. Then it turned out that the Newhouses had an agreement with the Pulitzers to combine operations — and share profits. That JOA gave the Newhouses $177 million in the years from 1986 to 2000, when the Pulitzers finally negotiated a new agreement. For a payoff of $306 million, the new agreement gives the Pulitzers 95 percent of the profits until 2015, when an undetermined final payoff will be made.

By the mid-1990s, according to biographer Thomas Maier, the Newhouse media company had become the largest privately-held communications giant in America, with some 19,000 employees. In sheer size, the Newhouse empire was ranked at the top — or close to it — in books, magazines, newspapers and cable-television franchises.[12] In the U.S., the Conde Nast group now includes not only *Vogue, Vanity Fair, New Yorker* and *House and Garden*, but *Self, Architectural Digest, Mademoiselle, Glamour, Gourmet, Bride's, Gentlemen's Quarterly (GQ)* and *Parade.* .

A magazine for computer users, *Wired*, was added to the Conde Nast family in June, 1998. A year later, "many *Wired* cultists . . .are griping about the changes in their beloved techno-bible," the *San Francisco Chronicle* reported, because "the magazine is edging away from big thoughts and placing more emphasis on business in the Internet age."[13] A year after the *Wired* takeover, Conde Nast paid $650 million to buy Fairchild Publishing from Walt Disney Co., adding *Women's Wear Daily, Daily News Record,* and fashion magazines *W* and *Jane.* In mid-2000, Conde Nast stopped publishing *Women's Sports & Fitness* and *Sport* magazines . A few months earlier, the men's magazine *Details* was suspended.

Meanwhile, the empire has extended its reach to overseas sites. The Conde Nast group gave Si Newhouse a foothold first in England and ultimately in Italy, France, Spain, and even Australia. By 1997, there were 41 magazines overseas, including such titles as *The Tatler, The World of Interiors, Maison and Jardin,* and *Vogue Bambini.*

Over and over in magazine articles and books, the role of family in running the Newhouse properties is emphasized, as it was in the long-running inheritance tax case. Donald makes most decisions about the newspaper and cable properties; Si makes decisions about magazine properties. But on big issues, especially expansion of the empire, there is discussion among family members, including cousins and aunts and uncles, before decisions are made. When considering a new property for purchase, a key question is whether a family member is available — and willing — to "oversee" it. If not, there is no purchase.

Family discussions in early 1998 led to a bombshell announcement about one of four branches of the Newhouse empire — book publishing. By then the Random House stable had joined Conde Nast in hemorrhaging red ink. In discussions with family members, especially Donald, Si became convinced that while it was okay to have one major money loser (magazines), owning two was not. This led to discussions with Thomas Middlehoff, representing the Bertelsmann media giant, for the sale of Random House. The sale was announced in March, 1998, with Bertelsmann paying an estimated $1.4 billion for the Random House group which Newhouse had bought for $65 million 18 years earlier. With the deal including imprints in England, Si Newhouse no longer had control of any book publisher. Biographer Carol Felsenthal comments that it was "indisputable . . . that he (Si Newhouse) had taken a venerable publisher and stripped it of its values and its intellectual tone."[14]

The sale of Random House came soon after announcement that the *New Yorker* was becoming part of the Conde Nast group and moving to a new Times Square building. Conde Nast has moved into 18 floors of the 48-story building completed in 1999. Now Conde Nast employees can go for meals to a fourth floor canteen designed by famed architect Frank Gehry.

Even as the Newhouse conglomerate has grown to enormous size, even though its properties are widely varied in both type and location, it has all remained within family hands. The temptation to put stock on Wall Street has been successfully resisted. Among other benefits of this privacy, the family can be secretive about the value of its properties. Today it is America's largest privately held media empire, and includes "TV and radio stations, part of a pulp mill, real estate that includes an airport in Massachusetts, Lifetime and the Learning Channel, 24 percent of the Discovery Channel, and other assorted properties here and abroad."[15]

Writing about Si and Don Newhouse in a 1987 *Fortune* article, Carol Loomis said, "Physically, they are short and inconspicuous, and they hug the background in their lives as well."[16] They have work habits similar to those of their father. Si gets to his office by six in the morning and starts home at about three in the afternoon. He lives with Victoria in a big townhouse on Park Avenue, with a spacious setting for a substantial, valuable collection of modern art, which both Si and Victoria admire. She is in charge of a foundation which publishes art histories.

Donald seems more straight-forward and friendly, even "sweet," than his older brother, whose friends use words like "complex," "idiosyncratic," and "odd" to describe Si's behavior.[17] Don also heads for his Newark office early in the morning. He often visits Advance Corporation papers in other parts of the country, flying by commercial airline. While Don is considered a liberal Democrat, his older brother is conservative but seldom indicates it to his liberal friends. Don and his wife Sue both work on projects for the New York Public Library and the National Dance Institute. The father of these wealthy brothers set up a foundation which gives several million dollars a year to a wide variety of causes. Biographer Felsenthal says, "Si continues to make almost no mark on American philanthropy."[18]

There is considerable speculation about who in the family will rule the Newhouse empire in the future. The likeliest to take over the magazine branch is Jonathan Newhouse, whose father, Norman, was brother to the late Sam Newhouse. Jonathan is now president of Conde Nast International. Steven Newhouse, Don's first born, seems likely to take over the newspaper and cable branches of the conglomerate.

Si is still clearly the dominant member of the Newhouse family. Two books in the 1990s — *Newhouse* and *Citizen Newhouse* — focused on S.I.Newhouse Jr. (Si), although both gave ample information on the rest of the family. At 73, he still works long days and meets regularly for business lunches with executives in his part of the empire. In summer, he relaxes on weekends in his Long Island vacation home, but he returns to his New York City home early Sunday afternoon, ready to set out for the office early Monday morning.

Billionaires often make headlines, but Si and Don seldom do. When they do, it's likely to be in the business section.

MICHAEL BLOOMBERG–
HE WANTS TO BE NEW YORK'S MAYOR

11

Michael Bloomberg is a relative newcomer to the billionaire class. His name first showed up in the *Forbes 400* in 1996. By 2001, his fortune had jumped to $4.5 billion. At age 57, he owns one of the fastest-growing companies in the country. And now he plans to run for mayor of New York.

He works hard and puts in long hours, and his well-paid New York staff of 350 reporters and editors, part of 1,100 employees in 79 news bureaus worldwide, do the same. He calls them "workaholics." To encourage them to stay in the office at lunchtime, Bloomberg supplies a continuous flow of snacks, soft drinks, cereal, coffee, vegetables and fruit. The average age of Bloomberg staffers is 30.

Bloomberg Financial Markets, his bedrock agency, feeds financial data via computer from offices in New York City; Princeton, New Jersey; Frankfurt, Germany; London; Hong Kong; Singapore; Sydney; and Tokyo; with plans to add bureaus in Johannesburg and Beijing. His customers, who pay $1,650 a month for one user and $1,285 apiece for more than one, include the Bank of England, the Vatican, World Bank and every Federal Reserve Bank. And "the company's increasingly diversified units — wire service, television, radio, publishing, interactive trading — all set records the last 12 months."[1]

Bloomberg News, a younger venture, supplies information on financial markets. With a worldwide staff of 1,100 reporters and editors, it has become a major supplier of customized news via computer, radio and satellite TV. The BN terminal, nowadays called simply "the Bloomberg," provides thousands of news stories a day on business and related topics. The related topics include analysis of securities, histories and current activities of companies and dividend records.[2] It also provides movie reviews, scores on a wide variety of sports, weather forecasts, ski reports, airline schedules, travel services, real estate listings, even horoscopes. Indeed, a subscriber can punch out a request for an on-line summary of the day's *Wall Street Journal*.

The first broadcast venture came in the 1992 purchase of WNEW, an AM station in New York, for $13.5 million. Bloomberg quickly converted it to an all-news station. Then he worked out an arrangement with Maryland Public Television to broadcast Bloomberg News at 7 am on TV, starting in January, 1994. By mid-1995, the Bloomberg syndicate was sending news to 125 radio and five TV stations, as well as 200 public TV stations and 500 National Public Radio stations. Bloomberg Information Television is broadcast 24 hours a day in English in four different versions — one each for US-and-Canada, Europe, South America and Asia. Then there are also French, Japanese, Spanish, Portuguese, Italian, Dutch and German BITs. The "Charlie Rose" program on PBS originates in a Bloomberg TV station in New York. By 1995, Bloomberg also owned WBBR-AM, with all-news reporting focused on business. The company sends out 4,000 stories a day, and many can be heard on Bloomberg Radio and its 200 -plus affiliates.

While Bloomberg News is broadcast on radio and TV, the company's main profits come from "the Bloomberg" — leased out to carry "a data flow to 110,000 trading desks, executive suites and newsrooms -- anywhere that instantaneous financial information is in demand."[3] That number has now jumped to 140,000, some at $1,650 a month, some at $1,285 a month.

Another Bloomberg enterprise is *Bloomberg Personal Finance* , a 24-page glossy magazine which carries features on personal finance and which reaches 215,000 subscribers. Still another is *Bloomberg,* a monthly magazine. Any one of the many thousands hooked up to a company terminal gets *Bloomberg,* which had a 90,000 circulation in mid-1995. Finally there's "Bloomberg Forum," which provides audio-visual interviews with executives. In recent years, with such ventures as the *Bloomberg* magazine, he has tried to reach individual investors rather than financial professionals.

When a staff member from a new Bloomberg bureau in Washington, DC applied for Capitol Hill credentials in 1989, he was turned down. At about the same time, a *New York Times* editor asked for a Bloomberg terminal, saying that the paper could not pay for it. Knowing that service to the *Times* would give his company credibility, Bloomberg asked only for the cost of installation and telephone service, but he added that he'd like Bloomberg News to be given credit whenever one of its stories was used. Before long, the service was going out to 120 papers.[4] The "free" service to newspapers was ended by Bloomberg early in 1999, but news organizations were expected to get discounted rates.

Born in Medford, Massachusetts, in 1942, he's the son of a dairy bookkeeper and his wife. Little is known about his childhood, but he attended Johns Hopkins University in Baltimore. In order to pay college expenses, he worked as a parking lot attendant at the faculty club. He majored in electrical engineering and physics, and then went on to Harvard Business School for a master's degree in business administration.

His first post-graduate job was in the Salomon Brothers trading room. It was a rock-bottom   job. But now he tells how he made it a point to get to the office at seven every morning so that he could talk with William R. Salomon when no other employees were present. Then, by working beyond the normal day's end at six, he'd leave at the same time as John Gutfreund, who usually invited Bloomberg to ride in his car. Later he said, "So the managing partner, Gutfreund, and the heir apparent, became my friends when I was just a clerk."[5]

He rose fast. Six years after he started, Bloomberg became a Salomon partner in 1972, and three years later he was promoted to director of the company's block trading operations. The new job demanded 12 to 15 hours a day, always under high pressure. He became so sure of his judgment that he openly showed impatience with the ways in which company officials operated. He was demoted in 1979 to director of computer operations. Finally, when Salomon's merged with Philbro Corporation, he found himself out of a job.

Undaunted, Bloomberg started his own business in 1981, using some of the $10 million in cash and stocks that came with his Salomon departure. It wasn't enough for what he wanted to do, so he approached a number of companies, finally arousing interest at Merrill Lynch. To convince hesitant officials there, he spent six months devising a system that performed complex calculations not only on government bonds but also on the Merrill Lynch inventory. On the strength of that, Merrill Lynch advanced Bloomberg $30 million for a 30 percent stake in his new company, Bloomberg Inc. That was in 1981. By 1996, Merrill's $30 million investment had risen in value to $600 million; three years later, Bloomberg had bought back enough to reduce Merrill's share to 20 percent. He now owns 72 percent and six longtime employees have a total of eight percent of the Bloomberg empire.

He has a house on New York's upper east side, a weekend home in Westchester, and a condominium in Vail, Colorado. He married English-born Susan Brown. Probably because he was gone from home so much of the time, they were divorced in 1993 after 18 years, but remain friends. They have two daughters, Emma, born in 1976, and Georgina, born in 1979.

One of the workers in his New York office calls Bloomberg a "benevolent despot," indicating that while he has a large ego and likes to be the one in charge, he is generous to his employees. One example of his generosity was the $2.5 million Christmas party he hosted in London for all his British employees. The party, spread over four floors of an office building, cost about $800 per guest. The company's Christmas party in 2000 at the New York Museum of Natural History had a $2.5 million pricetag. Every summer, he is host for an expensive picnic at his Westchester County home. Overseas employees are flown in from as far away as Asia at company expense to attend. For the several thousand guests, including the families of all employees, there are pony rides, a magcian, jugglers, a petting zoo and amusement park rides.

A workaholic himself, Bloomberg expects his employees to be workaholics, too. He and other managers frown on a staff member who leaves the office for lunch. Many of those who quit say they did so because the pressures were too great.

"A certified multimedia mogul" was the description given Bloomberg by Stephen I. Johnson in a 1995 *Forbes* article.[6] "Street Fighter" was the appellation used by *Time* magazine.[7] "Michael Bloomberg has been described as 'charming, quick-talking, and cocky,' 'brash, vulgar and hot-tempered,' and 'over-flowing with self-confidence.'

He is well-known for fierce competitiveness, 'often raw aggression,' a tendency to make 'outrageous, off-the-record pronouncements,' and skill at 'cutting complex ideas down to size with a few slashes of his sharp tongue'."[8] His ego shows up in almost everything he does. The name Bloomberg is pinned to his company, his terminals, his magazines, his radio and TV outlets, and transcendentally, to the title of his autobiography, *Bloomberg by Bloomberg*.

As early as 1998, he floated the idea that he might run for New York mayor. A New York magazine reported that he had "been whispering to friends that he might just try" for the job.[9] In 2000, his intention to run became quite clear when he bought up a series of "Web site domain names he could use for a campaign — everything from bloombergformayor.com to mayor2001.net,"[10] And in October, 2000, he changed his registration from Democrat to Republican, apparently because the Democratic field for the 2001 election was too crowded. Inside his New York offices, Bloomberg began to hold special sessions with senior staff members to prepare them to take over their departments. And reporters were added to the staff to "add coverage of city news outside the world of business."[11] He made clear that he would do no fund-raising, but finance the campaign himself. There were reports that he was prepared to spend up to $20 million to become mayor. By spring 2001, he had hired experienced political consultants from Washington.

Until recently, his bonus system made most employees quite happy. It was based on the number of new customers each year. But Bloomberg overhauled the system, reducing the sales base on which bonuses are figured. It seems clear that he is exercising tighter control over all kinds of costs. He has no secretary and there are no private offices.

But not all employees are happy. There have been three lawsuits by former women employees charging sexism, especially in the sales section of the empire. Bloomberg told a *Fortune* reporter in 1995 that "we have a game plan. It is to provide all the useful information in as many different forms as possible to people who need it. You try different areas, and some will be very profitable down the road."[12] Bloomberg's programs have the ability not only to present data, but to manipulate it.

He is licensed to pilot not only helicopters but fixed wing airplanes. He chairs the board of trustees at Johns Hopkins, and often flies his helicopter to the campus. He has given $55 million to the university, one of the largest gifts any university has ever received. His initial contribution was made in 1996, the same year that he made two other million dollar gifts to educational and charitable organizations. He is trustee of many other organizations, including the New York Jewish Museum, Lincoln Center for the Performing Arts, Spence School, and New York Police and Fire Widows' and Children's Benefit Fund. In 1998, he was benefit chairman for the Committee to Protect Journalists. He endowed a fellowship at Harvard to study philanthropic programs. He talks and writes often about the obligation of the rich to make such gifts before they die.

His company and his fortune have grown with great speed since 1981, and he has already moved into the Internet. He agreed with America Online (AOL) early in 1998 to be its primary provider of business news and information on a web site titled Bloomberg. In doing so, he replaced Dow Jones. There has been no report of how much AOL is paying for the service. Earlier the same month, he worked out a deal for his news to be provided on CNet's two web sites — News.com.Investor and Snap.Finance. So Bloomberg is well started on the Internet. His other main competitor, Reuters, also sends financial news to Internet web sites, including one operated by *Fortune* magazine. Moreover, in December, 1999, he moved "into interactive TV — the first ever in the industry. . . the system provides stock quotes and e-commerce transactions on demand, and is expected to be in 25 percent of U.S. homes, making for a $10 billion market."[13]

In August, 2000, he helped FBI agents arrest two Russian extortionists who "penetrated security at his company, which provides data direct to the terminals of (London) City terminals," a story in the London *Sunday Times* reported, adding that the hackers had demanded $200,000 after convincing Bloomberg that they had stolen his personal computer passwords, and "two men from Kazakhstan were arrested in a classic police sting involving Bloomberg himself, the FBI and Scotland Yard."[14]

Bloomberg still gets up at 5 am every weekday morning to put in those 12-hour days at the office. Back in 1992, he commented, "The future belongs to multimedia, not one-product companies. I'm going to make sure that we're one of those New Age companies."[15]

So far, Michael Bloomberg has kept up perfectly with his game plan. Now he's looking ahead to the top seat at City Hall.

THE SCRIPPS FAMILY–THE DIVIDED DYNASTY

12

The Scripps empire, created in the last century, has been torn apart by so many family feuds that it has been called "the divided dynasty." What makes the division easy to see are the two listings in the *Forbes 400* for 1998 — the E. W. Scripps family at $4.4 billion and the James E. Scripps family, some 200 strong, sharing $1 billion. The wealth of the E. W. Scripps family rose to $4.5 billion in 2000. The James E. Scripps family disappeared from the *Forbes 400* after their empire, the Scripps League, was sold.

There are three corporate strands to the Scripps story: the Evening News Association (ENA), formed by James E. Scripps, the immigrant who started the family's first paper, and sold to the Gannett newspaper chain in 1986 for $717 million; the Scripps League, formed by descendants of James G. O. Scripps, the eldest son of E. W. Scripps, and sold to Pulitzer Publishing Co. in 1996; and the present-day E.W. Scripps Co., descended from Scripps McRae and Scripps-Howard. The only corporate body remaining today is titled the E. W. Scripps Company.

Some explanation of the complicated Scripps family geneology is in order. Edward Wyllis Scripps shared the same father -- the Englishman who immigrated in 1844 and settled on an Illinois farm after marrying his third wife in Cleveland -- but had a different mother than James E. Scripps, Ellen Scripps and George Scripps. The mother of E.W. was that third wife, Julia Osborn. James E., Ellen and George were all born in England.

James E. Scripps, an innovator, became business manager and part owner of the *Detroit Tribune* in 1873. There, he introduced market strategies to appeal to blue collar workers, including a two-cent price. When the building that housed the *Tribune* burned down one Sunday a few months later, the insurance money allowed James to build a new plant. He renamed the paper, which he co-founded with

George Scripps — also a half-brother to Edward Wyllis Scripps —, the *Detroit News*. While he started or helped start other papers over the years, the *Detroit News* remained James's favorite.

When James E. began the *News*, he already had several years experience as a reporter and editor. "In his dark, vested suits, James was a cautious model of maturity. 'A fossil,' thought E. W., himself a rakish redhead who wore flannel shirts and high boots and carried a flask of whiskey in his hip pocket."[1]

Edward Wyllis Scripps went to work at his half-brother's *Detroit News* a few months after it started. In 1878 he borrowed from his brothers and sisters — mostly James — to launch the *Cleveland Penny Press*, from which *Penny* was soon dropped. The paper used the same working class appeals as the *Detroit News*, and carried features sent from Detroit by an older sister, Ellen Browning Scripps.

The family continued to buy or start papers — the *Buffalo Evening Telegraph*, *St. Louis Chronicle* and *Cincinnati Post*. Twenty years before the end of the century, they had the country's first newspaper chain. The Cleveland and Detroit papers grew rapidly. All the Scripps papers were strenuously pro-labor and anti-business. E. W. Scripps "made protest the spirit of the Scripps papers," one of his biographers wrote.[2] It is no longer.

As early as 1877, James E. incorporated the Detroit Evening News Association, taking 30 of the 50 shares for himself, with George H. Scripps getting 16, and Ellen, E.W. and John Sweeney only one or two each. It became known as the Evening News Association, or ENA.

The decade starting in 1880 marked dramatic changes for the family. The partners started a penny paper, the *St. Louis Chronicle*, in 1880, putting E. W. in charge. It faced formidable Pulitzer opposition, and struggled for years to stay alive. While E.W. was working hard in St. Louis, James E. bought the *Buffalo Evening Telegraph*, which lasted only a few years, and started the *Cincinnati Penny Paper*, destined to become the cornerstone for the 20th century E.W.Scripps empire.

In late 1880s the Scripps Publishing Company was formed by the family to control the papers in Cleveland, St. Louis and Buffalo — but not Detroit.[3] In St. Louis, E.W. was working very hard, fighting to build circulation against the Pulitzers. "In adversity, he showed himself to be mulish, egotistical, petulant, short-tempered, super-sensitive, depressed, impatient, melancholy, disgusted — trying to run away when he couldn't have his own way. He spent himself physically, through hard work and mental torture, resulting from emotional stress, continued hard drinking, and sexual adventuring. His already poor health eroded into an illness which a physician was to say gave him but a few more months to live."[4] He blamed everybody but himself for the continued losses of the paper in St. Louis, demanding that James send others to help him, and then finding fault with those who came. In Detroit, "James showed more patience, kindness, tolerance, and affection for the younger brother than could be expected in view of the provocation."[5]

The doctor's warning to Edward Wyllis in 1881 was much like the warning given the same year to James E. But E.W.'s doctor was wrong; E.W. lived 45 more years. That was not the case for James, destined to die in 1906, twenty years before his younger half-brother.

Edward Wyllis Scripps heeded the doctor's warning and, with his sister Ellen, headed for Algeria in the fall of 1881. Algeria was good for his health; his chronic colds and bronchial hemorrhages both ended. The pair spent a few months in Paris, returning in June 1883 after more than a year and a half abroad. During his long stay overseas, E. W. decided that he wanted a paper of his own, as James had in Detroit. He chose Cincinnati and found it easy to buy out his relatives to give him control of the paper which had been started by his half-brother. Thus was the E. W. Scripps empire born with the *Cincinnati Post.*

The Buffalo paper, never a strong contender, was sold in 1885. That year also marked an important event for Edward Wyllis Scripps. For some years he had lived with a succession of women he called "mistresses." Now he decided it was time to marry. Attending a church social, he met Nackey Holtsinger, the daughter of a Presbyterian minister. After a brief courtship, they were married. Nackey was 12 years younger than her new husband. They had six children: James George, John Paul, Dorothy Blair, Edward Wyllis McLean, Robert Paine and Nackey Elizabeth.

After years of drifting apart, the final break between James E. and his half-brother, E.W., came in 1889. After James returned from a trip to Europe, he became furious over the changes made by E. W. at the *Detroit News* during his absence. The younger half-brother "had rushed the *News* toward modernization, planning to print eight pages and maybe more. James E. was especially outraged by E.W.'s unauthorized decision to build a new pressroom and install a complete new set of presses."[6]

The result: E.W. was deposed as president of the Evening News Association and removed from management of the *Cleveland Press*. He was left with only the *Cincinnati Post* and *St. Louis Chronicle* under his control. "In 1890 the two brothers separated forever, notwithstanding an overlap of stock ownership. In the split, George H. sided with James E.; Ellen with (E.W.). Scripps."[7]

The "overlap of stock ownership" led to one last fight between James and his younger half-brother. When George Scripps, now back in the E.W. camp, died in 1900, he left his one-third interest in the ENA and its *Detroit News* to E.W. "Thus, when James died, E.W. would be in a position to vie for control of the (Detroit) *News*. James would not stand for it. Years of litigation followed. Before he died in 1906, James agreed to swap his holdings in the Cincinnati, Cleveland and St. Louis papers for the bulk of E.W.'s stock in the *News*."[8] The *Detroit News* was, of course, the paper James E. Scripps loved most; it was the first he started.

The Evening News Association was destined to remain in the hands of James E. Scripps's heirs until his descendants sold it to the Gannett chain in 1986. By then the family had expanded ENA to include TV stations in Mobile, Alabama; Tucson, Arizona; Oklahoma City; Austin, Texas; and Washington, D.C., as well as a group of small newspapers in New Jersey and a small daily in Palm Springs, California. The two most valuable, of course, were the Washington TV station and the *Detroit News*. All of it went to the Gannett empire for $717 million in cash in 1986. That settlement was the basis for the $1 billion today shared by 200 heirs of James E. Scripps.

Back in 1892, when George H. broke with James E. and brought the *Cleveland Press* into the newly-formed Scripps-McRae League, E.W. had created the League to distinguish his holdings from those of his half-brother in Detroit. The partnership with McRae was lop-sided. McRae continued as business manager and got one-third of the profits, while E.W. got two-thirds.

Now E.W. began to look toward what he called "retirement." He went all the way to southern California and found a sage-covered mesa north of San Diego. Starting with 400 acres, he ultimately purchased 2,100 acres and built, over a period of nine years, Miramar Ranch. At first, he and his growing family stayed at Miramar Ranch only in the winter, summering in West Chester, Ohio. The last three of his six children were born at Miramar.

Although he had announced his retirement, he still maintained control over his growing press empire. He chose both the editors and business managers carefully, in much the same manner as Joseph Pulitzer and Samuel Newhouse. Each hire was told he could have 10 percent of the paper as soon as it was profitable.

The papers all started with a pro-labor, anti-corporate editorial position, but they all gradually became more like the rest of the country's press. That resulted partly from local management autonomy. But it contradicted one of Scripps's famous disquisitions: "I have only one principle and that is represented by an effort to make it harder for the rich to become richer and easier for the poor to keep from growing poorer."[9]

Ellen's human interest features gave E.W. the idea for the Newspaper Enterprise Association to distribute features, including cartoons, to any newspaper wanting to buy them. Years later, NEA was merged with other Scripps operations into United Media, owned, of course, by E.W.Scripps.

When his editors reported that they had trouble joining the Associated Press, E.W. started the Scripps-McRae Association, which became United Press in 1907. He believed competition between the two wire services would be healthy for "correct news." United Press was only a year old when Roy Howard was put in charge in 1908. He built the wire service, both in the U.S. and abroad, so rapidly that he was made business director of Scripps-McRae. He remained a key figure in the empire until his death in 1964. UP was later combined with Hearst's International News Service to become UPI. Its history has been rocky in recent years.

E.W. was growing blind when he was only 46, much as Pulitzer had. He hired a doctor to be with him constantly. At age 55 in 1909, he was both heavier and bearded. "The big fellow wore a full white scraggly beard, baggy pants and English Wellington-style knee-high boots, a frontiersman's cotton shirt and a billed cap."[10] The portrait of him most often used today shows that he wore a skull cap, with thick-lensed glasses on his forehead. A personality portrait is drawn in a Scripps-Howard *Handbook:* "He smoked cigars and drank whisky until almost the day of his death. He enjoyed pleasures of the flesh. He liked a rowdy game of poker. In his later years, he was gruff in manner; he wore boots and dribbled cigar ashes on his vest. His language was not always elegant. He was, in fact, a tough customer."[11] And a later biographer writes that "there was a streak of meanness as well as stubbornness in him."[12]

E.W. left his misnamed "retirement" during the first World War to take over active editorial management of the growing Scripps-McRae chain. But before the war ended he was paralyzed by a stroke, and his doctor ordered a six-month rest. Now, his two sons, Robert and James G., bickered constantly. More and more, E.W. showed his preference for Bob rather than Jim. He made Bob the editor-in-chief of Scripps-McRae papers and gave him full power-of-attorney for the chain.

After a quarrel with his father in 1920, "Jim (James G. Scripps) walked away with the seven Western newspapers -- the *Los Angeles Record, Portland News, Sacramento Star, San Francisco News, Seattle Star, Spokane Press* and *Tacoma Times*. He was accompanied by local executives whose stock support allowed Jim to take control. The *Dallas Dispatch* and *Denver Express* later joined the fledgling chain."[13] When James G. died at age 34 in 1921, his widow Josephine and their sons took control of the western papers, which they re-named the Scripps League, based in Seattle. Josephine, the daughter-in-law of E. W. Scripps, and her sons — his grandsons — were left out of E.W.'s will and its trusteeship.

The Scripps League continued for 75 years, when it was sold to Pulitzer Publishing Co. for $250 million. By then — 1996 — it had expanded to 16 papers in eleven states spread across the country — Vermont, Massachusetts, Illinois, Wisconsin, Arizona, Montana, Oregon, Utah, Washington, California -- even Hawaii.

Before he died at 72 in 1926, the paralyzed E. W. Scripps had continued to explore new frontiers. In 1921 he started Science Service to report about American research in simple terms. The service was discontinued in 1970, but it still publishes the monthly magazine *Science News*.[14] He also helped in founding the Scripps Institute of Biological Research at LaJolla, California, now part of the University of California and titled Scripps Institute of Oceanography.

E.W. outlived all but one of his sons, Robert Paine Scripps -- Bob -- who inherited control of papers in 15 states as well as UPI, NEA, ACME Newsphotos and United Features Syndicate. By then Scripps-McRae had become Scripps-Howard, with Roy Howard managing the business end and Robert Scripps the editorial.[15] In 1926, the same year Scripps died, the company bought the *Rocky Mountain News* in Denver. By 1935, there were 35 dailies, but as papers were closed or sold, only 16 were left by 1977.

Robert Paine Scripps agreed with his father's philosophy, but was not as vigorous in its application. Partly, but not entirely, because of heavy alcohol use, he also suffered illnesses and was in virtual retirement when he died, at age 38, in 1938. By then, Roy Howard had taken over greater control of the empire. Howard was just as strong-minded as E.W. and Bob had been, but in the opposite direction, at least editorially. When FDR announced his plan to change the Supreme Court, Howard made sure Scripps-Howard opposed Roosevelt in the 1940 election campaign. He had Scripps-Howard papers supporting GOP candidates all the way through 1960. But his control faltered after World War II, when the new Scripps heirs took over key trustee posts. Edward W. Scripps II, who was put into the top editorial spot by the heirs, understood and agreed with most of his grandfather's basic beliefs. In turn, his brother Charles E. Scripps took over active control in 1953 and stayed there until 1994, when he retired at age 74.

Because E. W. Scripps left his son James out of his inheritance, control of the empire remains in the hands of his son Robert's descendants. "The dynasty has been divided — and subdivided --for more than sixty years," a Scripps biographer wrote in 1993.[16] Descendants of James E. Scripps were cut out of the inheritance because he -- James E., the one who started it all -- dared to disagree with E.W. on both money and policy issues.

In recent years the Scripps empire has become more and more business orient-ed. Even before its 1997 acquisition of a block of six newspapers in Texas and South Carolina from Harte-Hanks Communications, almost two-thirds of its total income came from daily and community newspapers. The Harte-Hanks purchase, at more than $600 million, increased its newspapers to 22 daily and six community. It already owned six ABC-TV stations and three NBC-TV stations. The Harte-Hanks deal added a CBS-TV station in San Antonio, Texas, and brought the number of TV holdings to ten, all in major markets.

Home and Garden Television (HGTV), developed in the nineties for the Scripps empire by Ken Lowe, is a highly successful operation with 66 million cable sub-scribers. The TV Food Network, bought early in 1997, augments the HGTV oper-ation. United Media syndicates 150 comic strips including "Peanuts" and "Dilbert," and news features. HGTV programs are seen and heard in Europe and Japan. The Scripps Company makes prime-time TV programs, including documentaries and miniseries, and sells to 60 countries overseas. Cenetel Productions makes programs for both cable TV and television networks. Due in the last half of 2001 is Scripps' fourth TV and Internet network, Fine Living, which will serve higher income view-ers in the $200 billion luxury goods and services markets.

But while the new media properties of E. W. Scripps Co. flourished at the end of the 1990s, its leading newspaper, the *Rocky Mountain News*, was in serious trou-ble in its continuing long-time battles with the *Denver Post*. To increase its circula-tion, the tabloid *News* had dropped its newsstand price to as low as a penny a day. Early in 2000, it picked up its first Pulitzer since it was born 141 years earlier. But it had been losing money — $123 million since 1990.

Then, suddenly, in May, 2000, Scripps empire CEO William Burleigh announced that the company had paid $60 million to bring the *Rocky Mountain News* into a 50-year Joint Operating Agreement (JOA) with its rival, owned by Dean Singleton's MediaNews. "The war was over, and the *News* had lost," commented an article in the *Columbia Journalism Review*.[17] The JOA provides that the two papers will have a single management, quite apart from editorial content, and share profits.

The Scripps Howard Foundation today carries on a long tradition of gifts to both scholars and universities. The E. W. Scripps School of Journalism at Ohio University in Athens, Ohio, was founded in 1982 with $1,250,000 from the Foundation, which adds another $100,000 a year against a million dollar grant to support visiting scholars. The Foundation also funded a $1 million chair at Indiana University, and in March, 2000, announced a $2.3 million grant to Hampton University's journalism program in Virginia.

In mid-1988, Charles E. Scripps and then-CEO Lawrence Leser took the Scripps company public, with stock selling at $16 a share. By mid-1997 it had risen to $39.5 after it sold its huge cable holdings to Comcast for $1.6 billion in 1995. The bottom-line oriented Scripps management, led by CEO Bill Burleigh, is proud of the fact that income has been rising steadily. Ken Lowe became E.W. Scripps Company CEO in October, 2000. Burleigh said Lowe "has strong roots in the traditional media outlets that are the foundation of the company, and a deep understanding of the growth potential and power of new media applications and the Internet."[18]

Even though company stock is for sale on Wall Street, the Scripps Trust continues in full control, with ownership of more than 53 percent of Class A shares. The trust created in 1926 won't die until the last of E.W.'s grandchildren dies. They are Charles E. Scripps and Robert Paine Scripps. Twenty-eight great-grandchildren of E. W. Scripps will ultimately share a fortune of more than $4.5 billion.

The dynasty has been divided, but the fortune of the E. W. Scripps branch grows every day.

THE CHANDLER FAMILY–
IT DOESN'T RUN THE *L.A. TIMES* NOW

13

Merger mania broke out again in March, 2000, when the *Los Angeles Times* was swallowed up by the Tribune Company of Chicago. "The $6.3 billion transaction would create the nation's third largest newspaper company," a pair of *Times* reporters wrote.[1] Already big before the buyout, the Tribune empire stretches from New York with *Newsday*, to Chicago with the *Tribune*, to Los Angeles with the *Times*.

The Chandler family, now numbering more than 100, will have four seats on the 16-member Tribune board of directors, and 40 percent of the seats on the new *Los Angeles Times* board. So, despite the takeover, the Chandlers are still in the media. After the deal is settled, they will own 10 percent of the conglomerate Tribune's stock. In October, 2000, their collective worth was put at $3.8 billion in the *Forbes 400*.

Family members had initiated the secret negotiations with John W. Madigan, Tribune's president and CEO. Even when *Times Mirror* board members were debating the terms and voting on it, Otis Chandler knew nothing about it. But when the deal was announced, he gave his enthusiastic approval, calling it "a win-win situation," and commenting, "We're not a major presence in the Internet world, and they are. We don't have TV stations any more, and they do. There couldn't be a better fit."[2]

The arrangement giving 40 percent of the seats on the new Times Mirror board had nothing to do with *management* of the paper by descendants of famed General Otis. It resulted from terms in the Chandler family trust stipulating that the paper could neither be sold or merged. Significantly, six months after the merger, the *Los Angeles Times* shut down 14 neighborhood sections and eliminated 170 editorial and advertising positions. A reporter for the *Baltimore Sun*, also owned by the Tribune, commented that "when Tribune bought Times Mirror, the word everywhere was that the Tribune demanded higher profits."[3] The staff cuts in Los Angeles were clearly ordered in Chicago.

Otis and other members of the Chandler family had been unhappy with the management of the Times Mirror empire under Mark Willes, who had taken over in 1995, coming straight from General Mills, with no journalism background. The Tribune negotiations were also kept secret from Willes, who announced his resignation..

The Times Mirror empire had faltered in the years after Otis Chandler began his long withdrawal from management of the *Los Angeles Times* in 1980. Otis had transformed the *Times* from one of the country's worst big city dailies to one of its three best — ranking alongside the *New York Times* and *Washington Post*. In the early 1990s, with Otis Chandler almost completely out of the picture, southern California suffered a series of economic blows with shutdowns of defense and aerospace industries which had prospered during the Cold War years. For the *Los Angeles Times*, that meant a dramatic drop in circulation and profits.

Through the late '80s, non-Chandlers assumed more and more control. Tom Johnson took over as publisher and in 1986 a company lawyer, Robert Erburu, assumed the corporate spot Otis had held.   Shelby Coffey, who had worked at *U.S. News & World Report*, *Washington Post* and then the *Dallas Times-Herald* before the Chandlers sold it, became executive editor at the *Times*, but the paper's downward slide continued on Wall Street.

Mark Willes brought dramatic changes to the Times Mirror empire, and the early reports were negative both inside and outside the newsroom. His first moves were to cut 930 jobs from the *Times* payroll, drop several *Times* sections, close the New York city edition of *Newsday*, and shutter the evening edition of the *Baltimore Sun*. A year later, he traded the Times Mirror's higher education publishing business to McGraw Hill in exchange for Shepard's, a legal publishing operation, which joined Matthew Bender & Co., Times Mirror's legal publishing subsidiary.

After announcing that he had taken on the title of publisher, Willes cut the newsstand price of the *Times* to 25 cents to build circulation, and it gradually rose to more than 1,050,000 a day, still far short of the 1.5 million goal he had set, and only 40,000 more than the circulation when Otis Chandler retired.   In October 1995, four months after he took over, Willes announced plans to demolish the historic wall between the newsroom and the advertising department, declaring that he wanted the two sides of the paper to "work closely together in an effort to strengthen the paper."[4] As he explained it, that meant advertising salesmen could talk to journalists, and each section would have a business manager to conduct "strategic planning" with the section editor. All sections, he said at a staff meeting, "will have both readership objectives and revenue objectives."[5]

But in the fall of 1999, the broken wall led to an explosion in the *Los Angeles Times* newsroom. By then Willes had handed the title of publisher to Kathryn M. Downing, who also had no journalism background, while he retained the chairman title. Under a secret deal with Staples, Willes and Downing agreed to production of a 164-page magazine, with article after article — 22 of them -- by *Times* staff members, all vigorously lauding the new Staples Center Sports Arena. The deal called for a split of the $2 million in advertising revenues from the magazine between the *Times* itself and the owners of the Staples Center. When the deal was exposed in a local alternative weekly, Otis Chandler expressed his outrage in a long letter to the newsroom staff and all executives, calling the deal a "fiasco" and saying, "Trust and faith in a newspaper by its employees, its readers and the community is dearer to me than life itself."[6] More than 300 *Times* reporters and editors signed a petition in protest as soon as they heard about the deal. Then, admitting that she had planned the Staples deal, Publisher Downing issued a mea culpa to the staff, "saying it reflected her 'fundamental misunderstanding' of the role of publisher."[7] But the Wall Street price of Times Mirror stock had more than tripled, from $17.25 before Willes' 1995 arrival to $64.63 by the time of the Staples "fiasco," which was followed by a drop to $37.69 just before the Tribune merger.

The Chandlers are descendants of General Harrison Gray Otis, who took over the *Los Angeles Times* in 1882. General Otis's editorial policies were quite reactionary, and his militantly anti-union policies lasted until his great grandson, Otis Chandler, assumed command in 1960. The *Times* grew explosively during World War II because Norman Chandler, Otis's father, eliminated advertising from the paper for the duration. The city and its region had a tremendous influx of war workers and servicemen, so even without ads, the paper flourished. Chandler's wife Dorothy came from the Buffum Department Store family and after the war she became a cultural leader in the city, where the famous Dorothy Chandler Pavilion is named for her. Three years after the war, Norman and Dorothy launched an afternoon tabloid - the *Mirror*. That paper died in 1962, but its name remains in the title of the Times Mirror Company.

The *Mirror* closing was part of a deal for the shutdown of Hearst's morning paper, the *Examiner*. That left the *Times* with no competition, and although the deal was illegal under the Sherman Act, Robert Kennedy's Justice Department did nothing because the head of its antitrust division had suggested the idea to a Hearst official.[8]

In the years before Otis took over, the *Times* had been quite conservative, its strong support greatly aided Richard Nixon's political career. But under Otis's direction, the paper became more objective and its editorials more liberal. A five-part investigative story on the reactionary John Birch Society was so sharp that Otis's uncle Philip resigned from the board; his wife was a Birch Society member.[9] While Nixon had been strongly supported by the *Times*, that changed when he ran for California governor in 1962. Otis ordered equal treatment for the Democratic opponent, and Nixon "was deeply offended."[10]

Otis had spent seven years grooming for the publisher job, working in almost every department of the *Times*. In the 16 years after he took over, the editorial budget jumped from $3.6 million to $19 million. Both the size and the quality of the staff improved. One result was a doubling of circulation, from 536,000 to 1,010,000 daily.

The *Times* was the first family-owned paper to go public, with a listing on Wall Street in 1964. Otis Chandler made clear that the paper was not aiming for low income readers. In a 1979 talk he said, "The target audience of the *Times* is the middle class and the upper middle class," adding later, "We are not trying to get mass circulation, but quality circulation."[11] In seven years after he took over, the paper's annual income almost tripled and its net profit jumped from $4.5 million to $19 million. He got his board to approve a variety of new investments, buying the *Dallas Times-Herald* and *Long Island Newsday*, the *Sporting News* magazine, two TV cable systems and five TV stations, none in California.[12] The cable systems were both sold to Cox Communications in 1994. Except for the *Long Island Newsday*, all the rest were sold by the Willes regime, which got rid of *Sporting News* just before the Staples Center affair. But Willes arranged in 1999 for the purchase of five weekly papers in Massachusetts by the *Hartford Courant*, one of the dailies still owned by Times Mirror.

At the time of the Tribune Co. takeover, the Chandler family empire included no TV or radio stations and no cable systems. Its properties were all in print and computer services. The Times Mirror banner still waves over eight newspapers: the *Stamford Advocate* and *Greenwich Time* in Connecticut, the *Baltimore Sun*, *Hartford Courant*, *Morning Call* (Allentown, Pennsylvania), *Newsday* (Long Island), half of *La Opinion*, Spanish language paper in southern California, and of course, the *Los Angeles Times*. The company also has the *Los Angeles Times* news syndicate and its half of the *Los Angeles Times-Washington Post* news service. Then there are 18 magazines including *Field and Stream*, *Outdoor Life*, *Popular Science*, *Golf*, and *Ski*. Under the heading of professional information services, there are seven subsidiaries: AchieveGlobal, Allen Communications (technology), Apartment Search (listings), Jepperson Sanderson (aeronautical), ListingLink (real estate listings), MD Consult (online information for doctors), and Staywell (health and behavior programs). Operating close to Tinseltown, it has Hollywood Online, giving entertainment information. While all these media still operate under the Times Mirror banner, they are now owned by the Tribune Company.

In 1986, 26 years after he took control of the *Times* and its empire, Otis Chandler began to retire, holding only the post of executive committee chairman. It soon became clear that no other Chandler was able — or wanted — to succeed him as he had succeeded his father.

He and his first wife, Marilyn Bryant, had five children after their 1951 marriage, including three boys, but none indicated interest. A year after his 1980 divorce from Marilyn, he married Bettina Whitaker, who had been an executive at Shakey's International. The two live quietly on a 150-acre ranch estate near Redmond, Oregon, and he "spends his days surfing, hiking and tending to his own antique-automobile museum in Oxnard, California."[13] He has been a classic car enthusiast since well before his retirement. The National Press Association gave Otis its Distinguished Contribution to Journalism Award in February, 2001.

Despite its three Pulitzer prizes after Willes took over, it seems clear that the overall quality of the *Times* has declined, especially in the all-important local and suburban coverage. "There is far less depth in the local report," according to former editor Bob Waters, who is now an editor at the *Raleigh News and Observer* in North Carolina.[14] Waters says, "The bean-counters killed the entire suburban staff of 60 writers, editors and photographers" and now "the suburbs are covered by underpaid novices." In the *San Francisco Chronicle* after the Staples Center affair, reporter Ken

Garcia said, "Morale at the *Times*, not very high to begin with, is at a record low."[15] The paper goes to only 23 percent of the families in its market and is 450,000 short of Willes' goal of 1.5 million circulation.

And the Tribune Company?   In the half century since the death of the arch-reactionary Col. Robert R. McCormick, who ruled the *Chicago Tribune* during both the Roosevelt and Eisenhower years, the quality of the paper has improved remarkably. Now the Tribune empire reaches from both coasts, with its hub in the center. After the takeover, the folks of Los Angeles have good reason to be hopeful about the *Times*. And Chandler family members, who got 2.5 shares of Tribune stock for each of their Times Mirror shares, can now clip Tribune coupons.

DAVID GEFFEN–HE'S BOTH MAGNETIC AND SCARY

14

In the bottom tenth of his high school graduating class and a two-time college flunkout, David Geffen was worth $3.4 billion in 2001. At age 57, he is a key player in the infant DreamWorks SKG. He made his fortune mainly in record albums, but he also successfully invested in movies and a number of Broadway shows, including musicals.

He was born in February, 1943, in Brooklyn, the son of Russian immigrants, Abraham and Batya Geffen. His mother, the family breadwinner, sold corsets in a store near the family flat, where she also made them. David took an early interest in show business, especially movies, and his first job, at age 14, was as a movie theater usher. In high school, he paid more attention to music and drama activities than all his other studies. When the University of California, Los Angeles (UCLA) refused to admit him because of his low grades, he went to the University of Texas, but quickly flunked out. After the same thing happened at Brooklyn College, he gave up on college, moved to Los Angeles, where, at 21, he got a mailroom job at the William Morris talent agency, in part by stating on his application that he had graduated from UCLA. Early every day he went to the office to check incoming mail until he spotted a letter from UCLA, which he opened and edited to say he had graduated; then he re-sealed and returned it. Within 18 months, he was promoted to junior agent, working to get bookings for musicians.

At Morris, he discovered Laura Nyro, singer and song-writer. Even though she had been booed when she sang at the Monterey Pop Festival, Geffen liked what he heard in a recording of her Monterey song and signed her to a contract. He encouraged her to write more music and together they started Tuna Fish Music to publish her songs. In 1968 Geffen left Morris to work at Ashley Famous Agency, but left after a few months to manage Nyro as a singer full time. Under his careful guidance, she became so well-known that she was booked twice into a packed Carnegie Hall for concerts. Three years after he joined with Laura Nyro, they sold Tuna Fish Music, the main products of which were Nyro records, to CBS, with each getting half of the $4.5 million proceeds.

In 1970, he launched Asylum Records together with Elliot Roberts, an old Morris Agency friend. The two also started a talent agency, Geffen-Roberts, which specialized in folk-rock musicians, including Linda Ronstadt, Joni Mitchell and Jackson Browne — one of his discoveries -- among other big names. Browne's first album included "Doctor My Eyes," which sold more than a million copies.

Roberts and Geffen sold Asylum Records to Warner Communications for $7 million in 1971. At the same time, Geffen signed a contract to continue managing Asylum, which was merged with Warner's Elektra label in 1973. Buying a house near Bob Dylan in Malibu, he became friends with the very private singer and before long signed him up. In one year, three stars managed by Geffen — Dylan, Joni Mitchell and Carly Simon — produced records which sold more than a half million copies each. He also managed Crosby, Stills and Nash. "As far as David Crosby was concerned, Geffen was an obvious shark — but he was *his* shark."[1] When he took over the Crosky, Stills and Nash trio, Geffen eased out Paul Rothchild, who had been with the group since its startup. Rothchild is quoted in *The Mansion on the Hill*, a book about rock music, as saying, "When David Geffen enters the California waters as a manager, the sharks have entered the lagoon . . . It used to be 'Let's make music, money is a by-product.' Then it became 'Let's make money, music is a by-product'."[2]

During this early '70s period, Geffen lived with Cher, the singer, after she separated from Sonny Bono. While their relationship didn't last long, it got lots of publicity for both. Then he lived with Marlo Thomas. By now, he had become friends with Steve Ross, the legendary head of Warner Studios, which had been earning much of its profits from music when Ross took over; Ross made him vice chairman of Warner Brothers Pictures in 1975. During his one year in that job he produced *Oh, God, Greased Lightning,* and *The Late Show.* "But as a studio chieftain, he would prove a washout."[3] He was given a meaningless job as "executive assistant." But his contract had three years to run, and Ross refused to release him. "Sitting at home with nothing to do was torture for Geffen, a workaholic who for so long defined himself by his career."[4] To vent his anger, he began to make nasty comments about Ross whenever he had a chance. Indeed, more than 15 years after his Warner contract expired, Courtney Ross refused to invite Geffen to her husband's funeral because he "had chosen to vilify Ross as he was dying."[5]

In 1976, his doctor told Geffen that he had bladder cancer, so for the last few years of the 1970s, Geffen stayed outside the media world, giving most attention to his health, but also to California real estate, his art collection and teaching about the music industry at both UCLA and Yale. Then his doctor found that the cancer diagnosis had been mistaken, and suddenly Geffen was back in the media, especially the music industry, which by then he knew very well.

Many of the rock performers in the '60s and '70s gave inspiration and support to two major causes — civil rights and the anti-war movement. Geffen was one of two leaders in showing them how to tie these causes to amassing money — big money -- out of every performance and every recording. A reviewer of *The Mansion on The Hill*, a book about rock music, commented that Albert Grossman, agent for Bob Dylan, and David Geffen were the ones chiefly responsible for "rock's sad meta-morphosis from a quasi-moral force to an unstoppable money machine."[6]

In 1980 Geffen introduced a new label, Geffen Records, which soon had a range of top stars, including Cher, Guns 'N Roses, Eddie Brickell, New Bohemians, Yoko Ono, John Lennon, Whitesnake, Aerosmith and Elton John. He also branched out to produce shows like *Cats* on Broadway and *Risky Business* in Hollywood. The 1980s were boom years for Geffen. In addition to *Cats*, he produced or helped fund *Miss Saigon, Dreamgirls, Little Shop of Horrors, Good,* and *Master Harold ... and the Boys* on the New York stage. The productions lasted from as short a time as three months to as long as ten years.

Also in the '80s, the Geffen Film Company operated under a five-year contract with Warner Communications. Its films during the decade included *Personal Best, Risky Business, After Hours, Little Shop of Horrors, Lost in America, Beetlejuice, Defending Your Life* and *Men Don't Leave.*

As early as 1988, Geffen was listed by *Forbes* as one of America's wealthiest, but there was more to come. When in 1989 he sold Geffen Records to Music Corporation of America (MCA), he didn't take cash but 10 million shares of stock, guessing that the company was for sale. That turned out to be a brilliant stroke of timing. Only eight months later, when MCA was sold to Matsushita Corporation of Japan, Geffen's $545 million investment brought him $710 million.[7] By that time he had a chauffeur-driven limousine and a $20 million Gulfstream jet. A 1990 *Forbes* profile of Geffen was headlined, "The Richest Man in Hollywood."[8]

Between the 1990 sale of MCA to Matsushita and the creation of DreamWorks SKG, Geffen did much the same as he had during the 1980s. One difference was his purchase of the Jack Warner mansion and estate for $47.5 million. During the next eight years, he reorganized and remodeled the mansion and surrounding build-ings, finally moving in early in 1998. He also continued to add to his valuable col-lection of American art, gave time and money to AIDS causes, and created the David Geffen Foundation, which gives "between $5 and $8 million per year to social, political, and charitable causes."[9]

DreamWorks SKG was fashioned by three Hollywood mega-producers — Geffen, Steven Spielberg, who directed the Oscar-winning *Schindler's List,* and Jeffrey Katzenberg, who was second in command at Disney Studios during its big decade before the 1995 merger with ABC-Capital Cities. When Jeffrey Katzenberg approached Geffen to join in the DreamWorks venture in October, 1994, Geffen agreed to discuss it. Katzenberg had been fired by Michael Eisner at Disney Studios only two months before, and Geffen had great sympathy for him. The three met in their homes several times and then the plan was turned over to the lawyers. After a few days, they held a press conference to announce plans for the first new Hollywood studio in 75 years. Katzenberg was to be the organizer and detail man, and the one who concentrated on animated films, which he had produced so well for Disney. Spielberg would direct movies; and Geffen would be the major talent scout for films, TV programs and animated features, preside over the music division, and above all, would be the chief financial negotiator. Folded into the new studio were Spielberg's Amblin Television and Geffen Films. For financing their early projects, the three main players each invested $33.3 million and set a goal of $1 billion, a figure later doubled. The trio was so well-known and highly regarded that their new company quickly attracted investors. Paul Allen of Microsoft came up with $500 million, $27 million came from Ziff Brothers Investments, and $300 million from Korea's Samsung Investments.

The young partnership focused on production of movies, TV programs, music and interactive media. Its subsidiary Amblin Entertainment soon produced *Twister* and then *The Peacemaker*, a suspense action story set in Russia. Animated films so far have been *Prince of Egypt*, the story of Moses, and *Antz*. When Edgar Bronfman, Jr. took over MCA and renamed it Universal, the DreamWorks trio quickly worked out a deal to produce both films and TV programs there. The three also worked out a production deal with ABC for TV programs, movies and miniseries to be shown on both TV and cable. DreamWorks and ABC each invested $100 million.

The group produced two TV shows in 1995 — *Champs and High Incident*. In the fall of 1996, Michael J. Fox appeared in *Spin City*, a situation comedy on ABC, and Ted Danson and Mary Steenbergen showed up in *Ink* on CBS. *Ink* died quickly, but *Spin City* was still on the air in 2000, although it had lost Michael J. Fox because of illness.

However, by the fall of 2000, DreamWorks, "which planned works in a wide range of entertainment media, finds true success only in movie making, with its films grossing on average 15 percent more per film than any other studio; and ranks a close second behind Walt Disney Co.'s Buena Vista which has released nearly twice as many movies.[10]

Time magazine listed the DreamWorks early hits as *Saving Private Ryan*, "one of the 25 highest-grossing films in history," *Deep Impact*, which brought in $140 million, *Prince of Egypt*, which had a $100 million box office, and *Spin City*. But *Amistad* did poorly, as did *Ink* and *In Dreams*, a movie thriller.[11]

DreamWorks SKG already has a payroll of more than a thousand, 400 of whom work in Katzenberg's animation division. Media forecasters are predicting that either the animation or the music recording units of DreamWorks will be most profitable. In 2000, Geffen signed DreamWorks to co-production contracts with both Fox and Warner Brothers studios. Plans have been drafted for a big studio complex in Glendale. Meantime, most operations are quartered in Amblin's studios on the back lot of Universal Studios. The trio had hoped to build a major film studio combined with a technology complex in the Playa Vista wetland area, but that was called off because of serious environmental problems. During the protracted debate about the project, some environmental protesters approached Geffen at a Clinton fundraiser in Beverly Hills. He told them, "If you want to save the frogs, go to a French restaurant."[12]

He is a major contributor to, and fund-raiser for, the Democratic Party, and slept overnight at the Clinton White House several times. His DreamWorks partners are also strong Democratic Party supporters.

Partner David Geffen follows a Pritikin diet and interrupts his endless hours on the telephone with a daily workout, so he is in good health. He is seldom away from a phone, from early morning until midnight. When he moved into the remodeled former home of Jack Warner, he brought with him an extensive collection of American art. His signature clothes consist of a T-shirt, jeans and sneakers, whether at home or away. He's described as "a schmoozemeister with a vast network of important connections and a wicked sense of mischief."[13] Biographer Fred Goodman calls him "the great robber baron of pop culture."[14] A *Vanity Fair* reporter wrote that his personality "is at once magnetic and scary — a kind of cross between Peter Pan and Jack the Ripper."[15] He is forthright about his bisexuality. One reporter quoted him as saying, "I date men and I date women. . . say what you will about bisexuality, you have a fifty percent chance of finding a date on Saturday night."[16] But his relationships seem to be mainly with men. His most lasting romance was with Robert Brassel, who was 23 and worked at Liz Claibourne in New York when they met. Brassel moved to California and the two exchanged gold rings. That fell apart after a few years, mainly because of Brassel's alcoholism. At 57, in the year 2000, "he (Geffen) continued to pursue men who were half his age," but "there was no longer a 'significant other' in his life."[17]

Geffen has been a major contributor to a number of AIDS causes, giving millions to such organizations as AIDS Project in Los Angeles (APLA) and Gay Men's Health Crisis (GMHC), and organizing fund-raisers for them. *The Advocate*, a gay magazine, gave Geffen the title "Man of the Year" in 1992.

Tom King, a *Wall Street Journal* reporter, published a lengthy biography of Geffen early in 2000. *The Operator: David Geffen Builds, Buys, and Sells the New Hollywood* is loaded with unsavory revelations about Geffen's dealings. In one of the many articles about the book, a *San Francisco Chronicle* reporter recounted the following anecdote: "At one point, he wanted to renegotiate Geffen Records' deal with parent company Warner Bros. Music. He knew that his old friend Mo Ostin was tough to bargain with. So he engineered the end of the friendship. That would, and did, leave him free to negotiate with Steve Ross, who rarely denied his protégé Geffen anything. Geffen destroyed the friendship by taking Ostin's wife to lunch and telling her that her husband didn't really care about her."[18] That was in the 1980s. When DreamWorks was organized in 1994, Geffen hired Mo Ostin to run its music division. An excerpt from the book in *People* magazine quotes author King as saying that "Geffen is a man whose moral compass seems to be off kilter. He'll sabotage any relationship, personal or professional, to get what he wants."[19]

In 1990 a pair of *Forbes* reporters called Geffen "the most powerful man in the $22 billion record industry." They quoted him as saying, "I started the 1980s with $30 million. In one decade it went into (nearly) a billion dollars. The world is presenting itself for people who have cash."[20] A decade later, his wealth had more than tripled to $3.4 billion — evidently the world is still presenting itself to him.

THE BRONFMANS–EDGAR JR. SLIPS FROM FIRST TO SECOND

15

After the dramatic merger of America Online (AOL) with Time-Warner-Turner in January, 2000, media observers asked, who's next? During the next few months, Seagram-Universal CEO Edgar Bronfman Jr. repeatedly denied that his family's liquor and entertainment conglomerate was for sale. He had been Number One at Seagram since 1992 and at both Seagram and Universal since 1995. But in June he went to Paris, there to embrace Jean-Marie Messier, head of the Vivendi media and utility giant, and to announce the Vivendi takeover of Seagram-Universal. Vivendi was already "Europe's biggest pay-television company, France's second-largest mobile telephone operator and a major publishing house."[1]

The price Vivendi paid to acquire Seagram's huge liquor company, its Universal Studios, and its gigantic array of music holdings, came to $34 billion. Vivendi was joined in the buyout by CanalPlus, the French pay TV giant partly owned by Vivendi. Messier heads the new conglomerate, with the 45-year-old Bronfman as second in command. Pierre Lescure, top officer at CanalPlus, was scheduled to head the combined movie and television operations. Bronfman was expected to run Universal Music, the largest music company in the world, as well as its Internet operations. The complicated merger was finalized by the end of the year. In Brussels, European regulators cleared it in October. Despite his critics, "Bronfman has better than doubled Seagram's value in six years, and gotten a price half again Wall Street estimates."[2]

The merger married Vivendi's extensive distribution network to Universal's rich content -- music and film properties. In that respect, the deal was much like that of the marriage of AOL to Time Warner. Less than a year after the Vivendi-Universal merger, Bertelsmann's chief executive Thomas Middelhoff resigned from Vivendi's board of directors. The two conglomerates compete in both music and publishing.

Six months after the merger, the huge Seagram liquor empire was bought by a British-French consortium — Britain's Diageo PLC and France's Pernot Ricard SA. The price: $8.15 billion. The deal included Seagram's wineries. Vivendi had already announced plans to sell its water and waste management companies.

An important property of the new Vivendi-Universal is Vizzavi, an Internet portal jointly owned by Vivendi and Vodaphone Air Touch. The brand new Vizzavi is expected to become the "Internet entry point for 80 million Europeans using wireless devices such as cell phones and digital assistants such as the Palm," according to the *Washington Post*, which added that Bronfman had said it will be an Internet site that is available on "all devices, all the time, all the places."[3]

Indicating that he expects to spend time in the States, Jean-Marie Messier paid $17.5 million for a Park Avenue apartment in New York in March, 2001. Vivendi-Universal will be focused entirely on entertainment. The Bronfman family will control eight percent of the new company's stock and hold five of the 18 seats on its board. Seagram shareholders will own a little less than 30 percent of the new combine.

Bronfman had taken over the entertainment conglomerate Music Corporation of America (MCA) and its Universal Pictures only five years earlier, in April, 1995. For a four-fifth share of MCA, he paid $5.7 billion to the giant Japanese company Matsushita Electric, which had bought MCA for $6.6 billion in 1990. Bronfman soon dropped the name MCA in favor of Universal.

Three years after taking over MCA, Bronfman risked an even larger stake — $10.6 billion — in the purchase of the world's largest music empire — PolyGram — from the Dutch firm Philips Electronics. This added Mercury Records, Island Records, Motown Records and A&M Records, as well as its huge library and movie studio, PolyGram Filmed Entertainment, to the family. With MCA, Bronfman already had captured Universal Records, MCA Records, GRP Recording Co., Geffen Records and half of Interscope Records.

A month before the PolyGram purchase, after a two-year feud with Viacom's Sumner Redstone, Bronfman paid $1.7 billion to buy Viacom's 50 percent stake in USA Network. Then he made a complicated deal with Barry Diller and the Home Shopping Network in order to secure access for Universal's film and TV programs to 70 million cable homes and 25 TV stations. Diller, in turn, got management control of USA Network, with Seagram keeping "the option to increase its stake to no more than 50 percent in the future."[4] The value of the Seagram share of USA Networks rose from $1.7 billion in 1998 to $7 billion in 2000.

With MCA-Universal, Bronfman got theme parks, several record companies, a TV production company and, above all, Universal Pictures, a major movie production company. Bronfman says he is convinced that control of entertainment *content* is more important than delivery systems. That was also the belief that led Messier to the buyout of Seagram-Universal.

To buy MCA-Universal, Bronfman had sold most of Seagram's 163 million shares of DuPont stock, a 24 percent holding, which had gone up almost 300 percent in the years since it had been bought in 1981. The sale brought in $8.8 billion. Bronfman said he had seen DuPont as a passive investment while the MCA-Universal buy gave him a hands-on opportunity to make any changes he wanted.

To help pay for PolyGram, he sold, at a profit of $2.8 billion, Tropicana Products, the huge fruit juice company he had bought ten years earlier. In the same period he gradually sold off PolyGram's film library to Hollywood's MGM/UA and the Carlton media group in England for $400 million. Early in 1999, he sold PolyGram's film and TV division for another $400 million to a Saudi prince, Muhammed Bin Bandur Abdul Aziz. Obviously, the PolyGram music holdings were his chief interest.

He moved quickly after the MCA-Universal takeover in 1995. In less than three months, he had reached a valuable distribution agreement, expected to generate $1 billion a year, with DreamWorks SKG. He also made two important appointments: Frank Biondi came over as Chief Executive, and Ron Meyer came from Creative Artists Agency as Chairman. The management style of the new leadership was far more collegial than that of their main predecessors at MCA. The tone of the new regime was made clear in invitations to an all-day meeting soon after Bronfman took over: "Wear jeans."

Bronfman is described as soft-spoken and courteous. He is a lank 6'3" and his handsome face is accented by a reddish beard. Born in New York in 1955, Bronfman has been interested in both movies and music since childhood. In 1970, when he was only 14, he found a script sitting on a family table. He coaxed his father, who then had investments in MGM Studios and Broadway plays, into bankrolling production of the film *Melody* in England. His father contributed $450,000 in up-front money for *Melody* and he hired producer David Puttnam and screen writer Alan Parker. Like Edgar Jr., they were both beginners in movie-making. Young Bronfman spent the summer in London, where he was paid all of ten pounds a week to run errands for Puttnam and Parker. *Melody* disappeared from the screen quickly.

In the summer of 1972, the young Bronfman was back in London, again as an assistant to Puttnam. Somehow he managed to raise funds to co-produce a movie titled *The Blockhouse*, with Peter Sellers as the star. The film told how seven men were trapped in an underground bunker during World War II. The depressing film found no more audience than *Melody* had.[5]

By now he was 16 and finishing his senior year at Collegiate, a private high school in New York City, where his Canadian-born father had taken out American citizenship long before. After graduation, he moved to Hollywood, having made clear to his father that he would not go to college. During the next few years, he tried his hand at a variety of Hollywood activities. He made friends easily and some of them were movie celebrities. One of his activities was music composition, and after he met Dionne Warwick, he wrote a song for her titled "Whisper in the Dark." Warwick, in turn, introduced him to her African-American actress friend, Sherry Brewer, a stunning beauty. They fell in love with each other.

He wanted to marry Sherry immediately, but because of his age and his father's strenuous opposition, his mother persuaded him to wait a year. An elopement to New Orleans came in November, 1979, when he was 24, leading to estrangement from his father. A year later, the first of their three children was born while Bronfman was co-producing a movie titled *The Border*, with Jack Nicholson as the star.

He invited his father to the New York screening of *The Border*, and a meeting followed, with Edgar Sr. urging his second son to come back to Seagram's New York headquarters and prepare ultimately to take over company control. The younger Bronfman said only that he would discuss it with his wife, Sherry, who turned out to be enthusiastic. After he had also obtained the approval of his older brother Sam, he agreed. That was in 1982. Ten years later, Edgar Jr. was voted into Seagram's highest executive office.

Although the Seagram company had started in Canada in the 1920s, it had operated in the United States for many years under the name Joseph Seagram and Sons, and indeed had been the top American distiller for more than 50 years. Edgar Sr. had taken charge of American operations many years before, and had moved his family to New York at the same time. His brother Charles was in charge of Seagram's Canadian operations before the Vivendi merger and then the sale of all Seagram liquor operations.

When Edgar Jr. moved into Seagram management in 1982, both he and his father had considerable background in the entertainment industry, and both were fascinated by it. But for the time being, both focused on production and sale of spirits. After awhile, Edgar Jr. came up up with a plan for reorganizing the company, dropping the cheaper brands and concentrating on the better ones. By 1992, Seagram profits were rising dramatically.

Meantime, Edgar Jr. and his wife Sherry had three children — a son and two daughters. But the marriage was troubled, and they agreed to a friendly divorce in 1991. He still sees the children every day when in New York.

A year before the divorce, on a trip to Caracas, Venezuela, he met the beautiful Clarissa Alcock, daughter of a rich oil company executive, and herself an executive in a major Venezuela company. Her family had a New York apartment, and when she visited, Edgar Jr. took her to *The Phantom of the Opera*.[6] Not long after, Edgar proposed to Clarissa, the first of many proposals. The relationship was complicated by the fact that she is Roman Catholic, he Jewish. Late in the long-running courtship, he composed a song, "If I Didn't Love You," and that apparently convinced her. This time the marriage proposal was made by Clarissa herself. A priest and a rabbi conducted the marriage ceremony in Caracas in 1993, with Edgar's brother Sam as best man. The marriage seems to be working well, with Clarissa continuing in her job and the couple taking his children for alternate weekends at the 127-acre Pawling estate. In 1996, their child, Aaron Edgar, was born, and later they had twin girls, so now they entertain six children on weekends. Sherry joins them when any of her children celebrate birthdays.

After long study, Edgar Jr. was convinced by 1993 that the time had come for Seagram to invest somewhere in the communications field. That decision led to purchase of Time Warner stock, just below the five percent mark at which Seagram would have to make a public announcement of intentions. But Time Warner's Gerald Levin considered the Bronfmans hostile and had a "poison plan" inserted into company rules to prevent a takeover. At that point Bronfman turned away from Time Warner.

The uneasy relationship with Time Warner led Edgar Jr. to turn his attention elsewhere — to MCA. With MCA, Bronfman got a vast empire. Universal Pictures has produced in recent years *Apollo 13, Babe, Casper, Schindler's List, Jurassic Park, The Lost World, ET, Erin Brokovich, Shakespeare in Love, Patch Adams* and co-produced *Gladiator*. It also owns the second largest film library in the world -- 4,700 films -- topped only by Ted Turner's movie holdings. Among its TV series have been *Murder, She Wrote, Coach, Miami Vice, Law and Order, Dragnet* and *Columbo*, all highly rated and lasting years before going into syndication.

MCA-Universal theme parks in Hollywood and Florida attract 12 million visitors a year. A second Florida park has opened near Orlando, this one costing $2 billion, and another in Osaka, Japan, all joint ventures with England's Rank organization. In Orlando, Universal's five-part theme park competes with the huge Disney World. Recording artists under MCA-Universal labels include Meat Loaf, Reba McEntire, Wynona Judd and Aerosmith. Its publishing company is Putnam, and its Cineplex Odeon Company operates 361 movie theaters in the U.S. and Canada.

Despite all these holdings, the money magazines were pointing out that MCA-Universal's performance record in recent years had been weak. Bronfman soon learned that movie studios have ups and downs. While the Seagram stock had risen 139 percent in the five years after the MCA buy, it was well behind the Standard & Poor 500, which had risen 193 percent. The poor showing was traced primarily to the film business, which was still in the red at the time of the Vivendi merger. The films *Erin Brockovich, The Green Mile* and *Gladiator* enjoyed good box office in 2000, but not enough to overcome losses for *Dudley Do-Right* and *Man on the Moon*. But it improved after the merger, and a film critic commented on what he called "the miracle season for Universal," adding, "A year ago, the studio was struggling to escape a prolonged box office slump. Today it's a hit-making powerhouse."[7]

In recent years, Bronfman and Universal-PolyGram were sharply criticized on two fronts -- offensive lyrics on recordings and Seagram liquor commercials on TV. In 1996, Universal Music was attacked for the lewd and violent lyrics recorded by some of its popular musicians. "They're marketing death and degradation as a twisted form of holiday cheer," said Senator Joseph Lieberman of Connecticut, speaking about albums by shock rocker Marilyn Manson, gangsta rapper Snoopy Dog Dog and the late Tupac Shakur.[8] Former Education Secretary William Bennett said Bronfman and MCA had violated a promise not to distribute vulgar and violent music, and were "peddling filth for profit."[9] But Bronfman was clearly determined to hold onto the recording properties. Demonstrating that determination, Universal Music joined Bertelsmann BMG Entertainment in the spring of 1999 in forming getmusic.com to sell music on the Internet, and in April, 2001, Universal Music Group bought Emusic.com Inc, which also sells songs on the Internet.

Indicating Bronfman's influence even after the merger, the next month Vivendi Universal bought the online music provider, MP3.com for $372 million. A company spokesman said the buy will help create an online digital music subscription service.

The young Bronfman seems to have prepared for the outbursts against both Universal Records and Seagram ads. Seagram was the largest 1996 donor to the Democratic Party and fourth largest to the Republicans. The result: no strong words from either party about the TV ads or the sordid lyrics. The criticism quickly died down. In the spring of 2000, Bronfman joined media billionaire Michael Bloomberg in hosting fund raisers for Republican John McCain in New York, Boston and Connecticut.

The elder Bronfman, Edgar Sr., listed at $3.3 billion by *Forbes* for July 9, 2001, spends much of his time working on affairs of the World Jewish Congress, having served as president since 1981. He is an especially effective fund-raiser, and in recent years has devoted close attention to recovering Holocaust victims' assets from Swiss banks — property, art and money.

There is constant discussion among Bronfman family members about a wide variety of issues. After the merger with Vivendi, Edgar Jr. told *Business Week*, "Three people have to be in concert before Seagram makes any major move. Two are named Edgar and one is named Charles."[10] Charles, of course, is Edgar Jr.'s uncle, whose fortune in 2001 was $3.4 billion.

Even as he considered the sale or merger of his family's company in the fall of 1999, Edgar Jr. joined his wife Clarissa and the six children in moving into their new 15,000 square foot town house on New York's East Side. Now he expects to make frequent trips to Vivendi headquarters in Paris, but as Number Two in the Vivendi-Universal empire, he'll have more time to write poetry and songs than he did when he was Number One in the Seagram-Universal empire.

GEORGE LUCAS–NOW HE'S MAKING MORE *STAR WARS*

16

A master of special effects in both film and television, with one blockbuster after another, George Lucas has, in the process of becoming a billionaire, changed the way most movies are made. *Forbes* for July 9, 2001 listed him at $3 billion, and his technology-loaded Skywalker Ranch north of San Francisco is worth $5 billion.

Born in May, 1944, in the California farm town of Modesto, which furnished the background for some of his movies, he grew up like his friends, loving cars, especially those that went fast. Modesto is quiet and surrounded by flat land, ideal for highway racing. Driving his car the night before he was scheduled to graduate from high school, Lucas had an accident that almost cost him his life. He lived only because his seat belt failed and he was thrown from the car.

He had low grades in both elementary and high school, but after two years at Modesto Community College, he gained admission to the cinema program at the University of Southern California. There he began to produce short films for class assignments. He also became friends with Francis Coppola, and signed on as Coppola's administrative assistant. While he was still at the university, they worked together on *Rain Man*, and the 22-year-old Lucas began to consider Coppola his mentor. After he got his bachelor's degree, he tried to enlist in the army but was rejected because he suffers from diabetes. So he started to work on documentary films for the U. S. Information Agency.

He met Marcia Griffin in an editing room at the Information Agency, and three years later they were married, moving into a rented house in Mill Valley, north of the Golden Gate Bridge. By then Lucas was working in a San Francisco "community" of young filmmakers led by Coppola. The group, called Zoetrope, spurned the Hollywood scene. Together, they developed scripts for seven films and delivered them to the president of Warner's, who quickly rejected all seven. Meantime Lucas went ahead with his first feature film — *THX-1138* — a science fiction story, set in the 25th century, with all human beings living underground like robots with numbers instead of names. Financed by Zoetrope and distributed by Warner Brothers, it scored poorly at the box office.

Lucas turned to production of *American Graffiti*, a story about the sunset-to-sunrise activities of four adolescent boys, one a rebel, another a square, the third a nerd, and the fourth "king of the road." Cars and his high school years clearly furnished the ideas for the film. "I was trying to re-create something that had been a huge thing in my life," Lucas is quoted as saying.[1] *Graffiti* got five Academy Award nominations, won best screenplay awards from both the National Society of Film Critics and the New York Film Critics Association. Moreover, it made Lucas a millionaire at 28, two years earlier than the goal he had announced to his conservative father before he left Modesto.

Even before he had finished *THX -1138*, Lucas had been thinking about ideas for the first *Star Wars*. Well before he started the first of the series, he had visualized many of the pictures in his mind, but to work out a story line he went to books on mythology, especially Joseph Campbell's *The Hero With a Thousand Faces*, published in 1959. After the success of *American Graffiti*, he was able to get a contract with Twentieth Century Fox for the first of three *Star Wars* pictures. He loaded the film with technology, spending $3 million on special effects alone. Along with their action-packed, high speed pace and limited dialog, the *Star Wars* series carried morality lessons — "that good is stronger than evil, that human values can triumph over superior technology, that even the lowliest of us can be redeemed, and that all this is relatively free of moral ambiguity."[2] The appeal to children was also central in Lucas's mind. "I wanted to make a kids' film that would strengthen contemporary mythology and introduce a kind of basic morality," he explained to Orville Schell in March, 1999.[3] He also told Schell that "I'm dealing with the need for humans to have friendships, to be compassionate, to band together to help each other and to join together against what is negative." The film opened in May 1977 and before long won a world box office record of $524 million. It also won his wife, Marcia Lucas, an Oscar for editing.

With the $20 million he got from the first *Star Wars*, Lucas expanded Industrial Light and Magic, the special effects studios he had set up in Marin County. Although *Star Wars* was not a musical, it included a good deal of memorable music, most of which Fox put into a two-record album, which brought in more millions. Lucas went on quickly to produce a second *Star Wars* film, *The Empire Strikes Back*, but he hired the director for it. During that period, he had lost his joy in directing. Carrie Fisher (who played Leia in *Star Wars*) "complained of Lucas's monotonously repeated direction, 'Faster and more intense'."[4] After *THX 1138*, Lucas himself said, "I dislike directing."[5] The directors Lucas hired for the second and third *Star Wars* episodes were thoroughly briefed by him at the start of each day.

Before taking on the third *Star Wars* film, Lucas joined Steven Spielberg in producing *Raiders of the Lost Ark*, the first of the Indiana Jones films, released in 1981. Jones is the adventurous professor who engages in a competition with Nazis and a French archeologist to find the lost Ark of the Covenant. *Raiders* was another blockbuster, with $335 million in tickets sold worldwide.

In 1983, Lucas produced but did not direct what was then the last *Star Wars* film, *Return of the Jedi*. By now he was worth $60 million and his Skywalker Ranch had grown to 3,000 acres with more than 900 employees. In the *Jedi* story, Luke Skywalker has come of age, and rejoins his old comrades to combat the Deathstar, victoriously, of course. Like all Lucas movies, this one was super-loaded with special effects. In 1996, a *Forbes* reporter said, "The *Star Wars* series has been the most profitable movie product in history."[6] Books, toys, videos and games added more than $3 billion to the *Star Wars* take by 1996.[7] Along the way, mythology scholar Joseph Campbell and Lucas became good friends and Campbell came to Skywalker Ranch's library to videotape discussions with Bill Moyers on *The Power of Myth*.

Indiana Jones and the Temple of Doom was the second in the Lucas-Spielberg series; the third, *Indiana Jones and the Last Crusade*. The three *Indiana Jones* movies enjoyed a box office of more than $1 billion. While Paramount financed these three films, and Spielberg directed them, Lucas owns them.

When Marcia and George Lucas were divorced in the late 1980s, her settlement was $50 million. They share joint custody of their adopted child, Amanda. He has since adopted two more children, but has not remarried.

A Special Edition of the *Star Wars* series was launched early in 1997, aimed at both youngsters who were born since the first showings and older folks lured to theaters by announcements that the special effects had been enhanced. It included a few new scenes and enhanced digital imagery. The Special Edition *Star Wars* releases have brought in $1.3 billion, while toys and merchandise associated with them have sold another $4.5 billion, most of which went to Lucas and his empire.

The first of a series of prequels to *Star Wars*, the stories of Luke Skywalker and Obi-Wan Kenobi growing up, was released with great fanfare in the spring of 1999. The hype, orchestrated by Lucas, began weeks before the opening day. Asked about the avalanche of toys, books and video games inspired by *The Phantom Menace*, Lucas said, "I'm an independent filmmaker from San Francisco and I have to make sure that I have exploited anything I can."[8] The prequel contains even more than usual of the special effects for which Lucas is now world famous. For this, Lucas returned to directing. Titled *Star Wars: Episode 1 — The Phantom Menace*, the prequel was expected to top the box office of *Titanic's* $600 million in North America, and it chalked up $430 million by October, despite some critical reviews. It was attacked in Mexico as anti-Catholic, and in the U.S. "where film reviewers, antidefamation activists and academics found racial stereotypes represented by alien creatures."[9] In the *New York Times*, columnist Brent Staples wrote, "The characters who most resemble Asians here are greedy, rapacious and disturbingly similar to Asian hordes in the 1940s serials."[10] Columnist John Leo, in *U.S. News & World Report*, called it racist. "Fractured English is one of the key traits of racist caricature from all the 19th century characters named Snowball to Amos 'n' Andy."[11]

The first of the next two *Star Wars* "prequels" began shooting in Australia in 2000, in cooperation with Fox Studios Australia, half of which is owned by Rupert Murdoch's News Corp. Needless to say, Lucas owns all the prequels and their merchandising rights.

Spielberg relied heavily on Lucas for the special effects involved in *Jurassic Park* in 1996 and *The Lost World* four years later. The two communicated by satellite three nights a week while Spielberg was in Poland working on *Schindler's List*.

LucasFilm has won 17 Oscars while Industrial Light and Magic and Skywalker Sound have a combined 24 Oscars. Writing about Lucas in 1996, Randall Lane said "he has put a powerful new tool at the service of the human imagination, enabling filmmakers to marry fantasy and reality."[12] Examples abound. In *Forrest Gump*, we see the hero shaking hands with President Kennedy. Stunts by Sylvester Stallone in *Cliffhanger* and Tom Cruise in *Mission: Impossible* are all made possible by LucasFilm and its Skywalker studios. It's all done with digital technology, inserting one image next to another and deleting cables and other extraneous material.

In 1992, Lucas turned to television, producing *The Young Indiana Jones*, featuring the adventurous young Indiana and his father. In the TV movie, which uses special effects heavily, Indiana "serves as a courier at the WWI battle of Verdun, meets the young Picasso in Paris, goes big game hunting with Teddy Roosevelt, matches wits with Sigmund Freud, and even has a hot romance with Mata Hari."[13] As special effects produced by Industrial Light and Magic became more widely known, Lucas took orders from a number of Hollywood film makers and still does, and by 1996 a fourth of ILM income came from special effects used in TV commercials. Because of Lucas' work with computer graphics (CG), predicted a *New Yorker* writer, we can look forward to a CG film starring a cast of "synthespian" actors. The writer asked if we could expect "a new James Dean movie in which Dean is a synthespian made up of bits lifted from old images of him?"[14]

The seven light and sound subsidiaries of Lucasfilm Ltd. -- LucasFilm, Lucas Arts Entertainment, Industrial Light and Magic (visual effects), Skywalker Sound, Lucas Learning, Lucas Licensing (toys and games) and THX (sound systems for movie theaters) — are located in Marin County. Now Lucas plans to move much of the company to the famous San Francisco Presidio, abandoned by the army and designated a national park. The Presidio Trust approved his application for a part of the old Letterman Hospital site. The Trust decision was opposed by no fewer than 56 environmental organizations, led by the California League of Conservation Voters, Natural Resources Defense Council, Audubon Society and Wilderness Society. They argued that the 1994 Presidio Plan envisioned "a global center dedicated to the world's most critical environmental, social and cultural challenges" — not making digital films.[15] However, as it was unveiled by Lucasfilm President Gordon Radley, the design emphasized environmental values. The plan, said Radley, "will provide a pastoral experience," adding, "We're trying to integrate man and his place in nature."[16] The plan called for 15 acres of open space in the 23-acre hospital site, with four three-story buildings to house employees coming from five of the companies at Skywalker Ranch. The Advisory Council on Historic Preservation approved the plan in late 2000.

Skywalker Ranch, where Lucas has worked almost 30 years, has four restaurants for its 1,500 employees, as well as a health club and trails for hiking and jogging. Every employee gets a turkey for Thanksgiving. Some of them have spun off companies of their own, like Digital Domain, Tippett Studios, Matte World and

EDNet. Most of them continue working at Skywalker Ranch for many years.

Lucas himself puts in long days. He is slightly stooped, wears horn-rimmed glasses, has thick wavy hair and a salt-and- pepper beard and mustache, and wears plaid shirts, dark jeans and sneakers. He spends only two days a week at the Ranch studios, devoting the other five days to work at home. There, he sets time apart for his adopted daughters, Amanda, 17, and Kate, 11, and his adopted son, Jet, 6. "Although hectically busy running his film empire, he is a fiercely devoted, if some-times indulgent, single parent," according to a long article about Lucas in the *New York Times*.[17] He says he spends a little more than a third of his time with the children.

Almost from the start, Lucas had critics as well as fans. Recently, David Ansen in *Newsweek* said, "What Lucas inaugurated was the triumph of kineticism over con-tent, action over plot, comic book simplicities over real life complexities."[18] In his 1983 biography, Dale Pollock wrote, "The major criticism of Lucas is that he's inca-pable of making a movie about today, concerning adults who live and love and work and die. He seems permanently stuck in adolescence."[19] As far back as the late 1970s, *New Yorker* film critic Pauline Kael "suggested that in sacrificing character and complexity for non-stop action, *Star Wars* threatened to turn movies into comic books."[20] However, Lucas defenders insist that there is meaningful content in *Star Wars*. The Force, they argue, is God. The death of Obi-Wan Kenobi can be inter-preted as the sacrifice of St. Stephen. "The message of *Star Wars* is religious: God isn't dead. He's there if you want him to be," Pollock wrote in his Lucas biography.[21]

Lucas is called generous by many of those who have worked with him. After the success of *American Graffiti*, he made millionaires of at least three of those who helped produce it. He has given more than $6 million to his alma mater, the University of Southern California, to be used for a cinema-and-television center and a digital film studio. He also funds the George Lucas Educational Foundation (GLEF). It collects success stories from the nation's schools and circulates them to educators, legislators and parents, using films, CD-ROMS, books. newsletters and a Web site. The program, called Edutopic, was started in 1991.

Apart from his children, Lucas is focused on planning for the second prequel, which won't be released until 2002. The third prequel is five years off. He now says that the three prequels will finish off *Star Wars*. That means there will not be a *Star Wars 7, 8, or 9*, as had been expected.. But Lucas fans can be sure he will keep on producing action-packed, special effects-loaded films well into the new century. *Forbes* reported that his estimated one-year earnings for 1999 came to $400 million. Looking at his bank balance, the Force still seems to be with him.

JERRY PERENCHIO–HIS NETWORKS KEEP GROWING

17

He's Italian-American and doesn't speak Spanish, but Jerry Perenchio operates the biggest Latino broadcasting network in the United States — Univision. — and it hasn't stopped growing.

The network had been started under another name 31 years earlier by Mexico's media mogul Emilio Azcarraga. Hallmark Cards Inc. had bought it from Azcarraga in 1986 for $600 million, but under the greeting card company managers, Univision's audience declined. When Perenchio bought it for $550 million in 1992, its name had been changed to Univision. To buy it, he got Ascarraga's company, Televisa, and Gustavo Cisneros, owner of Venezuela's main TV network, Venevision, to share in the funding and become minority owners. Televisa and Venevision each still own 25 percent of the network, a foreign ownership permissible under FCC rules.

Latino activists, especially in the Los Angeles area, protested to the FCC against the sale, arguing that with Televisa and Venevision as partners, most of the programs would be imported. But the FCC gave its blessing, leading a *Forbes* reporter to comment that "Jerry Perenchio doesn't speak a word of Spanish, but he can sure speak legalese."[1]

At first, the Latino protesters turned out to have been right; much of Univision's programming *was* imported, especially the telenovelas, a Latino variation of the American soap opera. But Perenchio promoted Mario Rodriguez, a Cuban-American who had been on the staff since 1990, to the post of program director. "His main programming qualification was that he was a walking encyclopedia of Spanish-language TV," a pair of *Los Angeles Times* reporters wrote.[2] With Perenchio and Rodriguez in charge, the programs strove to appeal to both immigrant Latinos and those who have been in the country long enough to become Americanized.

Born in Fresno, California, Perenchio got his bachelor's degree at UCLA in

1954, and soon went to work at the talent agency, MCA. In 1962, he launched his own agency, Chartwell Artists and after a few years had signed up such Hollywood stars as Elizabeth Taylor, Marlon Brando and Jane Fonda. After running Chartwell for 11 years, he joined Norman Lear and Bud Lorkin, who had been his MCA clients, and helped them build the highly successful TV programs of Tandem Communications Lear had already started *All in the Family*.

Lear and Perenchio bought Avco Embassy, a company making both movies and TV programs, in 1982. Among other shows, Avco produced *The Facts of Life* and *The Jeffersons*. Then they sold both Avco Embassy and Tandem Communications to Coca Cola for $485 million in 1985. Perenchio then bought the Loews theater chain, soon sold that, and partnered with the Zanuck Company in the late 1980s to produce films, which included *Driving Miss Daisy*.

Thus, by the time he bought Univision in 1992, Perenchio, at 61, had more than 35 years' experience in the entertainment industry. And, like Ted Field and some of the other Hollywood moguls, he had learned how to protect his privacy. When *Variety* reporters sought an interview, he replied by letter. "I was fortunate to work as an agent for MCA when it was run by Mr. Lew Wasserman," he wrote. "One of his basic tenets was 'Stay out of the limelight, it fades your suit.' I adhered to his rule of the road then and still follow it today."[3]

It's less than a decade since Perenchio assumed command, but he has overseen dramatic changes in both strategies and program content at Univision. In addition to putting Rodriguez in charge of program development, he brought in Henry Cisneros, former Secretary of Housing and Urban Development, to become Univision's president and CEO. Perenchio's title is Chairman. But Cisneros stayed only until mid-2000, when he resigned to return to San Antonio to start building low income housing. While he was still at Univision, he emphasized the need for Univision programs to be in pure Spanish, "preventing the use of slang or themes that demean Spanish" and "declining to take English advertising that has been dubbed."[4]

Perenchio arranged for Univision stock to go public in 1996, and by 1999 it was called "a Wall Street darling" because its commercials were bringing more and more income. Univision's stock price tripled in the two years ending in July, 1999. In July, 2000, it announced its second two-for-one stock split, to make the stock more affordable. Univision's success reflects the country's growing number of Latinos, who are expected to be the largest minority group by 2010. In some parts of the country, Hispanics are a swing vote already. In 2000, the Latino population in the U.S. reached 33 million, and that number is expected to double by 2030.

By the end of the 1990s, Univision programming had been dramatically changed. It still carried plenty of novelas produced by Televisa in Mexico, but their quality improved -- better writing and better acting. Each novela episode lasts an hour, and in prime time there are three in a row, one for children at 7, another for teens at 8, and a third for adults at 9. The telenovas are like soap operas, but while the soaps last years, the novelas end after a few months. Univision also began *Despierta America*, a three-hour morning program quite similar to ayem programs on ABC and NBC. Another new program is *Sabado Gigante*, a kind of *Price is Right* "

Latino style, with ladies in skimpy outfits and a boisterous host named Don Francisco."[5] Probably the most popular Univision show is *Cristina,* featuring Cristina Saralegui as a talk show host much like Oprah Winfey. Early in 1999, the network launched a prime time news magazine show, *VisionTV.* Later, Univision carried the first program of a series reporting on each elimination match leading to the 2002 World Cup.

In 1999, Univision also began *Ultima Hora* (Last Hour), running from 11:30 pm to midnight, in competition with NBC's *Nightline.* The anchor is well-known Enrique Gratas, who told a *Los Angeles Times* reporter that "we will have a selection of the most important news, plus one longer story with a debate by experts."[6] Like all other Univision news programs, *Ultima Hora* looks especially for stories that affect Latino communities. The network won an Emmy award for its coverage of Hurricane Mitch. Another popular news anchorman is Jorge Ramos. "In Los Angeles, Miami and Houston, more people watch Ramos than watch Rather, Brokaw or Jennings."[7]

Early in December, 2000, Univision "confirmed that it would buy 13 wholly owned television stations and minority stakes in four more from USA Networks for $1.1 billion."[8] At the end of the century, Univision had 33 TV stations, 21 affiliated TV stations and 740 cable affiliates. Most of the network-owned stations are in Latino population centers such as New York, Chicago and Los Angeles. In his 1992 purchase of Univision, Perenchio also got *Mas,* "which has the largest circulation of any Spanish-language magazine in the United States."[9] Univision also has Galavision, a cable network that carries bi-lingual youth-oriented programs.

In the fall of 1998, both Univision and Galavision began to offer Spanish-language programs to the DISH network, a digital satellite provider. Galavision, now the leading Spanish cable network, offers sports, music, variety, news, novelas and monthly specials aimed especially at young Hispanic Americans.

While it continued to carry Televisa-made novelas, Univision announced plans to make its first self-produced movie, and to broadcast 10 to 12 made-for-TV films a year, with some to be released in Latin America. Moreover, it announced in May, 2000, its first U.S.-produced sitcom. The new daytime series, which premiered in the fall with the title *Estamos Unidos,* is about a Latino family adjusting to life in the United States. And the network set up an Internet web portal, Univision Online, with sports, news, and entertainment as well as a tie-in with Home Shopping Network. It was "expected to devote plenty of air time to educate consumers on computer use and aggressively promote its own Web site, along with low-priced hardware and software deals with major manufacturers."[10]

By 1998, Perenchio could say that Univision had grown 14 percent a year, and its prime time audience was bigger than Time Warner's WB network or Viacom's UPN, according to a *New York Times* story[11]. The reporter added, "Researchers say that Hispanics watch an average of 15.3 hours a week of Spanish programs and 10 hours of English."

According to the same reporter, Perenchio is "a deal maker who is described as shrewd, tough, straight forward and visionary." He is a Republican and often supported conservative California Governor Peter Wilson. At age 69, he has three children and has been divorced twice. He owns lots of real estate, including the Bel Air mansion that was the setting for *The Beverly Hillbillies.*

As the year 2000 dawned, Perenchio's future seemed bright. The *Forbes 400* for 1999 had listed his wealth at $2.7 billion. And advance sales of ads "were 42 percent more than in 1999 and more than triple the growth rate of the big networks combined."[12] By July, 2001, his wealth had gone up to $3 billion. Still, Perenchio had no plans to learn Spanish.

JOHN MALONE–FROM DARTH VADER TO PA BELL

18

John Malone, the Denver billionaire who made his fortune in the cable industry's Telecommunications Inc (TCI) and Liberty Media, has been called "the most powerful man in television."[1] His fortune jumped from $750 million in the *Forbes 400* listing for 1997 to $2.5 billion in its 1998 listing after the estate of Bob Magness, founder of TCI., was settled and soon after the sale of TCI to AT&T Corp. for $48 billion in July, 1998. As a result, he became AT&T's largest shareholder with an estimated 1.5 percent -- worth $1.8 billion -- of the mammoth company's stock, and a position on its board. In 2001, his fortune was listed at $2.4 billion, reflecting the stock market's drop during the year.

One headline identified him as "Pa Bell."[2] He has also been called "the king of cable," "the man who makes the networks tremble," "the tenacious tycoon," "the Darth Vader of the communications highway," and "the patron saint of channel surfing."[3]

Malone's fortune dropped steeply in 2000 as AT&T and Liberty Media Corp. stocks went down. His AT&T stock dropped $750 million. Still, he's now the second largest stockholder in *both* Time Warner and Rupert Murdoch's News Corp. And his five percent stake in Liberty was worth $1.57 billion at the end of 2000.

Even with the sale of TCI to AT&T, Malone continues to manage Liberty Media, the cable programming arm of TCI, with stakes in Time-Warner-Turner, USA Networks, Discovery Networks, Black Entertainment Television, and some two dozen other program services. Liberty has been called a "programming juggernaut."[4]

Malone is an aggressive deal-maker, "a master at putting together highly complex financial structures."[5] Malone's politics, which he inherited from his father, are ultra-conservative. He stays up beyond his regular bedtime to listen to Rush Limbaugh.

He was born March 7, 1941 in Milford, Connecticut, the son of an inventor who worked for General Electric. The elder Malone taught his son that he must work hard in order to succeed professionally. When young Malone heard about surplus GE radios, with broken or missing parts, that could be bought for a dollar, he quickly learned how to fix and then sell them for $10 each. He was still in public high school when he won a scholarship to Hopkins Grammar School in New Haven. From there he went to Yale, where he excelled in science and math classes as an electrical engineering major. He found the professors in social science classes to be "socialistic," while he considered himself to be an "individualist conservative."[6]

When he graduated from Yale in 1963, his degrees were in both electrical engineering and economics, and his grades won him election to Phi Beta Kappa. He went quickly to Bell Laboratories, a research arm of AT&T. Here he showed such promise that AT&T helped finance four years of post-graduate study, leading to a master's in industrial management in 1964 and a doctorate in operations research in 1967, both at Johns Hopkins University. But by that time, Malone had decided that he didn't want to live out his professional life at Bell. So in 1968 he became a management consultant at McKinsey & Company, where he stayed only two years. Then he moved to General Instrument Corp. as president of its subsidiary, Jerrold Electronics, which made equipment for cable systems. Here he quickly learned about the infant cable industry, and was introduced to the intricacies of corporate finance. John Malone had found his niche.

Two years after he started at Jerrold, Malone's reputation led Steve Ross to invite him to New York to run the Warner cable business. He turned that offer down and instead accepted a job at a floundering cable company headquartered in Denver. The offer was made by Bob Magness, who had sold off his ranch herd to start a small cable company in Memphis, Texas, and then expanded into Montana and Colorado. When he set up a permanent office in Denver, he changed his company's name to Telecommunications Inc.[7]

When Magness invited Malone to join him in 1972, TCI was bogged down with debts of $130 million and income of only $19 million. But Malone saw the company's possibilities and accepted the invitation to become TCI's president and CEO at a salary of $60,000 a year, half of what he had been getting at Jerrold. It took him five years to work the company out of its debt morass, dealing week after week with Boston and New York bankers, so that by 1977, TCI was operating profitably. As the 1980s began, Malone was rapidly expanding TCI's cable holdings.

In seven years, TCI acquired at least 150 cable systems. During the same period, Malone bought large chunks of United Artists Communications and Heritage Communications. *Fortune* magazine reported in mid-1989, "In 16 years as CEO, Malone has done 482 deals — an average of one every two weeks — and four have been for $1 billion. The company has grown so fast that some of its secretaries are worth more than a million dollars, compliments of the stock in the TCI retirement plan."[8] In the same year, a study by Paul Kagan Associates in California found that TCI stock had risen 91,000 percent — a 58 percent compound interest rate of return, third highest of 4,000 stocks listed in Standard & Poor's stock guide. The stock bought at $1000 in 1974 was worth $913,350 in 1989.

The 1980s were a time of explosive growth for TCI. By the end of the decade, the company owned and operated a thousand cable systems. In the same decade, it bought, and later sold, United Artists Entertainment Company, which gave it control of some 2,500 movie screens across the country, at least for awhile. In the same decade, TCI became a major content provider, with control of Black Entertainment Television, the Discovery Channel, Cable Value Network (CVN) and American Movie Classics (AMC). To operate these systems, Malone launched Liberty Media. Through Liberty, Malone bought a 21 percent stake in the financially floundering Turner Broadcasting System. This meant Malone could sit on Ted Turner's board and help run CNN, TBS and TNT.

Local communities seldom resisted TCI's rate increases, even though they complained about them. In one case, Malone closed off programming in Vail, Colorado, for a whole weekend, telling viewers to blame the mayor and city manager, who had rejected a proposed rate increase, and giving their names and phone numbers. The Vail government gave in quickly. All over the country, TCI subscribers complained about poor service and difficulty reaching the company's poorly staffed local offices.

The poor service and steadily rising rates got the attention of Senator Albert Gore, and by 1993, "in Congress, bashing cable companies had become the king of indoor sports."[9] The complaints and bad press had an effect on Malone's wife, Leslie. "Her husband had been denounced on television and in the press. There had been letters and threats. The house was surrounded by a new security fence. Guards had been hired."[10]

Malone failed in one huge venture, a 1994 merger with Bell Atlantic in which, according to the Bell Atlantic chair, Ray Smith, a new giant would offer "wire and wireless service, video on demand, and interactive media," all of which would make "a reality of the electronic superhighway we've been talking about."[11] The $32 billion deal collapsed for two reasons: the dealers learned that the FCC had ordered a seven percent cut in cable TV rates, and there was a four-month drop in Bell Atlantic stocks. But Malone didn't give up his hopes for a merger or buyout of TCI; management of the now huge company was increasingly demanding and time-consuming.

Even before the failed Bell Atlantic merger, Malone had begun a program to install fiber optic wiring in TCI cable systems. The purpose was to increase dramatically the number of channels that could be carried. Newspapers reported Malone's prediction that before many years passed, TV viewers could tune into as many as 500 channels.

The collapse of the Bell Atlantic merger didn't stop Malone from becoming a major player in the 1995 negotiations for Time Warner to take over the Turner Broadcasting System. Gerald Levin, chairman and CEO of Time-Warner, offered a huge stake in his empire to Turner, enough to make Turner $2 billion richer. Turner would not only become Time-Warner's biggest shareholder, he would get control of two seats on the board and the title of vice-chairman, second only to Levin. Both Turner and his wife Jane Fonda liked the proposal. But the deal stumbled when Malone learned that TCI would receive only nine percent of Time-Warner shares in return for its 21 percent stake in TBS; Malone demanded more. Levin's response was to offer him the right of first refusal on any shares of Turner's new Time-Warner stock, should Turner decide to sell. If that happened, however, it would bring the TCI and Time-Warner control of the country's cable to more than 40 percent of all subscribers — and that would violate the FCC regulation setting 30 percent as the limit. To solve that problem, Malone agreed to put his stock in a voting trust controlled by Levin. The Federal Trade Commission also ordered an end to discounts TCI had been getting for programs coming from Turner channels.

Despite the failure of the Bell Atlantic merger, Malone continued to seek a way out of TCI and its management. The way out came with the offer from Michael Armstrong, who was eager to combine the AT&T telephone empire with the country's largest cable empire. The $48 billion deal gave AT&T the power to offer phone, cable and computer access to 60 million homes. Happy to leave TCI, Malone told a *Forbes* reporter after the sale, "It isn't a lot of fun fighting through the politics and irrationality of heavily regulated businesses."[12]

Malone's business deals are always extremely complicated, but they always work out well for him. In addition to his 1.5 percent stake in AT&T, he owns five percent of Liberty Media, worth $1.57 billion. He also owns eight percent of Rupert Murdoch's News Corp., a share second only to the 30 percent owned by the Murdoch family. He acquired that in April, 1999, when the Liberty Media Group traded its half interest of Fox/Liberty Sports, which owns regional sports cable networks, for 51.8 million shares of News Corp., an eight percent stake. In the same deal, Liberty Media got 44 percent of *TV Guide*, reduced to 19 percent in a 2000 deal. He also owns a big chunk of Time-Warner-Turner, now AOL-Time-Warner, and 21 percent of USA Networks. His most recent investments have been in Sprint wireless communications and General Instruments set top cable boxes. And in June, 2000, he concluded partnerships with the leading cable operators in Japan, Europe and South America.

While Malone's business story is complicated, his personal story is simple. He met Leslie Ann Evans when she was only 15 and married her five years later, in 1963. He still leaves his office in time to drive home for lunch with Leslie. He returns to the office after lunch, but leaves three hours later, usually to rejoin his wife at a health club, where he keeps in top physical shape. He and Leslie live alone in a Denver suburb in Douglas county, with 93 acres surrounding their 6,000 square foot home. They have no servants. Their daughter, Tracy, and son, Evan, are grown and live elsewhere. Like Warren Buffett, Malone says he will leave only a little of his huge fortune to his children. Rather, he announced in January, 1998 that he has set up the Malone Family Foundation, with 42 million shares of TCI and related company stock, then valued at $1.5 billion, to be used for education after his death.

Like Ted Turner, he loves sailing. Some years ago, he and his wife bought a 200-acre farm on Boothbay Harbor, Maine. There, in summer, he sailed aboard a 59-foot Hinckley yacht.[13] More recently, he sold the yacht and bought a custom-built one, 80 feet long, named Liberty. In 1992, the Malones bought a large recreational vehicle, and use it for January and June trips from Denver to Boothbay Harbor. In winter, they ice skate on their small pond. In 1995, he bought a seven-story "lodge" and 900 acres of land around Spencer Lake in Maine near the Quebec border. He has since enlarged the property to 16,000 acres. His seaplane in Boothbay harbor makes it possible for him to fly to his other properties on the Mosquito Islands in Penobscot Bay and Tibbets Island on Boothbay's Black River.

But Malone is all business when he goes to his Denver office. Before the sale to AT&T, he was concerned about the reputation of both TCI and Liberty. Early in 1994, Liberty bought a two-thirds ownership of the *Jim Lehrer News Hour* on PBS public television. Press observers interpreted it as a move to increase TCI's influence. "For TCI, the investment into a well-respected journalism outfit may help better its influence with Washington insiders."[14] But when Malone ran it, TCI didn't enjoy public admiration. A reporter in his home town, Denver, wrote in 1994, "Regulators, independent cable industry consultants, consumer groups and lawyers representing cities for years have complained that TCI employs a ruthless policy designed to muffle critics, smother competition and saddle local governments with huge legal bills."[15] In the same story, reporter John Accola quoted a New York cable consultant as calling Malone "a modern day robber baron, who has plundered America in the worst tradition of the country's early railroad and western land moguls."

AT&T's Armstrong was probably well aware of TCI's reputation when he closed the deal with Malone. But it took almost a year for AT&T to replace the TCI initials on bills to customers around the country. The name change had public relations value. "AT&T's name evokes images of financial strength, fair dealing and high quality service," wrote a *Newsweek* reporter, adding, "The image of TCI is junk bonds and crummy service."[16]

Malone is now working primarily with the Liberty Media Group, an empire itself. But he is handy to give Armstrong advice, or answer questions, about TCI operation. Under his management since 1972, TCI became a major gatekeeper in this country, with a variety of interests in both business and entertainment. In a 1995 *New York Times* Malone profile, two reporters wrote, "Telecommunications is only one part of his staggeringly complex portfolio of businesses. In addition to the cable systems, the company has overseas investments like TeleWest, a partnership with U. S. West that is building a combined cable and telephone system in Great Britain. TCI has also spent $600 million to $700 million in a joint venture with Sprint Corporation and two cable operators to build a nationwide communications network."[17]

Armstrong's goal in buying TCI -- and then the cable company, MediaOne, for $58 billion -- was clearly to combine telephone, cable and Internet services. Almost at once, AT&T launched a $40 billion program to upgrade the lines in its cable systems, which are now second only to Time-Warner-Turner in the number of customers they reach. When the FCC approved AT&T's takeover of MediaOne, "it ordered divestiture of significant cable holdings by May 19, 2001."[18] That could leave the door open for Malone to assume full control, and possibly even ownership, of Liberty Media. When the Internal Revenue Service gave its tax-free ruling in April, 2001, AT&T prepared to spin off Liberty Medea by summer, making it possible for Liberty to issue shares and settle competitive problems. Malone was expected to resign from AT&T's board.

Meantime, Liberty joined with Klesch & Co in purchase of 55 percent of Deutsche Telecom's cable business, which serves more than 10 million customers. It also invested $1.4 billion in UnitedGlobalCom (UGC), a company that controls United Pan-Europe Communications. UPC is Europe's second-largest cable company and serves about 11 million subscribers in 14 European countries. This move clearly put Malone back into the cable business. He has also promised to come up with $500 million if and when Rupert Murdoch buys DirecTV, the one satellite company in the U.S. that has been most successful.

Important to AT&T in the TCI buyout was its 39 percent ownership of @Home, a quite new network services company that uses cable TV wires for access to the Internet at a speed far faster than a telephone line. Even though it has only about 100,000 customers, Malone told *New Yorker* reporter Ken Auletta that a major factor in the deal was "high-speed Internet access" made possible by @Home.[19] Less than a year after TCI joined the AT&T family, the At Home Corp. was merged with Excite Inc. and the combined service became Excite@Home.

Malone's awards have all been in recognition of his work at TCI. The National Cable Television Association, a lobbying group, gave him its Vanguard award in 1983; the Wharton School at University of Pennsylvania, an Award of Merit for Distinguished Entrepreneurship; the University of Denver, an honorary doctorate in 1992; and *Financial World* named him CEO of the Year in 1993.

Since the sale of TCI, he apparently is not working quite so hard. He goes home earlier in the day, and has given top staff members more authority than in the past. He's also bought three cattle ranches, one outside Denver, and one each in Wyoming and New Mexico.

After the AT&T deal closed, a *Forbes* reporter asked if he missed TCI after 26 years, "You don't cry in the corner because they call you Darth Vader, but sure it bothers you," he said, speaking of his TCI reputation.[20] "I'd rather be a good guy than a bad guy — but I'd rather be a rich bad guy than a poor good guy." No longer at TCI and, with $2.4 billion, maybe he's become a rich good guy.

MCGRAW FAMILY–
THEY CATER TO STUDENTS AROUND THE WORLD

19

They publish business and financial information in a wide variety of venues — computers, magazines, books, television, even CD-ROMS. They also publish textbooks — lots of them — for elementary, high school and college students. They're the McGraw family of McGraw Hill Publishing Companies. Even though they own only twenty percent of the companies, they control them, and they're worth $2.3 billion, according to *Forbes* in July, 2001.

Nepotism is a feature of company operations. Harold "Terry" McGraw III is currently the company president and, since the retirement of Joseph Dionne at the end of 1999, chairman of the board. His brother Robert is executive vice president of the Publishing Group, probably the most important unit of the empire. A third McGraw, James, is vice president for strategic programs.

A great grandson of the founder, Terry moved into the top position in 1993 at age 44, after joining the company in 1980 and rising to supervise its many operations in 1992. There were some company workers who saw Terry's rapid rise as resulting from his last name. A lengthy *Wall Street Journal* story quoted "former and current McGraw-Hill employees" describing him as "a decisive manager with strong competitive instincts" but adding that "many view him as autocratic and . . . prone to discourage dissent."[1]

The *Journal* story added, "Terry McGraw grew up in privilege, graduated from Tufts University and started, if not at the top, within striking distance of it. Trim and sandy blond, he is sometimes known around McGraw Hill as 'our Dan Quayle'."[2] Another story about the empire, in the *New York Times*, quoted "many outside and inside McGraw-Hill" describing Terry McGraw as a "tightly wound young man with a guarded demeanor. He maintains a polished exterior that covers feelings that are kept hidden."[3] While his father is profiled in the 1997 edition of

Who's Who in America, Terry is not listed.

In descriptions of Terry, there's a strong hint that he resembles his great grandfather, James McGraw. The author of a company history wrote that "James McGraw was deeply serious . . . for him the theater was out of bounds. Cards, genial drinking, the most innocent ribaldry were foreign to his nature. He rarely smiled or laughed, at least in business hours, and these were about twenty-four a day."[4*]

Begun separately in 1888 by James McGraw, who started a railway appliances magazine, and John Hill, then editor of *Locomotive Engineer*, both companies began technical book publishing within a few years. They merged in 1909 to form McGraw-Hill Book Company. Hill died in 1916 and a year later his five magazines were merged with McGraw Publishing Company. The new operation was titled McGraw-Hill Publishing Company. While the McGraw family is still very active in company management, the Hill family dropped out of sight as long ago as 1917.

Business Week, the most important of McGraw-Hill's magazines, was launched only a couple of months before the 1929 stock market crash. Just before the magazine launching, McGraw-Hill had published an economics textbook predicting confidently that there would never again be another market meltdown. *Business Week* contradicted that with the prediction that hard times were coming. While *Business Week* lost money in its first six years, it's been a leader in total advertising carried by a news magazine since 1937, and now enjoys a circulation of one million.

When the Depression was in its second year, the 33-story McGraw-Hill Building was completed on New York's 42nd Street between Eighth and Ninth Avenues. The building was later sold. More recently, company headquarters have relocated to 1221 Avenue of the Americas.

The company grew explosively during both world wars, publishing a variety of manuals. During World War II, the manuals reflected new technologies such as radar, sonar, loran and proximity fuses. After the victories over Japan and Germany, the company expanded rapidly into new fields, with books and magazines on electronics, nucleonics, plastics, data processing and computers. Textbook publishing expanded as huge numbers of veterans took advantage of the GI Bill of Rights to go to college.

In 1960 McGraw-Hill acquired F. W. Dodge Company, which publishes construction information, and six years later took over Standard & Poor's Corporation, which rates a variety of financial data around the world 24 hours a day. Another reorganization came in 1985 to coordinate the growing variety of McGraw-Hill output in books, magazines, newsletters, broadcasting and electronic services. During that period, the company's operations were carefully screened. When Harold McGraw Jr., the retired chairman, was asked by a *Wall Street Journal* reporter to comment on the reorganization, he said, "I don't talk to reporters."[5] But there's no evidence that Terry is as stiff as his father.

The company has been publishing books for use abroad since the 1950s. This overseas business has continued to grow, with much of the publishing done outside the United States, and today, McGraw-Hill publishes "in 16 languages from 23 distribution centers around the world."[6] And the company churns out 2,000 new titles every year. With 16,000 employees in more than 400 offices in 30 countries,

McGraw-Hill has 101 publications in four major divisions — corporate, financial services, educational and professional publishing, and information and media services. In addition to *Business Week*, it publishes *Aviation Week* and computer publications such as *BYTE*. Its four TV stations, all affiliated to ABC, are in San Diego, Bakersfield, Indianapolis and Denver.

The company defended itself from a possible takeover by American Express in 1979. Amex wanted it because McGraw-Hill was "cash rich." To solve that problem, McGraw- Hill spent $103 million to buy Data Resources Inc., an economic forecasting company. Joseph L.Dionne and Terry McGraw "were intrigued by DRI's business of delivering economic data electronically." They overlooked the fact that DRI made most of its money simply renting space on its computers. "The rental market fell off precipitously with the advent of personal computers."[7] Terry was also apparently intrigued by Numerax, a supplier of transportation data. "He paid $45 million for Numerax in 1986 only to see the profits spiral downward; Numerax was written off in 1989."[8]

As the overseas and home markets for books boomed, McGraw-Hill acquired the Times-Mirror Higher Education Group in 1996. In the transaction, it turned over its Shepards/McGraw-Hill to the Times-Mirror Group, which published a number of college-level texts. The acquisition was followed by more than 340 layoffs. But it put McGraw-Hill at the top of book publishers in twelve fields, most important of which are economics, accounting, finance, biology and psychology.

The company ran into trouble when it began running advertisements in its textbooks. Its subdivision, Glencoe, published 1,539 commercial images in a math text for sixth graders. The math problems featured Gatorade, M&Ms, Nike shoes, Pop Secret popcorn, and Raisinettes. A *San Francisco Chronicle* reporter noted that there are "thousands of examples of brand names, sports teams, movies and commercial logos scattered through many of the math textbooks approved by the state (California) for use in kindergarten through grade 12."[9] The San Francisco school board promptly approved the Commercial Free Schools Act, banning textbooks that unnecessarily mention brand names. A spokesman for McGraw-Hill told reporters that his company receives no payments from companies whose products appear in the books.

At about the same time in 1999, Texas education advocates were "urging the state's 1,200 school districts to scrutinize a math textbook series published by McGraw-Hill Inc. that features promotions for Burger King and Nike but still made the state's list of textbooks approved for purchase."[10]

In the same year, problems also faced subsidiary CTB McGraw-Hill, which provides tests in basic skills for schools across the country. Associated Press reported , "An error by school testing company CTB McGraw-Hill that may have sent almost 9,000 New York City pupils to summer school or held them back a grade has also affected test results in four other states."[11] The other states were Nevada, South Carolina, Tennessee and Wisconsin. "This wasn't Tennessee's first problem with CTB results," the story continued. In 1996, the company gave a faulty reading comprehension test to 60,000 Tennessee fourth-graders. In Indiana, administrators have faced a similar problem. It happened as well in Missouri. CTB also took the blame in Florida in May 1998, when flawed results were issued for a statewide test to assess reading and math skills."

The company has been moving away from sidelines. Eight years before the Times-Mirror deal, it sold off its trade book division, then 58 years old. The division, under the Whittlesey House imprint, had published books by Raymond Carver, Leon Uris, Jack Kerouac, Taylor Caldwell and Nobel prize-winner Heinrich Boll, as well as biographies of Shirley Temple Black and Bob Dylan.

Constantly reaching for efficiency and eager to try new technologies, in 1989 McGraw-Hill found a way to "customize" the making of textbooks. It joined R.R.Donnelly & Sons and Eastman Kodak in developing the electronic system. The McGraw-Hill Custom Publishing System makes it possible to work with individual professors who select the parts of an already-published book they want to focus on, add the instructor's notes, study guides and syllabus, put it all in a personalized jacket and ship copies of the book in two days. In one hour, twenty copies of a customized book of 300 pages can be printed by the system.

The company's emphasis on children's books was underscored by the June, 2000, purchase of the Tribune Company's scholastic publishing unit. At the same time it gave a new name to McGraw-Hill Consumer Products -- McGraw-Hill Children's Publishing.

In the fall of 1993, McGraw-Hill paid $337 million for Maxwell Communications' half-interest in the MacMillan-McGraw-Hill School Publishing Company. The joint venture had been formed with Macmillan four years earlier. In November, 2000, the company bought Mayfield Publishing Co., producer of college learning materials.

Terry McGraw's interest in new technologies was again demonstrated by the company's alliance in the fall of 2000 with Ilearn.com, a British company that offers courses online. "Subscribers have access to scores of McGraw-Hill courses."[12]

The Standard & Poor's financial information services company now has 50 offices around the world, and it provides a variety of financial services, rating stocks, bonds and currencies with letter grades from AAA to D. The information is available to computer terminals worldwide, as well as in newsletters, fact sheets and special reports. Now, more than 90 percent of the company's products, including *Business Week*, are available in digital format. There are more than 80 websites.

As 2000 ended, Terry McGraw was leading his company into the 21st century with seven years in a row of double-digit growth. His eyes are focused on the bottom line just as closely as those of his great grandfather were 115 years ago.

STEVEN SPIELBERG–
SOME MOVIES FOR KIDS, SOME FOR ADULTS

20

Although Steven Spielberg produced the somber, multi-prize winning *Schindler's List* and the World War II drama *Saving Private Ryan*, he still thinks of himself as a maker of children's movies. Even as he directed *Schindler's List* in Poland, he was in almost daily contact with George Lucas and other *Jurassic Park* workers in California. He says he "can always trace a movie idea back to my childhood."[1] But that comment veils a double meaning: his childhood was sometimes happy, some-times troubled.

He was born in Cincinnati in December, 1946. His mother had been a concert pianist and his father had returned the year before from the Asia-Pacific war theater after serving in the Army Air Force. The G.I. Bill of Rights enabled Arnold Spielberg to earn an electronic engineering degree, which led to a career in computer engineering.

Young Spielberg grew up hearing his parents and grandparents talk about the Nazis and their hatred of Jews. The grandparents told about pogroms (attacks on Jews) in Russia. Both parents were reformed Jews who seldom visited a synagogue and served kosher-style food only when their parents visited. As Arnold Spielberg moved up the job ladder, the family moved first to Haddonfield, New Jersey; then Phoenix, Arizona; and finally Saratoga, near San Jose, California. The frequent moves to different parts of the country were unsettling for Steven and his younger sisters, Anne, Sue, and Nancy, contributing to what he later remembered as his sometimes troubled childhood. Entertainment provided the children with some escape from the troubles. It was the dawn of the television era, and before long, Steven was watching movies on TV. "Undoubtedly the single most pervasive influ-ence on Spielberg in his early childhood was television. 'I was, and still am, a TV junkie'," he has said.[2]

His father had owned small movie cameras since his own teens and still enjoyed making home movies, so it wasn't long before young Steven wanted to make his own. After the family moved to Phoenix, Arnold gave him a new movie camera, and soon young Steven persuaded his father to drive with him and a few fellow Boy Scouts out to the desert to make *The Last Gun*, a Western. Steven directed and Arnold operated the camera. By the time he was 13, he had experimented with a number of home movies, each with his own plot. Then he went back to the desert to make *Escape to Nowhere*, a story about a group of American soldiers surrounded by Nazi troops in North Africa. When their breakout attempt was over, only one American survived. The film was silent, but somehow young Steven had obtained several cameras and rounded up all the needed props, including a machine gun. *Escape to Nowhere* won first prize in a state amateur film contest. As the son of an Air Force veteran, Spielberg has always been interested in World War II; by 1999 had made four films about the war.

At seventeen, he produced *Firelight*, a feature film lasting two and a half hours. He showed it to ticket buyers, mostly family friends, in a Scottsdale movie house rented by his father for the purpose. *Firelight* was about mysterious lights in the sky. Later he said it was based on his experience as a young boy, awakened at three in the morning by his father, who drove his son out of town to lie on the grass and gaze up at a meteor shower. Even today, he talks about that experience.

At Saratoga High School in California, Spielberg endured anti-Semitic attacks, mostly verbal. He later said these experiences were part of the impetus for *Schindler's List*. During his high school years his parents engaged in escalating arguments, which he and his three sisters could easily hear through their bedroom doors. For all four children, the period at Saratoga was the most troubled. Arnold and Leah Spielberg were divorced just before Steven went to college. He enrolled at Long Beach State University because his mediocre high school record was too poor to gain him admission to either of the two major film schools in Southern California.

In college he spent at least as much time going to movies and Universal Studios as to classes. During a bus tour of Universal Studios, he slipped away and walked around the studio on his own, asking questions of anyone who would give him attention. He made many forays into the studio after he found that he could enter the gate simply by wearing a suit and carrying a briefcase.

Still in college, he persuaded a friend, Denis Hoffman, to put up money for a short film. Hoffman was managing a rock group and wanted their music to be used in a film. Spielberg's 22-minute movie, *Amblin*, told the story of a boy and girl hitch-hiking from the Mojave Desert across southern California to the ocean. It won an award at the Atlanta film festival. By now he had friends on the Universal lot, including Chuck Silvers, who worked in the studio's film library. Silvers took the *Amblin* print to Sydney Sheinberg, the Universal head, who was so impressed that he offered Spielberg a seven-year contract. It was 1968; Spielberg was twenty-two. He began to direct TV dramas, starting with segments of a series called *Night Gallery*. Then came episodes of *Marcus Welby, M.D., Columbo, Owen Marshall, The Psychiatrist* and *The Name of the Game*, all one-hour segments, each with several writers.

His first made-for-TV movie was *Duel*, assigned in November, 1971. The story is simple: a traveling salesman is driving down a country highway when he realizes that he is being followed by a menacing truck. No matter where he turns, the truck follows, but the psychotic truck driver remains unseen. The truck driver finally is lured to drive over a cliff. *Duel* was shown on American TV, then released in Europe and Japan.

Sheinberg had enough confidence in Spielberg by 1974 to assign a theatrical movie to him, and the 27-year-old based his script on a real news event. The *Sugarland Express* was about a young couple, determined to keep their baby from its foster parents, driving across Texas with police cars in hot pursuit. While the film won favorable reviews, it did poorly at the box office. Then Spielberg directed his first blockbuster, *Jaws*, an adventure thriller about a great white shark lurking off a southern California town. This time the reviews were extremely favorable and the box office reached $458 million worldwide. It merited a *Time* magazine cover story. Also in 1975, Universal gave him a new contract calling for him to direct four feature films by 1981 and allowing him to direct for other studios.

Working from 1976 to 1978 in great secrecy at Columbia Studios and in an abandoned dirigible hangar in Mobile, Alabama, Spielberg wrote and directed *Close Encounters of the Third Kind*. It was an elaboration of his teenage film, *Firelight*, which depicted space aliens as friendly. Although Spielberg later mentioned his early film as its model, *Close Encounters* was far more complicated and sophisticated. *Close Encounters* was also a megahit, garnering $270 million in worldwide box office, plus an Oscar nomination for its director. While he was working on the film, Spielberg met Amy Irving, an actress who is the daughter of TV producer Jules Irving. She moved in with him and they married in late 1985, when their son Max was five months old. They were divorced four years later and have joint custody of Max. Amy got $100 million, $25 million for each year of their marriage. By the time they were divorced, Spielberg was living with another actress, Kate Capshaw. They had known each other since she acted in *Indiana Jones and the Temple of Doom* in 1983.

His next film, *1941*, was a comedy about events on the California coast soon after Pearl Harbor. It was based on the fact that only two months after the U.S. entered the war, a Japanese submarine sent shells into oil fields near Santa Barbara, the first attack on the U.S. mainland since 1812. There was little damage. Intended as a satire on the anti-Japanese hysteria after Pearl Harbor, the film bombed at the box office.

But two years later Spielberg was back with a new blockbuster, this time working with George Lucas to produce *Raiders of the Lost Ark*. The first of a new series, the film is about the adventures of archeologist Indiana Jones who seeks the lost Ark of the Covenant in which the Ten Commandments were stored. To make the film, Spielberg and Lucas traveled to Tunisia, England, France, Hawaii and Long Beach, California. It was clearly a commercial enterprise, depicting "good guys beating bad guys," as Lucas said, with Nazis usually the bad guys. Released in 1982, the worldwide box office came to $363 million, then the highest grossing film in Paramount history. Again Spielberg was nominated for an Oscar; again he didn't get it.

With *E.T., the Extra-Terrestrial*, Spielberg returned to Universal Studios -- and to

125

his childhood fantasies. Here a spaceship deposits its young, childlike "alien," called Puck, in a suburban neighborhood where a young boy, Elliott, becomes his friend and custodian. Puck and Elliott have a series of adventures, but after a while Puck begins to long for his home in space. Ultimately, the space ship returns to pick up E.T. Again Spielberg had a megahit, with the domestic box office reaching $399 million and ultimately a worldwide gross of $701 million. Also, of course, another Oscar nomination for Spielberg, praise from *Time* magazine and a *Rolling Stone* cover story. *Poltergeist*, which Spielberg wrote and produced but did not direct, was also released in 1982. It told a story of ghosts in a southern California home and carried special effects by George Lucas. It made no waves at the box office.

Spielberg formed Amblin Entertainment in 1984, and the new company got space for studios on the Universal back lot, where it still is. Its launching drew plenty of press ballyhoo. In a cover story, *Time* magazine called Spielberg "the Prince of Hollywood," and said he was "still a little boy at heart." The story put his line, "I dream for a living," in large type.[3] During its early years, Spielberg was usually producer rather than director. One after another came *Twilight Zone, Gremlins, Back to the Future, Who Framed Roger Rabbit?, Young Sherlock Holmes, The Money Pit* and *Joe Versus the Volcano.*

But while he produced these films, he directed *The Color Purple*, based on Alice Walker's Pulitzer Prize winning novel. Some critics asserted that he wanted to prove he could direct a serious film that would win an Oscar. The film contains not only feminist themes, but deals with incest, domestic violence and, in a limited way, lesbianism. The film starred Oprah Winfrey and Whoopi Goldberg, neither as famous as they are today. While it got thirteen Academy Award nominations, *The Color Purple* won no Oscars. The movie was good enough to gross $143 worldwide against production costs of $15 million. It got both favorable and unfavorable reviews.

Spielberg then tried two more serious films. One, *Empire of the Sun*, about a British boy's survival in a Japanese prison camp during World War II, was released in 1987, the year Spielberg got the Irving G. Thalberg Memorial Award from the Academy of Motion Pictures Arts and Sciences. But *Empire* did poorly at the box office. The movie-going public was also unkind to *Always*, a 1989 remake of *A Guy Named Joe*, which had been a successful 1943 film. The original story told about a pilot — killed while fighting a fire — whose ghost returns to advise a young man courting his former love. The new version had much the same plot.

Meanwhile, the three-picture deal with George Lucas had been moving along. *Indiana Jones and the Temple of Doom* was a big success in 1983. The last of the trilogy, *Indiana Jones and the Last Crusade*, came out in 1988 and earned a worldwide box office of $495 million. By May 1989, Spielberg's 25 films had sold more than $2 billion worth of tickets.

Up to now, aside from 1941, *The Color Purple, Jaws, Sugarland Express* and *Empire of the Sun*, almost all his movies were aimed primarily for children. But he had not forgotten either his father's war stories or his grandparents' experiences with anti-semitism in Europe. After the book *Schindler's List* was published in 1982, Spielberg began to think about making a movie based on the true story. The year of publication, he met Leopold Pfefferberg, a Pole who had been one of those saved by

Schindler. By then, Steven had arranged for Universal to buy the film rights to the story. But it was 10 years before he felt ready to start the project.

After *Always,* he took two years to direct *Hook,* based on several Peter Pan stories, with Robin Williams playing a growing up Peter Pan, again a story for children The 1991 film enjoyed a $288 million worldwide box office. While *Hook* was in production, Steven and Kate Capshaw had their first child, Sasha, who joined an adopted African-American child, Theo. Capshaw converted to Judaism early in 1991 and they were married that fall. By then he had begun major preparations for the production of *Schindler's List*

When he took off for Poland in 1993 for the filming of the Schindler story, Spielberg brought with him his wife and five children including Max, his son by Amy Irving; their own two children, Sasha and Sawyer; their adopted son Theo, and Kate's teen-age daughter Jessica. (The family grew to seven in 1996, when Steven and Kate had a third child, Dusty Allen, and they adopted a daughter, Mikaela.) He later said his three-month stay in Krakow during the dead of winter was made bearable by the presence of his family.

Jurassic Park, the dinosaur movie made jointly with George Lucas, was in its final stages while *Schindler's List* was being shot. Spielberg kept in touch with Lucas via satellite, working three nights a week, with Spielberg in Krakow and Lucas in his Marin County studio. The juxtaposition of what was a fact-based film about the Holocaust with a dinosaur fantasy didn't seem to trouble Spielberg. Indeed, he welcomed the *Jurassic Park* intervals as relief from the shattering war story. *Jurassic Park* was released in June, 1993, and enjoyed a worldwide gross of $913 million, topping even the $701 million of *E.T.*

Schindler's List runs three hours — long for a theatrical film, but it easily recaptured its $22 million cost. The film "became the transforming experience of Spielberg's lifetime," according to one of his many biographers, Joseph McBride.[4] He quotes Spielberg as saying that "Jewish life came pouring back into my heart . . . I cried all the time." The movie's worldwide gross came to $321 million, another blockbuster figure. Spielberg finally got an Oscar for directing while the film drew Best Picture and five other Oscars.

Much of his income from the picture has gone to Survivors of the Shoah Visual History Foundation, which is funding videotaped testimony of Holocaust survivors. More than 250,000 such survivors live in various countries and the Foundation has now reached its first goal of videotaping 50,000 of these. Spielberg's Righteous Persons Foundation has also given funds to a number of Jewish organizations and the Holocaust Memorial Museum in Washington, D.C. In spring, 1999 he released *The Last Days,* a Holocaust documentary featuring five survivors from the final weeks of the war in Hungary.

Soon after he won his Director's Oscar, Spielberg joined David Geffen and Jeffrey Katzenberg in creation of DreamWorks SKG, a studio to produce films, TV programs, records and games. He folded Amblin Entertainment into DreamWorks. The idea for the combination was worked out by the three in discussions at their California homes. From the start they made clear that Katzenberg would be manager. Press reports said they intended to produce live-action and animated films, music, TV programs and interactive games and software. Each of the trio contributed $33.3 million. A $500 million investment in DreamWorks came from Microsoft's Paul Allen; at the same time Bill Gates and Spielberg announced DreamWorks Interactive, a partnership to produce computer games.

By 1996, Spielberg was back churning out more films. In midsummer came *Twister*, about a couple trying to find a way to give Oklahomans a longer warning time before the arrival of tornadoes. In the same year DreamWorks launched two TV comedy series, *Ink* starring Ted Danson as a newspaper columnist, and *Spin City* with Michael J. Fox as deputy mayor of New York. Neither was outstanding and only *Spin City* lasted through 2000. Much higher ratings went to the TV hospital series, ER, which Spielberg co-produced. In the summer of 1997, the sequel to *Jurassic Park*, titled *The Lost World*, got mixed reviews. One reviewer commented that *The Lost World* had "more dinosaurs, better special effects and more action than the original *Jurassic Park* . . . but the inspiration is gone and with it most of the fun."[5] However, the reviews and box office returns for the animated comedy *Antz*, as well as the animated story of Moses, *The Prince of Egypt*, were very good.

Spielberg then went to work on *Amistad*, based on the true story of 53 Africans on board a Cuban slave ship in 1839. They killed all crew members except the captain and mate, who cunningly sailed them to Long Island, where they were arrested. In the end John Quincy Adams, played by Anthony Hopkins, argued successfully before the Supreme Court and they were freed to sail back to Sierra Leone. The reviews were respectful but not enthusiastic; the same can be said about its box office returns.

Spielberg returned to a World War II theme in 1998 with release of *Saving Private Ryan*, which dramatized the American D-Day landing on Omaha Beach. Its simple plot was the story of a company ordered to find and save Private Ryan, whose brothers had all been killed in other theaters of the war. It became one of the 25 highest grossing films in history and won several Oscars — but neither Best Picture nor Best Director.

Spielberg is a shrewd businessman. His later film deals have always allowed generous percentages of profits for the director. He gives up any salary for a percentage of box office gross. He is called "an unusually tough businessman, a ferocious, canny, and obsessively secretive negotiator, and not a terribly generous one."[6]

His tousled head is usually covered by a baseball cap and his legs by corduroy jeans; he has a greying reddish beard and wears glasses; and he enjoys an occasional cigar. While he is now on excellent terms with both parents, his troubled childhood is reflected time and again in his movies. Witness the *Last Crusade, Always,* and *Hook*. He tries to be a perfect dad to the seven children, ranging in age from two to twenty-two, living in a big, lively household in Pacific Palisades just outside Los Angeles. He's happy that his younger children enjoy the two Saturday morning TV comics for which he is founding producer — *Tiny Toon Adventures* and *Animaniacs*. He talks freely to reporters and often focuses on his childhood. Indeed, "No other film maker has mined his childhood more obsessively or profitably than Spielberg," according to biographer Joseph McBride.[7] The same biographer comments that in some of his movies, he has enjoyed frightening people, as he enjoyed frightening his young sisters. Examples are the shark in *Jaws*, the huge truck in *Duel*, and the ghost in *Poltergeist*.[8]

In addition to his funding of the Shoah project, he gives substantial sums to a variety of causes, but the gifts are now always anonymous and private. He says he learned the pleasure of such charity from the late Steve Ross, who ran Warner Brothers for many years and who, along with Sydney Sheinberg of Universal Studios, he considered his mentors.

He became a Knight of the British Empire in a ceremony at the British Embassy in Washington in January, 2001. He received the National Medal of the Arts in September, 1999. Word that he was to become Sir Steven Spielberg coincided with news that he had withdrawn an application to build a huge horse ring in Brentwood for his wife, Kate Capshaw. Neighbors objected strenuously to plans for the massive five-story project.

Spielberg produced or directed seven of the 20 highest-grossing films of all time and has been "enshrined as the most successful film-maker in history, a man with a seemingly flawless golden touch as both director of his own projects and producer of other people's."[9] He is widely admired in Hollywood, where the question is often asked: what next? Right now, he plans a futuristic science fiction thriller, *Minority Report*, with Tom Cruise, *Memoirs of a Geisha*, and *A.I.*, a robot film first considered by Stanley Kubrick. Through DreamWorks, he will produce *Into the Setting Sun*, telling about the building of the transcontinental railroad. Recently he backed out of directing a film based on the first Harry Potter story. He disagreed with author Rowling over the actor to play Harry Potter. In June, 2000, he was in England directing a 10-part TV series, *Band of Brothers*, a follow-up to *Saving Private Ryan* due on HBO in late 2001. He has plenty on his plate.

At age 54, and worth $2 billion, he still enjoys the role of the man behind the camera. And Jeffrey Katzenberg helps him arrange the day's activities to end in time for him to be home with Kate and their large family by suppertime at six o'clock. As a child he was sometimes troubled, but today Steven Spielberg is a happy man.

EDWARD L. GAYLORD–
NEWSPAPERS, TV, RADIO AND COUNTRY MUSIC

21

Edward Lewis Gaylord, Oklahoma's media mogul, doesn't like to give out information about himself or his far-flung empire. Now 81 and worth $2 billion, Gaylord adheres to the extreme political conservatism of his father, who died in 1974 at age 101, and makes his views clear in *Daily Oklahoman* editorials attacking those he calls the "liberal bubbleheads" in Congress. To a *Business Week* reporter, he once insisted that the Associated Press was left wing politically.

His father founded the family empire when he bought into the *Daily Oklahoman* in 1903. The paper has been a dominant influence in the state's capital for many years. It is militantly *against* taxes and militantly *for* business. His father also helped organize the John Birch Society. When he died at age 101, his properties included two Oklahoma City dailies, a radio and a television station in Oklahoma City, TV stations in Houston, Tampa, Ft.Worth-Dallas, and Milwaukee, a trucking company, an oil and gas development company, and an offset printing plant.

The empire has grown since his son Edward, then 55, took over the conglomerate. Up to then Edward had lived in his father's shadow. It was a lengthy shadow, reflecting the power which had not only made Oklahoma City the state capitol but had also drawn in Tinker Air Force base. Not much is known about Gaylord's childhood. He was sent to the Ashville School for Boys in North Carolina, and then went on to Stanford University, receiving his bachelor's degree in June, 1941. He enrolled at Harvard Business School but quit to enlist in the army a few months after America entered World War II. He stayed in the army until the war ended, leaving with the rank of captain in 1946.

Although he returned home to start work at the *Daily Oklahoman*, his father continued his tight control of the paper and all the other properties. The younger Gaylord showed little interest in the newsroom side of the paper, while the elder

Gaylord continued active management, putting in a full day's work even on the day of his death in 1974, 18 years after Edward Lewis returned from the war.

Gaylord's marriage in 1950 to Thelma Fragen Horton was opposed by his father, who considered her to be socially inferior; she was his secretary. The couple had four children, three daughters and a son. The son, now 42, is Edward King Gaylord II, called "EK," is listed as President of the *Daily Oklahoman* and in the spring of 1999 briefly took an active role in the family paper. Up to then, he showed more interest in riding horses and roping cows than in journalism.[1] He graduated from Texas Christian University in 1979, and now owns the Lazy E Arena, in Guthrie, Oklahoma, a venue for the National Finals Steer Roping Competition. Also interested in films, he co-produced *My Heroes Have Always Been Cowboys*, and was executive producer of the feature film, *With Friends Like These*, released in 1999. EK was also a co-producer for two *Bonanza* TV sequels. Gaylord's daughter Christy Everest is listed on the *Oklahoman* masthead as vice president, but her main interest is in community health programs.

Edward Lewis Gaylord merged the two Oklahoma City dailies in 1983, killing off the *Oklahoma City Times*. He also pushed the *Daily Oklahoman* further to the right. "The Worst Newspaper in America" was the headline description of his paper in a lengthy *Columbia Journalism Review* article early in 1999. The article hit the paper on all counts: skimpy news coverage, slanting of stories in a conservative direction, and a radical right editorial page. Summing up, it called the *Oklahoman* "a virulent, compromised beast that sucks intelligence from its readers and replaces it with intolerance, triviality and false scandal."[2]

The CJR article appeared in January, 1999. Three months later, the young Gaylord -- EK -- took over management of the paper because his father was at home caring for his dying wife. EK hired a new editor, Stan Tiner, who came from the *Mobile Register*, where he had been a Pulitzer Prize finalist. Tiner brought "a dramatic redesign, reorganized the paper's sections, brought in a female sports columnist and focused more on minority issues and individuals."[3]

Tiner's changes were so dramatic that CJR editors prepared a laudatory piece for their January 2000 issue, not knowing that by then Tiner had already disappeared from Oklahoma City. Mrs. Gaylord had died and Edward L. Gaylord was back in charge of the paper, clearly unhappy with Tiner's changes. In mid-December, while Tiner was still editor, the *Oklahoman* ran the first of what was promoted as a three-part series on contamination of workers at the Kerr-McGee plutonium processing plant, now closed. The other two parts didn't appear, apparently because Kerr-McGee officials complained to the elder Gaylord. Three weeks after the Kerr-McGee story appeared, Tiner left the paper. The *Columbia Journalism Review* commented that "recently, The *Daily Oklahoman* gave us a classic case of an irreconcilable clash between a reformist, liberal editor, Stan Tiner, and an entrenched, conservative publisher-owner, Edward L. Gaylord."[4]

Tiner was replaced by Sue Hale, who had worked on the paper 34 years, and had been "its most ardent defender against the recent journalism reviews, commenting that CJR based its criticism largely on the opinions of 'liberals'."[5]

Gaylord is back keeping a watchful eye on his Oklahoma media properties, but he still loves country music, an affection that led him as far back as 1983 to create the Gaylord Entertainment Company and buy the "Opryland complex" in Tennessee for $270 million.. That gave him the Grand Ole Opry, as well as a pair of radio stations — WSM-AM and WSM-FM — plus the Opryland theme park, Opryland Hotel and most of all, the Nashville Network, a cable system for country music, which has now been sold. He has expanded the Opryland Hotel so much that it is now called the biggest hotel-convention center in the world, with 2,283 rooms. He also owns the huge Broadmoor Hotel in Colorado Springs, with Pike's Peak nearby. Gaylord Entertainment plans another Opryland Hotel near Disney World in Orlando, and still another near Dallas. He also owns TV stations in Houston, Tampa, Dallas and Milwaukee, radio stations in Nashville and Oklahoma City, as well as the Texas Rangers baseball team in Ft. Worth and a number of golf courses. In 1995 he sold 27 cable systems in California and North and South Carolina for $370 million.

Plans for a huge $200 million development, Opry Mills, in the Opryland complex were announced in November, 1997. The project added a sizeable retail complex to the numerous entertainment venues in Nashville. The Gaylord Entertainment Center also contains the Nashville Predators of the National Hockey League. The "enhancements" announced by Gaylord Entertainment were expected to bring the number of visitors to 17 million a year.

Gaylord put his broadcast and entertainment properties, all of which were under the Gaylord Entertainment Company umbrella, on Wall Street in 1991, with shares for sale to the public. He still owns 60 percent of the company. He kept private only the *Daily Oklahoman.*

The Opryland complex jumped in value from its 1983 purchase price of $270 million to more than $800 million in March, 1993.[6] The same year, Gaylord decided to test the popularity of country music in Europe. He created CMT Europe with a budget of $20 million to be spent over five years. Nashville CMT produces the music and sends it to an uplink in Connecticut, from where it's beamed to a satellite above Europe. From the satellite, the music signal goes to owners of TV dishes and operators of cable channels. "We think there's a large potential over there," says Ed Benson, the head of Country Music Association.[7] Five months after the launch, Gaylord Entertainment Company officials reported that requests for service had come not only from Europe, but even Israel.

Early in 1997, Gaylord bought the Christian music company's Word Records for $120 million. A month later, he got $1.5 billion in Westinghouse stock in return for a pair of valuable networks — Country Music Television (CMT), which is carried by a fourth of all American cable systems — and the Nashville Network, which he had bought in 1983. CMT Europe was not included in the deal with CBS. The rest of his Nashville empire still flies the Gaylord banner. That group includes Opryland Productions, which every year turns out more than 30 stage show productions, specialty acts and bookings for country artists into venues all over the country. Gaylord Entertainment now has a country music site on the Internet — www.musiccountry.com — which is one of three Internet sites carrying the Grand Ole Opry.

Gaylord lives in a ranch-style house in Nichols Hills, a well-to-do Oklahoma City suburb.. On the front lawn stands a tall pole flying an American flag. He is developing Gallardia, a gated community north of the city, with 400 lots, country club, golf course, tennis courts, and pools, for wealthy Oklahomans.

Even though he hangs up when a reporter calls to request an interview, contrasting images of his personality have emerged, both from those who work with him and those who know him socially. One side of the image portrays him as witty and warm with his family, friends and employees. The other side shows him as cool, aloof, and in many ways hostile. In 1984, *Daily Oklahoman* editor Jim Standard argued that Gaylord's shyness explained the "impression of aloofness."[8] Frosty Troy, who publishes a weekly in Oklahoma City, says, "If personality was money, he'd be one of the truly needy."[9] A brief 1982 profile of Gaylord in *Forbes* magazine described him as "reclusive," "caustic" and "heavy-handed," quoting a local journalist who said, "The general opinion of Eddie is that he is a cold fish."[10] In a short paragraph in 1995, *Fortune* magazine called him a "blunt right-winger." His secrecy is demonstrated by the contract his ex-daughter-in-law signed at the time of her divorce, agreeing not to talk about him or risk losing income.

Even though the Gaylords are conservative, both politically and economically, the Oklahoma City papers have been technologically up-to-date since E. K. Gaylord took over in 1903. The papers were the first in the country to set both news and classified ads by computer in 1963. The paper's attitude toward African-Americans, hostile during his father's regime, continued after he took over in 1974. "Midlevel editors in the late 1970s remember periodic edicts banning pictures of blacks from the front page," a lengthy profile of Gaylord reported in 1984.[11] Of the 145 reporters and editors on the staff today, only three are African-Americans. The newsroom staff size is considerably smaller than most papers with similar circulation, but its news space is also smaller. "Over the years, dozens of his (Gaylord's) reporters have been classified as part-time, thirty-nine-hour-a-week workers, to avoid paying them benefits," according to the 1999 *Columbia Journalism Review* article.[12] The *Daily Oklahoman's* extreme conservatism and inadequate news coverage probably account for its low circulation. Its ad rates are among the highest in the country, higher even than those for the *New York Times*. Profits are far higher than the 20 percent industry average.

When the Murrah Federal Building was bombed in April 1995, the paper's staff worked hard to report the running story. Afterward, the Society of Professional Journalists gave it an award for its coverage. But the Pulitzer Prize judges found the quality of its stories wanting, so it didn't get a Pulitzer for its thousands of stories about the event and its aftermath. Indeed, in its 95 years, the *Oklahoman* has won only one Pulitzer — for cartoons, in 1939.

While Gaylord pays close attention to everything in the *Oklahoman* and writes editorials frequently, he is also very interested in Texas, especially Dallas. His Oklahoma Graphics, a substantial printing company, has customers in Dallas. He also owns 150 acres of prime real estate in the North Dallas area. His Lazy E Ranch is in St. Joe, Texas, and his Windward Ranch is in San Saba, also in Texas.

He is a heavy contributor to the University of Oklahoma, and a few months after

Stan Tiner's departure, he gave UO $22 million to establish a college of journalism and mass communications. He also vigorously supports the Oklahoma Christian University, located in the capital city. Gaylord has received honorary degrees from Oklahoma City University, Oklahoma Christian University, and Pepperdine University. He's on the board of directors of the Oklahoma State Fair, the National Cowboy Hall of Fame, and the Western Heritage Center. He was named to the Oklahoma Hall of Fame in 1974, and was the first to receive the Spirit of America award of the U.S.Olympic Committee in 1984.

Edward Lewis Gaylord is clearly trying to repeat the record started by his father. He had more than 100 guests at his 80th birthday party in June 1999. His son, EK, has made clear that the empire will remain in family hands, and that he will run it. There are no signs that the *Oklahoman* will become a better paper when that happens. The thousands of Oklahoma City residents who buy the *Dallas Morning News*, published 200 miles away, will continue to sidestep what they call the "Daily Disappointment."

PATRICK J. McGOVERN– HE'S NO DUMMY

22

His company publishes all those books "For Dummies," but Patrick McGovern is no dummy. He started publishing *ComputerWorld* in 1967 and since then has run his fortune up to $2 billion.

Born August 11, 1937 in New York and raised in Philadelphia, he became interested in computers when he was still in high school. Before he graduated, he had built his own computer and programmed it to play tic-tac-toe in a way that was unbeatable. The feat led to a scholarship at MIT, where he majored in neurology.

A *Boston Globe* reporter recently wrote that McGovern's "career, dating to his first job in a one-room office in Newtonville (Mass.) in 1959, has moved seamlessly from the days of the mainframe behemoths, to the microcomputers of the '70s, to the PCs and Macs of the '80s, to the Web, handhelds, wireless, B-to-B (Business-to-Business), and whatever sizzle of the next nanosecond is likely to be."[1]

He was still a student at MIT when he became associate publisher of the first computer magazine, called *Computers and Automation*. The magazine was started by Edmund Berkeley, a computer pioneer, whose book, *Giant Brains,* was important to young McGovern — and still is. He continued working at *Computers and Automation* after his 1959 graduation, but five years later, he launched his own business, International Data Corporation, which at first offered statistics on information technology (IT) markets to the computer industry. IDG today is the parent of his many companies. His rule for creation of new companies is simple: when the number of workers in an operation gets to between 200 and 300, the unit is spun off as yet another subsidiary. As of 2000 there were 120 such units, each one operating independently.

In 1967, he began publishing *ComputerWorld*, the weekly paper that still keeps computer owners and buyers up-to-date on computers and the industry.

ComputerWorld was so successful that within five years he launched *Shukan Computer* in Japan, making sure that the paper's staff — managers, editors, reporters — were all Japanese, to cater to local buyers. Today, IDG operates 290 computer magazines and newspapers in 75 countries, including *MacWorld, Network World,* and *PC World.*

McGovern launched IDG Books in 1990, to put in book form the kinds of information computer users need. While IDG headquarters are in Boston, IDG Books operates in Foster City, California, with John Kilcullen in charge. IDG Books did poorly with information technology books until one day Kilcullen over-heard a conversation in a computer store. A customer complained about the need for a simple primer for computer users, adding "something like DOS for dummies." Before long Kilcullen stocked bookstores with books titled exactly that, *DOS For Dummies.* Five million copies of that book have been sold. Indeed, it sold so well that Kilcullen found authors for more books with titles ending "For Dummies." Now he runs IDG Books Worldwide, and the self-help reference books have a wide variety of topics, including finance, gardening, birds, golf, cooking, lifestyle, even sex. IDG Books now has more than 700 titles, including 400 books for dummies, with translations in 31 languages, and some 70 million copies sold.

In 1998, IDG Books bought Cliff Notes, which publishes study guides for college students, and in 1999 it acquired Macmillan General Reference. In addition to the For Dummies line, it has Betty Crocker cookbooks, Frommer's Travel Guides and Weight Watchers books. IDG Books became a public stock offering in 1998, the first such offering made by McGovern.

McGovern commented to a reporter early in 2000, "In the mainframe era (1960s and '70s), we predicted that based on miniaturization and other factors, there would be one billion users by the year 2000," and he added, "By the end of 1999, there were 950 million users."[2]

International Data Group sponsors numerous high tech trade shows, including the annual Macworld Expo. For Microsoft's unveiling of Windows 2000 early in 2000, IDG's events division brought out nearly 15 books on Windows 2000 and developed a special Web site. The events division, which is called IDG World Expo, now produces 168 computer-related expositions world-wide.

New in the late 1990s was *Industry Standard,* an Internet business magazine published by IDG in San Francisco. A European edition of *Industry Standard* was due in the fall of 2000. Launching another magazine in Europe is an indication of McGovern's focus on foreign markets. In addition to IDG's *Shukan Japan,* there is *China ComputerWorld,* and *Russian PC World* in Russia. "After more than three decades in business, IDG now boasts publications on all seven continents," a *New York Times* story reported in 1997, adding, "Earlier this year, Mr. McGovern trekked to the South Pole to start ComputerWorld *Antarctica,* IDG's 280th publication."[4] By that year — 1997 — IDG was well- established in the Internet, with more than 140 Web sites offered by its companies.

IDG has been publishing in China since 1980, starting with *China ComputerWorld,* which has more circulation than any other publication in that country. All the publications are joint ventures with Chinese partners. McGovern was the escort for the head of China's Ministry of Electronics in Silicon Valley in the mid 1980s. The guest met many Chinese engineers working there and when he asked why they didn't return to China with their skills, the answer always was "because there's no opportunity in China." That guest was Jiang Zemin, now China's president, and he has done a great deal to transform information technology in his country. IDG continues to expand in China, with the 1998 launch of a monthly magazine, *Internet World in China*, bringing to 17 the number of IDG computer publications in China.

IDG employees work under such good conditions and get such good rewards that few ever leave. Hundreds have become rich as the result of the employee stock ownership program (ESOP). All the employees are eligible for the ESOP, which gives them a bonus of 10 to 15 percent of their annual salary, depending on how well their unit has done during the year. The bonuses are handed out personally by McGovern to the more than 5,000 staff members in the U.S., taking the first two weeks of December to complete the rounds. By 1997, at least 100 workers were millionaires and another 400 had over a $500,000 stake in the company.

McGovern is tall and speaks softly. He dresses in ordinary business suits. At 63, he told a reporter in 1999, "Although I have no thought of retiring, I realize I am not eternal." The comment was made as Kelly Conlin, who had been president of IDG since 1995, was named CEO and McGovern stepped down to become Chairman and a self-described "chief encouragement officer." The South Pole trip was a small part of McGovern's travels that year. "He logged 400,000 miles and spent 20 weeks in airplanes last year," the *Boston Globe* reported in April, 2000, adding, "Even at IDG headquarters, he can't settle. He works at a standup desk."[5] He is also clearly an outdoor enthusiast. In addition to exercising daily at home, he goes on several bike trips every year and even does some mountain climbing.

His homes are on both sides of the country, one in San Francisco, the other in Hollis, New Hampshire. When he is not at work, he enjoys classical music and supports the teaching of such music at Boston schools. His wife, Lore Harp McGovern, was born in Germany and had two children by her first husband before she married Patrick. They have two grown children. She has worked in technology for almost 30 years and was co-founder of Vector Graphics, which made desktop computers starting in 1976. Now she works with Silicon Valley startups.

McGovern and his son, also named Patrick, were pictured on the cover of the *Forbes* June 12, 2000, issue as examples of "How to Raise Your Kid in an Age of Wealth, Rich But Not Spoiled." When his son was 10, McGovern gave him a Commodore Pet computer, "then a rare and exotic gizmo," the article said.[6] "That gift was key to Patrick's future. By 16 he was working in Dad's office, preparing spreadsheets and building an online service." The same *Forbes* article tells about Michelle Harp, McGovern's step-daughter, who grew up in a wealthy San Francisco suburb, went to Smith College, "joined Web TV, picking up a pile of stock options shortly before Microsoft bought the company."[7] Now she's working on an MBA at MIT.

To cap his long-time support for his alma mater, early in 2000 McGovern and his wife gave $350 million to MIT to set up the McGovern Institute for Brain Research. He has been interested in the ways the brain works since he was in college. "The McGoverns decided to devote a major portion of their wealth to brain research because they believe neuroscience is poised to make major advances in understanding human behavior," the *Boston Herald* reported.[8] McGovern and his wife are paying close attention to the startup of their brain research institute, as plans are made for a building to house the 300-member staff.

As the year 2000 began, McGovern's IDG was publishing 300 magazines and newspapers and 4,000 book titles. It was also offering online users a huge network of technology-specific sites around the world, with some 270 Web sites in 70 countries. In August, 2000, IDG Books bought Hungry Minds Inc. of San Francisco, an Internet learning portal. "HungryMinds.com offers links to 17,000 online courses such as the UC Berkeley Extension, UCLA Extension and NYU Online," the *San Francisco Chronicle* reported.[9]

Patrick McGovern continues to prove that he's no dummy.

LOWRY MAYS–THE ACCIDENTAL BROADCASTER

23

Lowry Mays, the Texas tycoon, didn't intend to get into broadcasting. With his MBA from Harvard, he was sitting at his desk as an investment banker when two friends persuaded him to co-sign a note for purchase of a San Antonio radio station. Before the deal closed, his friends backed out. Convinced that the station could become profitable, Mays borrowed $175,000 and, with the help of his friend B. J. (Red) McCombs, bought the station. That was in 1972. He ordered changes in the station's format and added salesmen to the staff. Two years later, he quit invest-ment banking to devote full time to the four stations he and car dealer McCombs owned by then.

Twenty-eight years after he went into broadcasting, billionaire Lowry Mays's Clear Channel Communications operates 1,200 radio stations, including a chain of Spanish-language outlets, 19 television stations and more than 700,000 billboards in the U. S., England, France, Australia and New Zealand. The radio stations are in 32 countries. No wonder a *Business Week* headline called him "The Biggest Media Mogul You Never Heard Of."[1] The total number of radio stations varies as he buys and sells, but it's been above 1,000 for at least two years. That's about ten percent of the country's radio stations and Clear Channel harvests 20 percent of radio's adver-tising revenue.

Spreading its wings even further, Mays' company announced at the end of February, 2000, that it had acquired SFX Entertainment Inc, the largest producer of live concerts, theater and sports events, for $3.3 billion and the assumption of $1.1 billion in debt. "The acquisition would create a diversified powerhouse with stakes in everything from Broadway theaters, television and billboards to monster truck rallies, radio and the Internet," the *New York Times* reported.[2] SFX "has 16 amphitheaters in the top 10 markets, including New York, Los Angeles and

Chicago" and "it staged more than 25,000 events last year which attracted about 60 million people, including 7,000 rock concerts and more than 13,000 theatrical shows."[3]

"The Accidental Broadcaster," as a news headline once called Mays, was born in Houston, July 24, 1935. He went to Highland Park High School, then on to a degree in petroleum engineering at Texas A&M, and an MBA at Harvard. He married Peggy Pitman in 1959; they have four children — Kathryn Mays Johnson, Linda Mays McCaul, Mark and Randall. Mark, Randall and Kathryn work at Clear Channel.

From the start, Mays emphasized service to his advertisers. He uses a variety of promotional gimmicks, including on-air contests, giveaways and -- most of all -- billboards. "I'm in the business of selling automobiles and tamales," he says.[4] He controls the world's second- largest outdoor advertising company. And he likes to sell broadcast time and billboard space directly to advertisers. "Mays makes it clear that he wants his sales staffs working directly with local merchants, not fighting to get their stations included in agency buys."[5]

The Mays technique of clustering stations makes it possible to send programs out from one station to listeners of several stations in the region. That, in turn, helps advertisers buy commercial time efficiently. In effect, they buy in one place for several or many stations. Mays has always paid much more attention to advertisers than to his program content. He offers one-stop shopping to advertisers for both regional and national markets. One argument Mays' salespeople can use is that Americans spend more time listening to radio, especially in cars on the highway, than in the past. The Radio Advertisers Bureau reports that "people listen to radio on average three hours and 11 minutes a day" compared to four hours a day for television[6].

The loosening of FCC rules on the number of stations one company could own has spurred many of Mays's purchases. Mays lobbied both the FCC and Congress for years for deregulation and for rules that would allow one owner to have more than one station in a region. "Wily as a coyote, Mays works on changing rules he doesn't like."[7] In 1984, the FCC allowed a company to own 12 each of AM, FM and TV stations. That year Clear Channel went public and bought dozens of stations. In 1993 there was more easing of rules. But in 1996, the Telecommunications Act transformed the industry, opening the floodgates for Mays. By mid-1998, he was one of four operators who had gobbled up almost a third of the radio industry. One of those four was Jacor Communications, which Mays bought for $4.4 billion in May, 1999, to make Clear Channel the second largest radio station chain, second only to Mel Karmazin's Infinity Broadcasting chain. Only five months after that, Mays bought AMFM Inc., an even larger chain based in Dallas, for $23.5 billion.

Suddenly, Clear Channel was the biggest radio station owner in the world, with a total of 1,200 stations in 32 countries. What's more, "Clear Channel is a Wall Street heavyweight, ranking as the fourth largest media company, behind Walt Disney, Time Warner and Viacom/CBS," a pair of *Business Week* reporters noted.[8] The company's stations have an estimated 110 million listeners in the United States, including listeners to Heftel Broadcasting's largest Spanish language radio chain in the U. S., which Clear Channel bought in 1996. But FCC regulations required Clear Channel to sell up to 125 stations, since it exceeded the station limit in many areas. The 1996 Telecommunications Act allows ownership of up to eight radio stations in the same market, compared with a maximum of four before, and eliminated limits on the total number of stations one owner can own nationally. The sell-off was expected to leave the company with 830 stations in the U.S.[9] Of the 830, five stations will be in New York, eight in Los Angeles, six in Chicago and seven in San Francisco.

At Clear Channel, Lowry Mays holds the titles of Chairman and Chief Executive Officer, while son Mark is Chief Operating Officer, son Randall, Chief Financial Officer, and daughter Kathryn, Vice President, Communications. Based in San Antonio from the beginning, Clear Channel has moved three times as it continued to grow. Now it's building a new home to house its growing staff, including personnel expected to move from Chicago and Phoenix after the Jacor and AMFM takeovers.

In 1996, Clear Channel bought the More Group, a billboard company based in England. Two years later, the More Group paid $87 million for the French billboard firm Sirocco, with 22,000 billboards. A year later it bought Dauphin OTA, France's biggest poster group. It also has poster subsidiaries in Italy and Switzerland.

An example of Lowry Mays's foresight was his decision to join a consortium of companies in 1999, planning to launch the XM Satellite. When it started in 2001, the satellite beamed programs from CNN, *USA Today*, Bloomberg and C-Span and many other channels to specially installed radio receivers in some General Motors cars. GM is, of course, a member of the consortium. Ford Motor Company offered the same kind of satellite program, called CD Radio, to its customers even earlier — before the end of 2000. In another move to exploit new technology, the Mays company joined e4L in June, 1999, in starting BuyItNow, a Tulsa-based Web retailer on the Internet, offering thousands of toy products. But he has more Internet plans. By the end of 2001, he says, "all the Web sites of the company's radio stations will have streaming audio," reports the *New York Times*.[10] "That, combined with SFX's concerts, could let it offer pay-per-view concerts over the Web."

After the AMFM purchase, warnings were sounded by the *New Yorker*'s media critic, Ken Auletta. Commenting that "control of advertising dollars leads to control of programming," he wrote,. "More and more programming decisions are made by financial engineers, not broadcasters, and they are made centrally, not locally. So the real threat is to diversity, and to a public trust that has been implicit in broadcasting since its inception."[11] The threat is what *The Industry Standard* called "stale content, resulting in radio stations that are indistinguishable from one market to the next and sometimes even from those next to each other on the dial."[12]

The National Association of Broadcasters elected Mays as its chairman in both 1990 and 1991. He has also been active in the United Way in his Texas region. He funded the Lowry Mays College and Graduate School of Business at Texas A&M, where he is a regent emeritus. He received the Golden Mike Award from the Broadcasters' Foundation in March, 2001.

In 1999, Mays joined Mel Karmazin of CBS in a call to other broadcasters to build a $1 billion investment fund for women and minorities. They and others in the industry had contributed $175 million to start it. The money would be used to help women, African Americans and other minorities buy radio stations. Here they were acting in support of William Kennard, then the FCC chairman, who made minority ownership of more radio stations a priority. Another reason was suggested in press comments. Mays and Karmazin hope to "buy some good will at FCC . . . because they want the FCC to loosen broadcast ownership restrictions."[13] A *New York Times* story said Mays and Karmazin "brushed off suggestions that the fund is meant to sway regulators" who were then studying the acquisition of CBS by Viacom and the Clear Channel deal to buy AMFM Inc.[14] Not long after the Mays-Karmazin announcement, Black Entertainment Television (BET) revealed that it would pay as much as $1 billion to buy 20 or 30 of Clear Channel's newly-purchased AMFM stations. The FCC gave its final approval of the AM/FM purchase by Clear Channel in August, 2000.

Only a month later, as the National Association of Broadcasters held its annual convention in San Francisco, a group of progressive organizations staged a protest outside. They were protesting against Clear Channel Communications domination of radio.

And what happened to Red McCombs, the car dealer who helped Mays buy the first station in San Antonio? He owns the Minnesota Vikings football team; he runs the McCombs Enterprises real estate and oil company in San Antonio; he's on the Clear Channel board; and the *Forbes 400* says he's worth $2.1 billion.

Mays is a heftily-built mogul who speaks softly with a Texas drawl; always carefully dressed, he has a powerful handshake. He's "an affable bear of a man, 6 feet 3 inches tall, with a shock of wavy grey hair, (who) can lapse into a country-boy mode," according to a Houston reporter.[15] He and Peggy "live in a comfortable, if not lavish, five-bedroom house in San Antonio," the *New York Times* reports.[16] "On weekends, they often retreat to a 2,000-acre ranch near Spring Branch, 40 miles north of San Antonio, where they raise registered longhorns." At 64, he makes it clear that he has no intention to retire soon, even though he'd like to spend more time quail hunting and driving his Jeep around his ranch. While his 36-year-old son Mark is clearly in line to take over, the man listed by *Forbes* in July, 2001 at $1.9 billion, says, "I'm still at my work station."[17]

THE FRANK BATTENS–THEY PROFIT FROM THE WEATHER

24

The Frank Battens, senior and junior, run Landmark Communications, a network of newspapers, TV stations, book publishers, software provider Red Hat and — best-known of all — the Weather Channel. Frank Senior was listed at $1.5 billion in the July 9, 2001 *Forbes*. After 40 years building the company from two daily papers and a TV station in Norfolk, Virginia, Frank Senior on January 1, 1998, handed the reins over to his son, who is now chairman of the Landmark board.

The elder Batten inherited the two Norfolk papers from his uncle, Samuel Slover, in 1967 after he had served his apprenticeship at the Norfolk *Virginian-Pilot* and its sister paper, the Norfolk *Ledger-Star*. With the papers came a TV station.

Born February 11, 1927, in Norfolk, Batten served in the U.S. Merchant Marine during World War II, then went on to get his bachelor's degree at the University of Virginia in 1950 and an MBA at Harvard two years later. He started to work on his uncle's paper soon after he left Harvard. Partly because Batten's father had died when he was young, Slover developed a father-son relationship with him. Batten was only 27 when his uncle named him publisher of the *Virginian-Pilot*. Under his leadership, the paper strongly supported the Supreme Court's school desegregation decision, and his editor Lenoir Chamber won a Pulitzer Prize for his editorials opposing those who resisted school integration.

When Batten took over the company, Landmark Communications, in 1967, he was eager for expansion. Creating TeleCable Corp., he bought cable companies in North Carolina and West Virginia, and began to look for other possible acquisitions.. By the time he sold TeleCable to John Malone's TCI in 1995, it operated 21 cable systems in 15 states.

Meantime, he had started the Weather Channel in 1982, a cable program available to a huge share of American homes. By 1997, the channel, based in Atlanta, was beaming weather news to 70 million subscribers and was pulling in $100 million in profits on $200 million in revenues. "Its web site, www.weather.com, is now the 30th most popular destination on the Internet."[1] In the fall of 1999, the Weather Channel began to provide weather news to America Online (AOL). By then, the Channel's value had risen to $1 billion, according to media research firm Paul Kagan Associates.[2] A *New York Times* reporter wrote, "Reaching 70 million homes and offering programs that may cost less to produce than anything else this side of C-SPAN, the Weather Channel is a 'cash machine' in the estimate of Jessica Reif, a media analyst at Merrill Lynch."[3] That estimate was made in 1999; by August, 2000 the number of cable households had gone up to 76 million — 93 percent of the country's cable homes.

In mid-2000, the Weather Channel learned about competition from WeatherPlus, a cable channel in the Netherlands planning to come to at least 10 U.S. markets. It already had competition from AccuWeather, a forecasting service at State College, Pa. AccuWeather provides weather news for about 1,400 Internet sites, including MSNBC.com and CNN.com.

To meet the competition, staff members at Weather Channel began to increase the number of local updates, aiming ultimately for each of the biggest 200 markets in the U.S. They also planned to use the Internet to expand overseas. "Weather Channel executives say Web sites are cheaper, easier alternatives to getting on cable systems across the globe."[4] The channel already has two networks in Latin America, one in Spanish, the other in Portuguese.

In March, 1999, the Battens put the Weather Channel on the Internet with a Web site, weather.com. It also has "Wireless Weather," available to cellular subscribers for a monthly fee.

The Weather Channel was strengthened early in 2000 when Landmark bought Weather Service International from Litton Industries. The new acquisition, based in a Boston suburb, brought a 230-member staff, 40 percent of whom are meteorologists. The Weather Channel is set up in an eight-floor building on Atlanta's outskirts. Eighty staff meteorologists analyze data coming from the National Weather Bureau as well as military sources. The programs are transmitted by satellite, maps are sold to 52 newspapers, and regular reports go to 250 radio stations. The Weather Channel's website offers forecasts for 70,000 locations, as well as weather by e-mail. Through the Weather Channel, Landmark now owns half of Pelmorex, which does nothing but provide weather news to cable networks in Canada.

Currently growing even faster than the Weather Channel is Red Hat, which markets software called the Linux operating system, available free on the Internet. By mid-1999, Linux had "some 12 million users, and the number is growing fast," the *Economist* reported.[5] The magazine added that "anyone can download (the Red Hat programs) from the Internet, copy them and even alter them. Because the software is written by hackers for hackers, it is often hard to install. Most users rely on online *newsgroups* for technical support." An article in the *Financial Times* called Red Hat "the leader in the growing market for open source software based on Linux, which is used to run corporate IT (information technology) systems."[6] The article added that by buying Cygnus Solutions in the fall of 1999, Red Hat aimed "to extend the use of the Linus operating system, which competes with Microsoft Windows." Cygnus produces software systems that enable programmers to create programs based on Linux. If Red Hat is free, how does it stay in business? "It sells packaged versions for sophisticated business users" and "expects to make money by selling advertising on its Web pages," according to a Richmond paper.[7]

While Red Hat lost $14.9 million in the first quarter of 2000, by the end of the year, Deloitte and Touche Fast 500 called it one of the fastest growing technology companies on the continent. The reason for its explosive growth is that it provides a common platform for developing, deploying and managing open source across Internet's infrastructure. The Red Hat Network helps companies all over the world deliver open source products, service and information on-line.

The Battens started to buy Red Hat shares in August 1997, at 29 cents a share. By February, 1999, the company had expanded so much and become so profitable they paid $3.14 a share. By then, they had "22 percent of the company, a stake worth about $3.79 billion."[8] Eleven months later, a *Fortune* reporter wrote that Red Hat was "worth more than British Airways, Japan Airlines, and KLM Royal Dutch Airlines combined."[9]

In addition to the Norfolk papers, Landmark owns the *Roanoke Times* in Virginia and the *News & Record* in Greensboro, North Carolina, as well as a string of 79 community papers — some shoppers and some paid circulation weeklies — all across the southeast and midwest. Its television stations are in Las Vegas and Nashville. Just before he gave control of Landmark to his son, the elder Batten sold the Travel Channel to Paxson Communications. But it still owns Falcon Publishing, based in Helena, Montana, which provides guidebooks about hiking, camping, climbing, mountain biking, fishing and birding at sites all over the United States. Some examples: *America On My Mind, Hiking Shenandoah National Park, National Forest Service Scenic Byways,* and *Traveling the Lewis and Clark Trail.*

Another indication of Landmark's broad range is Travel, a broadcast program in London, targeting audiences in the U. K. and Europe. The program, in English, provides many kinds of travel information. In 1996, the company launched Voyage, a French language travel channel for the French market. It goes out as a service to the Canal satellite digital package of CanalPlus.

The Battens don't hesitate to join other companies in launching new programs. They are 50-50 owners with Cox Enterprises of Trader Publishing Co., a network of publications providing photo guides advertising automobiles and boats. It issues both paid and free weeklies. Landmark also has half of Capital-Gazette Communications, which publishes *Washingtonian* magazine..

While Frank Junior now has day-to-day control of Landmark, he checks with his father, who's in charge of Landmark philanthropies. The senior Frank Batten lives in Virginia Beach. He gave the University of Virginia, his alma mater, $60 million in 1999 to create the Batten Institute, for entrepreneurial programs in its business school. His 42-year-old son, now the top official at Landmark, is married, has two sons and lives in Norfolk, the headquarters for Landmark.

When Frank Batten Jr. took over Landmark in 1998, he had served a lengthy apprenticeship. Born in Norfolk in 1958, Frank Junior went to Dartmouth College for his bachelor's in history and then to the University of Virginia for an MBA. After that, he became a reporter at the *Roanoke Times* for two years, and then spent 18 months in London working for the Associated Press, finally coming home to work at Landmark.

The Battens, father and son, are both press shy, so little is known about them except their ability to make money. The Weather Channel was Frank Senior's idea, and the Red Hat investment was Frank Junior's idea. Both Senior and Junior seem to have a golden touch.

STANLEY HUBBARD–THE BROADCAST VISIONARY

25

An early pioneer in satellite television, Stanley Hubbard followed in the footsteps of his father, who built one of America's first radio stations in 1923 and then one of the world's first TV stations in 1948. Now 67 and still just as visionary as his father, Hubbard has run his family's fortune up to $1.5 billion.

Born in St. Paul May 28, 1933, Hubbard went to Minnesota University's School of Journalism for his bachelor's degree. He married Karen Holmen in 1959 and they have five children. He was driving one of his sons to school one morning when "it came to me like a vision that DBS (Direct Broadcast Satellite) was nothing less than a broadcast license."[1] The 1981 "vision" may have been more than a coincidence because 1981 was the year the FCC set out new direct-broadcast-satellite rules.[2] In any case, that year was when he applied for a satellite license under the name United States Satellite Broadcasting (USSB). It took twelve years, but by December, 1993, USSB was on the country's first direct-broadcast satellite, sharing it with DirecTV, then co-owned by Hubbard and Hughes Communications.

The long period between the license application and USSB's first broadcast tells a lot about Stub Hubbard. A local magazine in his home town quoted colleagues as saying that "Stanley Hubbard is much like his father: a visionary, a workhorse, a risk-taker."[3] *Broadcasting* later reported, "To keep alive the dream, Hubbard gave hundreds of speeches and presentations and spent millions of dollars on lawyers, researchers and consultants."[4] In a June, 2000, telephone interview, Hubbard said the years of delay were because "we couldn't borrow money," because "the cable companies were opposed."[5] But then, "with Hughes' help, we got it going."

USSB offered 20 digital channels of programs. Hubbard owned five of the 16 transmitters on his part of the satellite. By then USSB was worth more than $100 million, most of it advanced by Hubbard Broadcasting, but with several other important stockholders, including Nationwide Mutual Insurance, fire alarm maker Pittway Corp. and cable operator Burt Harris. Late in 1995, USSB began to sell shares on Wall Street.

Before the satellite was lofted, Hubbard said, "You'll see a lot of programming that will be produced by local stations and by major Hollywood producers who want to have a window on this market and want to start out and grow with the business."[6] After the satellite had been in operation four years, *Broadcasting & Cable* reported that "USSB offers premium and basic program packages that include five channels of HBO, three channels of Showtime, Flix, Sundance Channel and pay per view events."[7]

A year after USSB got its license, Hubbard helped launch Conus Satellite News Service. "We were able to package a set of existing technologies," he later said.[8] With remote satellite uplinks at their core, creating a video news exchange among TV stations and networks (including TV Asahi in Japan), Conus had more than 100 members worldwide by 1992.

In order to draw more customers to USSB's news and entertainment channels, he worked with electronic engineers to find a smaller receiver and hit upon an 18-inch disc. Later, a *Wall Street Journal* reporter wrote, "A few years ago, Stanley S. Hubbard was laughed out of cable conventions when he promised to offer a direct-broadcast satellite service on an 18-inch disc he held under his arm."[9] The story went on to quote Hubbard, "They'd say, 'DBS stands for Don't Be Stupid'." And the *Journal* reporter added, "But nobody -- particularly anyone in the cable industry — is laughing today." In 1996 Hubbard was able to report that sales of those DBS dishes had reached a million and there were more than four million subscribers, who of course no longer needed cable. By then, the price of the backyard satellite dish had dropped to $200. In late 1999, USSB had 2,192,000 subscribers, scattered from coast to coast, who paid $23 per month for 25 to 30 channels

As the year 2000 approached, the Hubbards' partners -- Nationwide Insurance, Pittway Corp., and Burt Harris -- who held big chunks of USSB stock, put pressure on the Hubbards to sell. "The industry was consolidating, and the cable companies were consolidating," Hubbard said in the June, 2000 telephone interview. "If it had been up to us, we would have kept it, but we owned only 51 percent," he added. So in December, 1999, USSB was sold to owners of DirectTV, operated by Hughes Communications, who thus took over the whole of the satellite which they had shared from the start. The price tag was $1.25 billion. Of this, the Hubbard family got an estimated $674 million.

All members of the Hubbard family sit on the Hubbard Broadcasting board. They are: Stanley S., his wife Karen and their five children, Virginia, Robert, Stanley E., Kathryn and Julie.

After the sale of USSB, the Hubbards still own nine television stations and two radio stations. They have also set up the new Hubbard Media Group, which operates three satellite channels that are linked to DirecTV. They also own F&F Productions in Tampa, Florida, specializing in remote productions, and Diamond P Sports, which produces auto racing programs.

The family set up the Hubbard Foundation in 1959, and it contributes to community organizations such as hospitals, health agencies and arts groups, with some $20 million to work with. The Foundation is directed by daughter Kathryn Hubbard Rominski. Stanley Hubbard has received some 27 awards, including the Golden Mike Award of the Broadcasters Foundation, Pioneer Broadcaster Award of the Minnesota Broadcasters Association, and the Golden Plate Award of the American Academy of Achievement.

As of 2001, *Forbes* listed Stanley Hubbard at $1.5 billion, but it seems pretty clear that the wealth is shared by all the Hubbards. They don't own USSB any more, but they're not entirely divorced from satellites. Under Hubbard's far-sighted management, they own and operate those three channels that carry their signals from satellite to listener-viewers. Stanley Hubbard is still a visionary. Like father, like son.

STEVE CASE–HE SITS ATOP
THE WORLD'S BIGGEST MEDIA CONGLOMERATE

26

He's the hard-driving mogul who, early in 2000, negotiated the America Online (AOL) $183 billion buyout of media giant Time Warner in history's largest takeover.

Steve Case has been Chief Executive Officer of AOL only since 1992 and Chairman since 1995. But he was key to its evolution from the 1983 upstart Control Video, which brought Atari video games to home computers, to Quantum Computer Services, offering on-line services to computer users. Quantum, in turn, was renamed America Online in 1991. As recently as 1994, *Business Week* reported "talk that Time Warner might want to pick up" AOL.[1] Six years later, AOL "picked up" Time Warner.

Case popped into the *Forbes 400* in October, 1999, a few months before the merger, when he was listed at $1.5 billion. By then, AOL had 22 million subscribers, each paying $21.95 a month. Only three years earlier, it had 6.3 million subscribers.

Stephen M. Case was born August 21, 1958, on the island of Oahu in Hawaii, the son of a corporate lawyer and a school teacher. He has an older sister, Carin; an older brother, Dan; and a younger brother, Jeff. As they grew up, Steve and Dan called themselves "entrepreneurs" and ran "Case Enterprises," based mainly on selling a variety of goods to owners of homes where they delivered papers. "Case has been selling almost since he left the crib," a *Time* reporter noted after the Time Warner takeover.[2]

He attended a private prep school, Punahou School in Honolulu, and then went to Williams College in Williamstown, Massachusetts. There, "he ran the student entertainment committee, put on campus concerts, and founded a company that produced an album representing the best college bands. He also sang for two new-wave rock groups."[3] His 1980 degree was in political science, which he considered closest to marketing of all college majors.

His first post-college job was at Proctor & Gamble in Cincinnati, where he strove — unsuccessfully — to increase sales of Lilt and Abound, two women's hair care products. After two years, he moved to Wichita, Kansas, to take charge of developing new toppings for Pizza Hut, Pepsi Cola's subsidiary. During his long trips to Pizza Huts around the country, he brought a Kaypro personal computer for amusement in hotel room evenings. That started his computer education — and infatuation.

In 1983 in Las Vegas he visited a consumer electronics show attended by his brother Dan, who had shares in a new company, Control Video Corp.. Dan introduced Steve to company officers. Then and there, Steve Case switched from pizzas to computer services, going to work for Control Video. When the company had serious financial problems because video game sales were tanking, its board of directors appointed Jim Kimsey as its CEO and Case as financial officer. Together, Kimsey and Case changed the company's product to provide access to news, soap opera updates and a variety of games. They also changed its name to Quantum Computer Services Thus AOL was born in 1985, even though it was seven years before it took on that name.

The new 1985 product was in the form of on-line services, which Apple Computers began to use on its operating system. In the fall of 1989, America Online was added to Quantum's products, offering e-mail, travel and other information in addition to the games and news already available. In 1990, Quantum added Promenade as a service on the new IBM PS/i. Then Tandy Computers and the (Chicago) Tribune Company also began using it on their operating systems. The IBM, Apple, Tandy and Tribune deals were made by Case, again demonstrating his marketing skills.

Quantum's name was changed to America Online in 1992, the same year AOL's stock was posted on Wall Street and Case was named CEO. As CEO, Case moved aggressively to increase services and thereby attract more customers. By 1993, Microsoft co-founder Paul Allen had bought 24.9 percent of AOL's stock and Case persuaded him to refrain from a takeover, which would have been easy, considering Allen's growing wealth. More formidable was the proposal by Microsoft's Bill Gates, "whose overtures to buy AOL prompted an AOL board vote in 1993. . . . . by a narrow margin, the AOL board declined Gates' entreaties to begin negotiations."[4]

Now began a number of Case-inspired purchases and alliances, all intended to increase the usefulness of AOL to its growing number of customers. Purchases included Advance Network Services, BookLink Technologies, Global Network Navigator, Redgate Communications, Medio Inc., and Wide Area Information Services. Alliances were made with Broderbund Software and Novell. These all made it possible to use Internet's fiber optic lines, the World Wide Web (www) and graphics to expand and make easier the use of AOL's information and entertainment war chest. Altogether, "AOL spent more than $1 billion building up its system."[5] Each of the moves advanced Case's marketing plans.

Not content with AOL's growing reach in the United States, Case worked out a $100 million joint venture with Bertelsmann, Germany's huge media conglomerate, so that AOL could be used on European computers. The venture is titled AOL Europe. By 1999, AOL Europe had 10 million of AOL's 20 million subscribers and Bertelsmann's Thomas Middelhoff was on AOL's board of directors. He resigned after the AOL merger with Time Warner in 2000, and less than two months later, Bertelsmann sold its $6.75 billion stake in AOL Europe back to AOL. AOL also severed its relationship with Vivendi, the French entertainment company that bought the Bronfman family's entertainment and liquor conglomerate in the same year. Case's company was expected to be more active in management of AOL Europe. "The company expects that by 2004 there will be twice as many online consumers outside the U.S. as inside."[6]

The fast growth rate and huge expansion of services caused problems toward the end of 1993, when AOL customers complained that they were unable to get what they wanted online when they wanted it. Case agreed that more action was needed and hired more technical staff and customer service personnel. Even so, the grumbling continued as the company was called "America On Hold." The problems were underscored by AOL's charges, still based on hourly rates, which added up fast for many customers. In October, 1996, AOL announced a flat monthly rate of $19.95, which was hiked to $21.95 eighteen months later. 1996 was also the year that Case was the subject of a *Business Week* cover story and a profile in *Current Biography*.

Also in the mid-1990s, AOL and Microsoft made a trade-off. It called for Bill Gates to include access to AOL's services in Windows 95. In return, AOL customers can use Microsoft browsing software to work on the World Wide Web.

By then Case had become AOL chairman, having replaced Kimsey in October, 1995. Along the line, AOL bought rival CompuServe. A *Fortune* reporter noted in March, 1998, that "With CompuServe, AOL captures about 60 percent of home use of the Internet, overwhelming the hundreds of big and small companies competing to take people online," adding that "AOL has more subscribers than *Time*, *Newsweek* and *U.S. News & World Report* combined."[7]

Those three news-weeklies devoted page after page to the marriage of AOL and Time Warner in January, 2000. As an indication of AOL's explosive growth, a *Time* reporter noted that "in December, 1998 . . . . Time Warner was worth more than AOL. By December, 1999, AOL was worth 2.5 times more than Time Warner."[8]

Commentators noted that Case was eager for AOL to have the enormous Time Warner audiences, including its huge cable system with 13 million customers, its movie studios, its television network, its Warner Music Group, its 33 magazines led by flagship *Time*, its Warner Books and Little Brown, and its huge Turner holdings at home and abroad. The magazine group was enlarged in the fall of 2000 when Time Inc. bought a group including *Golf, Field & Stream* and *Ski* from the Tribune Company for $475 million.

Talks about the possible partnership had started when Case and Time Warner's Gerald Levin met in Paris while attending the Global Business Dialogue in September, 1999. Their conversation was friendly and tentative. It was continued at a *Fortune*-sponsored event in Shanghai and Beijing only two weeks later. Then, in early October, Case phoned Levin to propose the merger, adding that Levin would be CEO of the new behemoth. The nitty-gritty negotiations began secretly in mid-November, with Levin suggesting 1.42 shares for each Time Warner share, which would give AOL shareholders 55 percent of the new company. Negotiations climaxed at a dinner in Case's home in northern Virginia, and the deal was announced to the press January 11, 2000.

For Case, it meant an enormous increase in the amount and variety of *content* available to AOL users. For Levin and Time Warner, it meant a vast increase in its ability to *distribute* news, information and entertainment. And for consumers, "the combination represents, in its barest terms, the potential for getting whatever they want — books, movies, magazines, music — whenever they want it, whatever way they choose, whether on a TV, a PC, a cell phone or any of the myriad wireless devices that are hurtling toward the marketplace."[9]

But AOL also brought content, in addition to its unparalleled service, to the deal. "People can get most of the content and services they want, including shopping, travel reservations, chat, instant messaging, e-mail, news, and financial services, without ever leaving AOL's comfy confines."[10]

Reporters for London's *Financial Times* commented, "The deal is scattered with superlatives. It is the largest takeover ever. Based on a market value of around $335 billion, the combined company . . . will be one of the world's five largest companies, along with Micrcosoft, General Electric, Cisco and Wal-Mart."[11] It also brought added wealth to both Levin, with $350 million, and Case, with $1.375 billion in vested and unvested stock options.[12] Not only his wealth but also his fame jumped after the merger. *Vanity Fair* commented that "he's become a celebrity: Hollywood legend Tony Curtis recently interrupted Case and his wife Jean at a Washington restaurant to have his picture taken with them."[13]

The new behemoth has Case as its Chair, Levin as CEO, and Time Warner's Richard Parsons and AOL's Bob Pittman as co-chief operating officers. The employee count adds up to more than 80,000. Even though experts correctly estimated that it would take nine months to a year for the merger to get approval by federal agencies, in less than a month new AOL 5.0 software was stocked at the Time Warner store on New York's Fifth Avenue, and the Warner label Electra Records joined AOL's Spinner.com in releasing a single record by The Cure.

The ink was barely dry on the marriage certificate before Time Warner announced a merger of its already-huge music group, Warner Music, on a 50-50 basis with England's EMI, to create the world's largest music conglomerate. But that merger was called off in October as Case and Levin concentrated on FTC negotiations, and regulators in the European Commission approved the AOL-Time Warner merger. Less than two months after the merger announcement, AOL said that Time Warner cable TV lines would be opened to rival Internet services, giving consumers more choices. And in late July, Case assured FCC regulators that "if America Online and Time Warner are allowed to merge, consumers will see the Internet taken to the next level — connecting, informing and entertaining people around the world as never before."[14]

But there were critics, including Professor Robert McChesney, author of *Rich Media, Poor Democracy*, who told a *New York Times* reporter that the merger shows "the Internet is being brought fully into the circle of commercial corporate interests."[15] McChesney had called attention to the government origins of the Internet: "The government created and subsidized the Internet and its predecessors for three decades. Private sector firms wanted no part of it because they couldn't figure out a way to make a buck from it. Then in the early '90s, without a shred of public debate or deliberation, with no media coverage whatsoever, the prohibition of commercialism was lifted and the Internet was privatized and turned over to corporate America."[16] Also opposing the merger were Disney-ABC and General Electric-NBC.

However, almost a year after the merger was announced, the Federal Trade Commission approved it in mid-December, 2000, after AOL agreed to give its rivals access to the huge Time Warner cable TV network. Time Warner had already "agreed to carry AOL's chief Internet service rival, EarthLink, on its high speed cable systems."[17] By then, many AOL executives had already moved to New York. Plans were being made to build a new corporate headquarters in Manhattan. Meanwhile, because of the sharp stock market decline, the value of the merger deal, originally touted at $183 billion, had dropped to $106 billion.

After the FTC approval, the Federal Communications Commission stepped in. In a separate opinion, the FCC ordered AT&T to get rid of its stake in Time Warner Entertainment, a subsidiary that owns most of the huge Time Warner cable system. AT&T had bought the huge cable system, then known as Telecommunications Inc. (TCI) from John Malone only two years earlier. When the FCC's final approval came almost exactly one year after the deal was announced, it required AOL to open its instant messaging services to rival providers over Time Warner's cable lines. The services include video teleconferencing, sharing of files and sending messages over interactive television.

The huge conglomerate waited until the final federal approval to lay off 2,400 employees, three percent of its 85,000 workers, including 725 AOL people and more than 1,700 from Time Warner and Turner. It also announced plans to close the 130 Warner Brothers retail stores.

As part of corporate America, AOL has done very well indeed. While its subscriber lists grew in the last five years, its profits zoomed. In just the last three months of 1999, "it enjoyed $352 million of income on advertising and electronic commerce, quite apart from its $1.1 billion income during the same quarter from its monthly subscriptions."[18] Those monthly fees went up to $23.90 in July, 2001. During the first month of that year, Internet users spent 532 million hours on AOL service

AOL-Time Warner doesn't have the global reach of Murdoch's News Corp., but it's well-established in foreign markets. It's already England's biggest Internet provider. It's meeting resistance in Germany from Deutsche Telecom, that country's number one Internet service provider. But AOL added about two million overseas subscribers in 2000 and now enjoys 32 million in 16 foreign countries.

One explanation for the growing AOL profits was revealed in a lengthy *Forbes ASAP* article in early 2001. It seems that growing numbers of "volunteers" -- as many as 14,000 in 2000 -- have been working for AOL.[19] Their only reimbursement has been free use of AOL's programs instead of the monthly fee. The "volunteers" have such titles as AOL Live Typist, AOL Live Proofreader, AOL Online Tutor, AOL Database Monitor, AOL Online Promotions, and AOL Librarian. On behalf of these volunteers, attorney Leon Greenberg filed a class action lawsuit in May, 1999. AOL immediately laid off about 500 volunteers who it determined were under 18 years old. The suit was to be heard in a New York federal district court. Greenberg says the "volunteers" should be paid at least minimum wage, and points out that each one works at least ten hours a week.

Almost two years before the AOL-Time Warner merger, a *Fortune* reporter summarized Case's personality in a paragraph: "He's so, well, ordinary. Nothing about him says media mogul — he wears polo shirts and khakis, lunches on turkey sandwiches and Sun Chips, and has the boyish good looks of an aging fraternity brother. He's brainy but not in the 'out of the box' way prized by famous techies who launch their careers with nifty pieces of software or a breakthrough technology."[20]

In AOL's early days, he was shy and uncomfortable in big groups. But as the company grew and he found himself in more and more social situations, Case consciously remade himself. Ultimately, he learned how to initiate conversations and respond easily to those around him. "He pushed himself out front and made himself AOL personified."[21] At a White House dinner in the spring of 1999, President Clinton introduced him to Chinese Premier Zhu Rongji, adding with emphasis, "He's the head of America Online!"[22]

He was divorced in 1996 from his first wife, Joanne, with whom he had three children during 11 years. Now he lives with his second wife, Jean M. Villanueva, who worked in a Republican congressman's office during the 1980s, and who had become AOL's marketing vice president. Their two children have joined the three who remained with him after the divorce. In 1998, Case paid $2.2 million for a mansion outside Warrenton, in the Washington, D.C. area. In July, 2001, a *Forbes* list showed that his wealth had dropped from $1.5 billion to $1.4 billion.

His friendship with President Clinton fits in with his lobbying activities in Washington. Unlike Bill Gates and other cyberspace leaders who are hostile to the government, he maintains a lobbying staff in the capitol. Late in 1998, he spoke at the National Press Club.

After the merger with Time Warner, he spoke of the "Internet Century." In that century's infancy, he's making lots of money with the gigantic technology-and-profit-driven AOL and its new Time Warner partner.

MORTIMER ZUCKERMAN–THE BILLIONAIRE PUNDIT

27

Mortimer Zuckerman popped into the media billionaire class in 1998, listed by *Forbes* at $1 billion. The number rose to $1.2 billion in 1999 and stayed there in 2001. After amassing millions in real estate over a 15-year period, in 1980 he shifted his interests to publishing, where they have remained since.

First, he bought the venerable *Atlantic Monthly*. Four years later he bought the weekly *U.S. News & World Report*, for which he still writes a regular column. And in 1992 he took over the *New York Daily News*, a tabloid which competes with Rupert Murdoch's *New York Post*. More recently he launched *Fast Company*, a business magazine aimed at young readers, at first a by-monthly, but soon moved to monthly publication.

Controversy seems to dog Zuckerman, whether in real estate or publishing. At the *Atlantic*, *U.S. News* and *New York Daily News*, the problems stem mostly from his habit of changing editors often. This has been especially true at *U.S. News*, which had four editors in the five years after he bought it in 1984. "The *U.S. News* goes through editors the way Italy does governments or the Yankees do managers," commented *Forbes* in July, 1990.[1]

He was born in Montreal, Canada, June 4, 1937, the son of Jewish immigrants Abraham and Esther Zuckerman. His father was a tobacco and candy wholesaler. During childhood, Mortimer avidly read books and newspapers, including the *New York Times*, and even today often talks about his early interest in journalism. At Strathcona Academy in Montreal, he wrote in the yearbook that gossip columnist Walter Winchell was his role model. He found, as did other Jewish applicants to McGill University, that they had to score above gentiles to gain admission. Once in, he performed so well that he was elected president of the Skull & Bones honor society. He was only nineteen when he graduated with a degree in economics and political science. He stayed at McGill long enough to earn another degree — in law.

Then he moved to Boston and went to Harvard Law School for a master's degree in law. After that, it was on to Wharton School of Finance at the University of Pennsylvania for an MBA. Demonstrating his preference for business over law, he got his first job at the real estate firm, Cabot, Cabot & Forbes, where he quickly became chief financial officer. Zuckerman hoped to reach a wealth of $1 million by his 30th birthday; by his 32nd he had banked $5 million after winning a $4 million lawsuit against Cabot for his share of a deal he had helped broker.

He and another Cabot dealer, Edward Linde, left Cabot in 1969 to form Boston Properties. Within two years, Zuckerman ran into trouble with his proposal for a huge office-and-apartment complex beside Boston's Public Garden and the famed Boston Common. Public opposition led to downsizing the project by about a third. But after seven years of wrangling, Zuckerman backed away and the project was completed by another developer. Several years of fighting also led to his withdrawal from a project close to the famous Walden Pond.

While all this was going on, Zuckerman was an associate professor at the Harvard Graduate School of Design, where he taught city and regional planning from 1966 to 1974. During two years of this period, he taught the same subject as a visiting lecturer at Yale. He was still dealing in real estate and teaching at Harvard when he bought the *Atlantic Monthly* in 1980 at a cost of $3.6 million. Once again, only two months after taking control, he was caught in controversy when he fired the *Atlantic* editor, Robert Manning. Manning fought back in a suit settled out of court for an amount he claimed was $430,000. Another larger suit was brought by five *Atlantic* shareholders when Zuckerman refused to pay the second of four installments on the purchase price, arguing that he had been misled as to the property's value. When the court ruled that there had been an "unintentional breach of warranty," the cost of the magazine to Zuckerman was $2.6 million, a million less than the original amount.

In the meantime he replaced Manning with William Whitworth. By 1992 the circulation grew by 135,000 and advertising pages more than doubled. Moreover, the magazine won five National Magazine Awards. Whitworth was still editor in 1998, and had lasted longer than any of Zuckerman's other editors. But he was replaced in the fall of 1999, after Zuckerman sold the magazine for a reported $15 million to the National Journal Group, and David Bradley took over as publisher.

Only three years after buying the *Atlantic*, Zuckerman moved Boston Properties to New York, where he built a highrise office building, bringing *Atlantic* headquarters with him. Interested in expanding his holdings in media, in 1984 he found that with $182.5 million he could buy *U.S. News & World Report*, a newsweekly based on a Washington site where Boston Properties owned half of the land. Within seven months he had replaced editor Marvin Stone with Shelby Coffee, III, announced that he himself was editor-in-chief and started writing a regular column for inside the back page. Coffee resigned in less than a year because, he said, Zuckerman interfered too much in editorial decisions. His replacement, David Gergen, was in turn replaced by Roger Rosenblatt, who in 1989 resigned and was replaced by co-editors Michael Ruby and Merrill McLoughlin. Through all this, according to critics, the magazine gradually improved, with better and more analysis of national and foreign news and new interview features, so that in 1990 *Forbes* commented editorially that *U.S. News* "today is the most useful, readable newsweekly," adding that "Zuckerman has confounded the skeptics."[2] Zuckerman's column still alternates with those of at least two others, including David Gergen's. *U.S.News* sells 2.2 million copies a week and "stays in the black because of sales of its successful college guidebook."[3]

Zuckerman's name appeared again in mainstream headlines when he named James Fallows to edit *U.S. News* in April 1996, replacing Ruby and McLoughlin. Fallows, who had been an editor of the *Atlantic* and a ferocious critic of the broadcast news media, was fired 22 months later because of his failure to give more space to such stories as the Versace murder and the Northern Ireland peace plan. Fallows told reporters that he had disagreed with Zuckerman over a variety of budget cuts. His replacement was Stephen Smith, former editor at both *Time* and *Newsweek*. The Fallows furor revealed that Harold Evans had been named the "editorial director" of *all* Zuckerman publications. Evans, who claimed the credit -- or blame -- for Fallows' departure, had been Random House president before Bertelsmann took over the book giant. In the fall of 1999, Evans left Zuckerman's magazines to become CEO of GeoCities, a Web site now operated by Yahoo and to write two books.

When Zuckerman bought the *New York Daily News* for $36 million in 1992, observers remembered that the paper had enjoyed a long but checkered past. It was launched in 1919 by Captain Joseph Medill Patterson of the famous McCormick family in Chicago as a tabloid which tried to match England's great tabloids. Its audience was working class, largely immigrants, and by 1947 its Sunday circulation topped four million, the highest ever for an American newspaper. By the time Zuckerman bought the paper, the circulation was down to 800,000 daily and 1.1 million on Sunday, still high figures. Zuckerman moved the offices to the West Thirties from its historic 42nd Street home, and started a new printing plant in Jersey City, also to cut costs. Debby Krenek, mother of two, was editor-in-chief from the fall of 1997 until she was replaced in March, 2000, by Edward Kosner, who again threw the newsroom into turmoil. Kosner was the fifth Zuckerman editor at the *Daily News*.

The tabloid *New York Post* is the main competitor of the *Daily News*, and it is a typical Rupert Murdoch product. The *Post*'s history goes all the way back to 1803, when it was founded by Alexander Hamilton; like the *Daily News*, it has had a variety of owners. Murdoch brought editors from both England and Australia to show how a tabloid should be run. The *Post* is as far right as other Murdoch publications, and relies on celebrity and sensation for its main news. Murdoch is accused of buying it to increase his power and expand his empire. "In both its news columns and its editorials, the *Post* has energetically boosted Mayor Rudolph Giuliani. Murdoch's critics charge that multimillions in tax breaks and incentives have followed."[4] Zuckerman's *News* is "a hair to the left of center," according to a long article in the *New Yorker*, which added, "There's simply more news in the News, and that news is presented in a more balanced, less distorted manner."[5] Daily circulation at the *News* was 723,000 in late 1998, against 437,000 for the *Post*.

Ad sales for *U.S.News* dropped 23 percent in the spring of 2000, and the magazine had lost money in 1999. Then its Tokyo bureau was closed, and then there was speculation that the magazine might be sold. *Washingtonian* magazine said Zuckerman "wants to sell" his weekly. In April Zuckerman responded to the rumors, saying, "Not only do I not plan to sell it, I happen to love the process and the product . . . I'm going in the other direction."[6] He was adding business and investigative reporters to the staff. "Beyond profits, the magazine (*U.S.News*) pays Zuckerman a big psychic dividend by making him a popular current events pundit," a *USA Today* reporter noted, adding, "He holds the title of editor-in-chief, writes a column for the magazine and is a frequent guest at MSNBC, *Charlie Rose* and *The McLaughlin Group.*"[7]

Zuckerman was described in the 1990 *Current Biography* as "a slim, athletic man with dark, thinning hair and a hyperkinetic nature that keeps him in perpetual motion between New York and Washington to oversee his various business ventures."[8] Before his 1996 wedding to Marla Prather, a curator at the National Gallery of Art, he seemed to enjoy dating celebrity women. Among them were Diane von Furstenburg, Gail Strickland, Betty Rollin, Arianna Huffington, Nora Ephron and Gloria Steinem. He figures unfavorably in Steinem's book, *Revolution From Within*. In the book, Steinem "makes Zuckerman seem like every woman's nightmare: a selfish, self-absorbed lover."[9] Betty Rollin's book, *First You Cry*, asserts that after she had breast cancer, Zuckerman dropped her because she couldn't have children.[10] A daughter was born to Marla and Mortimer in 1997, but the couple reportedly separated in 2000.

The quality of all three of the publications he bought improved after he took them over. The *Daily News* won a Pulitzer in 1999 for a series of editorials, its third Pulitzer in four years. *Fast Company*, the monthly business publication he started in 1995, made a profit in 1998, ahead of predictions. In addition to its printed magazine version, *Fast Company* operates online with business news and analysis, as well as classified advertising. By 1999, its circulation had risen to 402,000, its profits went to $10 million in 1999 and were expected to hit $20 million in 2000.

But only five days before Christmas, 2000, the *Financial Times* reported that *Fast Company* had been sold to the magazine division of Gruner & Jahr, a part of the Bertelsmann conglomerate. The reported price was $450 million.[11] That left Zuckerman with his magazine, *U. S. News & World Report*, and a newspaper, the *New York Daily News*.

Brill's Content reported in September 2000 that while Zuckerman's partner Drasner still has a minority stake in both *U.S.News* and the *Daily News*, their close relationship has faltered. "Although Zuckerman tries to paint their breakup as amicable, he is clearly unhappy with Drasner."[12]

Zuckerman obviously takes his media properties seriously, and he says he spends a major part of his time with them, even though the largest part of his wealth still comes from real estate. Boston Properties and its Real Estate Investment Trust controls 116 office properties, mostly in northeast United States, but now including San Francisco's Embarcadero Center as well as two sites in New York's Times Square.[13]

When Rockefeller Center went up for sale in 2000, Boston Properties was one of four bidders. Aside from real estate and publications, Zuckerman and his partner Drasner have $165 million of stock in Applied Graphics Technologies, which prepares digital images for advertisers and publishers, and $270 million in Snyder Communications, a direct marketing operation.

He also enjoys his triplex on Fifth Avenue in New York, his vacation home in Aspen, a very large beach house in East Hampton, and his place in Georgetown, where he can oversee and write for his news weekly. Zuckerman likes to think of himself as a pundit. He knows he is a very successful real estate magnate. And he's clearly an eminent magazine and newspaper publisher. He wants to bring *U.S. News* into e-commerce.

He obviously loves the media and the opportunities he gets for punditry. He says, "I'm a nut about journalism. It's an irrational pursuit, but there you are."[14] When he introduced his three-year-old daughter to the *Daily News* newsroom, he said she would be the paper's next publisher, adding, "And frankly, it's a fabulous job."[15] At 63, as he looks for new fields to conquer, Zuckerman remains no stranger to controversy.

DONALD GRAHAM– POWERFUL AND CONSERVATIVE

28

Donald Graham, who now runs the *Washington Post* empire, was born rich.. His family differs from the other famous media families -- the Hearsts, Chandlers, Pulitzers and Scrippses -- in that his grandfather, the late patriarch Eugene Meyer, started the media empire with purchase of its seed corn -- the *Post* -- for a bargain price at an auction sale. He also differs from all the other press barons -- even the Sulzbergers of the *New York Times* -- in two ways. His paper is located in the capital of the wealthiest, most powerful country in the world. And he owns a top national newsmagazine, *Newsweek*. He shares a national news service with the *Los Angeles Times* (now owned by the *Chicago Tribune* empire) and a popular overseas paper, the *International Herald-Tribune*, with the Sulzbergers. To top it off , the Graham empire includes 53 cable systems and TV stations in five major market cities. His family's wealth was listed at $1.2 billion in October, 2000.

His mother, who died in July, 2001, was called "Katharine the Great" in a book by Deborah Davis, was born into great wealth and enjoyed its perks all her life.[1] Up to her death, she was still called one of the most powerful women in the country and "the doyenne of the capital's political and media elite."[2]

The *New York Times* obituary after her death at 84 said she had "transformed the *Washington Post* from a mediocre newspaper into an American institution and, in the process, transformed herself from a shy widow into a publishing legend."[3]

Her father, Eugene Meyer, born into a banker's family, was sent to Yale in 1893, where he enrolled in a double course load and graduated in two years. Within nine years he had bought a seat on the New York Stock Exchange and opened his own brokerage, Eugene Meyer & Co. In 1910, he courted and married Agnes Ernst, a friend and admirer of modern artists in both France and America.

In 1918, he became director of the War Finance Corporation, formed to provide loans to World War I industries, beginning what became a long career of government service. This move was also part of his life plan. Meantime his wealth grew steadily, totaling $60 million by 1931. Early in the Great Depression, he bought the *Washington Post* at an auction for $825,000.

Of Agnes and Eugene's five children, Katharine was fourth, born June 16, 1917. She grew up in a household staffed with 12 servants, but was mostly ignored by her mother. Agnes Meyer was over the years a close friend to such famous people as Thomas Mann, Gertrude Stein, Madame Curie and John Dewey, and enjoyed frequent trips to Europe. The family had a big house in Washington and a summer home in Mount Kisco. Katharine went to Madeira girls prep school in Washington. In 1934 she went off to Vassar where, as a sophomore, she took part in founding the liberal American Student Union.

After an active sophomore year at Vassar, leading anti-war demonstrations and supporting New Deal legislation, Katharine decided to switch to the University of Chicago because it had launched an interdisciplinary program which sounded attractive. At Chicago, the tall, bright young woman with curly black hair continued her political activism but began to concentrate more on studies, especially her history major. After graduation she went to work on the *San Francisco Daily News* in a job arranged by her father, but soon came home because her father wanted her to work at the *Post.*

By now she was 22. At her sister Ruth's debutante party, she met Philip Graham, then a clerk for Supreme Court Justice Stanley Reed. He had graduated from Harvard Law School where he was editor of the prestigious *Law Review.* She was quickly attracted to the bright, handsome, outgoing Graham After only a few dates, Phil asked the attractive Katharine to marry him, at the same time warning that they would have to live on his earnings. She readily agreed and they were married in June, 1940. In her autobiography, she wrote that in the period after their wedding, "Phil and I had a very happy time," and added that he cemented relations with both her parents.[4] She lost their first baby, a boy, at birth.

When America went to war more than a year and a half after their wedding, Philip joined Air Force Intelligence and went to the Pacific, where he helped provide information for General MacArthur's two great victories in the Philippines. He was commissioned and won the Legion of Merit award.

Their second child, conceived during one of Phil's home leaves, was born in July, 1943, and named Elizabeth. She was nicknamed "Lally." In April, 1945, Donald Edward, also conceived while Phil was in service, was born. William Graham came in April, 1948. After a miscarriage in 1951, Katharine bore their fifth and last child, Stephen, in April, 1952.

Philip was back home by the fall of 1945, and in January 1946, Eugene Meyer brought him to the *Post* as publisher. Only six months later Meyer became head of the newly formed World Bank and left the paper entirely in Phil's charge. It soon became clear that Phil was an excellent newspaperman, and so Meyer gave complete ownership of the paper to the couple in 1948, with Phil getting 70 percent of the voting stock and Katharine 30 percent. She didn't mind the unequal division. She adored Phil and considered her job to be that of hostess and homemaker.

Six years after Phil took control, he worked with Meyer to pay $8.5 million for the *Washington Times-Herald*, which had been owned by the McCormick family and which they quickly closed down. Circulation of the *Post*, both daily and Sunday, almost doubled overnight. Some of Phil's friendships and his own background in Air Force Intelligence led to information exchanges between the *Post* and Central Intelligence Agency. CIA officials were often dinner guests at the Graham home. One of Graham's best friends was Frank Wisner, a CIA official.

Graham's political power was clearly growing. As a price for burying coverage of a Washington race riot in 1949, authorities agreed to integrate the city's swimming pools. Phil also wrote speeches for Lyndon Johnson and at the 1960 Democratic convention helped persuade Kennedy to choose Johnson as his running mate.

Katharine noticed that, increasingly, Phil's behavior alternated between intense activity and passivity. She also noticed his stepped-up consumption of alcohol. The six-year downhill slide that led to Phil's suicide began in October 1957, soon after passage of Senator Lyndon Johnson's Civil Rights Act. Graham had worked strenuously for the new law. One night that fall he suddenly woke up and began to cry, complaining of pains all over his body. Katharine stayed with him through the night and he gradually recovered. When she urged him to see a psychiatrist, he went to Dr. Leslie Farber, chairman of the Washington School of Psychiatry faculty, who opposed all use of drugs. It was more than 20 years before the drug lithium was prescribed for Ted Turner's manic depression. In her autobiography, Katharine Graham writes, "I didn't hear the term 'manic depression' until some years later."[5]

Phil stayed home most of the next year, recovering slowly. He still conducted some *Post* business, but it was mostly by telephone and memos. He saw no conflict of interest in political activism with officials on issues about which the *Post* reported and editorialized

Phil competed with other buyers who wanted to have *Newsweek* magazine, and he got it from the Astor family for $9 million in March, 1961. During the negotiations, Katharine withheld from Phil the news that she had been diagnosed with tuberculosis. The illness had been found early, and after six weeks in bed, she was cured. In 1962 Graham joined Otis Chandler in forming the *Los Angeles Times-Washington Post News Service*, a syndicated operation which gives subscribers access to both foreign correspondents and Washington reporters.

In late fall, he flew to Paris for a meeting about the Communications Satellite Corporation, to which President Kennedy had appointed him as chairman. Soon after arriving, he wrote a letter to CBS President Frank Stanton urging him to become a COMSAT official. Considering the message urgent, Graham arranged for a *Newsweek* reporter to fly to New York to hand-deliver it to Stanton. The letter carrier was Robin Webb, a young Australian who had just started to work for the magazine. She became Phil's lover.

The love affair was the beginning of events which speeded up the ultimate suicide. He took Robin with him almost everywhere. At one point he told Katharine that he wanted a divorce so he could marry Robin. Now Katharine began for the first time to think of herself as one who might take charge at the *Post*.

Graham went to London for a meeting of *Newsweek* correspondents in May of

1963, and while there spoke of journalism as "the first rough draft of history." He and Robin flew back and went on to Puerto Rico. He returned to New York clearly depressed. In mid-June he told Dr. Farber that his affair with Robin was over, adding that he wanted to go back to Katharine. When he did, she persuaded him to return to Chestnut Lodge. She had just learned about manic depression and realized that this was his condition. After he had been at Chestnut Lodge a few days, he talked the doctors into letting him go to Glen Welby for a weekend. All seemed well when he and Katharine got there. But after a quiet lunch, while Katharine took a nap, Phil quietly went downstairs and shot himself in the head.

Even before the funeral a few days later, Katharine met with the *Post* board of directors. She assured them that the paper would stay in her hands, "a family operation." Within a month she was elected president of the board. She had been involved in affairs of the paper since her father had bought it 32 years earlier; they had talked about problems of the news and business ends frequently. The transformation of the shy, soft, withdrawn wife to the shrewd, confident, forceful -- but always polite -- businesswoman was rapid after Graham's death. At first she sat quietly in editorial meetings, then began to ask questions and ultimately to make comments. Thirty years later she told Nicholas Coleridge that while she was once shy, "I've to a large extent overcome it because I've lived this life for such a long time."[6] During her long tenure, the analogy to Catherine the Great, who ruled Russia for 34 years after her husband's death, began to emerge.

She backed away from the kind of personal involvement in the government that had characterized Phil Graham's management. She continued to attend dinners at the White House and to host government officials, including Oval Office occupants, but made no effort to use personal influence on federal policy. That became important to her as she made speeches on press issues.

Until his death, the paper had been Philip Graham's tool. He had done wonders with it, the circulation had thrived, but it did not rank with the *New York Times* or *Los Angeles Times*. "Under Phil Graham, the *Post* had a well-respected editorial page and mediocrity nearly everywhere else," according to David Remnick in the *New Yorker*.[7] It had never won a Pulitzer Prize.

It took about a year for Katharine to begin a makeover of the paper. She started with Al Friendly, who had been managing editor since 1955. He was transferred to a job as London correspondent. Over lunch, Katharine met with Ben Bradlee, then head of *Newsweek's* Washington bureau. When she asked if he would like to be managing editor of the *Post*, his reply later became famous: "I'd give my left one for it." She gave him an interim appointment as deputy managing editor for six months, after which he took over Friendly's job as executive editor. Bradlee quickly got Katharine's agreement to enlarge the newsroom staff with young reporters and to build a larger foreign service. Before long the newsroom numbers were doubled. The quality of the paper began to climb.

Three years after Philip Graham's death, Katharine's friend Truman Capote decided that she needed more social exposure. So he organized what became famous as the Black and White Ball in a major New York hotel. Invited were celebrities from the worlds of movies, politics, broadcasting and publishing. Three months later

Vogue ran a warm profile of Katharine by her friend Arthur Schlesinger. The same year, 1966, her young son Donald enlisted in the army to demonstrate his support for U.S. involvement in Vietnam. After only a week in the embattled country, Don joined the growing number of Americans who believed the war was a mistake. Meantime his younger brother Bill was at home taking part in anti-war demonstrations. Yet the *Post* continued to support both President Johnson and the war.

In 1967, Philip Geyelin left the *Wall Street Journal* to become editor of the *Post* editorial page. Before he started, however, he had long discussions with Katharine about his discomfort over the paper's pro-war position. Result: during the next half-year, with Katharine's blessing, Geyelin's editorials gradually distanced the *Post* from both Johnson and the war. But as David Remnick says, "the *Post* performance (on Vietnam) was nearly an embarrassment."[8]

Both Presidents Kennedy and Johnson had dined at Katharine's home, but Nixon refused to come and ordered his staff to stay away. Now she was staying scrupulously out of newsroom matters, leaving reporters and editors to make decisions on what to cover.

Equal opportunity law suits were filed at *Newsweek* by women staff members who were limited to research and never given writing or editing assignments. The first suit, in 1970, was settled out of court. Two years later, a second similar suit led to a commitment for hiring quotas. Ultimately, Katharine Graham became a feminist and helped finance Gloria Steinem's MS magazine.

Early in 1971, Katharine was persuaded to put *Post* stock on Wall Street in a program that kept the company under family control. Two days before the initial stock sale, the *Post* ran the first installment of what came to be known as the Pentagon Papers. The *New York Times* staff had obtained the papers from a then-obscure official named Daniel Ellsberg and had gone through thousands of pages to prepare their own series. They had published only two installments when Nixon officials got an injunction to halt further printing. Ben Bagdikian, then the *Post* assistant managing editor for national news, went to Boston, met Ellsberg and got a cardboard box full of disorganized papers, bringing them back to Washington. At Ben Bradlee's house, a group of reporters joined in sorting out the more than 5,400 pages. Chalmers Roberts wrote the story. Despite the fierce opposition of *Post* lawyers, Katharine Graham gave permission to publish the first of a series in the next edition. She did this knowing that the *Post* stock was about to go on the Wall Street market.

That was June 17, 1971. The Nixon administration immediately went to court to halt the series. The cases of both the *New York Times* and *Washington Post* worked their way rapidly through the courts until the U.S. Supreme Court ruled on June 30 that both papers could complete publication of their Pentagon Papers series. Now, as Bradlee said, the world would "refer to the *Post* and *New York Times* in the same breath."[9]

The Pentagon Papers story, Katharine Graham later said, "prepared us for Watergate."[10] The break-in at the Democratic National Committee office took place in the Watergate complex in June of 1972, a year after the Pentagon Papers story. The two young reporters assigned to the story were Bob Woodward and Carl

Bernstein. Katharine didn't meet with the pair until they had worked on the story seven months. By then, Woodward had begun to refer to his informant as "Deep Throat" and she asked for his identity, then hastily withdrew the request. In the course of his investigations, Bernstein picked up a report that a secret Republican program, headed by former Attorney General John Mitchell, was trying to dig up information on the Democrats. For comment on the report, Bernstein called Mitchell. An angry Mitchell shouted into the phone that "Katie Graham is gonna get her tits caught in a big fat wringer if that's published."[11] It was published, along with a carefully edited version of the Mitchell quote.

By mid-September, the five burglars had been indicted along with E. Howard Hunt and Gordon Liddy, both former aides in the Nixon White House. Meantime, Nixon had been making a variety of threats to the *Post*. Despite the stories in the *Post* and on CBS, Nixon was reelected.

At the end of 1972, renewal of licenses for the two *Post*-owned stations — one in Jacksonville, one in Miami -- in Florida were challenged. At least two of the challenging companies involved friends and supporters of Nixon -- George Champion, Ed Bell and Glen Sedam. It took more than two years and a million dollars in legal fees to fight the challenges, but the licenses were renewed after Nixon's resignation.

Liddy and McCord were convicted in late January 1973. By then the five burglars had all pleaded guilty to the charges against them. Nixon had barely started his second term when the Senate voted to investigate Watergate.

Events followed rapidly. In May, the *Washington Post* won a Pulitzer Prize for its Watergate reporting. Impeachment proceedings against Nixon were started before the House Judiciary Committee. Vice President Spiro Agnew resigned in October 1973 after pleading no contest to a charge of income tax evasion and Gerald Ford became Vice President. In February, 1974, the House voted 410 to 4 to go ahead with the impeachment process. During the last three days of July, the House Judiciary Committee approved three articles of impeachment. Nine days later, Nixon announced his resignation on television.

All the President's Men, the book by Woodward and Bernstein about these events, became the title of a movie starring Robert Redford. Katharine Graham later wrote, "I loved the movie."[12] In her autobiography, she says, "Watergate was the transforming event in the life of the *Washington Post* — as it was for many of us at the paper and throughout journalism."[13]

During the Watergate period, the already-famous investor Warren Buffett had written to Katharine to tell her that his Berkshire Hathaway company had bought 230,000 shares of class B stock in the *Post* company and planned to buy more. He told her about his early purchase of Walt Disney stock and also mentioned his ownership of Sun Newspapers (weekly) in the Omaha area. She met Buffett the following summer in Los Angeles. By September 1973 his *Post* holdings had climbed to 410,000 shares. In September 1974, Buffett and Donald Graham went onto the *Post* board of directors. Buffett left the board in 1985 when ABC was merged — with his help -- with Capital Cities and he went onto the ABC/Cap Cities board. But he was to return to the *Post* board after the Disney merger with ABC/Cap Cities 10 years later. His Berkshire Hathaway owns the largest single block of *Post* stock outside the Graham family — 16 percent. Katharine and Buffett have been good friends since they met in the 1970s, and he stays at her house when he is in Washington.

Katharine Graham had what she considered serious problems with the unions whose members produced the *Post*. There was a printers walkout in 1973 caused by the firing of a printer for failing to work during an eight-hour shift. The pressmen supported the printers, and management had to take the fired printer back. A Newspaper Guild strike in early 1974 was settled after two weeks. But the *Post's* union troubles exploded in a major way in October 1975, when a pressmen's strike erupted with serious damage to nine presses. Most Guild members continued to work and the paper was printed at other plants during the two weeks it took to repair the presses. A final settlement offer by *Post* management was rejected December 10, after which the management began to hire non-union workers. In the end, the strike was broken. One by one, members of the other craft unions returned to work.

Fourteen years later, the Graham paper was called "The Union Busting *Post*" in an article by John Hanrahan, executive director of the Fund for Investigative Journalism, who had worked for the *Post* for eight years. The eight-page piece appeared in the liberal *Progressive* magazine, edited by Erwin Knoll, who had also worked at the *Post*.[14] Hanrahan quoted labor reporter A. H. Raskin of the *New York Times*, who charged in 1987 that the *Post* had "turned the clock back to the long-discredited tactics of the take-it-or-leave-it era of management authoritarianism." Hanrahan added that the "swing to the right in labor relations had been marked by a corresponding rise in conservatism in *Post* editorials and on the op-ed pages."[15]

Katharine Graham in the years after Watergate "committed herself more and more to profit, to winning Wall Street's approval," according to David Halberstam in his book, *The Powers That Be*, about Bill Paley of CBS, Henry Luce of *Time* magazine, the Chandlers of the *Los Angeles Times*, the Sulzbergers of the *New York Times*, and the Grahams of the *Washington Post*.[16] She was quoted frequently as expecting 15 percent profit, and defending that number as a minimum. During her nearly 30 years in control until she stepped down as chief executive in 1991, *Post* Company revenues rose from $84 million to $1.4 billion.

After Watergate, the higher profits were rolling in from all the *Post* properties. When *Fortune* magazine elected Katharine Graham to its National Business Hall of Fame in April, 1993, a share of *Post* stock bought in 1971 for $6.50 was selling at $230.[17] All the cable systems had been bought at once in 1985, at Warren Buffett's urging, for $350 million, from Capital Cities Communications. .

"During the 1980s, profits in several sectors of the company were spectacular — a profit margin of 39 percent for the TV stations in the middle of the decade," Carol Felsenthal wrote in 1993.[18] And she went on, "but profits at the *Post*, which contributes about half of the company's profits and sales, gave new meaning to Warren Buffett's assertion that a monopoly newspaper is like an 'unregulated toll booth.' The *Post* enjoyed profits four times higher than the national average for newspapers."

Nothing tells more about her relationship to the wealthy and powerful than the roster of attendees at Katharine's 70th birthday party in June, 1987. She asked her daughter Lally, who organized the event, to invite only her "friends." Felsenthal describes the affair: "At dinner, she sat between the President (Reagan) and Secretary of State George Schultz. Also in attendance were justices of the Supreme Court, senators, ambassadors from several countries, the heads of Sony, IBM, Ford, General Motors, Dow Jones. Among the others were Oscar de la Renta, Malcolm Forbes, Rupert Murdoch, Otis Chandler, William Paley, Punch Sulzberger, Barbara Walters, Ted Koppel, H. Ross Perot, Warren Buffett, Helmut Kohl, former British prime minister James Callahan, Israeli Prime Minister Itzak Rabin, I.M.Pei, Jack Valenti, Clare Booth Luce, Brooke Astor, Ethel Kennedy and Gordon Getty."[19] Toasts were made by Art Buchwald, George Will, Mike Wallace and, finally, President Reagan.

The range of "friends" at the birthday party was a good indication of how important celebrities and powerful people were to Katharine Graham. That is a underlying theme that runs through her 625-page autobiography. Publication of her book led to many reviews and articles in magazines. One, by Sally Quinn, Ben Bradlee's wife and a *Post* columnist, was titled "Katharine the Great" and appeared in *Vanity Fair.*[20] Another longer and even more complimentary review appeared in *Vogue* the same month. The book won a Pulitzer Prize for biography.

Donald Graham was only 31 when he became general manager of the *Post* in 1976. Three years later he became publisher as Katharine took on the title of chief executive officer, a post which she held until her final retirement in 1991. Donald has a markedly different personality and management style than his mother had. After services in Vietnam and on Washington's police force, Donald had worked through a *Post* job program similar to those of Otis Chandler at the *Los Angeles Times* and Punch Sulzberger at the *New York Times*. He stayed in most departments long enough to understand their operations. He had also completed an executive management program at Stanford University; as a result, he now tends to pick financial officers for the empire with MBAs from prestigious universities. The *Post* vice president and controller since 1984 is Margaret Schiff, an MBA at George Washington University; Alan Spoon, vice president for finance, got a master's degree at MIT Management School.[21]

In 1967, Don married Mary Wissler, a graduate of Radcliffe who had gone to the New York University law school. She had worked with him on the Harvard *Crimson*. Very little is said about her in the many books about the Graham family and the *Post*. She is clearly a very private person. While Don says he grew up in a household where conversation was always about Washington politics and personalities, in his home that's not the case, according to David Remnick in the *New Yorker*.[22] He and Mary don't entertain as often as Katharine did. He spends a lot of time with his family, and likes to read, garden and play tennis. Of Don, Remnick says, "His temperament, his interests, and his style are quite different from his mother's."[23] And he adds that Don's "friends are, for the most part, not especially famous."

When he came into control of the *Washington Post*, Don chose a long-time staff member, Leonard Downie Jr., to be executive editor. Both have a great interest in news of Washington and its suburbs, and both are private, family men. In 1993 he said the most important thing he had done as publisher was to name two key editors -- Meg Greenfield to control the editorial pages and Downie to succeed Bradlee as executive editor.

That the *Post* management no longer considers the paper liberal is attested by both its contents and a telling statement by Don. During the Reagan 1980s, long-time liberal Joseph Rauh submitted a comment about a presidential appointment for the op-ed page. When it was rejected, he was invited to an editorial board meeting. After the session, Don told Rauh, "You have to remember one thing. This is not the liberal paper you remember."[24]

He has pushed for and succeeded in the hiring of blacks in both the newsroom and advertising. There are now many more than there were before his ascent to power. But he is barely mentioned in Jill Nelson's account of her four and a half years as a *Post* reporter, starting in 1986. In *Voluntary Slavery*, the African-American Nelson writes critically about how many of her stories were either heavily edited or not printed at all.[25]

After looking closely at *Post* contents in 1995, Amy Waldman wrote in *Washington Monthly* that "On economic issues, the *Post* is far from a gadfly — because it is not liberal."[26] She called attention to Robert Samuelson and Jay Matthews, both conservative, who "play critical roles" in coverage of the economy and business. And she compared the handling of stories about the 1995 transgressions by Squibb, DuPont and Maytag, which were buried inside *Post* pages with the front page coverage of both the *Wall Street Journal* and *New York Times*. The *Post's* own media critic, Howard Kurtz, was quoted by Waldman as saying, "I'm often amazed how significant wrong-doing by corporations is not always treated as a page-one story."[27] Consumer-friendly reporter Morton Mintz retired in 1988. Since then, wrote Waldman, much "of the business coverage serves as a press-release based bulletin board for company profits, mergers, and personnel moves."

Katharine Graham at age 80 was the only woman in a two-page picture spread in the July, 1997 *Vanity Fair*, showing 23 members of "The New Establishment" at an annual meeting of powerful media people in Sun Valley, Idaho. Others in the picture included such media moguls as Rupert Murdoch, Bill Gates, Warren Buffett and John Malone.[28] It was during this group's 2001 meeting at Sun Valley that she suffered the fall that led to her death.

In his 1977 book about the first 100 years of the *Post*, long-time staffer Chalmers Roberts wrote that "Today, a *Post* editor, reporter or editorial writer can move a President or the Congress, influence the courts, cleanse a regulatory agency, affect elections, protect the public in myriad ways."[29] Roberts updated the book 12 years later under a new title, and he used the same sentence in his conclusion. While that might exaggerate the situation today, it is still close to the mark.

Nicholas Coleridge, in his 1993 *Paper Tigers* wrote, "As a newspaper property, the *Post* scores high with all three criteria: reputation for strong journalism, consistent profits, and the unquantifiable element of swank and consequence."[30] More critical is the comment of biographer Tom Kelly that Don Graham "can, perhaps, in time, with luck and persistence, make it what it has always claimed to be -- complete, accurate, well-written, well-edited, and fair. It has been most of these things, here and there, now and then, but never all of them at once."[31]

What Kelly wrote in 1983 seems still to be true today. Donald Graham, whose eyes are always focused on the bottom line, is still quite conservative — and more and more powerful.

PULITZER FAMILY–
THEY'RE NOT CRUSADERS LIKE JOSEPH PULITZER WAS

29

The name Pulitzer is familiar to most of us because it's attached to all those awards in journalism, literature and music. The first Joseph Pulitzer set up the awards program shortly before his death in 1911. Nine years earlier, he gave $2 million to Columbia University to create the country's first graduate school of journalism.

More than 20 years after his death, a 1934 poll of American editors named Pulitzer as the greatest editor of modern times, even though E. W. Scripps had died only eight years earlier and W. R. Hearst was still very much alive. The legacy he left was two papers - the *New York World*, now long dead, and the *St. Louis Post-Dispatch*, now run by fourth generation Michael Pulitzer for the family, whose wealth comes to $1.2 billion. But the crusading spirit of the original Joseph Pulitzer is gone. Forgotten in the P-D news and editorial rooms is the masthead admonition of 1907: "Always oppose privileged classes and public plunderers."

There have been four generations of Joseph Pulitzers but the last one, Joseph Pulitzer IV, has made it clear that he's not interested in his family's paper. Ed Bishop, editor of the *St. Louis Journalism Review*, says the fourth Joseph Pulitzer was "bought out" by the family in the mid-'90s when Pulitzer Publishing Company was made public.[1] His father died in 1993.

Michael Pulitzer, who was both chairman and CEO from 1993 to 1998, is now chairman. Robert C. Woodworth is president and CEO, and Terrance C. Z. Egger is publisher. Michael announced plans to retire from the chairmanship in June, 2001, staying on as "senior advisor." Nicholas Penniman IV, a BMA type, manages the business side of the newspaper group. Emily Pulitzer, widow of Joseph Pulitzer III, visits the newsroom regularly. She is providing the funds for a $17 million building to house the valuable paintings collected by her husband, including works by Picasso, Rodin, Modigliani, Warhol and Monet. The building will be open to the public.

In recent years the empire has been dramatically reorganized. First, it bought 16 papers from the Scripps League for $230 million in 1996. Mostly in the West and Midwest, the papers range in circulation from 13,000 in Flagstaff to 32,500 in Provo, Utah. Then in 1998 the company sold all its broadcast properties -- nine TV stations and five radio stations -- to Hearst-Argyle, a subsidiary of the Hearst empire. At about the same time, Penniman announced a new "strategy to concentrate on small and medium-sized papers."

The handover of broadcast properties was complicated but it accomplished three things: it cleared Pulitzer books of debt; it gave Pulitzer shareholders a substantial stake in Hearst-Argyle stock; and it gave the Pulitzer empire $450 million in cash. It also meant that the Pulitzers still have a major financial interest in broadcasting. Because of the $1.15 billion in Hearst-Argyle shares taken in by the Pulitzers, Michael Pulitzer and Ken Elkins, who had run the TV and radio stations, went onto the Hearst-Argyle board. There was irony in this for journalists who recalled the history of Pulitzer's *World* and Hearst's *Journal*, with their fierce competition in New York City in the 1890s and into the 20th century.

The Pulitzer Company now operates only two major papers — the *St. Louis Post-Dispatch* -- and *the Arizona Daily Star* in Tucson. In 1999, it bought the Bloomington, Illinois, *Pantagraph*, and seven community papers in central Illinois, for $180 million. That brought the total number of Pulitzer dailies to twenty. But the family is still clearly focused on its St. Louis paper, where the empire was started.

The *Post-Dispatch*, founded by the original Joseph Pulitzer in 1878, has had a bumpy ride, especially since William Woo, the first non-Pulitzer to be editor, was pushed out in March, 1996. Circulation had declined and the crusading spirit of the founder had disappeared. It's now more than 40 years since the paper has won a Pulitzer Prize for reporting.

The struggle for increased circulation has meant reaching for readers in surrounding municipalities, as well as inside St. Louis with its 49 percent African-American population. An attempt to introduce "public journalism," which calls for deeper involvement of the staff in the community, was started in 1997. It was one of many efforts to seek better reporting and increased circulation, according to Professor J.T. Johnson, who tried to involve the company more in the digital revolution during a 15-month period in 1997-1998. The San Francisco State University faculty member left, he says, for a variety of reasons. "The Pulitzer executive team doesn't understand the full impact of the digital revolution," he says.[2] "The corporation is much like that of the 1940s," he adds.

Early in 2000, Ed Bishop, editor of the *St. Louis Journalism Review*, commented that "the *Post* editors have created an atmosphere . . . where the newspaper's image is far more important than news, where corporate agendas are made to appear as if they were civic agendas, and where 'groupthink' has become a byword for leadership."[3]

Bishop was writing about the era of "public journalism" which had started in October, 1997, when publisher Michael Pulitzer brought in Cole Campbell as editor. Campbell introduced "public journalism," a reform concept that calls for readers to become involved in the making of news decisions, to the *Post-Dispatch*. Strongly supported by the staff at first, reporters gradually lost interest. "Campbell spoke in New Age jargon that many found difficult to grasp," a report on the Campbell era said in the *American Journalism Review*.[4] "Editorial writing, Washington reporting, design and online enterprise improved. Investigative reporting also thrived. . . But day in and day out, according to interviews with numerous *Post-Dispatch* staffers, many felt the paper wasn't covering the news as well as it could and should." The staff also got tired of the overly frequent meetings.

Staffers unloaded their grievances on publisher Terry Egger in a bar one evening, pointing out that many reporters and editors had left because of Campbell. Less than two weeks later, Campbell resigned in April, 2000.

Here we need to jump back more than a century for a brief review of the Pulitzer story. The first Joseph came to America from Hungary in 1864 and soon joined the Union Army, staying until he was mustered out at war's end in 1865. He went to St. Louis, became a citizen in 1867, served briefly as editor of a German language paper and then bought another German language paper. It had an Associated Press franchise, which he sold for enough to buy both the *Post* and the *Dispatch*, which he quickly merged.

He bought the *New York World* while he and his wife were on the way to Europe for a vacation in 1882 and settled in to build his new paper, using the same approaches he had used in St. Louis, all intended to appeal to working class readers. The *World's* story is marked by dramatic circulation increases coming from sensational news treatment, crusading for the rights of workers and the poor, and introduction of the "Yellow Kid" comic strip. When Hearst took over the *Journal*, he also snatched the "Yellow Kid" cartoonist. Soon both papers were called the "Yellow Press" to mark their sensationalism.

By 1890 Pulitzer had not only gone blind, but his health had deteriorated so seriously that he announced his "retirement." Now he began 21 years of sailing on private yachts all over the world, with at least two secretaries reading aloud the latest editions of his New York and St. Louis papers. Before the end of the Spanish-American war in 1900, Pulitzer had ordered the *World's* jingoism and sensationalism to stop.

As the country moved into the new century, the term "people's champions" was being used to describe the papers of both Pulitzer and Edward Wyllis Scripps, who was gaining ground in the Midwest. Although the *New York World* declined after Pulitzer's death in 1911, and died in 1931, the *Post-Dispatch* continued to flourish under the editorship of Joseph Pulitzer II. The paper itself won five Pulitzer awards and staff members won six more. The *New York Times* obituary when the second Joseph Pulitzer died in 1955 said he had "carried on the policy of militant journalism of his father . . . noted for his crusades against crime and injustice."[5]

Joseph Pulitzer III came into power on the death of his father and remained editor and publisher until his retirement in 1986. At that point, the first non-Pulitzer, William Woo, was named editor of the *Post-Dispatch* and he held that post for ten years. Joining Joseph Pulitzer III as chief overseer of the paper was his brother Michael, an attorney who had worked as a reporter in both St. Louis and the

Washington bureau. Joseph III held the title of board chairman until his death in 1993. Michael Pulitzer was both publisher and CEO from 1993 until 1998, and then chairman until his June, 2001, retirement. Just before his retirement, the company launched a Web site, STLtoday.com, to offer an array of news and information.

The billionaire family continues to enjoy good returns. Former editor Woo says, "The editor is no longer the dominant person; he is subordinate to a business person.[6] Bishop adds that "since it went public, the stockholders have had influence."[7]

In a study of "The State of the American Newspaper," Carl Sessions Stepp wrote that by 1999, "the *Post-Dispatch* was far more pleasing visually (than in 1964), with a larger newshole and more sports, business and features. Reader service material, almost unknown in the '60s, was plentiful."[8] He also revealed that *Post* circulation had dropped from 345,000 in 1964 to 312,000 in 1999.

But the era of public journalism ended in December, 2000, when Cole Campbell was replaced by a traditional editor, Ellen Soeteber, who had been managing editor of the *Sun-Sentinel* at Ft. Lauderdale, Florida. Ed Bishop of the *St. Louis Journalism Review* commented, "After three and a half years of goofy experimentation, endless reorganization and constant staff meetings, after years of declining circulation and poor news quality . . . former Editor Cole Campbell was sent packing."[9]

The income from the Pulitzer empire is still good, but the family can't be happy about a Joint Operating Agreement made by Joseph Pulitzer III with Sam Newhouse in the 1960s. Newhouse owned the *St. Louis Globe-Democrat*, and the JOA called for an even split of profits from both papers. That agreement gave $177 million to the Newhouses in the 14 years up to 2000, when a new kind of joint venture was signed, under which the Pulitzers own 95 percent. The agreement called for a $306 million payment to the Newhouses right away, and another payment to be agreed upon when the joint venture finally ends in 2015.

The Pulitzer enterprise is today run as a bottom line business. Members of the family enjoy handsome incomes that increase every year. The crusading spirit of the first Joseph Pulitzer has been lost along with much of the *Post-Dispatch's* quality journalism.

ROY E. DISNEY–
HE WORKS IN ANIMATION, JUST LIKE HIS UNCLE WALT

30

Roy E. Disney, nephew of Walt Disney, has been listed in the *Forbes 400* since 1982. But he didn't join the billionaires club until the year 2000, when his net worth was listed at $1.1 billion. He was responsible for the new *Fantasia* in 2000. Now he's vice chairman of the vast Disney empire..

Currently in charge of animation productions at Disney Studios, Roy E. has worked at Disney for more than 30 years; he has played a major role in the business even longer. Starting in 1953, he worked at various jobs for Walt Disney Productions, most notably the *Dragnet* series on TV. As assistant director of films, he was involved in a number of movies, including Academy Award winners *The Living Desert* and *The Vanishing Prairie*.

After his uncle Walt died in 1966, Roy E. was one of a committee advising his father, Roy O. Disney, who was put in charge of the studio. From the beginning, Roy O., Walt's older brother, had been important to Walt's projects. In 1924, the two opened a store in Hollywood with the sign "Disney Bros. Studio." In 1941, Roy O. became president of Walt Disney Productions. Roy O. died in 1971, and after a fractious period, Card Walker was appointed president of Walt Disney Productions, and Ron Miller, husband of Walt Disney's daughter Diane, was put in charge of motion picture production. Miller and Roy E. Disney shared a dislike for each other. By 1977, Roy E. had become so unhappy about working with Miller that he resigned as vice president. However, "While no longer active in day-to-day operations of the studio, he was still the company's largest shareholder."[1] When Roy E. left, the well-known animator Don Bluth also left, and many other animators followed.

During the years away from Disney — he returned in 1984 — Roy E. organized his Shamrock Holdings Inc., based in Burbank, which now owns a number of TV and radio stations as well as real estate, a chain of Los Angeles music stores and

Sound Warehouse, a chain of home entertainment stores in the central and south-west U.S.. In 2000, Shamrock bought a major share in the New Central Bus Station complex in Tel Aviv. Its other investments in Israel include Gilat Communications and Taderan Communications. It also bought an $11 million stake in Open Mobile Corp. in Scandinavia. The *Los Angeles Times* said, "The company (Shamrock) is building a global platform for mobile communications."[2] In late 2000, it bought a half-interest in cellular phone provider Pelephone Communications for $593 million.

The Disney studio performed poorly during the years he was away. Moreover, there were troubles in the construction of the Epcot Center project near Orlando, Florida, which had been conceived by Walt Disney before he died. During this peri-od, Roy Disney's holdings in Disney Studios dropped in value from $80 million to $40 million.

However, all that changed in 1984, when Roy E. helped bring Michael Eisner into management of Disney Studios. "Eisner, who knew Roy E. personally — both happened to be board members of Cal-Arts — called him rather than (Ron) Miller to explore the possibility of joining the studio."[3] When , in June 1984, the Disney stock plummeted, Roy E. joined Walt Disney's widow, Lillian, in ousting Ron Miller, the president during the years of decline. Roy E. was then brought back to the board. "The studio was finally back in the hands of a blood Disney," a biogra-pher of Walt Disney comments.[4]

A few months later, the board appointed Eisner and his long-time associate, Frank Wells, to head Walt Disney Productions. Disney output in both film and TV soon began to improve dramatically. Among other actions, Eisner "mandated a return to the studio's glory days of animation, beginning with the revival of a proj-ect that had languished for years under Ron Miller, *Who Framed Roger Rabbit?*"[5] And of course, animation was where Roy E. Disney wanted to work. By 1988, only four years after Eisner's arrival, the studio grossed more than $1 billion.

When Roy E. returned to the Disney studios, he was asked to take over the ani-mation department, and he is now both Chairman of Disney Features Animation and Vice President of Walt Disney Company. "Disney turned things around with the release of *The Little Mermaid* in 1989, launching a rebirth that has made the company the king of the animation mountain," a Minneapolis reporter wrote, adding, "The last step in bringing the animation department full circle was to revive and revise *Fantasia*," released in January, 2000.[6]

In 1995, Eisner and Roy E. Disney were able to merge the Disney empire with the ABC television network. The $19 billion merger was the second largest such corporate transaction in U.S. history. It combined the film and TV production facilities of Disney with the distribution power of a huge network. ABC has 225 affiliated TV stations, 10 of which it owns. It also has one of the country's largest radio networks, with 21 stations. It enjoys controlling interests in sports networks ESPN and ESPN-2, and part of the Arts & Entertainment and Lifetime cable net-works. Its Fairchild Publications at the time of the merger included *Women's Wear Daily, L.A. Magazine,* the Chilton trade journals, and seven newspapers, the four most valuable of which were sold to the Knight-Ridder chain for $1.65 billion more than a year after the merger. The magazines also went on the auction block. Abroad, ABC has interests in German and French TV production companies, a one-third interest in Eurosport, the London-based cable sports service, and partial interests in cable programming in Japan, Germany and Scandinavia.

On the Disney side by then were four movie studios: Walt Disney, Touchstone, Hollywood, and Miramax. The Disney studios produced *The Lion King*, the highest grossing animated film ever. Buena Vista Home Video Entertainment produces the long-running TV comedy series, *Home Improvement*. Also included are the Disney Channel cable network and KCAL-TV in Los Angeles. Then there are the theme parks: Disneyland in Anaheim, Epcot Center in Florida, Disneyland Paris, and Tokyo Disneyland. Associated with these are 21 hotels, three water parks and many golf courses. The Disney empire also includes more than 600 retail stores, selling a wide variety of children's merchandise; four magazines under Disney Publishing; the Disney ice shows; the Mighty Ducks hockey team in Anaheim and a fourth of the California Angels baseball team; and finally, Walt Disney Records. The two huge companies — Disney and ABC — together enjoyed annual revenues of $22.4 billion in 1994, the year before the merger.

Frank Wells had been a long-time right-hand man to Eisner before and after his arrival at Disney. After he was killed in a plane crash, Eisner replaced him with Michael Ovitz as Disney president. Jeffrey Katzenberg, who had expected to be Wells' replacement, was outraged. He sued for $250 million from Disney. The settlement, reportedly at or near $250 million, was made in 2000. Roy E. Disney apparently watched all this from the sidelines.

The Katzenberg suit was part of a host of troubles which followed the Disney-ABC merger: ineffective management by Ovitz and other staff leaders, especially at Disney; boycott campaigns; attacks on Disney's "sweatshop" operations; a steadily declining audience share at ABC; and a half-billion dollar loss at Disneyland Paris.

Ovitz had built his own empire, Creative Artists Agency, the biggest Hollywood talent agency, with 500 employees. At Disney, with 65,000 employees, it soon became clear that he had a lot to learn. But Eisner held back from allowing Ovitz real power. Technically, the new Disney president was in charge of theme parks, film divisions and consumer products as well as the ABC network. But Eisner continued to make the decisions and give the orders, "always treating Ovitz not like a co-chairman or real Disney CEO but like just another junior executive."[7] In many of the articles about the Disney empire, Eisner is described as hard-edged and ego-driven. The articles say nothing about his relationship to Roy E. Disney or about Disney's attitude toward his style.

The sweatshop revelations came in 1995 when a National Labor Committee official reported that workers in five factories in Haiti were making toys based on characters in *Pocahontas* and *The Hunchback of Notre Dame*. In response to the report, wages were raised to only 30 cents an hour for making a Pocahontas T-shirt that sold at WalMart for $11.97 At about the same time, a daily TV show owned and produced by Disney, *Live With Regis and Kathie Lee*, got national attention when the National Labor Committee revealed that a sweatshop near the ABC studios where

Kathie Lee then taped the show was paying very low wages for production of garments with her label. But the mainstream press didn't pursue the story. "In 1995, Disney sold more than $15 billion of its merchandise worldwide — more than seven times as much as the global box office for Disney movies."[8] Disney products were reportedly made in sweatshops in Haiti, Burma, Vietnam and China.

More serious for the Disney Company were threats of boycotts. A Southern Baptist convention voted to boycott the Walt Disney Company as a protest against its "gay friendly" policies, which include spousal benefits to gay employees. The decision followed the announcement that the star of the ABC sitcom character *Ellen* was a lesbian. The Baptists also objected to the violence in such movies as *Pulp Fiction.* Their boycott coincided with attacks by the American Family Association in its *AFA Journal.* The Association complained about "images hidden in Disney animated films," also insisting that "*The Little Mermaid* shows a priest becoming noticeably aroused while presiding at a wedding."[9] Eisner responded on *60 Minutes* to the Baptist charges that Disney products had become "anti-Christian." "That's ridiculous," he said, adding that the boycott "hasn't had a financial effect."[10] All this went on without any public comment by Roy Disney.

Also unlikely to affect Disney profits were attacks by Chinese government officials on the Disney film *Kundun,* a story about the Dalai Lama, who lives in exile, and who doesn't exist in Beijing's view. Another boycott was announced by the Arab-American Anti-Discrimination Committee against the movie *Operation Condor* because it used the "cliche of violent, unscrupulous and irrational Arabs."[11] And a Catholic anti-defamation group objected to the ABC series *Nothing Sacred* for trivializing the priesthood.

Disney's output has critics on other fronts. The syndicated columnist Marcia Meier expressed concern about the impact of Disney products on her four-year-old daughter, emphasizing the animated films over which Roy E. Disney presides. "Nearly all the old favorites (*Cinderella, Sleeping Beauty, Snow White, One Hundred and One Dalmatians*) feature evil stepmothers or female villains," she wrote.[12] She found "underlying tones of sexual desire and sadism" in *The Hunchback of Notre Dame.*" Meier added that "the Disney Channel is even more disappointing. Rampant commercialism is only part of the reason. While there are occasionally very good, wholesome movies featured, the bulk of the programming is cartoons that feature bastardized characters from Disney movies. The story lines are superficial and often stupid." *Mother Jones* magazine also criticized the Disney channel, calling it "one single-minded 24-hour-a-day advertisement for Disney."[13]

Still the "family entertainment" image created by Walt Disney in the 1930s seems to overcome all obstacles. In New York City, a stage version of *The Lion King* replaced *Beauty and the Beast* at the remodeled New Amsterdam Theater, with a new Disney store beside it. By the spring of 1997, the Paris Disneyland enjoyed a complete turnaround with more visitors — even French visitors — than the Eiffel Tower and the Louvre. And Disney launched its Animal Kingdom theme park in Orlando in 1998.

Today it's hard to keep up with developments in the many-sided Disney empire, let alone the huge ABC conglomerate. Since the mid-'80s, there has been a think tank — Disney Imagineers — developing ideas for a wide variety of projects. There are now "almost 2,000 robot mechanics, theme park designers, aerospace engineers, Goofy sculptors and other craftsmen who work in a string of unmarked offices and warehouses in Glendale."[14] In 1998, the Disney Cruise Line launched the 83,000-ton "Disney Magic," the first of three cruise ships. In the same year Walt Disney Company bought a 43 percent interest in Infoseek Corporation, an Internet search and directory service. "Tomorrowland" was also unveiled in the old Disneyland — another sign of the retirement or updating of old Disneyland features. Also in 1998, Disney began to furnish news, sports and entertainment from an e-mail address on the web site Excite. Opened in February 2001 was the new $1.4 billion theme park in Anaheim, called California Adventure. It was expected to add another seven million visitors to the 14 million who go to Disneyland.

Through all this, Roy E. Disney has tended to remain focused on the animation projects, varied as they have been. He's Vice President of Disney, but his job as Chairman of Disney Features Animation has been the one he loves.

Like Ted Turner, the 70-year-old Disney loves to sail -- he belongs to the Los Angeles, San Diego and Transpacific yacht clubs -- and enters a variety of races in his yacht, *Pyewacket*. In July, 2000, *Pyewacket* won first place in a 20-mile race during Ireland's Cork Week. One of his homes is 30 miles from Cork.

Born in Los Angeles January 10, 1930, he received his bachelor's degree from Pomona College in 1951, and married Patricia Ann Dailey in 1955; they have four children.

The Disney-ABC empire faltered financially in 1999, and Roy did not get his usual annual bonus, but he's not planning to retire. "I've got the best job in the world, and I get to work with the smartest, most talented people I've ever known," he told a reporter.[15] On the first day of 2000, he was Grand Marshal for the Rose Parade in Pasadena, California, just as his uncle Walt had been 40 years before.

Even though he didn't get that bonus, the *Forbes 400* noted that the wealth of 70-year-old Roy E. Disney went up from $900 million in 1999 to $1.1 billion in 2000.

PRINCE ALWALEED–THE DESERT FOX

31

Prince Alwaleed bin Talal bin Abdulaziz Al Saud is the proper title for the Arabian prince with a personal fortune of $20 billion. He is sixth on the *Forbes* July 9, 2001 list of the world's richest persons.[1] While not as well-known as Gates or Murdoch, "Alwaleed" is all it takes to bring up thousands of references on the Internet to his worldwide investments.

Although Alwaleed is the grandson of Ibn Saud, founder of modern Saudi Arabia, and nephew of Saudi Arabia's current King Fahd, he is more interested in business than politics. He buys undervalued stocks and keeps them, but he also likes to trade. With banks of TV sets in his offices, he keeps track of world markets. A Saudi adviser says, "With the prince it is like playing Monopoly with real money."[2]

At 44, he is chairman and sole shareholder of Kingdom Holdings Co., with substantial interests in Murdoch's News Corp., Netscape Communications, Apple Computer, Italy's Mediaset, Germany's KirchMedia, America Online, Kodak, Teledesic, Paris Disneyland, London's Canary Wharf and luxury hotels around the world, including sole ownership of the George V in Paris and the Fairmont Copley Plaza in Boston, and a half-interest in New York City's famous Plaza. He is also developing his Saudi Arabian interests in banking, cable and wireless technology and real estate.

His father, Talal, a former ambassador to France, and his mother, Princess Mona, divorced when he was a child. He grew up with his mother's family in Beirut until his father put him, as a swinging, overweight teenager, into the military academy at Riyadh. The discipline there carried him on to a business degree at Menlo College in California and a master's in social science from Syracuse University in New York. Slim and fit now, he exercises regularly and neither drinks nor smokes.[3] He is equally comfortable in desert garb or an exquisitely tailored tuxedo.

Twice divorced, Alwaleed lives in a new 317 room palace in Riyadh with his 22-year old third wife, Princess Kholood, his son, Khalid, 22, and daughter, Reem, 18. He has given his son an American education by importing professors from the University of New Haven in Connecticut for classes with five of his son's friends; he plans to do the same for his daughter. He says this avoids the "great temptations" in America "to do things against religion."[4] Khalid has already started playing in the stock market via his computer. He graduated in May of 2000 and will work with his father for awhile before going to graduate school in the U.S., probably majoring in information technology.

Renowned as a brilliant, clean-living, generous businessman, the prince was upset by an article in the *Economist* early in 1999, questioning both the origin of his wealth and his business acumen. The article examined Alwaleed's kingdom and concluded that his sums didn't add up -- that the prince gave inconsistent figures for his earnings and assets — the two basic measures of his success. A box in the investigative report admitted that if there is any question about the origin or conduct of Alwaleed's business, it would be hard to get the facts, since most of the investments are held in tax havens. More then 120 firms are registered in the Cayman Islands under the name Kingdom 5-KR. K and R are the initials of his children.[5]

He rebutted the article in a letter to the *Economist* published in the next month's issue, in which he defended his financial beginnings as well as the return on his investments. "Their performance wasn't as good as Warren Buffett's," he wrote, " but *Economist* readers would be more than content with returns like his."[6]

In a series of interviews with *New York Times* reporter Douglas Jehl, Alwaleed said it was true that "an early source of his capital was hundreds of millions of dollars in commissions paid by foreign and Saudi businessmen to provide services for handling government relations" but added that the money had been hard-earned. The prince's $5 million investment in Citicorp, when it was in trouble, was his first spectacular success. After Citicorp recovered and merged with Travelers Group, his original investment grew to $5 billion in Citigroup. His investments in Netscape, Apple Computer and News Corp. have also done well. Some, notably Euro Disney, Planet Hollywood, the theme restaurant chain, and Proton, the Malaysia automobile company, have not, nor has Priceline stock which dropped to $3 per share after Alwaleed bought it for $50. Euro Disney has improved somewhat and is becoming Europe's leading tourist attraction. It is building a combination theme park and working studio set to open in 2002. Alwaleed does not invest in tobacco or alcohol stocks and insists that income from drinking, smoking or gambling in his hotel holdings be contributed to charity.

The prince's new palace in Riyahd sits on 8.6 acres, has five wings and is staffed by 150 servants. It is five times the size of his old palace down the street, which he has set aside for his son. Jehl says the prince goes from wake-up at 10 a.m. to exercise, then office hours from 11 a.m. to 4 p.m., a family lunch and rest from 4 to 7 p.m., then work from 7 p.m. to 2 a.m., after which he exercises again, has dinner, and finishes his day with dawn prayers before retiring at 5 a.m. It takes a staff of 30 at his office to keep up with him. He also has a helicopter, three jets and a huge yacht, formerly owned by Donald Trump and the Sultan of Brunei. Two of Jehl's four interviews were conducted by telephone as the prince cruised the Caribbean on his yacht.[7] He usually spends the month of August anchored off the Cote d'Azur.

For relaxation Alwaleed often spends time in princely style at a campsite in the desert with associates and servants. Even here, he is in instant touch with his advisers and investments through phone, television, fax machines and laptops; and he often works through the night.

One of the prince's current projects is Kingdom Center, a 990-foot tower in Riyahd which is the country's commercial and diplomatic center. Rejecting dozens of plans and models, the prince finally chose a design by Ellerbe Becket, of Minneapolis, which has Kingdom Holdings on the top office floor and a whole floor for Saks Fifth Avenue. The tower, which is shaped like the eye of a needle, will have an observation deck on top. It will match the Eiffel Tower in height. "If I'm going to do anything, I do it spectacularly or not at all," the prince says.[8]

Another spectacular investment is with Microsoft's Bill Gates and telecom pioneer Craig McCaw in Teledesic, based in Seattle. Its aim is "to launch a network of 288 low-earth orbit satellites around 2002 to provide fiber optic-like access to telecommunications services such as broadband Internet access, video conferencing and high quality voice digital data."[9] It is expected to transmit voice, data and the Internet to every spot on earth..

Perhaps the most bizarre of Alwaleed's investments is Kingdom Entertainment, a fifty-fifty venture with Michael Jackson that includes a record deal with Sony and an interest in Landmark Entertainment Group, a theme park developer. Alwaleed sent his media consultant to help revive Jackson's flagging career. Although his draw in America is still slow, Jackson remains a top star internationally and his 1996 Asian tour and 1997 European tour were both financial successes. "The prince's advice and guidance have been extremely helpful to me," Jackson says.[10] But then nothing seems too far-fetched for a prince who owns 50 percent of Domino's Pizza in the Middle East.

Alwaleed has avoided the stock market, which he considered overpriced before it fell. Instead he searched for investments with humanitarian goals as well as financial gain. He is buying into South Africa, for example. He believes that it has gone peacefully through one transition and the next one from Mandela to Mbeki looks to be peaceful. "I look for countries that have a democracy, have got through a transference of power and have liberal economic policies," he says.[11] He already has direct investments in Uganda, Mozambique, and Senegal and has established a Kingdom Holdings office in Zimbabwe.

Another of his investments is in Toshka, a project to build a canal from Lake Nasser to Egypt's South Valley, near Aswan, to irrigate 500,000 acres of desert. He expects to sink a billion dollars to reclaim land and create an agricultural area capable of growing cereals, vegetables, fruit and cotton and of supporting breeding livestock. It's a long-term business proposition which he believes will eventually produce 20 percent profits. Sun World International of Bakersfield, California, and the company that owns it, Cadiz of Santa Monica, have a contract to develop 100,000 acres. Alwaleed expects to attract other investors as plans develop. It is a coup for Egyptian President Mubarak, who hopes it will solve the high unemployment and overpopulation of the Nile Valley.[12]

Like Warren Buffett, to whom he is often compared, Alwaleed is an investor rather than a manager of investments. "It is virtually impossible for me or the Kingdom Holdings Company to run 150 companies, not taking into consideration the subsidiaries and affiliates that amount to more than 5,000 companies across five continents," he told a reporter for the *Middle East Newsfile*, in May, 1999.[13] But he also sees himself as "in a helicopter over the forest. If he sees trouble he lands and fixes it," according to an *International Herald Tribune* story. "And once he's done, he goes back up."[14] The story, by Vernon Silver, also speculates about the possibility of Alwaleed's succession to the throne.

In a Dec.6, 1999, *Fortune* cover story, Andy Serwer says the prince gives away $60 million a year in charity, without details of where or how. He is "bringing digital technology to the Arab world by backing an Arab web portal, an ISP and huge satellite wireless network," Serwer says.[15] He is also spending $90 million to build a school to train technicians and teachers. While the school will conform to Islamic principles with separate areas for male and female students, it will be on the cutting edge in technical equipment. Every student will have a computer and Internet access.[16]

Alwaleed's life is a delicate balancing act. Somehow he manages to stay true to his religious principles while accumulating billions of dollars.

ROBERT KUOK–SUGAR DADDY BUYS INTO THE MEDIA

32

You may never have heard of Robert Kuok but he is the world's shrewdest businessman, according to a *Forbes* Magazine cover story mid-1997. He and his family were then worth at least $7 billion dollars.[1] By July 9, 2001, the Asian financial crisis had brought his worth down to $3,7 billion.[2] He makes the multi-media mogul list because a very minor part of his business is a controlling interest in the *South China Morning Post*, one of the world's most profitable newspapers, plus a Chinese language daily, both published in Hong Kong, a stake in Television Broadcasts, Ltd, Hong Kong's leading TV station, and cinemas in Malaysia.

His career began with trading in rice and sugar and has grown to include the Shangri-La Hotels, one of the largest hotel chains in Asia, and other real estate; the Hong Kong-based Kerry Group, a conglomerate of firms which include luxury apartment buildings in Hong Kong and Canada and a controlling interest in a dozen other private concerns that range from France to Australia.

An ethnic Chinese, Kuok was born Oct. 6, 1923, in Jahore Bahre, British Malaysia. His parents had come from Fujian Province in China and his father was a prosperous merchant who sent Kuok and his two brothers to Malaysia's finest British-run schools. His studies at Raffles College in Singapore ended when the Japanese bombed Singapore and declared war.

He went back home to Malaysia, at 18, to work for the local office of Mitsubishi, a Japanese trading company, until the end of World War II. Then he began working for his father who had won a contract from the British to supply produce for 50,000 Japanese prisoners of war. After his father died in 1948, he and his brother Philip, his mother and a couple of cousins formed a family business called the Kuok Brothers. His brother William became an organizer for the Malaysian Communist Party and was killed by the British in a Malaysian jungle in 1952. Philip became a

Malaysian diplomat leaving Robert to run the business.

Robert turned the business primarily to sugar and through old school ties with Malaysia's political elite won a license to build the country's first sugar refinery. He eventually became known as Asia's sugar king. At one time he controlled about 10 percent of the world sugar market.[3]

In 1963, Kuok moved to London, where he made lots of money trading in the sugar market, but where he took many chances. He told Andrew Tanzer of *Forbes* that he still shudders when he thinks of the chances he took. "I risked everything without realizing it. It was all rhythm. Have you ever seen Michael Jordan play when he's on a rhythm run? It was exactly like that," he said [4]

When Malaysia won independence from the British in 1957, Kuok returned with his trading knowledge and connections to expand his family's business. "Robert took off like a bomb," an associate said. He bought land for sugar cane in Malaysia and Indonesia and "moved from chartering ships to carry his commodities to owning them; from just owning plots of land in Malaysia and Singapore to developing them into housing estates and hotels. In 1971 he opened his first hotel, the Shangri-La Hotel in Singapore. He also built hotels in Kuala Lumpur, Penang and Hong Kong and acquired resort properties in Fiji."[5]

Kuok recruited Westin Hotel & Resorts to help run the Shangri-La Hotel in Singapore which was typical of his ability to rely on professionals. By July, 1997, Shangri-La Hotels and Resorts operated 36 properties in Asia, including 12 hotels in China and was building eight more there. In 1974 Kuok moved his headquarters to Hong Kong to take advantage of its lower tax rates. In 1988 his Kerry Properties bought a string of luxury apartment buildings there.[6] He also has stakes in the Western Harbor Tunnel Crossing, an airfreight terminal at the new Hong Kong airport, and in Kerry Securities.

One of the most potentially profitable investments fell into his lap in 1993 when Coca-Cola chose R.K., as his associates call him, to open their bottling venture in China. "My God, this is a gift from Heaven," Kuok told *Forbes*. With his excellent command of English, of Malay and five Chinese dialects, he was the perfect choice. He worked all over Asia and with the Chinese as far back as the Cultural Revolution. "I adapt like a chameleon to the particular society where I am operating at the moment," he says.[7]

This huge empire is run by family members and executives, many of whom have been working for Kuok for years. He is eminently fair. One of the executives of Kuok Philippines Property International, Rufo Colayco, says Kuok is always willing "to leave some meat on the bones for the other guy."[8] He watches the bottom line as carefully as any of the tycoons and maintains his connections with a wide range of Asian bankers and businessmen. In Asia, guanxi (connections) carries a lot of weight.

Kuok has eight children from two marriages. Two of his sons, Beau and Ean, two of his nephews and a nephew-in-law have leading roles in the businesses. Ean, 42, became chairman of the *South China Post* in January, 1998. He had been a director since his father bought a controlling interest in the paper from Murdoch in 1993.

Kuok has established several charitable foundations which his daughter Ruth helps run.[9] A niece, Kay, is chair of the Singapore Environment Council and a director of the family holding company in Singapore. His daughter Sue is married to a prominent Malaysian financial-services tycoon.

In February of 1998 Kuok moved his Hong Kong office into a new China-owned building on the site of the former British naval base. His suite on the 22nd floor is surrounded by four of his five closest managers, sons Beau and Ean, nephew Chye and nephew-in-law Richard Liu. "Robert is trying to get away and take more of a back seat these days," Ye Longfei, a vice chairman of the Kerry Group,[10] told Bruce Gilley of the *Far Eastern Economic Review*. The move was viewed with anxiety by some who thought Kuok was turning over the reins to the next generation. Chew Fook Aun, chief financial officer for Kerry Properties says that "although such transitions can be unsettling, in this case the family has worked closely together and the patriarch is very much here and involved on an active basis."[11] Adding to the anxiety, of course, was the Asian economic crisis of 1998 which, according to some experts, halved the value of Kuok's empire.

How freedom of the press would fare in Hong Kong in the transition from British to Chinese rule was another cause for anxiety. Article 27 of the Basic Law for Hong Kong's relationship with China guarantees "freedom of speech, of the press and of publication" but Article 23 instructs the Beijing-appointed Provisional Legislature of the Hong Kong government to pass its own laws prohibiting "treason, secession, sedition, subversion against the Central People's Government or theft of state secrets."[12]

Before the June 30 handover, the *South China Morning Post* appointed a retired Hong Kong pro-Beijing editor, Feng Xi Liang, as a consultant. After retiring as founding editor of the *China Daily*, he was adviser to the avidly pro-Beijing *Window* magazine, now defunct. One Hong Kong journalist says, "It now seems like a move from self-censorship which is widespread now, to overt censorship. None of us thought this would actually happen. Not so soon and not so openly either."[13]

Larry Feign, whose popular 12-year-old *Post* strip, "The World of Lily Wong," was dropped in May, 1995, immediately after a strip character said that a citizen agreeing with the suggestion that "Li Peng is a fascist murderous dog," would become an instant organ donor. Feign, whose cartoons have appeared in renowned newspapers and magazines worldwide, says, "There is no clampdown on free speech in Hong Kong and there won't be after the takeover. We're doing it all ourselves." Feign has left Hong Kong and now lives in London with his family. He has won two Amnesty International Human Rights Press Awards.[14]

There was a bit of a dust-up in March, 1999, when Mainland Chinese authorities invited 30 Hong Kong journalists to cover a mass murder trial in the southern city of Shatou. When the reporters asked questions outside the courtroom they were taken to a police station and detained for an hour before being released.

More serious was the resignation, in November, 2000, of Willy Wo-lap Lam, political columnist and China editor of the *South China Morning Post*. Kuok had written a letter to the editor accusing Lam of "exaggeration and fabrication" in his coverage of a visit of Hong Kong tycoons (including Kuok) to Beijing. Lam was relieved of his duties as editor and subsequently resigned because of intimidation and efforts to get him to tone down his aggressive coverage.

Lam said, "It's a sign of self-censorship that is getting worse by the day. It's not a precipitous decline, but it's there.[15]

Kuok's 46-year-old second son, Ean, resigned May 8, 2000, from Pelangi Bhd , a property development company in Johor, to concentrate on the *South China Morning Post,* according to the Singapore *Business Times.*[16]

It's a bit much to expect someone with Kuok's connections and investments in the mainland to keep an unbiased point of view. He helped found Citic Pacific, the Chinese cabinet-controlled Hong Kong company; he was one of a dozen Hong Kong tycoons at a special meeting with Chinese President Jiang Zemin in Shenzhen in 1995 to discuss who would be the territory's first chief executive and he sat on the Beijing-appointed Preparatory Committee which oversaw Hong Kong's transition to Chinese sovereignty.[17]

At least two books are in process on press censorship in Hong Kong. Moreover, anyone interested in how freedom of the press is playing out now that the British and Chris Patten are gone can read the *South China Morning Post* on the Internet daily. The whole world is watching to see what will happen to Kuok's very important media holdings in Hong Kong.

AKIO MORITA–SON MASAO CARRIES ON

33

Sony is a global electronic and entertainment colossus that now stretches all over the world and is listed on stock exchanges worldwide. It not only made TV sets and marketed them worldwide, it developed the enormously successful Walkman transistor radio, the first video cassette recorder for home use, the Triniton system for TV, CD's, the floppy disc, the latest sensation — the Play Station — then branched into movies, TV shows and record labels.

Akio Morita, co-founder of Sony and the grand old man of Japan's electronic industry, retired in 1993, after suffering a stroke while playing tennis. He was in a wheelchair until his death Oct. 4, 1999. Morita's second son, Masao, 45, entered the business and is a corporate vice president in Sony Music Entertainment (Japan). *Forbes* July 3, 2000 edition lists him and his family as worth $2 billion.[1] The first son, Hideo, heads the family brewery, of the sixteenth generation to do so, and take the title of *Kyuzaemon*. He is also president and CEO of both RayKay, Inc., the family holding company based in Tokyo, and the Morita Company, Ltd.[2]

Sony got into the entertainment business after Akio Morita became convinced that software should be married to hardware. It started with the $2 billion purchase of CBS Records from Columbia Broadcasting System's Laurence Tisch. Because it was Japan's first invasion of an American media company, there was a storm of protest.[3] Only a year later, Sony acquired Columbia Pictures and TriStar Entertainment from Coca Cola for $5 billion. A *Newsweek* cover showed the Columbia logo lady dressed in a kimono. At first it was a costly and embarrassing venture but it was finally turned around. Movies and music are but a small part of Sony's vast empire which in 1999 had revenues of $64 billion.[4] It is among the leading motion picture and television production companies in the U.S. and worldwide.

Morita realized that the company name, Tokyo Tsushin Koggo Kabushiki Kasha, was unwieldy even in its translation as Tokyo Telecommunications Engineering. Searching for a name in 1958, Morita and his partner, Masaru Ibuku, found the Latin word for sound -- sonus -- in the dictionary. It sounded happy like sonny boy and so Sony became a trademark, one of the best-known and respected in the world. "Sony bears the stamp of Morita's character, a blend of drive, chutzpah, and calculated playfulness," according to Richard J. Barnet and John Cavanaugh in *Global Dreams*.[5]

Akio Morita was born January 26, 1921 in Kasugaya, Japan, the child of wealthy brewers of sake, the Japanese wine made from rice, and reared from childhood to take over the business. He was more interested in electronics, making his own ham radio transmitter, and chose to study physics at Osaka University. Immediately after he graduated in 1944, he became a lieutenant in the Japanese navy, which assigned him to a research center at Sagami Bay. There he met Masaru Ibuku and they both worked on thermal guidance weapons and night vision gunsights in the last year of World War II.

A few months after the war ended, Morita borrowed $500 from his family and teamed up with his friend Ibuku to start a company making electronic equipment. He had to get his father's permission to stay out of the family saki business. A year later the little company already had 50 employees and moved from cramped quarters in central Tokyo to a former barracks in the suburbs. Its first product was an expensive and bulky voltmeter and amplifier, impossible for the ordinary consumer to buy, but useful to Japan's post office and to the Japan Broadcasting Company.

Then came a tape recorder, also too expensive for home use. But the tape recorder turned out to be precursor to a standout product. When the Tokyo Art Institute bought one, a student named Norio Ohga complained about its quality. Morita promptly hired Ohga, who ultimately became Sony's president and is now chairman of the board.

Responding to the student's complaint, Morita asked company engineers to develop a smaller, less expensive tape recorder. Large numbers of these were sold to schools all over Japan, the company's first breakthrough in the marketplace. Then Ibuku learned about a new AT&T invention, the transistor, available to any company in the world willing to pay its licensing fee. The Ibuku-Morita partnership was delighted, and began to make and sell one transistor product after another. In the next six years, they launched a series of worldwide firsts, all using transistors -- radios, two-band radios, FM radios, video tape recorders and small screen TV sets. Most famous of all -- and the biggest seller -- was the Walkman, a transistorized tape player that could be used even while walking or jogging[6]

By the time the company had been re-named Sony in 1958, it already had world markets and Morita was making frequent trips to the United States, Canada and Europe. By then also, Morita was married and had a growing family of three children. The wedding to Yoshido Kamei took place in 1950 and the couple had two sons, Hideo and Masao, and a daughter, Naoko.

Morita was now ready to launch Sony Corporation of America, capitalized at $500,000 under a complicated U.S. law permitting shares of stock in a foreign company to be sold in America. Since 1967, the mother Sony company has been listed on the New York stock exchange.

Determined to understand Americans and their culture better, Morita careful-ly planned to move his family to New York for a two-year stay. Violinist Nathan Milstein was planning a two-year visit in Paris, so they rented his Fifth Avenue apart-ment, fully furnished. The children were sent to summer camp and then to private schools in the city. Morita's wife Yoshiko got a driver's license and used it on both company business and family outings. Aided by the family's Japanese maid, she began having dinner parties for both friends and Morita's business associates. Later she wrote *My Thoughts on Home Entertainment* as a guide for Japanese who want to learn how to entertain foreigners.[7]

The American stay was cut short by the death of Morita's father, and they returned to Tokyo after 15 months. The family's beautifully landscaped house is only a mile from the Sony office building in Tokyo. Morita helped design both buildings. In his many visits to France, he liked French cuisine so much that he had a duplicate of the famous Paris restaurant, Maxim's, built in the basement of the Sony headquarters.[8]

Sony's first American plant was built in San Diego in 1963 and the first in Great Britain was opened in Bridgend, South Wales, in 1974. In his 1969 book, *Made in Japan*, Morita asserts, "Our sets are more completely American than some famous U.S. brands that are actually built in the Far East by American companies and then shipped to the United States. One of the ironies of the situation today is that almost any 'American' TV set is about 80 per cent Japanese inside."[9]

He credited the high quality of Japanese products first to demands of American occupation authorities and second to W. Edwards Deming, the American engineer whose quality control ideas were welcomed in Japan after being rejected by American auto makers, especially Chrysler.[10] Morita's preoccupation with quality ran throughout his life.

The company suffered a major setback in the mid-1970s when it marketed the Betamax home video recorder. It presented the format to its competitors and urged them to accept it as a standard. The competitors banded together behind Matsushita's cheaper VHS and eventually Sony had to join them.[11] It had a similar experience with the compact disc (CD) in the early 1980s, when record companies were afraid the new format would harm their record and cassette sales. This time Sony set the standard.

Sony began to see the need for its own record company. That insight ultimate-ly led to the decision to buy CBS Records, Columbia Pictures and Tristar Entertainment. Columbia's library, the fourth largest in the world, controls 2,700 films, from *Lawrence of Arabia* to *Rambo*, and 23,000 television shows.

Sony left the management to Hollywood veterans who spent money on corpo-rate jets lavish quarters and films that failed. Columbia and TriStar had some suc-cesses such as *Remains of the Day, Sleepless in Seattle* and *Philadelphia*, but also embarrassing flops. The story of Sony's ups and downs in Hollywood is detailed in *Hit and Run: How Jon Peters and Peter Guber Took Sony for a Ride in Hollywood,* by Nancy Griffin and Kim Masters.[12] Sony finally took over management of the studio and turned it around. It is now called Sony Pictures Entertainment.

Nobuyuki Idei (pronounced ee-DAY) was named president of Sony in March,

1995, by former president Norio Ohga, who moved up to chairman and CEO. Idei came from the bottom up, having arrived at Sony when just out of a Tokyo university. He started Sony of France in the 1970s and moved through a series of important company positions in Japan. He had Morita's blessing. They had become close friends and tennis partners over the years.

As president, Idei has steered the company in the direction of the information superhighway, the new networking trends that connect individual consumers to others via phones, faxes, modems, and other equipment. In a *Fortune* article, he said, "We have to recognize that in the future most of our products will become part of a larger digital network. From now on, then, Sony's work is to build bridges between computers and consumer electronics and communications and entertainment, not mere boxes."[13] To this end Idei carried out a major restructuring of leadership in March, 2000.

The Play Station that Sony introduced in Japan in 1994 has been a phenomenal success. More than 80 million Play Stations have been sold and Play Station II, introduced in Japan in February, 2000, sold two million units in less than three months. It was released in the United States and Europe in October, 2000. Play Station II can use the software titles made for its predecessor and connect users to the Internet and a personal computer. Also well-received wee VAIO home-use PCs, Digital Handycam home-use camcorders and DVD-Video players.

Sony is developing digital networks for distribution of music and movies along with its insurance and financial services. In the spring of 2001, Sony linked up with Vivendi Universal and Yahoo to deliver music over the Internet. Vivendi and Sony also announced plans to create Duet, an online music distribution platform to rival Napster. To counter Nintendo's Game Cube and Microsoft's Xbox, rivals to its Play Station, Sony has made alliances with Cisco, which will provide infrastructure, RealNetwork and Macromedia to provide content, America Online and UK's Vodafone and Telewest to provide access. All three companies plan to release their game consoles in the fall of 2001. Earlier, Columbia House -- Sony's 50-50 joint venture with Time Warner -- expanded its online presence by merging with Cdnow, and Sony made a deal with Cablevision to install Sony-made set topo boxes for New York area subscribers. It also launched interactive versions of *Jeopardy* .and *Wheel of Fortune*, leading the way to interactive TV.[14]

The creative, innovative spirit of Akio Morita still dominates Sony, which continues to reinvent itself. Morita's father's decision to exempt him from his destiny to run the family saki business enabled him to bring pleasure to millions all over the world. His elder son, Hideo, is the father of triplets, two boys and a girl. The first-born son, by several minutes, has been named the seventeenth *Kyuzaemon*.[15]

Akiro Morita received many honors in his lifetime: three honorary doctorates from American universities, the French Legion d'Honneur, the Order of the British Empire and awards from other countries in Europe, Asia and South America. He was one of the most influential business geniuses of the 20th Century.

MASAYOSHI SON–
SOFTBANK'S SWEET SUCCESS AND THEN OUCH!

34

Masayoshi Son, the grandson of Korean immigrants, was born Aug. 11, 1957, on Kyushu Island in Japan. Often called Japan's Bill Gates, he is president and CEO of Softbank, a computer software firm he started from scratch in 1981. It grew rapidly and in July, 1999, *Forbes* said Son was worth $6.4 billion.[1] Eight months later, *Forbes* took out the period and said he was worth $64 billion, second only to Bill Gates.[2] That was before the tech market took a dive. Softbank's share price dropped 90 percent from its high and by July 9, 2001, *Forbes* estimate of Son's worth was at $5.6.billion.[3] Son doesn't seem to be worried and is optimistic about the future.

A soft-spoken, boyish-looking entrepreneur, Son came to California at 16 to learn English in a special language program at Holy Names College in Oakland. After several months of study, he entered Serramonte High School in Daly City as a sophomore but was bucked up to junior, then senior and within two weeks after his arrival at Serramonte had passed an exam and received a high school diploma. He returned to Holy Names College, studied there for two years, then transferred to the University of California at Berkeley as a junior. While at Holy Names he met his future wife, who was also born on Kyushu Island but of Japanese parents.

Son's grandparents immigrated to Japan from Korea; like all Korean immigrants they were discriminated against by the Japanese and forced to take a Japanese name, Yasumoto, for themselves and their descendants. When Son came to the United States, he proudly took back his Korean surname and has used it ever since.

He majored in economics at Cal, and working with some Cal professors, he invented and patented an electronic dictionary that he sold to Sharp for almost a million dollars. It became the prototype of Sharp's successful Wizard line. Forrest Mozer, a physics professor who worked with him said, "It was clear even then that he was some day going to own all of Japan."[4] Son asked Mozer and research physicist Chuck Carlson to keep track of the hours they worked on his inventions and paid them off after he sold the patent to Sharp. He also made another million by importing used computer game machines from his father's pachinko parlors in Japan, rebuilding them and placing them around campus. Within a year he owned the largest video arcade in Berkeley.

When he went back to Japan, Son spent a year and a half just thinking about what he wanted to do. He admits that he was worried and so were his parents, his wife and his friends, but it took him that long, he says, to research and plan his career.[5]

Son focused on software distribution and started Softbank in 1981. His first break came when he set up a big booth at a trade show in Tokyo and offered to display software for free. Almost no one was interested in displaying software but the booth project led to an offer from Joshin Denki Co., to supply software for a PC superstore. Son wrapped up an exclusive deal to supply Denki and within a year moved software into so many other stores that his monthly revenues went from $10,000 to $2.3 million.[6]

Son is not only Japan's top software distributor and the world's top producer of computer trade shows, he has also joined with international entrepreneurs to break down Japan's archaic business rules and, as a result, is reaching beyond Japan and the States in numerous joint ventures.

Like Richard Branson, Son believes that small is beautiful. While his businesses keep expanding, he organizes their personnel in small groups that can make their own decisions. He believes an organization that gets too big loses its vitality.

Also like Branson, Son spins off new projects at a dizzy pace. Softbank-linked companies swap capital ideas and expertise and collaborate on joint ventures. Son keeps track of them by frequent flights across the Pacific. He calls his empire an Internet Zaibatsu (Japanese cartel). Through Softbank, he has investments in more than 600 hi-tech companies and he rewards his executives' success with lavish bonuses and stock.

In 1996, he bought a 30 percent stake in Yahoo, the Internet search engine, and made a killing when it went public later that year. He has since launched the very successful Yahoo Japan, in which he has a 51 percent interest. In February, 1999, Son sold $410 million of his stake in Yahoo Inc., reducing his holding to 28 percent, to finance new investments. Yahoo!, E*Trade, GeoCities and others are not only leading companies in the U.S. but they account for 90 percent of all Internet companies in Japan. He operates a small incubator called Hot Bank in Mountain View, Calif., and another in Boulder, Colo., for cyberspace start-ups, and plans to run other incubators around the world. Each week dozens of applications pour in.

He has also established himself in Europe through joint ventures with Vivendi in France and News Corp. in England. In June, 1997, he and Rupert Murdoch acquired a 21 percent interest in TV Asahi, a base for a 150-station satellite network called Japan SkyBroadcast.[7]

In California's Silicon Valley, Son formed a joint venture with Novell Inc., one of the world's leading network software providers, which opened up Japan to its products. Also in Silicon Valley, Son has served on the board of directors of Cisco Systems since 1995. Cisco is now the world's number one supplier of internetworking products that link local and world area networks. These products allow spiders (computers) on one web to communicate with spiders on another network.

It isn't only in the U.S. that everyone seems to have a mobile phone glued to an ear. By March, 2000, the number of mobile phone subscribers in Japan exceeded the number of fixed phone subscribers. To take advantage of this trend, Softbank Technology set up a subsidiary to operate e-commerce businesses aiming at mobile phone users. Services in the new company will include online authorization, billing and settlement.[8]

Son and UT Starcom president and CEO Hong Lu met when they were students at Cal. Lu was night shift manager of an ice cream parlor; Son was working on his economics degree. Softbank now owns 50 percent of Hong Lu's UT Starcom Inc., headquartered in Alameda, California, which develops, markets and supports advanced telephony products and services for emerging markets, primarily in China, India, Southeast Asia and South America

On the other side of the globe, Softbank has joined with Finland's Nokia to invest in Riot Entertainment, a Finnish wireless publisher. Riot-E develops and distributes entertainment services and games to mobile terminals. In March, 1999, Softbank and News Corps' Epartners set up two Internet investment funds worth a combined $1 billion: one fund worth $450 million is devoted to the United Kingdom while the other $550 million will be used to invest in companies based in continental Europe. Riot-E was the UK fund's first European investment.[9]

Softbank has also formed a $500 million investment fund with the International Finance Corporation, the private sector arm of the World Bank, to build the digital economy of developing countries. The fund, Softbank Emerging Markets, is based in Silicon Velley and invests in small Internet projects in Latin America, China, and India. The operation is an attempt to include developing countries in the information revolution and close the digital divide between them and the rest of the world.[10]

In June, 2000, Softbank joined with Hewlett-Packard to create a Japanese website E-COMMERCE Corp. Hewlett-Packard will offer printers and other products and supply the infrastructure. In the same turbulent month Son teamed up with the National Association of Securities Dealers and the Osaka Stock Exchange to create Nasdaq Japan, which they plan to make a 24-hour marketplace for hi-tech shares by linking up with similar firms in the United States and Europe.[11]

Not everything has turned up roses for Son. In 1995 he bought Ziff-Davis, the world's largest publisher of computer magazines, including *PC Magazine, PC Week* and 80 more magazines plus some 200 instructional manuals. When advertising fell off, he sold its publishing division for $780 million in December, 1999, at a heavy loss but still has a 69 percent interest in Ziff-Davis' Comdex technology trade shows, online ZDNet and the Internet-based learning service SmartPlanet.[12] He has also unloaded his 80 percent interest in Kingston Technology, maker of memory boards, at a loss.

A disgruntled former employee, Kochi-Yoshida, wrote a book titled, *The Inside Report of Softbank's Warped Management*, in 1997, which presents an angry catalogue of alleged wrongdoing by Son and his company. It was a best seller in Japan and caused Softbank stock to drop temporarily. Son took offense and has sued the publisher for libel.[13]

There were times when Softbank was at odds with Japanese bankers because it moved too swiftly for them. Now the government invited Softbank and a consortium to take over the Nippon Credit Bank, which collapsed in 1998. The group agreed in June, 2000, to buy and recapitalize the bank.[14]

Only 42 years old, Son continues to pursue aggressively whatever opportunities turn up, buddies around with fellow billionaires Bill Gates, Paul Allen and Rupert Murdoch, and keeps on top of his rapidly expanding empire. Business associates call him Son-san, a title of respect. Friends simply say "Masa." He goes to the huge trade shows in casual clothes and is available for interviews and conferences. His infectious grin has appeared on the covers of numerous business magazines but he is relatively unknown to the general public. His family lives in privacy and comfort in Tokyo. Not even the International Who's Who carries a line about them. A top-notch golfer, Son keeps in practice with a virtual golf course in the basement of his home. It has an electronic range that reproduces competitive courses and simulated weather conditions, including wind and rain.

On March 8, 2000, the Softbank web page announced a reorganization of the company. Softbank is now divided into four parts: Softbank Corp is the parent company; Softbank Global Ventures oversees some operations outside Japan; Softbank Venture Capital manages all US operations; and Softbank International Ventures manages other operations outside of Japan and the US. The announcement's headline read, "Building the global e-Future," and Masayoshi Son seems to be poised to do just that when the market settles down.[15]

Ronald Fisher, chief executive of Softbank Global Investors, has said, "This is a great time to have money and courage." Son agrees. "Far from being the end of the line," he says. " It is still the beginning of a big thing coming." He plans to create a cyber conglomerate that will transform the Net into a truly global phenomenon.[16]

KERRY PACKER–AUSTRALIA'S WEALTHIEST MAN

35

If sportsman Kerry Packer sometimes seems larger than life, it may be because he is a stalwart six feet six inches tall. He's also Australia's wealthiest man. *Forbes* estimates his worth at $2.5 billion.[1] His Consolidated Press Holdings (CPH) is one of Australia's largest companies with business interests in TV, magazines, newspapers, and one of his favorite sports -- gambling. Once, when he won $7.5 million in Las Vegas, he tipped the dealer $1.7 million. Another story in the *Economist* tells of a Texas oilman who objected to Packer's behavior at a Las Vegas casino. He poked a finger at him and said, "Don't you know who I am?" Packer asked him what he was worth, and when the oilman replied, "About $300 million." "Right," Packer said, "let's toss a coin for it."[2]

Born in Sydney, Dec. 13, 1937, Kerry was educated at Geelong Grammar School in Victoria. He and his wife, Roslyn, live in the Sydney suburb of Bellevue Hill. They have two children, James and Gretel. James, like his father, went to Geelong Grammar; Gretel to Ascham School, an exclusive school for girls, where her paternal grandmother, her aunts and cousins were also educated. Packer gave $2 million for a theater on the Ascham campus.

Clyde Packer, Kerry's grandfather, started the newspaper business. Kerry's father, Sir Frank Packer, founded Consolidated Press Holdings in the 1930's and started the *Sydney Daily Telegraph* as well as Australia's first commercial TV station. Kerry worked in the family business for two decades, and on his father's death, in 1974, inherited control.

Packer became Australia's first billionaire in 1987 when he sold his Nine Network TV stations to yachtsman Alan Bond for $1 billion. Bond failed, and three years later Packer bought them all back for a fifth of the price.

Packer and former Australian, Rupert Murdoch, have been at one another's throats and in one another's pockets for decades, and the duel has continued into the next generation with heirs apparent, James Packer and Lachlan Murdoch, following in their fathers' footsteps. In May, 1998, James was appointed chief executive of Consolidated Press Holdings and chairman of Publishing and Broadcasting Ltd. In 1999, he became director of Melbourne's Crown Casino, Hoyt's Cinemas and Ecorp Ltd. Lachlan is CEO of News Ltd., the parent company of Murdoch's News Corp. The two heirs have been known to party together and to work together when their interests coincide.[3]

Publishing and Broadcasting Ltd. dates back to July, 1994, when shareholders agreed to merge two of Packer's biggest companies, the magazine group Australian Consolidated Press and TV Nine Network, into PBL. Two years later Packer resigned and turned his stake over to son James. Company holdings include the highly successful Channel Nine Australian television network and such popular Australian magazines as *Woman's Day* and *Cosmopolitan*. PBL also holds investments in casinos, cinemas, the Sky Channel TV network and the Optus Vision pay-TV concern.[4] CPH, the parent company, has interests in agriculture (Aussies call it pastorals), banking, resorts and chemicals, as well.

Back in March, 1996, when Packer resigned as chairman of PBL and turned his 45 percent stake over to James to manage, PBL managing director Brian Powers became chairman. When James was made chairman as well as CEO in 1998, Powers moved to John Fairfax Holdings newspaper group, severing his links to Packer. PBL holds a 14.9 percent interest in Fairfax, placed in the FXF trust, which is all the Australian Broadcasting Authority will allow under its cross ownership rules. No one is allowed to control both a television network and a newspaper group, and Kerry doesn't want to part with his television network. Both Packer and Murdoch have pressed the government to relax the cross-media and foreign ownership rules. Packer has long tried to take over the Fairfax newspaper group with its lucrative "rivers of gold" classified advertising earning a billion dollars a year. When Powers, the former Packer executive, turned up as publisher of Fairfax and announced plans to also take a 14.9 stake in the firm, there was strong opposition but the ABA ruled there was no conflict with PBL. Fairfax had been thrown into receivership when heirs chose to divide up the business — the third generation curse that so far the Packers and Murdochs have managed to avoid. Kerry joined with Conrad Black, a media mogul with interests in Canada and the United States as well as in Australia, in a buyout bid for Fairfax but regulators threatened to kill the deal and Packer backed out. Black then won Fairfax for $1.2 billion dollars.[5]

On other fronts Packer has battled not only Murdoch but Kerry Stokes, Australia's other media billionaire; the Fairfax group; and Conrad Black, the Canadian newspaper baron, as well as tax assessors and government regulators, winning some and losing others. A royal commission investigated him for tax evasion and possible drug schemes in the eighties.[6] He has astutely avoided paying taxes, all through legal methods. In 1998 he got $164 million in tax bills reduced to a small fraction after a seven year battle with Australian tax authorities.[7]

A bitter loss came when Showboat Inc., an Atlantic City gambling company and an Australian developer outbid him and Circus Circus Enterprises for Sydney's first casino. Packer's love for gambling is shared by many Australians who spend more on betting per capita than they do on food.[8] Refusing to give up, Packer kept up his legal fight for the casino, going all the way to the High Court. He lost the case but son James took up the battle and when PBL agreed to pay Showboat Inc. $340 million for a 10 percent stake in the casino and an 85 percent shareholding in the management company, the offer was accepted. The deal was pending for months until May, 1997, when Packer agreed to bow out to avoid a protracted investigation into his business and personal affairs by the Casino Control Authority.[9]

Not to worry. Packer has interests in other casinos. He took over the lavishly appointed Melbourne Crown in 1999 in a billion dollar share-swap deal. Every major city in Australia now has a casino. Gambling binges have caused many social problems: gambling chips from the Sydney Harbour Casino have even turned up in drug deals. Another of Packer's interests was revealed in an Associated Press story in July, 1995, about the trial of Los Angeles madam Heidi Fleiss, when he was listed as one of her clients.[10]

Kerry Stokes, who owns mining interests as well as Channel Seven, outfoxed Packer over the proposed Docklands Stadium at Melbourne. Originally planned as an underfunded government-built rugby stadium, it was changed into a privately funded multi-purpose stadium with a retractable roof suitable for all sorts of sporting events, concerts and theatrical performances. The funding would come from broadcast rights to the Australian Football League. Stokes has TV rights to AFL until 2001, when they are to be renegotiated. He put together a consortium which included Murdoch's 14.9 percent of Channel Seven and won the deal. Murdoch was afraid that if Packer won the stadium deal he would not honor his agreement to broadcast Murdoch's rugby Super League on his popular Channel Nine.

Packer's Channel Nine had outbid Stokes' Channel Seven for Murdoch's Super League rights after Murdoch launched the rebel rugby league to lure clubs and players away from the 88-year-old Australian Rugby League, for which Packer holds TV rights.

Then there's cricket, another of Packer's sports. The staid world of cricket competition was stunned 20 years ago when Packer launched a rival world series by luring the best of cricket talent, put his players into colored uniforms which gave rise to the public calling them "pyjama players," and put on night matches. Now cricket matches are sanctioned in all parts of the world; players are better paid but the level of playing has dropped and much of the excitement is missing.[11]

The sport which defines Packer is polo. Not only has he spent millions importing Argentine polo players and polo ponies but he has played with the best of them. He spends millions of dollars on horses, stables and players. In 1994 he played on the team that won the three top tournaments in Argentina: The Argentine Open, The Tortugas Open and the Hurlingham Open. Kerry suffered a massive heart attack while playing polo in October, 1990. Fortunately, an ambulance was standing by and he was resuscitated after being judged clinically dead. He was back in the saddle about five weeks later and his teams have continued to dominate the sport internationally.[12] A teetotaler but a heavy smoker, he has had a series of heart and kidney surgeries in the past few years.

To make money from sports Packer and Murdoch teamed up when Murdoch's News Corp. bought 50 percent of PBL's Sky Channel, which broadcasts racing and other sports events into 6500 pubs and clubs around the country. Both expect to reap huge revenues if they can offer interactive betting to Asia's gambling fanatics. Murdoch and Packer also jointly run Lotto, the lucrative lottery in New South Wales. Australia-based Pacific Magazines, which is 45 percent owned by News Corp., prints some of PBL's magazines.[13] Murdoch and Packer have an extremely complicated corporate relationship.

A new entry in Packer's enterprise division is Softix Pty Ltd., a wholly owned CPH subsidiary. The company develops, installs and supports entertainment ticketing software. Originating in the U.S. in 1974, it has support centers in the U.S. and Australia. The company provides clients in the Asia-Pacific region and in North America with tickets to sporting and multipurpose venues, stadia, sports teams, performing arts organizations, theme parks, cinemas, cabarets and casinos. It makes it possible for external computer systems such as Web browsers to connect to the ticket system.[14]

Packer's privately owned group, CPH, also owns the national Ticketek company, which has joined forces with Paul Dainty of Melbourne in Dainty Consolidated Entertainment to promote tours of plays and other kinds of entertainment in the Asia-Pacific area. The synergy of Packer's magazines, TV and Ticketek should give the new company great marketing power.[15]

Packer's PBL and Bill Gates' Microsoft joined forces on Oct. 30, 1997, to launch SideWalk, an on-line entertainment guide. Daniel Petre, who resigned from Microsoft as a multi-millionaire, came out of retirement to take the classified "rivers of gold" advertisements into the online world. It also provides online news, sports, travel, entertainment and weather shows, as well as financial and retail services. SideWalk was so expensive to launch that it lost money for the first several years. With about 20 percent of its homes owning computers, Australia is behind only the United States in home computers.[16]

Packer can't seem to lose for winning. His office in Sydney was robbed of A$5.7 million dollars of gold in 1995. It didn't bother him. He wins and loses that kind of money in one night in a casino. Besides, it was mostly covered by insurance. In a dispute over that insurance coverage, the Court, in February, 1997, gave Packer A$4.7 million, which was A$700,000 more than the Royal Insurance Company had offered.[17]

In April, 1996, PBL and two other companies rescued Australis Media Ltd., a financially troubled Australian company that provided satellite pay-TV services. The Australian Consumer and Competition Commission investigated to determine the control PBL would have with a 25 percent stake. Analysts argued that with PBL as part-owner of two of Australia's three cable-TV providers, relatively little competition would take place and reduced competition might lead to higher prices for consumers.[18] That ended in a three way settlement with James Packer and Lachlan Murdoch signing an agreement on June 20, 1997, to combine PBL's interest in Australis with Murdoch and Telstra's Foxtel to merge with Australis to form the country's leading pay-TV company.[19]

A joint venture with eBay Australia & New Zealand and Microsoft called Ecorp, includes ninemsn (a content portal), an auction business, online financial services, and a ticketing agency. CPH has also taken a five percent stake in California's Silicon Valley company Axon Instruments. Axon is expected to exploit commercial opportunities involving the human genome project, which began as a U.S. Government scheme in 1990.

Investment in India takes Packer in a new direction. In March, 2000, he joined with two Indian investors in a venture capital fund and with an Indian telecoms company in an e-commerce venture.

James Packer seems to be growing into his responsibilities as chief executive in the family empire. He has amassed a small fortune of his own by investing in property development in Sydney. In October, 1999, he was married to Jodie Meares, a 27-year-old model, in a lavish wedding at the Packer Bellevue Hill mansion, with Sir Elton John and blues legend B.B. King among the entertainers. The Murdochs, father and son, were guests at the wedding.[20]

The bitterness many Australians feel about the way the tycoons are eliminating competition and working to change government regulations is illustrated vividly in a Mediawatch Internet article by J. G Estiot. "Most of the companies involved in media own related businesses like advertising agencies and management groups," he writes. "When you see a show like *Riverdance* receive so much publicity, it is because the company staging the event and selling the merchandise is related to the media owner. In the commercial media, nothing happens by accident. They don't report the news, they launch the next step of the publicity campaign." He quotes Les Carlyon in *The Melbourne Age*: "Look up any list of mind-altering drugs. You'll see the usual suspects: coke and grass, ecstasy and angel dust. You won't see mention of one of the wildest hallucinatory drugs of all, a little number with an odd street name -- media regulation. This is because it's sniffed only by a tiny sect: politicians in power."[21]

Packer has also alienated Australian politicians. Former prime minister Paul Keating, especially bitter over losing Packer's influential support, has called him "a malignant force," and accused him of doing "everything in his power" to prevent Labor from winning an election.[22]

The public watches the tycoons' TV programs and buys their magazines and newspapers. There are no alternatives. The Packers generate a lot of social and governmental antagonism but they grow richer and more powerful every day while the country grows poorer in choice and diversity. Still larger than life, Kerry Packer casts a grim shadow over his native land.

THE ISRAEL ASPER FAMILY–LOVE BOAT NETWORK PAYS OFF

36

Canada's Israel (Izzy) Asper, tax lawyer and political leader turned media mogul, has built CanWest Global Communications Corp. into a multinational broadcasting empire from scratch. It extends from coast to coast in Canada and overseas west to Australia and New Zealand and east to Ireland. An aggressive entrepreneur, Asper has engaged in numerous lawsuits, many against friends and colleagues, most of which he has won. Critics, such as Friends of Canadian Broadcasting, say he made money by broadcasting cheap American sitcoms instead of creating original Canadian programs. True, but it paid off. *Forbes* says he is worth $1.8 billion dollars.[1]

Born in 1932, the son of Russian immigrant parents, he grew up in Minnedosa, Manitoba. His father was a distinguished violin teacher in Odessa who fled to Canada to escape the Bolshevik revolution. His mother, also a Russian refugee, was a pianist. The parents played in movie theaters until the talkies left them jobless. They bought a bankrupt theater and ran it, with Izzy working at everything from scraping gum off the seats to taking tickets. He chose to abandon the family business in favor of law school, graduating from the University of Manitoba in Winnipeg with bachelor's degrees in Arts and Law and a master's in Law. While at the university he wrote a music review column for the student paper which gave him entree to the jazz nightclubs in New York. His passion for jazz has continued all his life.[2]

Asper built a successful law practice in Winnepeg. At the same time, he wrote a nationally syndicated taxation column for the *Globe & Mail* and a book on taxation, *The Beacon Iceberg*, published in 1970. He served five years as leader of the small group of Manitoba liberals in the Legislature before devoting full time to a business venture. In 1975, with a couple of friends, he researched and built a distillery. It was an instant success, but to his disgust his friends opted to sell it within a year.

Then Asper and a couple of friends bought a small North Dakota television station, moved it to Winnepeg and named it CKND. They ran it out of an old Safeway store with programming help from the brand new Global television station in Toronto. When Global went into bankruptcy after only three months, Asper put together a group of investors to buy the station and soon turned it around. Global Ontario is now the flagship of the network that gradually grew with Asper's aggressive planning and the strategy of David Mintz, who was president from 1979 until he retired in 1993. During that time Mintz took Global from the station with the lowest ratings in the Toronto market to number one. He helped launch *Troopers,* a children's TV series of Canadian short stories, one segment of which won an Academy Award, and added such popular American series as *M*A*S*H* and *Cheers* to the programming.

Asper bought out his partners in 1989 after a bitter four-year legal struggle. Since then he has added constantly to the two stations, all of which have been re-branded under the name Global. In Canada, CanWest Global Communications now owns and operates the Global Television Network, as well as CanWest Entertainment, whose principal operation is Fireworks Entertainment Inc, a production and distribution company.

In March, 1999, CanWest created CanWest Entertainment International, headquartered in London, to distribute programs worldwide. Abroad, CanWest owns and operates New Zealand's TV3 and TV4 Television Networks and the More FM Radio Network. The company also has substantial investments in Canada's Western International Communications Inc. (WIC), Australia's Ten Television Network, the Republic of Ireland's new TV3 Television Network and Northern Ireland's Ulster Television.[3]

The story of Asper's legal efforts through the years to gain control of WIC would fill a book. He now shares WIC with Shaw Communications. They divided its assets after WIC's owners sold out and the legal battles were over. The plan gives Asper the Alberta stations he has always coveted and virtually completes his dream of a third national broadcasting system to compete with the government-owned CBC and the privately-owned CTV.

Several of Asper's ventures didn't pan out. An attempt to enter the recording business by investing in TeeVee records cost $4 million and a soccer team cost even more before Global unloaded it. The three-year battle to get Britain's Channel Five was lost to Pearson although Global's bid was higher. The English Independent Television Commission objected to the high percentage of repeat broadcasts and the low percentage of factual programming in Global's proposal.[4]

People dubbed Global "The Love Boat Network" because it depended so heavily on American sitcoms. A *Forbes* story, headlined "Bargain-basement broadcaster," said that by offering dramas instead of documentaries and sports summaries instead of live games, Global was able to improve ratings and margins. The government's bland CBC fare couldn't compete with Global's *Seinfeld, The Simpsons and The X-Files.*[5] Asper thinks the government should let CBC be owned by subscribers like the American PBS, with a government subsidy rather than government ownership. He also complains about the Canadian Radio-Television and Communications

Commission (CRTC), calling its commissioners "feudal lords" and urging an easing of restrictions on television content and advertising. "Governments and regulators must take off the shackles and understand that the viewer must come first," he told the Canadian Club.[6] CRTC has no control over newspapers but it is mandated to preserve media diversity in broadcasting. As more and more media companies merged CRTC began cracking down. The biggest media merger in Canadian history took place on July 31, 2000 when Asper's CanWest bought all of the major Hollinger Canadian newspapers, 50 percent of The National *Post*, Hollinger's Internet properties, the Southam Magazine and Information Group and the hockey portala, Faceoff.com, for $2.2 billion. An earlier acquisition of eight TV stations made CanWest.a truly national network and in August the company sealed a partnership with Medbroadcast, a specialty television channel devoted to health, with a medical information website.

When Leonard Asper talked of his dream of making journalists "content generation machines" reporting for print, TV and the Web, the Canadian Radio-television and Telecommunication Commission (CRTC) forced CanWest to agree to a journalistic code of conduct and ethics to preserve diversity of voices.

CRTC has criticized Global, charging that it spends only 18 percent of its revenues on Canadian production while CTV, the other commercial but less profitable station, spends 33 percent. Even stronger was movie mogul Robert Lantos' criticism in a speech at Ryerson Polytechnic University calling the private broadcasters "nothing but toll collectors between Canadians and their access to popular American shows and contribute nothing to anyone but their own estates."[7] This irritated Izzy to the point of filing a libel suit. Then Matthew Fraser, professor of communications at Ryerson, complained that the approval CRTC gave to Global for a PRIME TV specialty channel for the over-50 crowd had turned into a "shameless re-run channel for the same flossy American shows that had made The Love Boat so profitable."[8]

Asper protested that he had been so busy with day-to-day corporate business that he hadn't had time to spend on programming. Recent revamping of the six o'clock news in the Ontario market moved it out of the cellar. He believes that buying Fireworks Entertainment, a Toronto-based entertainment company engaged in the distribution, production and financing of film and television programs, will help. "A broadcaster is an exhibitor and scheduler and developer of audiences, but at the end of the day it comes down to the product.," he says. "With so many new technologies, like the internet and satellites, programming rules the roost."[9]

Global Ontario's 25th anniversary, celebrated in 1999, caused Asper to look back and to look ahead. The succession is taken care of. His son David is an executive vice president of CanWest, Leonard is president and CEO; daughter Gail is general counsel, secretary and managing director of The Asper Foundation and president of the CanWest Global Foundation.. It's a close-knit family that has played and worked together. Izzy and his wife Ruth (Babs) raised their children, David, Gail and Leonard in River Heights, Winnipeg. All three became lawyers like their father. People wonder why Asper has chosen to stay in the windswept prairie town of Winnipeg when his Ontario flagship station is in Toronto. He is happy there. Asper says he is a true Canadian. When he had a heart attack in 1984, he could easily have gone to the States for a triple bypass but he chose to wait six weeks for the Canadian health system to book the surgery.[10]

Asper stepped down as CanWest president in 1997. He now calls himself executive chairman. His offices on the 36th floor of the Toronto Dominion Centre overlook the area where the CanWest Centre for the Performing Arts was built with a $700,000 contribution from the CanWest Charitable Foundation, which he founded in 1983. The 7500 seat ballpark for the Winnipeg Goldeyes baseball team, was also built with foundation funding. The Asper Centre for Entrepreneurship and the Asper Chair in International Business and Trade are at the University of Manitoba. The former Faculty of Management at the University has been renamed the Asper School of Business. The Asper Jewish Community Campus is in a restored army barracks in Winnipeg.[11] Most recently CanWest gave half a million Canadian dollars' worth of free airtime to promote Ireland in Canada and an equal sum to Ireland to promote Canada tourism with the purpose of promoting cultural and historical ties between the two countries. In November, 2000, the Asper family gave $20 million Canadian dollars to be divided equally between the Winnipeg Foundation and the Jewish Foundation of Manitoba.

Izzy recalls when he was a boy that "Eaton's popular stores did not hire Jews. Or Indians. Or blacks. We've come a long way," he told a *Toronto Star* reporter, "adding that he believes firmly in multiculturalism and opposes providing a course in Hebrew in River Heights High School. "That's ridiculous especially when we teach too little Canadian history."[12]

He has received many honors. He was appointed Queen's Counsel in 1975, and received the Order of Canada in 1995. He has also received a Doctor of Law degree from the University of Manitoba and a PhD from Hebrew University.

Speaking at the World Economic Forum in Davos, Switzerland in February, 1999, Asper said broadcasters need not fear the new technology. He urged them to embrace cyberbroadcasting as an enormous opportunity to expand business. He said the broadcast industry survived the fragmentation of cable and of satellite competition and if it adopts and takes advantage of the new technology it will continue to attract and expand audiences.[13]

CanWest's tremendous expansion in the millennium year brought CEO and president Leonard Asper into the limelight. He handled the press when the Hollinger sale was announced with poise and fielded questions both in English and French. He plays tennis and hockey, is an accomplished pianist and is married with two small children. He runs a tight ship at the corporate headquarters with a staff of 30.

The Asper family works well together and seems to be in a position to move ahead in whatever direction the information highway takes.

KENNETH ROY THOMSON–LORD OF CYBERSPACE

37

Kenneth Roy Thomson, Lord of Fleet, is the richest man in Canada. He has sold off most of the newspapers which were the basis of his fortune and title to focus on electronic publishing in five areas: legal and regulatory matters, health care, education, financial services, and scientific reference. His goal of transforming his company into the world's leading information publishing company has earned him a new title, Lord of Cyberspace.

Law librarians were alarmed when, on June 20, 1996, Thomson, which had a reputation for jacking prices, acquired West Publishing Company from its 200-odd employees, at least eleven of whom became multimillionaires with the sale. West, an American company, had been the preeminent legal publisher dominating the U.S. market for case reports and publishing scores of treatises; Thomson had been the second biggest legal publisher and a major player in both case reports and secondary works.

The $3.4 billion merger of West Publishing Company with Thomson Corporation was maneuvered through the government review process with only minor divestitures of Thomson's legal portfolio, according to *The American Lawyer*.[1] Justice Department lawyers were skeptical about the merger and investigated it for several months. One sticking point was West's closely guarded page-numbering system, which the Justice Department had investigated in 1994. When Thomson agreed to license the page numbers in West's case reports to any rival publishers, the government settled.

John Morris, who interviewed people on both sides of the controversy for his article in The *American Lawyer*, said the merger casts doubts on a system in which arguments are held behind closed doors, and where little public discussion of the agreements that emerge, and little coverage in either the legal or business press occurs. He believes that the court-ordered divestiture of the minor pieces of the Thomson holdings is expected to have little effect on keeping prices down for legal information.[2] "The government appears to have become obsessed with competing seedlings and overlooked how the giants of the forest can black out the light."[3]

The giant in this case is the second Lord Thomson of Fleet of Northbridge in the City of Edinburgh, though he does not use the title and has never taken his seat in the House of Lords. He inherited the media empire from his father, the first Lord Thomson of Fleet, whose title was awarded by Queen Elizabeth II in 1964, and stems from his holdings at that time on London's traditional newspaper row on Fleet Street.

Thomson, chairman of the board of The Thomson Corporation (TTC) and with titles in numerous other companies, is overqualified for our billionaires' club. *Forbes* lists him as worth $16.4 billion, with financial interests not only in Canada and the United States but also in Australia, New Zealand, China, Japan, Mexico, Latin America, Germany and a growing number of other countries.[4]

Now 76, Kenneth Roy Thomson, was born in Canada and grew up there during the depression. Noted for frugality, he is apt to use a plastic bag rather than a briefcase, to travel coach class on business trips and to answer his own telephone. Tall and slim, he doesn't smoke and rarely drinks. He lives with his wife in a red brick Georgian mansion in Toronto. He married Nora Marilyn Lewis, a Toronto fashion model, in 1956. They have three children, David, Lynne and Peter.[5] He plays golf but his main hobbies are collecting paintings and antiques. He has been collecting the work of the Dutch-Canadian painter, Cornelius Krieghoff, since the sixties and houses some of the paintings in a gallery next to his office, which allows him to depreciate the paintings as a business expense. The collection is open to the public two afternoons a week.[6]

In February, 2000, the Thomson Corporation put all its newspapers in Canada and the United States up for sale except for its flagship, Toronto's *Globe & Mail*, and its related businesses including the Report on Business television channel (ROB-TV) and its web site. The bulk of the newspapers were sold in June to the Gannett Group and Community Newspaper Holdings Inc. to provide funds for hundreds of database acquisitions.

Now the Thomson Corporation is made up of Thomson's Legal and Regulatory Group, which provides information to law, tax, accounting and human resource firms; Thomson Financial, which serves the worldwide financial community; Thomson Learning, which provides learning information to educational institutions and corporations; Thomson Scientific Reference, providing scientific and business information for research, academics and governments; and Thomson Healthcare which serves the medical community .and its caregivers. Although a great deal of information in these areas is available on the Internet for free, the Thomson Corporation's specialized services are in much demand. Profits have increased dramatically.

Thomson's sons are involved in the business; David and his brother Peter are deputy chairmen of The Woodbridge Company, which controls the family assets. In May, 2000, Kenneth announced that David would take over from him as chairman of Thomson Corporation within the next two years. He has been groomed for the post since he was a teenager. Kenneth will retain his title of chairman of The Woodbridge Company.

David read history at Cambridge but his major interest is art, especially the work of John Constable. He owns a number of Constable's major paintings as well as drawings, watercolors and sketches. In 1989, he outbid the National Gallery of England to the tune of $14.6 million for J.M.W. Turner's *Seascape Folkestone*. It has since been valued at $50 million. He has homes in Toronto, New York and London, has two daughters from his first marriage and recently married for the second time. He told Peter C. Newman his "search is always to create new wealth."[7] Once a Thomson, always a Thomson.

Lord Thomson has always considered himself a financier, rather than a journalist, and neither he nor his father, Roy, ever took much interest in the editorial positions of their newspapers, preferring to leave that to editors of the widely scattered papers. Roy Thomson was primarily interested in the bottom line, as his son has been. According to John Miller, chairman of the journalism school at Toronto's Ryerson Polytechnic University, when some of Thomson's Canadian papers were sold, there were no layoffs because the papers were already down to the bone.[8]

The media empire began with Roy Herbert Thomson. Born in Toronto, Canada in 1894, he started work at age 14 for $5 a week. He was selling radios in the boondocks in Ontario during the depression when he thought sales might improve if reception were better. He acquired a transmitter, a broadcasting license and in 1931 began selling on-the-air advertising as well as radio sets. He started his first radio station in North Bay, then another in Timmins and another in Kirkland. In 1934 he bought a weekly paper in Timmins and within three years turned it into a daily. The family had little money and lived very simply until he bought the radio stations and began buying newspapers which proved to be little cash boxes.

The cash added up. By 1951, when he entered the Canadian commercial television field, he was already wealthy enough to spend winters on his yacht off the coast of Florida. He bought a newspaper in St. Petersburg and began buying small papers in southern states.

In 1953 he branched out across the Atlantic with publication of *Canada Review*, a weekly paper of Canadian news published in London. He also gained control of Edinburgh's distinguished morning newspaper, *The Scotsman*, and its companion publications, *The Evening Dispatch* and *the Weekly Scotsman*. Then he ran unsuccessfully as a Progressive Conservative candidate for the Canadian House of Commons. At this point he decided to make Edinburgh his permanent home and transferred control of his Canadian properties to his son, Kenneth, in 1956. He kept the title of Chairman of the Board.

He started a TV station in Scotland, then newspapers in England, Scotland and Wales. In 1966 he bought the debt-ridden *Times* of London and merged it with the *Sunday Times*. He appointed Kenneth chairman of the board and his son and family moved to London. That move didn't work out well. After three years, Kenneth decided *The Times* was just a drag on profits and moved with his family back to Toronto. Meantime his father had been aggressively expanding his empire, which by this time included 45 newspapers in Canada and 23 in the United States. Other investments included ownership of a British travel agency, an air charter business, a book and telephone directory publishing company, an insurance company, a 20 percent interest in the Piper and Claymore oil fields (which had been developed with

Jean Paul Getty and Armand Hammer) and 100 percent ownership of Dominion Consolidated Truck Lines.[9]

The first Lord of Fleet died in London on August 4, 1976 at the age of 82. In the British tradition his will stipulated that his son and his son's male heirs would control the family business.

The heir, Kenneth Roy Thomson, was born Sept. 1, 1934, in Toronto, one of three children and the only son. By the time he was in his teens his father was wealthy enough to send him to a prestigious private school and then to the University of Toronto. He dropped out in 1941 to join the Royal Canadian Air Force. He was posted in London and in the next three years wrote for an air force magazine called *Wings Abroad.* He was able to enroll as a graduate student at Cambridge in 1945 even though he didn't have an undergraduate degree, because as biographer Susan Goldenberg explains, his father persuaded the university to bend its rules. Kenneth earned a master's in law before returning to Canada to enter the family business.[10]

Assuming control after his father's death, he embarked on an aggressive acquisition campaign, winning control of Hudson's Bay Company, Canada's oldest trading establishment, chartered in 1670. It has since been sold, as has the *Timmins Daily Press.* Sentiment has never been a Thomson hallmark. In 1980 Thomson bought Canada's national newspaper, the *Toronto Globe & Mail,* and picked up other papers in Canada, Britain and the United States, mostly in one-paper towns. At this time he introduced a system of district managers, with 12 to 15 newspapers in a region, managed by an executive located in the regional headquarters.

The *London Times* continued to lose money because of work stoppages and union resistance to new methods of typesetting and composing. After a costly eleven month shutdown Thomson sold *The Times* and the *Sunday Times* in February, 1981, to Rupert Murdoch.[11] It took Murdoch until January, 1986, to transfer publication to a computerized plant in Wapping, a London suburb, break the unions and turn a profit.[12]

With Thomson's 1980 purchase of the *Toronto Globe & Mail* and other publications, only two Canadian companies, Thomson and Southam, Inc., owned 57 percent of Canada's newspapers. On May 1, 1981, the two chains were charged by the federal government with conspiring to reduce competition in four major cities, Montreal, Ottawa, Winnipeg and Vancouver, and ordered to stand trial.[13] The two chains were charged with conspiring to lessen daily newspaper competition and with unlawfully merging and monopolizing the production and sale of major daily English language newspapers. Anti-trust investigators conducted raids and seized papers at the offices of eleven newspapers owned by Thomson Newspapers Ltd. After a 31-day trial, which ended Dec. 9, 1983, both chains were acquitted of charges and the seized papers were ordered returned. Earlier that year, the federal government proposed legislation that would regulate the nation's newspaper industry, but the Daily Newspaper Act failed to pass Parliament.[14]

Despite this challenge to the extensiveness of his newspaper holdings, Thomson continued to buy and sell small daily and weekly newspapers in the United States and to invest in specialized trade publications such as *Jane's Fighting Ships, The*

American Banker and *Physician's Desk Reference,* plus four major data bases in the United States from Capital Cities/ABC, Access Co., West Publishing and a number of financial and educational publications.

The Thomson Corporation in 1995 sold 46 newspapers in the U.S. and Canada and the last of its newspapers in the United Kingdom, ending its ownership in the British Isles.[15] Gone also are the TV stations and the oil and gas division. The British travel service, airlines and all, was sold in May, 1998. In June, 1999, Thomson bought Macmillan Library Reference USA from Pearson. It includes Scribner's Reference, MacMillan Reference and Thorndike Press whose publications are used by high schools, universities and libraries. As a result of these transactions, TTC has transformed itself into a colossus for the Information Age. Thomson now sells data -- data to lawyers, data to doctors, data to bankers and accountants and securities advisers, data to anyone who needs data in the age of data.[16]

Critics have never stopped complaining about the continued consolidation of newspaper ownership. The Canadian Association of Journalists called for a public inquiry into the state of journalism, which it describes as seriously threatened. Among their concerns was the sale by Thomson Newspapers of more than 30 daily and community newspapers to Conrad Black's Hollinger Inc. which owned both dailies in Newfoundland and both dailies in Prince Edward Island and all four dailies in Saskatchewan. Hollinger also published 111 dailies in the United States--more than any other company.[17] Black sold most of the papers to CanWest Global Communications, Israel Asper's media empire, on Aug. 1, 2000. Black also sold his 50 percent interest in The Globe's television spinoff of the paper's financial section, ROB-TV to Can-West which has started legal proceedings for the other half, now under the umbrella of Bell Globemedia. *Forbes* predicts there will be a fight to the finish.[18] Everything changes, yet everything remains the same.

Although Canada's efforts to restrain monopoly control of newspapers in the eighties failed, the words of Thomas Kent of the Canadian Royal Commission which investigated concentration of ownership of newspapers ring true. "The only obvious measure of success is a quantitative measure, that is, return on the investment. The newspaper is a cash cow whose revenues can be milked not only to buy other papers but also to finance expansion into other ventures."[19]

Thomson continued to invest money from the sale of its remaining newspapers into new acquisitions which in the millennium year included: Dialog, a global provider of information services; Wave Technologies International, a provider of instructional products to information technologies; Prometric, a global leader in computer-based testing and assessment service, $1 billion for Primark, one of the world's top providers of financial analysis and a joint deal with Reed Elsevier for Harcourt General for $4 billion which gives Thomson adult testing and training programs. The more acquisitions, the more likely Thomson will be to jack up prices. Analysts wonder how the squeeze will play out over the next few years with the loss of diversity that accompanies merger after merger.

On a broader base, the Thomson Corporation, on Sept. 14, 2000, announced a joint venture with Bell Communications Enterprises (BCE), whose subsidiaries include the CTV television network and the Sympatico Internet server. Thomson tossed in the *Globe & Mail* and associated Internet assets. That was the last of the newspapers under Kenneth Thomson's direct control. Bell Globemedia, the new multimedia company with its leading print, broadcast and Internet brands forms a $2.7 billion media giant.[20]

Kenneth Roy Thomson is well-established as Lord of Cyberspace.

EMILIO AZCARRAGA JEAN–EL TIGRE'S CUB GROWS UP

38

Mexico's Emilio Azcarraga Jean has been the youngest person on *Forbes'* list of billionaires. His family's wealth, estimated at $3 billion in *Forbes* July, 2001 list, comes from owning more than half of Grupo Televisa, the top Spanish language media group in the world.[1] Grupa Televisa includes TV production and broadcasting, international distribution of TV programming, radio production and broadcasting, music recording, cable TV, professional sports promotion, including two soccer teams, dubbing film production and distribution, outdoor advertising, special events promotion and satellite communication.[2] The publishing group, largest in the Spanish market, includes *Eres, Vanidades*, and Spanish versions of *Cosmopolitan* and *Elle*.

Jean inherited control of the business from his father, Emilio Azcarraga Milmo, known as El Tigre, whose support of the ruling Institutional Revolutionary Party (PRI)), both financially and politically, was rewarded with clout enough to build a huge empire. El Tigre had, in 1972, inherited cinema studios and Telesistema Mexicano, a small group of radio and TV stations, from his father, Emilio Azcarraga Vidaurreta, nicknamed El Leon (The Lion). He promptly absorbed the rival Television Independiente Mexicana to create Grupo Televisa which gave him a virtual monopoly on Mexican television until 1993.

Indeed Azcarraga Milmo had a stranglehold on the Mexican communications market, a monopoly unrivaled except perhaps by the ruling PRI's grip on political power. For four decades Televisa supported PRI in newscasts which ignored or downplayed opposition forces, harassing especially the center-left Party of the Democratic Revolution (PRD) and its leader, Cuauhtemoc Cardenas, during his two presidential campaigns. El Tigre called himself "a soldier of the president" and the country's "No. 2 priista," or party supporter. In return Televisa got tax breaks by running public service announcements that earned it the "Ministry of Communications" moniker. It was so powerful that advertisers and entertainers were at its mercy. Sponsors could either buy a year of advertising in advance or pay triple the standard rate. Televisa actors were blacklisted if they worked elsewhere.[3]

There were two setbacks in El Tigre's long reign. First Milmo lost heavily when, in 1990, he launched *The National*, the first sports daily newspaper in the United States, and shut it down two years later after losing $130 million. Then in 1986-7 he was forced by the FCC to sell SIN, the U.S. Hispanic TV network based in Miami, which was founded by his father and which he had built up with satellite feeds from Mexico. Hallmark bought the network but failed to make a go of it. When proposed free trade agreements opened an opportunity, Milmo and a consortium of investors bought back the old SIN network, now named Univision. Televisa's U.S. cable network, Galavision, which reaches Hispanic homes from Chicago to Los Angeles, when coupled with Univision, gives the group a network of TV stations with access to 90 percent of Hispanic homes in the U.S., the richest Hispanic market in the world.[4]

Milmo's nickname, the Tiger, came from his aggressive business style as well as the blaze of white that swept the center of his black pompadour. For 25 years he had been president and chief executive of Televisa which employed 20,000 people and had revenues of more than a billion dollars a year. At the time of his death Televisa was the most prolific producer of programming in Spanish and was the world's largest publisher of Spanish magazines.

When Milmo was hospitalized for a heart attack in February, 1996, it was discovered that he had a brain tumor. He spent his last weeks aboard his yacht, Eco, said to be the world's largest, before dying of cancer at age 66, on April 16, 1997. Besides his son and heir, he left three daughters and his fifth wife, Adriana Asiscal.[5]

Televisa's cozy relationship with the government began to slip in 1993 when the Mexican government privatized a group of properties including two national TV channels. Ricardo Salinas Pliego, CEO of Electra, Mexico's largest retail chain, saw this as a way to promote social change as well as a business opportunity. He borrowed money and outbid competitors to start a rival TV chain called Azteca. He countered the sedate government-pandering news programs of Televisa's Jacobo Zabludovsky with a lively newscast called "Happenings." He hired smart young executives, set up a partnership with NBC, and began buying soap operas and generating scandalous telenovelas, a plan which captured a third of Televisa's prime time and advertising revenue. Telenovelas are a powerful force in Latin America. Millions plot their daily schedules around their air times.[6]

Battling back, Televisa sharpened the programming on its four networks and redesigned its news shows. According to a report by James F. Smith in the *Los Angeles Times*, Televisa has taken back much of the audience share it lost to Azteca.[7] Televisa has its own acting school in Mexico City, where it keeps stars under contract and is said to be the largest producer of broadcasting content in the world, generating five times as many hours of programming as Azteca. It sells its shows throughout Latin America and other countries, including Russia and the Philippines. Its stars have been leveraged through Televisa music albums and Televisa concerts in Televisa theaters and Televisa magazines. At one time any Televisa star who worked with a competitor would have been banned and destroyed but Azcarraga Jean has chosen to work with TV Azteca on several projects including "La Aventurera," a musical in Mexico City with a cast from both Televisa and Azteca studios; on successful telethons to benefit disadvantaged children; and on sharing broadcast rights to professional and amateur soccer games.[8]

Both Televisa and Azteca have been impacted by the collapse of the peso and the economic crises in Russia and Asia. Azcarraga Jean's problems have been further complicated by a power struggle within the company. Before his father's death in 1997 he was named president and CEO and Guillermo Canedo White became chairman. Because stock in the company was divided among his father's heirs, Azcarraga Jean had only 10 percent of the family's 75 percent, which endangered his control. His cousin, Burillo Azcarraga, had 16 percent. When Canedo White was ousted and Burillo became vice chairman and president of International Affairs, he pressured other stockholders to support Azcarraga Jean. It took awhile for the new president to win respect. Critics dubbed him "the kid" and "the idiot prince" but he has brought in savvy managers, including COO Jaime Davila, former chairman of Univision, the flourishing Miami-based Spanish language network in which Televisa owns a 19.8 percent stake, and business is improving.[9]

Much of Azcarraga Jean's financial problems stem from having the family's stakes scattered among his aunts, step-mothers, and cousins in Televicentro, the Azcarraga family holding company. He bought off some of them and traded with others so the pressure went down a notch.[10] But in May, 1999, the oldest of his three sisters, Alessandra Azcarraga de Sepul, began legal proceedings in the U.S. and Mexico, claiming that she has yet to receive her fair share of her father's fortune. Meantime, Azcarraga Jean engineered a complex combination of debt restructuring and a shareholder reshuffle in which his cousin and supporter, Alejandro Burillo Azcarraga kept a 25 percent stake. The Aleman family, partners in Televicentro for three decades cashed in their interest which was bought by Carlos Slim Helu, owner of Telmex, the Mexican telecommunications group, according to a story in the *Financial Times*, and share prices nearly doubled last year.[11] Then Burillo clashed with Azcarraga Jean and in July, 2000, sold a 20.62 percent stake in Televicentro to Maria Asuncion Aramburuzabala, heiress to a brewing fortune, and some of her family. They apparently have no interest in trying to control the holding company but wish to support Azcarraga's successful management strategy as a good investment. Televisa stock jumped again. Burillo will sell the rest of his 25 percent stake to Azcarraga Jean and Carlos Slim Helu. Azcarraga Jean has voting control over Slim's shares, so he now controls 75 percent of Televicentro, the holding company which controls over 50 percent of Televisa.

Azcarraga Jean was educated in Mexican schools, at Lakefield College, Ontario, and San Diego State University. He entered his father's firm in 1988, learning the ropes from the executives, and in 1990 was appointed vice president of marketing, then in 1996 was made COO. As he began to take on responsibility he grew closer to his father, who stepped down in March, 1997, naming his only son president and CEO.[12]

Since his father's death, Azcarraga Jean has been cutting costs by selling the corporate jets, reducing executive salaries, eliminating 4000 jobs -- some 20 percent of the work force -- and closing offices in New York and Los Angeles.[13] He also shut down Televisa's Cultural Center for Contemporary Art in Mexico City, planning to sell or rent the building but retaining the museum's permanent collection[14]. Management of the collection has been turned over to Casa Lamm, an institute run by Mexican women, which will lend exhibits from the collection to museums in Mexico and the U.S.

The break with political tradition was emphasized in 1998 when Azcarraga Jean told university students that Televisa no longer blindly supports the Mexican government's ruling party in order to maintain a monopoly on the viewing public.[15] Actually Televisa has already become fairer in its treatment of political parties, according to a report by the Mexican Human Rights Academy quoted in the *Houston Chronicle*. Dudley Althaus wrote that Televisa executives realized that favoring the PRI was not good for business and that the country had changed. Azcarraga Jean was quoted as saying, "Everything is changing. I'm not political, you understand. I'm a business man. I like entertainment. I like doing television."[16]

Azcarraga Jean is much more visible than was his reclusive father. He opened the Third Worldwide Television Industry Summit Conference in New York, Nov. 24, 1997, before the Emmy Awards and was the keynote speaker at the fourth annual News World Conference in Barcelona in November, 1998. In January, 1999, he was named one of the Global Leaders for Tomorrow at the 29th annual meeting of the World Economic Forum in Davos, Switzerland. And he takes a leading role in educational and philanthropic projects in Mexico City. In October, 1999, he married a Mexico City art dealer, Alejandra de Cima.

Even as competition cuts in on the home front, Televisa continues to expand in Central and South America, cutting deals with 17 networks in the region to exchange news stories. Eco, Televisa's news station, broadcasts news reports from an aligned network in Chile, Venezuela and Argentina.[17] And Televisa and Worldwide Television News (WTN) have a joint venture through which Televisa's regional coverage of South and Central America is distributed around the world. WTN covers more than 100 countries and is owned primarily by ABC News in the U.S.[18] In July, 1999, Televisa launched an internet service through its Cablevision. Internet access by cable is of interest to Mexicans who have an average of five personal computers per 100 residents. Later that year, Televisa formed an alliance with MGM Networks Latin America to bring the MGM channel and Casa Club TV to Mexico City

In May, 2000, Azcarraga Jean built a Spanish language internet portal called esmas.com which has access to all of Televisa's programming, news, sports, music, publishing and entertainment including also e-mail, search engines and chat rooms. The following September he attempted to break into radio, announcing a deal to buy a controlling interest in Grupo Aacir Communications which would add 194 radio stations to his 1112 television stations. The Federal Antitrust Commission ruled against the deal claiming it would drive competition out of the market. Jean is expected to appeal the ruling..

There is probably no argument against monopoly control of the media any better than the change wrought by TV Azteca in Mexico. Televisa had dominated the Mexican political scene for four decades, stifling opposition to PRI. The election of Cuauhtemoc Cardenas as mayor of Mexico City in July, 1997, was an indication of the waning power of the PRI and the change in its former life support. Both the Lion and the Tiger are gone, and the cub says he has no interest in politics. When Vicente Fox was elected president in the July 2, 2000, election, the power of the PRI was broken and a new Mexico has emerged.

Azcarraga Jean told James F. Smith of the *L. A. Times* that he believes Televisa's edge lies in its programming. "Technologically it is becoming easier to distribute entertainment," he said "Today there are 150, and if tomorrow there are 500 channels, the question is, what are you going to put on those 500 channels. So I believe we are in a privileged position to grow--to produce more, to produce better quality entertainment and to keep growing."[19]

Whether he can keep the family feuds under control as well as he has managed Televisa remains to be seen. So far, his performance has exceeded all expectations.

ROBERTO MARINHO AND FAMILY–
THEY DOMINATE BRAZIL'S MEDIA

39

Brazil's Roberto Marinho is still a potent force at 95. He has turned over management of the Globo Group to his three sons but goes to his office and is available for consultation. Despite Brazil's rocky economy and its currency devaluation which reduced his wealth, Marinho and his family are worth $1.5 billion.[1] The Globo group dominates Brazilian television and radio, it operates cable and satellite TV services, its *O Globo* is Rio de Janiero's leading newspaper, and Editora Globo is the country's second biggest publishing house.

At one time Marinho's power was sufficient to provoke an irate congressman to demand, "Who runs this country, the president of the republic or Mr. Roberto Marinho?" Another politician said, "There will never be democracy while there are forces like Globo."[2] In 1989, Julia Preston wrote in the *Washington Post*, "As an absolute ruler of a media empire that includes Rede Globo, the biggest television network in Brazil (and fourth largest in the world) and *O Globo* newspaper, one of the two biggest dailies, Marinho is quite simply the most influential man in Latin America's largest nation."[3] Like the Azcarragas in Mexico and Cisneros in Venezuela, Marinho has outlasted countless politicians and changes in government. His power is still a draw. The current president of the republic reportedly attended openings of Marinho's new printing press, the largest in Latin America, and his new TV studios.[4]

Marinho profited from laws barring foreigners from national television. Since these laws were lifted, many local and foreign groups have now cut into Globo's markets. When civilian rule was restored in the late 1980's, competition developed rapidly, opening up spaces for diverse expression and independent production. Many forces coalesced for change: the military abandoned government and Globo shifted its interest from controlling national politics to moving into international alliances.[5] Globo joined forces with Murdoch's News Corp., Azcarraga's Televisa and

223

John Malone's TCI in Sky Latin America, a Direct to Home service. Besides this satellite alliance, it has numerous joint ventures in cable systems including Globocabo which is majority owned and operated by Globo, Net-Brasil, a network for pay-TV programming and a consortium with AT&T in cell phone licenses.[6]

Rede Globo captures more than half of Brazil's prime time audience and up to 70 percent of ad revenue. The four top-rated shows in Brazil are Globo's flashy hour-long soap operas, called telenovelas, at 6 , 7 and 8:30 nightly and Globo's national evening news at 8 o'clock, all from the network's own studios. Globo produces 90 percent of its programming.[7] Most programs are produced at Projac, a sprawling facility Globo built for $60 million on the outskirts of Rio de Janeiro. There are six state of the art studios plus set-building facilities, costume shops, video libraries and storage facilities. The telenovelas are sold to more than 70 countries.

Television is powerful in Brazil because of the high rate of illiteracy. Nationwide, 21 percent of adults and up to 50 percent of those in the poorest regions are illiterate. Newspapers have a circulation of 8 million but television can reach 120 million, more than three-quarters of Brazil's population. The last census showed more households with televisions than refrigerators. In a country that reads little, television provides entertainment, information and a daily fantasy and this captive audience belongs for the most part to Roberto Marinho, according to a media study by Mac Margolis.[8]

Marinho's three sons from his first marriage worked with him in the Globo organization: Roberto Irineu, 52, at Globo TV, Joao Roberto, 46, at *O Globo* and Jose Roberto, 44, in the national radio network. When the sons gradually took over in the 1990's, they hired professionals to handle day to day business. " Now Roberto Irineu oversees strategic planning, Joao Roberto takes care of government relations and editorial policy and Jose Roberto handles community relations and the Roberto Marinho Foundation."[9] The empire includes Rede Globo, overseas programming sales, the newspapers, magazines, radio, cellular phone licenses, telecommunication equipment and real estate.

Marinho inherited *O Globo* from his father, who died shortly after he founded it. The son worked at most every job on the paper while he was finishing his university education. After six years, at age 21, he took over. He stayed at the paper even after he founded the Globo TV network with Time-Life in 1965. He borrowed money and bought out Time-Life four years later and soon moved into an office at the TV network. He kept close tabs on the TV news and often directly influenced coverage of politics. Globo TV helped elect Fernando Collor de Mello to the presidency and then helped drive him from office for corruption.[10] In the early days he delighted in occasionally scooping his reporters and there is no doubt that his wishes were respected in choosing and interpreting the news. As one reporter put it, "We are pretty well attuned to his likes and dislikes."[11]

Marinho would rather listen to classical music than watch television. A former champion horseman, he now mostly tends to his extensive art collection. Slightly built, dapper, with a neat mustache, Marinho is a teetotaler who prefers fish and vegetables to red meat. Reports of his retirement circulated for 20 years before he finally stepped down, according to a 1997 article in *Vanity Fair*. In his eighties he fell in love with Lily de Carvalho, a wealthy society widow, and left his second wife to marry her. They live in a ranch house in Rio de Janeiro.[12]

There have been a few setbacks even before the recent economic problems. Robert Irineu, the oldest son, lost $120 million on a failed venture with Italy's Telemontecarlo. The company wasted millions getting Pay-TV started and government environmental roadblocks kept Globo from building Projac for more than a year, at great cost to Marinho.

In spite of Brazil's economic situation, Globo successfully issued bonds on the U.S. market in March, 1998, for $300 million, using some of the money to launch a new newspaper, *Extra*, for lower income readers in Rio and a new weekly newsmagazine, *Epoca*, to counter rival publications.

Globo continues to forge alliances with domestic and foreign corporations. In August, 1999, Globo sold 9.6 percent of its cable TV unit to Microsoft. Microsoft paid $126 million and offered Globo high speed Internet services and online video images plus technology for e-commerce and interactive TV. Later that year Globo launched Virtua, a high speed residential broadband service available only to Globocabo's pay-TV subscribers. And in June, 2000, Telecom Italia agreed to pay $810 million for 30 percent of the Globo group's Internet portal. Globo.com will eventually make it possible for Globo to deliver content over wireless phones.[13]

Marinho has won recognition for his entrepreneurship. The Brazilian Advertisement Association gave him its Personality of the Year award in 1998 for his "business courage" in investing in the new printing plant and for launching the *Extra* newspaper and the *Epoca* magazine.[14] He has received numerous awards from countries in both hemispheres, including an Emmy in 1983. The American Chamber of Commerce gave Canal Futura, run by the Marinho Foundation, its Eco 1999 prize for its activities in schools, companies, hospitals, jails and communities.[15]

The 20-year-old Roberto Marinho Foundation provides educational TV programs to an audience in the millions every day in Brazil. Although almost all educational programs, including children's television, are sponsored by the government, Marinho's Telecurso 2000 is a special educational channel delivered direct to home by satellite TV Futura. Its only cost is the price of inexpensive materials which are available on newsstands and a TV set. Brazil has a population of 164 million and boasts a television set for every 4.8 persons. The channel is picked up by schools, penitentiaries, museums, hospitals and unions. Programs feature more than 200 hours of video lessons, each broadcast several times a week over four television networks at times that are convenient for working people. Futura's annual budget of $12 million is divided among its four partners, including Time-Warner-Turner.[16]

Despite the country's major economic problems, Globo continues to lead the market. After all, Roberto Marinho had a head start.

BORIS BEREZOVSKY–
PREFERS POLITICAL EXILE TO POLITICAL PRISON

40

When the Communist regime in the Soviet Union fell apart, a group of oligarchs was ready to grab anything that could be privatized. Chief among them was Boris Berezovsky, a former mathematician, who was able to pick up valuable state properties for peanuts in the early nineties and as a result, grew very wealthy. *Forbes* estimated his fortune at $3 billion in July, 1997.[1] Berezovsky and his fellow oligarchs were knocked off the *Forbes* billionaire list in 1998 because of the collapse of the ruble in August, according to reporter Paul Klebnikov, who says "the Berezovsky empire had been crippled by bad management, debts and endless schemes to funnel revenue offshore.[2] Berezovsky is suing for libel in a London court for an article in the Dec. 30, 1996 issue of *Forbes* by Klebnikov titled, "Godfather of the Kremlin?," which linked him to Chechen criminal gangs.

Berezovsky was a researcher at the Russian Academy of Sciences when he started Logovaz, a dealership for Russia's largest automaker Avtovaz. He was soon the largest Avtovaz dealer in the country. The *Forbes* article exposed the way in which gangsters control the lucrative Russian auto dealerships — how they steal parts and whole cars from the factory, which arrive at their dealerships in perfect shape; while cars ordered from competitors arrive with windshields smashed and tires slashed. Buyers pay up front for the cars, the dealers take a huge cut, and the automobile makers get their money late if at all.[3]

In his new book, also titled *Godfather of the Kremlin*, Klebnikov says that when Russian gangsters approached Berezovsky about an alliance, he said, "I already have a roof, (Russian slang for protection). Talk to the Chechens." The "talk" about the Moscow auto market took place outside a Logovaz showroom and led to a shootout with three killed and six wounded. "It was one of the bloodiest gang battles in Moscow in 1993." Berezovsky claims no knowledge of it.[4]

The biggest car dealer of them all — Berezovsky — bought prime real estate in Moscow and St Petersburg, a string of newspapers including one of Russia's most respected newspapers, a popular magazine and part of a new TV station called TV 6. He also owned 80 percent of Sibneft, one of Russia's largest oil companies before he sold it and part of Aeroflot, the national airline.

In 1994, Berezovsky barely escaped an assassination attempt. A remote-controlled bomb exploded next to his car, decapitating the driver. Berezovsky escaped with burns to his hands and face. No culprits were ever identified. After the attempt on his life, he moved to Israel and obtained Israeli citizenship. He gave that up and was back in Russia in 1996 helping to re-elect Boris Yeltsin as president. Yeltsin gratefully appointed him deputy secretary of the National Security Council, which coordinates military and law enforcement policy. He focused on implementing the peace settlement in Chechnya. Although he had promised to give up business activities in Chechnya, he continued to develop his interests there. As a result, he was ousted in November, 1997.[5]

Berezovsky's reputation was also damaged at the death of Vladislav Listiev, Moscow's most popular talk show host and its most successful TV producer. Early in 1995 Listiev persuaded the government to privatize Channel 1, Russia's biggest nationwide network, now known as ORT. The government kept 51 percent of the stock and businessmen got the rest. Berezovsky acquired 16 percent. Listiev was named head of the reorganized company. As with the car dealerships, most of the profits went to the middleman, in this case an advertising man named Sergei Lisovsky, who seemed to siphon off most of the profits while government subsidies kept the network going. On Feb. 20, 1995, Listiev announced he was breaking Lisovsky's advertising monopoly. Lisovsky demanded $100 million in damages. Listiev found a company willing to buy ORT's advertising franchise and asked Boris Berezovsky to act as transfer agent. Berezovsky stalled on delivering the money. Two weeks later Listiev was gunned down. There was a huge public outcry over his death, but no one was charged with the crime, least of all Berezovsky, even though he was widely suspected of involvement and by then controlled 49 percent of the network's voting stock.[6]

Aeroflot, Russia's national airline, was one of the crown jewels of Russian industry in 1995, according to *Forbes*. When Aeroflot was privatized, the state kept 51 percent and gave the other 49 percent to management and employees. With his connections to President Yeltsin and his family, Berezovsky was able to take over the airline. He brought in Nikolai Glushkov, an associate from the Logovaz dealership, as chief financial officer, and Aeroflot's money began moving back and forth within a network of Berezovsky-controlled financial companies in Russia and abroad. Andava, an obscure financial company in Lausanne, Switzerland, was set up as Aeroflot's foreign treasury center. It was mostly owned by Berezovsky and Glushkov. As *Forbes* reported, "It was time now to privatize the profits."[7] Within a few years Aeroflot foundered and things got so bad that Canadian authorities impounded an Aeroflot plane because the airline hadn't paid a $6 million hotel bill.

When Yevgeny Primakov became prime minister, he began to crack down on the influence of the oligarchs. Yeltsin's son-in-law, Valery Okulov, was appointed general director of Aeroflot in March, 1997, and he fired several managers and directors and all Berezovsky appointees who had not already resigned. On Feb. 4, 1999, police from the Federal Security Service raided Aeroflot's office looking for evidence of fraud, embezzlement and tax evasion. Logovaz offices were also raided. No charges were filed.[8]

Berezovsky had been helped in building his empire by his close friendship with President Yeltsin and his family. It began when the billionaire, one of seven bankers, spent more than $100 million to re-elect Yeltsin in 1996 when his campaign seemed doomed. Berezovsky lavished gifts of jewelry and cars on Yeltsin's influential daughter, Tatyana. But the big opportunity developed when Yeltsin was looking for someone to publish his second book. Berezovsky offered to publish it in Finland at his own expense. The ghost-written book, *Notes of a President*, was roundly ignored but Berezovsky deposited a $3 million advance in Barclay's Bank in London which generated $16,000 monthly interest for Yeltsin. Apparently the president was unaware that the book sales were fictitious but was grateful to Berezovsky for organizing the lucrative venture.[9]

Primakov continued his pressure on Berezovsky in the spring of 1999 and told a confidant he would like to see him behind bars or forced into exile.[10] On April 7, 1999, a warrant was issued for Berezovsky's arrest. He happened to be in France at the time. Both he and his friend and business associate, Nikolai Glushkov, were charged with illegal entrepreneurship and laundering of illegal income. They were suspected of transferring large amounts of money and putting some of it into the private Swiss company Andava, which handled 80 percent of Aeroflot's financial operations abroad. Nothing came of the charge. Berezovsky returned a couple of weeks later and began to fight back. He bought *Kommersant*, a business daily respected for its unbiased coverage, and several magazines. Under editor Raf Shakirov, the daily had been sharply critical of the billionaire and reported extensively on his suspected ties with Aeroflot's misfortunes. Berezovsky told the staff he would not interfere with editorial policy. Of course, Shakirov was replaced. He said he lost his job after he refused a cash bonus in exchange for his loyalty.

With his control of the media, Berezovsky set about discrediting his persecutors. So powerful was the media attack that Primakov and Moscow mayor Yuri Luzhkov, both prime candidates to succeed Yeltsin, withdrew from the presidential campaign, leaving the field to Vladimir Putin, a career intelligence officer with 16 years in the K.G.B. Putin became prime minister mid-year in 1999 and then acting president when Yeltsin resigned on New Year's Eve.

Forbes reporter Paul Krebnikov says that for the past several years Berezovsky has been making ransom payments to terrorists in Chechnya, boasting of his rescue efforts on news programs. The money allegedly helped finance the Islamic militias who are credited with a string of bombings, mostly in Moscow, that killed several hundred persons and led to the Chechen war. There have been so many kidnappings that the ransom has become a sort of currency. Berezovsky won points when he ransomed a British couple who had been working in a Chechen hospital and were held for 14 months. But when four telecom workers from England and New Zealand were held for ransom, Chechen president Aslan Maskhadov complained that Berezovsky was encouraging the kidnappers by paying ransom. With no ransom forthcoming, the heads of the four workers were found by a roadside within a month. Maskhadov said that in 1998 Berezovsky gave $1 million to Shamil Basayev, the warlord who is leading the Chechen rebel fight against Russia. While he admitted the gift, Berezovsky said it was not to finance the war but to begin the reconstruction of the Chechen republic.[11]

In the *New Yorker*, March 27, 2000, David Remnick quotes Igor Malashenko, a media executive, as saying, "For Berezovsky, television is a gun, a weapon, a propaganda machine." He also quotes a talk show host as saying, "Berezovsky is a tactician who wants to protect his turf and gain as much power as he can. He believes the country should be run by businessmen, the Russian version of 'What's good for General Motors is good for America.' He kicked and clawed his way into using the media and they're his best tool."[12]

Berezovsky is now at odds with the Putin government. Remnick, who covered Russia for the *New York Times* before becoming editor of The *New Yorker*, finds it incredible that in the spring of 2000, he heard Berezovsky give a lecture at Princeton University in which he put the oligarchs in a loving light and spoke well of Putin. He wrote, "Berezovsky is short and nearly bald with dark, intense eyes. Even his enemies who consider him evil say he is extremely smart. He won a seat in the Duma which his opponents claimed he wanted because it provided immunity from prosecution."[13]

Berzovsky offered Remnick a ride back to New York and told him that his father was a construction engineer; his mother, a nurse; that he got his doctorate in system-theory mathematics in 1973; that he has six children by three wives, and that he lives is an enormous well-guarded house in Moscow. He has various other residences, a couple of planes, and a yacht.[14]

Remnick reported in March, 2000, that Berezovsky took off in a new direction. He and his business associate, Roman Abramovich, bought up more than 60 percent of Russia's aluminum business — the country's biggest industry after oil and gas. The government found no problem with the deal. Putin wrote in a new book, according to Remnick, that he and Berezovsky talked fairly regularly, "And why not? He has a lively mind and many suggestions."[15]

Then Berezovsky resigned from the Duma in August, 2000, in protest against Putin's authoritarian policies, to form an opposition party. A month later he published a widely reported letter to the Kremlin outlining a plan to put his 49 percent interest in ORT and other media interests in a trust for four years to keep the government from taking them over. At about the same time he appeared on the *Charley Rose* program, saying that Putin's efforts to take government control of the media was why he was putting his business interests on hold to concentrate on politics. He was willing to go to jail, he said, if necessary, to resist Putin.

The president presented a different view. He said the Kremlin's actions were an attempt to free the media from the grip of rapacious monopolists and that the news media are not truly free because they speak for the rich instead of the ordinary people.[16]

Berezovsky countered in December, 2000, with $25 million to establish The

International Foundation for Civil Liberties to help the abused and oppressed in Russia, presumably including himself. The director of Moscow's Memorial human rights group expressed delight but also a concern that Berezovsky hoped to use the foundation to resolve personal issues. He also gave $3 million to the floundering Andrea Sakharov Foundation in Moscow . Sakharov's widow Yelena Bonner accepted the gift though she said she distrusted Berezovsky's motives.[17]

Roman Abramovich, close business ally of Berezovsky, was elected governor of the sparsely populated but resource-rich Arctic region of Chukotka in the December, 2000, elections. He seems to have made peace with Putin and reportedly bought Berezovsky's controlling interest in ORT, Russia's largest television network in January, 2001.[18]

Prosecutors seek to question Berezovsky about profit-skimming of Russia's formerly profitable airline, Aeroflot, according to Steve Crawshaw, of the *Independent* (London). He bitterly regrets helping put Putin in power and to avoid arrest, Berezovsky left Russia for exile in Europe and the United States in November, 2000. "I prefer to be a political emigre than a political prisoner," he told Crawshaw.[19]

In the epilogue to his book, *Godfather of the Kremlin,* Klebnikov writes, "In the late 1900's Communism was destroyed, the Soviet Union fell apart, democracy and free markets were proclaimed, huge fortunes were acquired. But what was left at the end of it all? Russia was ravaged and destroyed. Putin may well be the man to rebuild the Soviet Union but first he will have to deal with the corruption and crony capitalism of Berezovsky and the oligarchs."[20]

SILVIO BERLUSCONI—HEADING THE SHIP OF STATE AGAIN

41

Multi-billionaire media mogul Silvio Berlusconi has won a second term as Italy's premier after spending a large chunk of his fortune campaigning against the liberal, popular two-term former mayor of Rome, Francesco Rutelli. The election in May, 2001, gave Berlusconi's House of Freedom party a clear-cut majority in both houses of Parliament, which suggests that he might serve out his five year term. He was turned out of office after seven months in 1994 when Umberto Bossi's Northern League withdrew its support and Berlusconi's coalition fell apart. Berlusconi is in a much stronger position now while Bossi's has weakened . Supporters for both candidates felt passionate enough to stand in lines half the night in order to vote.

Berlusconi has promised to create new jobs, cut income taxes and increase pension payments. "A new era begins for Italians," he said after the election "I am convinced that you all feel the need for a government that governs and a premier who speaks less and works more."[1] Like Steve Forbes and Ross Perot, he could afford to run. He is worth $10.3 billion, according to *Forbes* magazine, July 9, 2001.[2]

His is a broad and varied empire: Italians live in houses built by Berlusconi, watch television on his TV stations, read his magazines, eat in his restaurants and wildly cheer his AC Milan soccer team, which has won three European Cups and six Italian League titles since he bought it in 1986. The money and the power, especially of television, helped Berlusconi break into politics. He says his purpose was to save his holding company, Fininvest, from the Communists. "The left would have given us a government with no business freedom where it wouldn't have been possible to work — one in which many entrepreneurs would have stopped doing business and many would have gone to foreign countries," he said.[3]

Widespread corruption in Italy led to the downfall of the Christian Democrat party which had been in power since 1945. Berlusconi created Forza Italia, named for the soccer cry, "Go Italy," and swept into power in March, 1994. It was a short-lived victory. His government lasted only from May to December.

Since then Berlusconi has three times been convicted of bribery, fraud and tax evasion and three times been acquitted on appeal. In October, 1999, because of the statute of limitations he was cleared of illegally financing a political party in 1991. Prosecutors alleged that he and his associates had funneled $6.6 million to ex-premier Bettino Craxi through a holding company called All Iberian. Craxi, who died in exile in Tunisia, in January, 2000, was cleared of the charges at the same time. Berlusconi was acquitted June 19, 2000, of bribing a judge in 1991 over control of the Mondadori publishing house.[4] He still faces half a dozen trials on bribery charges.

Berlusconi has profited from political patronage. Craxi, a friend since their university days, used his influence in Milan to change zoning regulations to facilitate Berlusconi's construction projects. In 1984, when Craxi became prime minister and pushed for deregulation of state television, Berlusconi was able to hang on to his three television stations that became the cornerstone of his empire. Since then he has been addressed in the press as Sua Emittenza (Your Broadcastship), a pun on addressing Roman Catholic cardinals Sua Eminenza (Your Eminence.)[5]

Denying any wrongdoing, Berlusconi says he is the victim of a vendetta by politically biased leftist magistrates. The disinterest of the electorate seems to indicate that they are tired of the litigation which dates back to the *mani pulite* or "clean hands" corruption probes which have dragged on since they began in Milan in 1992. Of the thousands of the accused, few have been convicted, and only a handful went to jail. Berlusconi was acquitted of tax fraud in March, 1999, claiming that the money involved was not a bribe but extortion by the tax collectors. Even Giulio Andreotti, who was prime minister seven times and fell from power when the *mani pulite* scandal erupted, was acquitted of consorting with the Mafia in October, 1999.

The political seas seemed to calm with the election of Carlo Azeglio Ciampi to the presidency in May, 1999, with broad support from the left and right after a single round of voting. Berlusconi said, "For once politicians were able to reach accord on a name, giving the country a strong sign of responsibility in a difficult moment."[6] The left's loss of the mayoral election in Bologna to the center right for the first time since 1945 was a big boost for Forza Italia. A jubilant Berlusconi got an even bigger boost April 16, 2000 when his Forza Italia party scored big in regional elections. Prime Minister Massimo d'Alema was unable to hold his bickering supporters together and resigned to be succeeded by the independent incumbent, Guliano Amato.

Berlusconi was born in 1936, the son of a bank official. He took a degree in law at the University of Milan, helping to pay for his tuition by performing with his own band during summers. The group was good enough to land bookings on cruise ships and at resorts. In the late 1970s he moved into construction, undertaking large projects. Borrowing money from banks, he was able to create Milano 2, an upmarket development on the outskirts of Milan, a yuppie city featuring expensive apartments, walkways, sports facilities and an artificial lake. It eventually accommodated 10,000 residents.[7]

Exactly how Berlusconi broke into television is an interesting story. In 1974, he created Telemilano, a closed circuit cable TV system to provide Milano 2 residents with entertainment and information about community events. Recognizing the potential of the medium in 1978, he used $2.5 million from his other businesses to launch a challenge to Radiotelevisione Italiana (RAI), Italy's state-owned, three-channel television network. Italian law permitted only the three government RAI stations to broadcast programs nationwide, but Berlusconi saw a legal loophole. By purchasing local stations and having them show tapes of the same program simultaneously, he could, in effect, operate a national television network while circumventing the law. Beginning in 1980, when Berlusconi established Canale 5, viewers all over Italy could tune in to programs ranging from Italian game shows to American offerings such as *Dallas*. Advertisers bought airtime to promote their products. In the end he formed Publitalia 80 which became the biggest advertising company in Europe.[8]

Later in the 1980's Berlusconi bought other networks outright -- Italia l in 1983 and Rete 4 in 1994. He spent $3 million to acquire American game shows, such as *Wheel of Fortune*, Hollywood movies and the largest library of sitcoms in Europe. The stations also broadcast original programs. He expanded his television operations outside Italy with outlets in Spain, France, Germany, Tunisia and Yugoslavia, and getting around Italy's ordinance against broadcasting live sports contests by beaming them from a facility on the Adriatic coast and collecting ad revenues in the process.[9]

When Berlusconi became prime minister the first time, there were grave concerns about the concentration of power in his hands. Fininvest, his holding company, was so huge that almost any political decision would affect some part of it. Despite Berlusconi's assurances that he would not allow his business interests to influence his political decisions, it was apparent that he recognized no distinction between his private concerns and the good of the country, according to a book on Italian politics, edited by Stephen Gundle and Simon Parker in 1996, which said, "His actions revealed that his aim was to conserve all his power and whenever possible to extend it."[10] Berlusconi said he would put his holdings in a blind trust if he came to power again but now he says he will resolve the conflict of interest question in the first hundred days of his administration, according to Tom Hundley, foreign correspondent for the *Chicago Trubune*.[11]

Because of new anti-trust laws, passed in 1997, governing the media, and to alleviate the conflict-of-interest charges that plagued his term in office, Berlusconi has been spinning off some of his holdings. He sold his 10 percent stake in Telepiu Grupo to French pay-TV Canal Plus in July, 1999. Mondadori, Italy's largest publishing company, owned 48 percent by Fininvest, has spun off its printing activities into an independent company which will absorb its five printing plants in Italy and perhaps find a foreign partner for its printing activities. It recently launched a new electronic publishing division.[12] Mondadori has also formed a partnership with Alta Vista, the U.S. search organ, for use on the Mondadori.com Internet pages. It will also be featured on the web pages of Mediaset, the commercial TV company, which is developing on-line services.[13]

Fininvest and Saudi Prince Alwaleed bin Talal joined Germany's Kirch Group in March, 1999, in a television joint venture with the understanding that Kirch would commit to an initial public offering in three years. Each will have a 3.2 percent stake in the subsidiary Kirch Media. Berlusconi is also joining Kirch to create a new European television production and distribution network. The venture, called Eureka, pairs their vast film and television operations with PubliEurope, Mediaset's dominant sales and advertising unit, combining the strengths of the two industry giants.[14]

In April, 1999, the *Financial Times* reported that Fininvest was planning to transform itself into a pan-European media and entertainment conglomerate to rival large U.S. media entertainment groups such as Time Warner, Disney and Viacom. The group hopes to attract French and United Kingdom partners. Claude Sposito, who is Fininvest's chief executive, says the expansion is necessary because they can't grow any more in Italy. "Our real core business is advertising," he says, and they aim to gain a slice of Europe's $20 billion a year advertising market.[15]

Berlusconi, now 45, is a short, balding well-tailored man who lives in well-guarded virtual solitude in a seventy room 18th century villa at Arcore, just north of Milan. He has five children. Two from his first marriage are active in the business. Marina, the eldest, is deputy chairman of Fininvest, sits on the board of Mondadori, and is chairman at Europortal Italia SpA, the developing Internet sector. Her brother, Piersilvio, is deputy general manager of Mediaset. Berlusconi divorced his first wife to marry actress Veronica Bartolini, who lives with their three children some miles away in another large villa.[16]

Berlusconi seems to be a teflon politician. Like former U.S. President Ronald Reagan, whom he admires, he has a charming persona that creates devoted followers. When the left-wingers won the November, 1998 elections, Berlusconi called up his followers to a gigantic rally in Rome. More than a million persons crowded Piazza San Giovanni to show support for the opposition and cheer their leader. When he was attacked savagely in the recent election, his ratings in the polls rose. Leftists and Communists will continue to try to annoy or destroy the newly elected. premier. He will have control of the three government TV channels, in addition to his own three channels, giving him a virtual monopoly, in addition to all his other media holdings. There is cause for alarm at the sheer magnitude of his power. Liberals both in Italy and abroad have expressed concern; conservatives, including Margaret Thatcher, have expressed delight. If he succeeds in bringing stability and economic reform to his fractured country, all the Italians will love him too.

SIR RICHARD BRANSON–ROCK MUSIC TO SPACE SHUTTLES

42

Brash, brilliant, unconventional, charismatic — meet daredevil Sir Richard Branson, who abandoned formal studies at 16 to start a business career which has grown to include more than 200 companies and at last count brought his personal fortune to an estimated $1.8 billion dollars.[1] It is difficult to know exactly how much Branson is worth since the private companies he owns are constantly dividing and multiplying, and many are based offshore.

Branson has been one of the most popular figures in England. Queen Elizabeth II knighted him in her Jan. 1, 2000 list of honors. His exploits, both economic and adventurous, have attracted attention worldwide. He makes the multimedia billion-aire gallery because of his entertainment, radio, television and publishing interests, which are just a small part of his Virgin empire.

His career began at Stowe, an exclusive public school, where he was more inter-ested in sports than in studies until a leg injury benched him and he turned to writ-ing. After he won a prize for a short story, he decided to start a magazine for stu-dents to circulate at other schools, colleges and universities. The magazine took over his life and he dropped out of school and moved to London with Jonny Gems, a col-league. The first issue of *Student*, published Jan. 16, 1968, was a critical and finan-cial success. He sold $10,000 worth of advertising for the first issue from a corner telephone booth and persuaded world-famous writers to contribute to it. He ran interviews with such famous personalities as David Hockney, Vanessa Redgrave and Jean-Paul Sartre. It operated on a shoestring and when it began losing money, in 1971, he ceased publication in order to open a discount record store. It flourished and the following year he built a recording studio in Oxfordshire.[2]

Tubular Bells, the first album under the newly minted Virgin label, featured an unknown artist, Mike Oldfield, but sold more than seven million copies worldwide and was used as background music for the hit movie, *The Exorcist*. The Sex Pistols, Boy George and the Rolling Stones were other sensations and the growth of the music company in the seventies and eighties was phenomenal. Branson was able to sell his Virgin Music Company to Thorn-EMI in 1992 for just under a billion dollars. It was a painful decision but he needed the cash for an airline venture.[3]

The Virgin brand name which Branson gave to his company to reflect youth and inexperience now extends to businesses as varied as airlines and vodka. It covers retail megastores, airlines, financial services, health services, hotels, radio stations, a publishing company, investments in railroads, travel, the Internet, cars and soft drinks. Branson says, "Consumers understand that all values that apply to one product — service, style, quality and fair dealing — apply to the others."[4]

The empire is run out of a mansion in London's Holland Park, two doors away from his family home, with none of the trappings of power except for three secretaries. He encourages executives and employees to send him ideas and suggestions and answers them all. He tends to immerse himself in each new project, carefully watch it develop and turn it over to competent people, give them a stake in the company and a lot of freedom, then back off and move on to something else.[5]

Branson is one of three children born to a barrister, Edward Branson and his wife, Eve, a former ballet instructor, glider pilot and flight attendant. He grew up in a 16th century farmhouse in Shamley Green, a picturesque village in Surrey where, as a youth. he tried various money-making schemes such as growing Christmas trees and raising budgies. He was sent to a prep school but cared so little for studies that his parents had to have him tutored to get into Stowe. He begged unsuccessfully to be sent to a technical school. After launching *Student* magazine he dropped out of Stowe and worked full-time selling advertising, doing interviews and attracting paid and volunteer staff.[6]

The magazine moved from the basement of Jonny Gems' parents' house in London to a house on Albion Street when Jonny left to continue his studies. Branson describes the scene in his autobiography, *Losing My Virginity*, as a house usually filled with young people working, smoking pot and falling in love. When one of his girl friends became pregnant, both realized that a baby was the last thing in the world they could cope with. After frantically trying to find help, she was able to get an abortion. The experience made them realize that there must be a lot of young people who needed information about birth control, social diseases and suicide prevention. As a result they started a Student Advisory Centre to help teenagers, which Branson still supports. Branson was arrested under an archaic law for using the word "venereal" disease in advertisements for the Center but was defended pro bono and released with a $17 fine.[7]

Several years later Branson married Kristen Tomassi, a blonde New Yorker he met at the recording studio. Tomassi felt neglected by Branson's absorption in business interests and left him after two years for another man.

He next fell in love with Joan Templeman. After living together for 12 years and having two children, Holly and Sam, they were married in 1989 on Necker Island, Branson's retreat in the British Virgin Islands, with 50 close friends attending. Branson joked that he thought they ought to get married before their children did.[8]

The Bransons manage a fairly conventional life style. Apart from the Holland Park home, they spend weekends at their country place on a river in Oxfordshire and from time to time go to Necker Island which boasts a staff with a gourmet chef. Between visits, the island is rented to the likes of Steven Spielberg and Oprah Winfrey for $23,000 a week or more.[9]

Daredevil stunts have brought Branson lots of publicity for his business interests. In 1985 he tried and failed to break the speed boat record across the Atlantic, but the following year in Challenger II he did break the record, gaining huge amounts of publicity. An attempt to cross the Atlantic the next year in a hot air balloon landed him in the Irish Sea; a 1990 attempt to cross the Pacific was successful but he landed in Arctic Canada. Both resulted in hair-raising rescues. Business advisers and his wife finally persuaded him to promise to give up the dangerous stunts. Later he begged to be relieved of the promise for a hot air balloon jaunt around the world; and in January, 1997, with two companions, he left from Marrakesh, Morocco, to circumnavigate the globe. After only one day off the ground, a leak in the helium tank forced them to land in Algeria. Again Branson's luck held when two tanks which could have caused a fatal crash were safely jettisoned.

Luck played a role, too, when in 1984, an American lawyer, named Randolph Field, asked Branson to invest in an airline for the Gatwick to New York route. Branson's business associates took a dim view of the project and Field turned out to be impossible to work with. The project appealed to Branson's sense of fun and he set it up under a separate company named Virgin Atlantic Airways. The financing almost threw the Virgin businesses into bankruptcy and the first trial flight ran into a flock of birds that blew up the engine of the leased Boeing 747. A replacement arrived in time for the inaugural flight and the plane began flying round-trips daily from Gatwick Airport just south of London and Newark, New Jersey. Virgin Atlantic Airways has grown to include flights from Heathrow to Kennedy, and London to Tokyo, Singapore, Hong Kong and Sydney as well as Chicago, Los Angeles, and other American cities.

Virgin Atlantic's popular perks for travelers lured customers away from British Airways, which fought back. Branson accused BA of unfair pricing policies, flooding the market with discount tickets, overcharging Virgin Atlantic for maintenance services and gaining access to its computerized booking system in a concerted effort to steal Virgin's upper class customers. He claimed that BA had hired a public relations firm to discredit Virgin and defame him personally. BA denied the allegations. But in 1993 the High Court ruled in Branson's favor, awarding Virgin Atlantic nearly one million dollars in damages as well as compensation for legal fees. Branson distributed the loot to his employees, who called it their BA bonus.[10] A similar suit in America was dismissed.

Atlantic Airways is part of the Virgin Travel Group which includes a tour group, a cargo service and a budget airline between European cities. Branson keeps a close hand on Virgin Atlantic which is noted for its lavish upper class, great food, even massages and manicures, and for video games and seat-back movies in economy. He expects to fly corporate jets daily to Dubai and New York in 2002 and expand to other cities. They will have the kind of flatbed seats available on Virgin Atlantic's Upper Class service and fill in for the grounded Concorde.[11]

The rest of the empire is divided into groups which are operated separately, some wholly Branson-owned and others in joint operations. Branson manages to keep control even when he has put up little or no funding.

The Rail Group has an interest in the British West Coast and Cross Country trains and the London & Continental Railways. These are profitable only because of state subsidies. Branson plans to get better, faster trains and improve the tracks.

The Retail Group has almost 200 megastores such as the one on Times Square in New York City which Branson launched by sliding down the side of the building on a big silver ball. The 75,000 square foot building offers 250 listening and viewing posts in addition to live performances, a bookstore, a travel agency, a cafe, and a movie theater. The megastore on the Champs Elysees in Paris has more visitors than the Eiffel Tower. The group also includes the Our Price record shop chain in Great Britain and other subsidiaries.

The Communications Group has an Internet service, television and radio stations, software productions and a book business. Virgin's Mobile Virtual Network Operator (MVNO) which was started in November, 1999, now has 750,000 subscribers in the United Kingdom plus expansion into Asia and Australia. A button on the phone can connect the subscriber to an operator for ordering plane tickets, records and other products. It is a joint venture with Deutsche Telekom unit One2One. Virgin Biznet provides websites for small business owners. Branson sold a 49 percent stake in Virgin Atlantic to Singapore Airlines to finance the Internet and mobile-phone businesses. Of the Singapore alliance, Branson said, "If you look at the route map, this really is a marriage made in heaven."[12]

The Hotel Group owns or manages several dozen hotels and night clubs, mostly in Britain, operating under different names. There is, of course, that extravagant complex on Neckar Island in the Caribbean and a couple of safari lodges in South Africa.

A financial services plan titled Virgin Direct sells tax-exempt savings plans, personal financial services and pension schemes. Half of it is owned by AMP, a financial service firm. The development arm, Voyager Investment, has a stake in the Eurostar London-Paris train service and also houses smaller oddities, such as Virgin Airship and Balloon that gives hot air balloon rides.[13]

Branson regretted having to sell his record business, the foundation of his empire, to finance the airline and is happy to have it back under a different name, V2 Music Group. To run it he hired Jeremy Pearce, a former lawyer, who opened offices in London, Europe, the States, Scandinavia and Asia and began signing up independent labels and bands. "We're doing immediately what it took Branson 15 years to do the last time," Pearce said.[14]

In 1996, the British Government chose a group headed by Branson and Bechtel Inc. to build and run a rail link between London and the Channel Tunnel, according to *Bloomberg Business News.* "It is scheduled to cost $4.6 billion dollars and to open in 2003. For Virgin, operating the 68-mile link fits Mr. Branson's plan to set up a pan-European rail and air network.[15]

Business has hit some rough spots. Branson took much of his company public in 1985 just before the stock market fell. That was a blow to the investors, so within two years he bought it back giving stockholders their purchase price which was twice the value of the market price after the crash. A bitter disappointment was the loss of his bid for the East Coast main rail line franchise to the incumbent in December, 2000.

There have been rough spots, too, with friends and associates from his first partner, Nik Powell, on down the line. Some of those who left, however, had become millionaires. Branson has been able to inspire loyalty in his employees and motivate them to offer suggestions for improving the company or spinning off another one.

Branson tangled with the law when he was caught by the Customs and Excise Department for evading purchase tax and duties on imported records. He was fined and bailed out by his family. After that he made sure that everything he did was according to law. However he learned the difference between tax *evasion* and tax *avoidance* and has taken advantage of every opportunity to avoid taxes, including transferring ownership of many of his company shares to offshore trusts which, while perfectly legitimate, have saved him tens of millions in taxes.[16]

There have also been problems. The British Government stopped his attempt with David Frost to take over Britain's Independent Television Network, and in 1993 he lost out in a bitterly contested bid to run the Government lottery. Branson spent a fortune to put together a team, which included Bill Gates, to bid for the next national lottery license; with plans to turn the profits over to worthy causes. To his chagrin the Lottery Commission again awarded the seven-year contract to Camelot, the incumbent in December, 2000.

Besides Branson's autobiography, there have been several other books about him. *Richard Branson, The Inside Story* by Mick Brown, published in 1988 and *Richard Branson: Virgin King,* by Tim Jackson, columnist for the London *Financial Times,* first published in 1994 and republished in 1996. Needless to say, both were out of date before they were printed. Branson moves too fast for the daily press, much less for a book. Two recent ones are like textbooks examining the Branson modus operandi: *Business the Richard Branson Way,* by Des Dearlove, 1999 and a segment in *The New Global Leaders,* by F. R. Kets de Vries and Elizabeth Florent-Treacy, 1999.

Tim Jackson says the public sees Branson as "the embodiment of all the great modern values, tolerance, informality, and human warmth, qualities not usually associated with business. But his success is due to his instinct for reducing risk, his drive for a hard bargain, the ruthlessness with which he will compete with his rivals — these are all characteristics that the most old-fashioned and least politically correct business men would find commendable.[17] A contrary view is taken by Tom Bower, in a new unauthorized biography, which displays Branson the businessman in a far from flattering light. The book, the loss of the lottery, the loss of the East Coast line and problems with Branson's train system have caused a shift in the public mood according to Martin Dickson writing in the *Financial Times.*[18]

Branson at 50 still has a boyish charm, a disarming grin and dresses mostly in casual sweaters and jeans. His sandy hair and Van Dyke beard are tinged with gray. He uses a notebook and a ballpoint pen to keep track of his interests. The notebooks are summarized and filed by his secretaries. He is a workaholic but says that his family is the most significant element in his life. He writes, "I spend much time traveling and treasure the moments the family is together. In many ways we are closest when we are all on Necker."[19]

What worlds are left for daredevil Branson to conquer? Virgin Space! Branson says, "I believe there are enough people willing to pay large sums of money to be passengers on space flights to make it feasible in my lifetime. Eventually Virgin Express will shuttle around in space like we do in Europe."[20] Plans are already underway for Virgin Galactic Airways to offer flights in space by 2010.

THE HOLTZBRINCK FAMILY–
INVADES AMERICAN PUBLISHING

43

Bertelsmann isn't the only German firm with a big chunk of the American book publishing business. The Georg von Holtzbrinck family has Henry Holt and Co., St. Martin's Press and prestigious Farrar Straus & Giroux plus many more. The family made the *Forbes* international billionaire list in July 9, 2001 with a worth estimated at $4.6 billion. Because it is privately held, not even *Forbes* can find out exactly how much money it makes. The family consists of Dieter, 56; his sister, Monika, 58; and their half-brother, Stefan, 34.[1]

Media interests in Germany include *Handelsblatt*, the largest business daily, and other newspapers, including the weekly *Die Zeit*, book publishing companies, printing plants, part interests in radio and television stations throughout the country, an on-line art portal, and shares in press and media elsewhere in Europe.[2]

The Holtzbrinck family history dates back as far as 1486, when the name, which means wooded hill, first appeared. Georg von Holtzbrinck, the patriarch for whom the firm is named, worked as a book salesman while studying law before World War II. After the war he started a book club in Stuttgart, added record clubs and expanded into other European countries. In the fifties he began buying shares in newspapers, business magazines and book publishing houses.[3]

His son, Dieter, took over after his father's death in 1983. Dieter was an indifferent student but eventually graduated from Hochschule St. Gallen, a prestigious business school in Switzerland. He worked at several publishing houses in the United States, including McGraw-Hill. As newlyweds, both he and his wife Richild, an artist, fell in love with New York City.

His father called him back to Germany in 1974 to head *Handelsblatt* in Dusselldorf and after four years brought him into the corporate headquarters in Stuttgart. His relationship with his father was an uneasy one but he gradually took over as his father aged. After his father's death in 1983, he looked back toward America for expansion. He bought *Scientific American* for $53 million, beating out competitors, including the late Robert Maxwell, by promising to preserve the magazine's quality and traditions, a pitch he used successfully in later transactions.[4]

Roger Straus asked him to buy Farrar, Straus and Giroux with its list of 20 Nobel laureates and such best sellers as Tom Wolfe, Philip Roth and Scott Turow because of his integrity and his reputation for letting subsidiaries run their own show. Other purchases include 70 percent of Macmillan Ltd., with its New York-based St. Martin's Press; W. H. Freeman; Hanley & Belfus; and Worth Publishers.

Before Georg died he turned over equal shares in the company to Dieter, Monika and Stefan, with one exception: Dieter got 55 percent of *Handelsblatt*. Each has a separate family trust and Dieter's three children already hold shares in his. On May 15, 2001, Dieter moved up to chairman of the supervisory board and his half-brother, Stefan, became CEO and chairman of the executive board. Monika Schoeller runs the venerable German publishing house S. Fisher, in Frankfurt. Corporate headquarters is on a hilltop overlooking the city of Stuttgart. Dieter mainly kept a hands-off policy with his family book publishers, including the 12 in Germany with 40 imprints. "They all know more about publishing than I do," he said.[5] Stefan is expected to follow Dieter's hands-off policy.

Von Holtzbrinck Publishers Services (VHPS) built a $30 million dollar high technology warehouse in Gordonsville, Virginia. The 435,000 square foot facility consolidates inventories of the company's American publishers. Laser wands can retrieve books so efficiently that 10,500 orders can be processed in a day with projected savings of $6 million a year. Dieter told the *New York Times'* Doreen Carvajal, "I just believe in America....America is the most important market in publishing." He flew in from Germany to cut the ribbon when the warehouse opened in September, 1998.[6]

In a long piece in *Vanity Fair* in June, 1998, David Margolick called Holtzbrinck a "stolid, contented, determinedly respectable man," who was admired by his executives. However, he also found some infighting among management teams both in Germany and New York. Several top executives resigned and changed jobs, taking prominent authors with them. Margolick also documents Georg's involvement with the Nazis both before and during World War II. He quotes Monika as saying that her father had indeed joined the Nazi party but it was a matter of survival rather than conviction. When he became a soldier in 1943, he had a wife and three children.[7]

Margolick says Nazi party records show Georg Holtzbrinck joined a student group two years before Hitler came to power and that "he managed to operate or own several publishing companies throughout the Nazi years, including one that produced books for German soldiers." The company's Nazi background was a problem when Dieter and Rachild came to New York in 1968. Richild said, "Most of our friends in New York were Jewish. We had to sort of prove that we were nice persons although we were Germans." A German "denazification" court accused Georg of profiteering during the war, but in the end he was fined a nominal sum and the charges were dismissed.[8]

Before he died, Georg donated money for a museum in Israel to commemorate

20 years of Jerusalem as a divided city. The family has continued its friendship with Israel into the third generation. "Monika's daughter volunteers at a clinic for handicapped Jewish and Arab children and speaks Hebrew."[9]

Like Mitterand, Georg had a longtime mistress and he adopted their son, Stefan, when he was 12, in 1963. At his funeral, Richild and their three children were seated in the first row and the mistress and Stefan in the second. Stefan worked at *Nature* magazine at Macmillan in London before moving up to CEO at Holtzbrinck. He recently married a Spanish television star. Like his father, Dieter has taken a mistress. His estranged wife lives in the family home recovering from cancer and severe depression. Margolick says Dieter still works hard and does little to relax, aside from jogging and brief sojourns at Lake Constance where he has a couple of cottages and a small yacht.[10]

The company continues to expand, most recently buying BookEasy, an English Internet-based inquiry and ordering service with 24-hour, seven-day access, which was launched in the United Kingdom in October, 1997 and is free to booksellers,[11] and a joint-venture with Springer, German Telecom, and Infoseek to create a new German search engine. Most recently Holtzbrinck traded some newspaper assets with Dow Jones in exchange for 49 percent of the *Wall Street Journal* Europe. Dow Jones got 22 percent of *Handelsblatt*. The two newspapers plan to use each other's reporting with each allowing the other to translate and publish on the same day.[12]

With Stefan at the helm, it remains to be seen how the company will fare with its expensive international ventures. So far it has been successful financially without lowering standards.

LEO KIRCH–SITS ATOP FAMOUS FILM ARCHIVE

44

Leo Kirch, Germany's second wealthiest media mogul, and founder of the KirchGroup, is an innovative entrepreneur who has run his empire close to the vest without benefit of boards or stockholders.

He changed that solo course in January, 1999, when he announced reorganization of the group into three separate units — KirchMedia, PayTV and Taurus Film — all under control of a family foundation with a board of directors and a supervising board. KirchMedia controls the publisher Axel Springer Verlag and the SAT1 broadcaster; Pay-TV handles the group's digital and pay-TV activities; and Taurus Film controls film and TV production and television rights. Outsiders would be offered shares only in Kirch Media.[1] Since then Silvio Berlusconi, Prince Alwaleed, Lehman Brothers, and Capital Research have all taken stakes in KirchMedia, and Murdoch's News Corp. has bought a 24 percent stake in Premiere, the former privately held Kirch digital PayTV business.

Leo Kirch began his media career in film distribution, then went on to film and television production and broadcasting on an international scale. KirchGroup is one of Europe's leading suppliers of films, TV series, classical music and children's programming for television. It also has a 40.5 percent interest in Axel Springer Verlag, Germany's biggest newspaper publisher.

Kirch has invested heavily in digital television. In the *Financial Times*, Judy Dempsey writes, "If digital satellite television proves lucrative, Kirch will unquestionably become one of the most powerful media groups in Europe if not the world."[2] Industry analysts, however, question whether the benefits of digital TV will outweigh its high cost and bring enough subscribers to make Dempsey's assumption come true. In 1996 Kirch spent billions to land German digital and pay-TV rights at major studios, including pacts signed with Viacom, Warner Bros., Sony, Disney,

MGM, Universal, and Regency, a Hollywood entertainment agency producing films, pilots and television series. His digital TV holdings contain 15 specialty channels on subjects such as romance, detective mysteries, cars and documentaries. Kirch DigitalTV has grown slowly but jumped to 300,000 subscribers for DF1 (Gesellschaft fur Digitales Fernechen) after the Telekom merger, but still has only one-fifth of Bertelsmann's 1.5 million subscribers. He has sunk $1 billion into this new digital-TV venture. "People have counted me out before," Kirch says. "Digital is long term."[3]

Kirch was born in Wurzburg in 1926, the son of a Bavarian vintner. His parents were poor, and because he served as an acolyte in his parish church, he came to the attention of the pastor who recognized his brilliance and made it possible for him to attend the Gymnasium. He went on to attend Munich University, receiving his PhD in business administration. He was serving as an associate professor in economics at the university when he got hooked on film and began to collect it. In 1956, Kirch was touring Italy in a VW bug when he discovered that Federico Fellini had exhausted funding for his half-completed film, *La Strada*. Kirch risked borrowing $54,000 from a bank so Fellini could complete the film. In exchange he received German rights. When the film turned out to be a smash hit, Kirch cashed in. He has been buying films ever since and has spent billions building the film archive which he stores in a climate-controlled vault in Munich. He now owns 15,000 feature films, ranging from silent film classics to current Hollywood hits, and 50,000 hours of TV programming. So complete is the collection that Hollywood studios sometimes borrow prints of their own classics because Kirch is the only one who has preserved decent copies.[4]

KirchGroup's Unitel, founded in 1966, is the world's leading producer of classical music programs for film, TV and video. In 1997 Unitel signed an exclusive contract to provide classical music for Japan's first digital pay-TV channel.[5]

In spite of being nearly blind from diabetes, Kirch often works seven-day weeks. Work and classical music are his only hobbies. Three decades of producing symphonies and operas for TV have led to friendships with leading conductors and artists ranging from Herbert von Karajan to Pavarotti. A recluse, who avoids the press and shuns the limelight, he lives simply in an apartment near Munich with his wife, Ruth. Their only heir, Thomas, now 41, co-founded PRO7 Media AG, which he took public in 1997. He also has a big stake in the cable channel, Kabelcanal, among other investments. Thomas is a billionaire in his own right.[6]

In June, 2000, Kirch consolidated his TV holdings by merging the Axel Springer Verlag publishing group with Kirch Media KgaG. The title of the new firm is ProSiebenSAT-1 Media AG. It is listed on the Frankfurt Stock Exchange. Kirch owns 52.5 percent of the new firm as well as his 40.5 percent of Axel Springer. The merger added the profitable ProSieben (PRO7) TV channel into Kirch's corporate empire. The new firm is estimated to have 25 percent of the national audience as opposed to the 19 percent credited to Bertelsmann and its partners, Pearson and Audofina.[7]

Kirch is a conservative and a devout Catholic. Offended by an editorial in Die Welt which supported the German constitutional court's ruling that there was no obligation to hang crucifixes in German schoolrooms, he demanded the editor's resignation. Liberals and politicians raised a storm of protest and the editor hung onto his job, but Kirch's arrogance caused a backlash which continues to this day.[8]

Die Welt is published by Axel Springer Verlag AG in which Kirch had bought an interest. Springer was incensed when Kirch began buying his company's stock and retaliated by using its stake in SAT1, one of Kirch's TV channels, to keep the channel from buying films from KirchGroup. This caused a cash flow crisis which Kirch resolved by selling films to Swiss retail king and business associate, Otto Beisham, who resold the films to Thomas Kirch's PRO7 and SAT1 in a deal worth several hundred million dollars even though the films never left Kirch's storage archive.[9] It is this deal which a government tax probe claims has allowed Kirch to make a huge profit and avoid paying $220 million in taxes, a claim which he vehemently denies.[10] The case has not yet been settled.

Kirch has been in trouble before but has always managed to outfox his would-be regulatory masters. Michael Radke, author of a critical biography, published in Germany in 1964, writes, "There is not a single institution in this country, not a single law, that can stop this power. It's a huge, ever-growing, incomparable concentration, a melange of business, media and politics."[11]

Critics have gleefully predicted that Kirch was over a barrel because of his huge investment in DF1, Germany's first digital television service. Rupert Murdoch withdrew from an option to acquire a 49 percent stake in DF1. An expected bank loan fell through amid accusations of special treatment. Kirch had trouble dealing with Deutsche Telekom, the telephone monopoly that controls all the cables that run under German streets. In the mid-nineties, Kirch was in a financial bind from the film and television deals in Hollywood[12] and from a deal with Sports Holding AG to acquire TV rights outside the United States for the 2002 and 2006 Soccer World Cups. Restructuring measures have reduced the indebtedness.

Kirch and the Swiss software company, Fantastic Corporation, have joined in a venture called Worldzap to offer coverage of the World Cup and other sporting events via mobile phones. They expect to invest $450 million in the next six years. Customers will also have access to stock market reports, news, games and concerts.[13] Kirch Media has also bought worldwide rights to Bundesliga, Germany's top football league, from 2001 to 2005. Games will be broadcast on Premiere, Kirch's pay-TV channel.

On April 24, 2001, the motor sports governing body granted a 100-year extension of the broadcasting and commercial rights to Formula One, to Kirch and EMTV. Big carmakers were concerned that Kirch might cut the free TV broadcasts which attract 300 million fans. Kirch assured the big carmakers that Formula One broadcasts would remain free with pay per view as an option for better coverage. He is still dickering over selling broadcast rights to the United Kingdom.

Kirch came out on top after a fight with his top rival, Bertelsmann, over set-top decoders for digital television. After years of infighting, Bertelsmann agreed to give up its plans for a different incompatible decoder — much as Sony had to give up its Betamax for Matsushita's home video recorder more than a decade earlier. Bertelsmann came in with too little, too late, and agreed to a three-way settlement with Kirch and Telekom, Germany's monopoly telephone company, to use the

KirchGroup decoder and adopt a common decoding system.[14] Critical to the agreement was the Deutsche Telekom announcement that it would adopt Kirch's technology for set-top decoders and customer verification and that it would provide the capacity to carry some 50 channels envisioned by Kirch and Bertelsmann. Previously, Kirch had only been able to transmit DF1 by satellite.[15] The system, from Nokia of Finland, now used by both, can turn an ordinary TV set into a multimedia station to which peripherals such as PCs, printers and CD-Roms can be connected. The box costs about $600 and users pay a monthly fee of $12.[16]

Telekom currently provides cable service to more than 16 million households. Analysts predict that it will take one million customers for KirchGroup to break even and two million for it to be solidly profitable.[17] A Bremen University study found that 99 percent of German households have TV sets and about one-fifth of those have cable, so Kirch's expectations may some day be realized.[18]

Looking ahead to the day when he will no longer be at the helm, Kirch, like Reinhard Mohn of Bertelsmann, set up a foundation in 1997. The foundation handles his diverse business interests and is intended to keep the holdings secure in the hands of the Kirch family until 2027.[19]

As for the political opposition, it will no doubt continue. Kirch has supported the conservative former Chancellor Helmut Kohl heavily since he first ran for office. Kohl, in turn, was supportive of Kirch's business plans and helped gain European Union approval for the PayTV alliance with Bertelsmann and Deutsche Telekom. An investigation into Kohl's Christian Union party revealed the existence of more than $13 million in illicit funding during Kohl's 16 years in office. Kohl has admitted he had $1 million in unaccounted funds but refuses to say where it came from. Some assume it came from Kirch. Kohl has also admitted that since he left office he accepted six free flights provided by Kirch, but insists they had nothing to do with his work as chancellor.[20] The liberals are outraged by these disclosures. In response, a Kirch spokesman said, "In the eyes of our critics, the right person (to control the KirchGroup) could only be a left-wing person." Kirch himself said, "To be sure I have a political viewpoint but no personal political ambition. I am a businessman. I don't want to exert political power, but I am a conservative." Less sanguine rivals call his empire "a political danger to democracy."[21]

Political danger or not, Leo Kirch continues to expand his financial empire. In addition to its German film, television and newspaper holdings, KirchGroup now has media interests in Austria, Italy, Switzerland, the Netherlands and Spain. And according to *Forbes*, he and his family are now worth $20 billion.[22]

JEAN-LUC LAGARDÈRE–
MUNITIONS, MAGAZINES AND SPACE

45

Because of his love for speed in race cars and race horses and for his boundless energy, French billionaire industrialist and media mogul Jean Luc Lagardère is nicknamed "Vroom Vroom." This energy has allowed him to rebound from crushing defeats to brilliant successes so often that a recent French biography was titled *L'Acrobate*.

Lagardère's successes have added up. The multi-billion dollar Lagardère Groupe has investments ranging from munitions to magazines. The munitions came first. When Lagardère graduated from the prestigious Ecole Supérieure d'Électricite and Aéronatique in 1951, he began working at the Dassault Aeronautic firm. He was head of research when Marcel Chassagny, founder and president of Matra (Société Méchanique Aviation Traction) invited him to join his firm as general director. Chassigny and chief stockholder Sylvain Floirat gave him carte blanche and let him run the company. Because neither had heirs to succeed them, they treated Lagardère as a son. Floirat said later that from the minute Lagardère arrived business went well. Matra developed missiles for the Mirage airplane as well as surface-to-air missiles, the Magic missile for air combat and the R530 surface-to-air missile used by Israel in the Six Day War of 1976. Because it was a private behind-the-scenes munitions business and Lagardère wanted recognition for the company, he worked out a plan to produce racing cars. His attempts failed at first but eventually the Matra-Simca entry won the 24 hour rally at Le Mans three years in a row.[1]

In the '70s and '80s Matra, along with Dassault Aérospatiale and Thomson-CSF, formed the famous band of four to sell enough arms to both Kadhafi and Saddam Hussein to make the Gulf a veritable powder keg.[2]   Lagardère had sold arms to both Iran and Iraq when they were fighting one another but he realized that the lucrative arms market could fluctuate wildly and so began to diversify. He entered into a dazzling array of joint ventures with Italian, German, Swedish and American partners. He poured profits from Matra into developing space launchers, satellites, optical lenses, automobile equipment and innovative transportation systems such as the driverless rapid transit railroad VAL in Lille. Under his leadership in the '70s, Matra moved into telecommunications and the manufacture of satellites and equipment related to space research.[3]

In 1982, the Socialist government under Mitterand followed through on its threat to nationalize businesses and took a 51 percent stake in the company. When Lagardère and his top managers threatened to resign, Lagardère was permitted to maintain strong managerial independence.[4] When the Conservatives and Chirac came to power, Lagardère looked forward to privatization. It took until 1988 for Lagardère to gain the right to be master of his own house again, just days before Mitterand was reelected president of the Republic.[5]

Lagardère was born in Aubiet, a small village in southwestern France, the son of a customs director. Because his ancestors came from Gascony, Lagardère likes to call himself a Gascon. Like D'Artagnan of *The Three Musketeers*, he loves a battle, which combined with his constant search for adventure, has made him a brilliant entrepreneur. He claims John Wayne as one of his heroes.

Lagardère is slim and trim, always deeply tanned. He neither smokes nor drinks and rises early each day for a half-hour of exercise. He is 72 now but looks 20 years younger. In 1958 he married Corinne Levasseur in an elaborate ceremony. Eleven years younger, she was the daughter of a wealthy Parisian family, a lover of music and horses. They had little in common but Lagardère became interested in horses and they began to raise thoroughbreds. Early in 1968 they registered their colors in her name and the following July won their first race at Chantilly. Lagardère was so absorbed in his work, his stables and the education of their son, Arnaud, that he neglected his wife and they gradually grew apart. When they were divorced in 1975, he immediately transferred their gray and pink colors to his name and later that year won his first major race in his own name. Corinne permitted their son, then 14, to choose which parent to live with and he chose his father. For some years Arnaud frequently visited his mother who had remarried and had two more children. As he grew older he spent all his time with his father.[6]

Lagardère worked days, nights and weekends, always searching for something new. He occasionally relaxed at the Polo Club; there, after three years as a bachelor, he fell under the charms of Elizabeth Pimenta Lucas, known as Bethy, a young Brazilian model at the House of Ungaro. After living together for 15 years, they were married quietly in a city hall in Paris in August, 1993.[7]

Lagardère's beloved son and heir was seriously injured in an automobile accident in 1981 when he was 20, but recovered after a long convalescence.[8] He is now co-director of Lagardère Groupe with Philippe Camus at the top of the management team directly under Jean Luc.

In 1980 Lagardère bought Hachette, the publishing house which dates back to 1826. The acquisition of Hachette was a gift from then President Giscard d'Estaing, a friend from the Polo Club where Lagardère played tennis. A financier called to tell him that a bank had options on 40 percent of the shares of Hachette and Lagardère had 48 hours to decide if he wanted them. The deal had been put together for

Havas Groupe, a mega-publisher, but d'Estaing considered Matra a safer deal. Overnight Lagardère found the necessary financing and the partnership of Daniel Filipacchi, publisher of *Paris Match*. Together they bought an additional 11 percent, to get the magic 51 percent majority.[9]

Lagardère has built Hachette into one of the world's biggest communications companies. It includes his popular radio station, Europe 1, which was also nationalized by the Socialists but later returned to private ownership. He made a big play for TF1 — channel 1 on French television — which was being denationalized but he lost out to a consortium which included the late media mogul Robert Maxwell. Still yearning for a television station, Lagardère decided to invest in La Cinq, a private TV station that had changed hands several times in its five years and was deeply in debt. It was a hopeless effort. In the end Le Cinq failed yet again and cost Hachette $643 million. To keep the company afloat, Lagardère set up a holding company combining Matra with Hachette under the new name of Lagardère Groupe. Matra stockholders received 13 Hachette shares for every five shares they held in Matra.[10]

Business has grown so rapidly that, according to company reports, Hachette, once a little company that Emile Zola worked for, now makes half its profits outside France. David Pecker, former chief of Hachette Filipacchi Magazines, based in New York, made *Elle*, the world's number two fashion magazine, second only to *Vogue*. Hachette also publishes *Elle Cuisine* and *Elle Decor* which are printed in multiple versions and languages. In July, 1999, Hachette announced a joint venture with Pacific Publications to publish *Elle* and *Elle Cuisine* in Australia and New Zealand. Pecker started *George* magazine with John F. Kennedy Jr. but left to run the *National Enquirer* and *Star* weekly tabloids. Jack W. Kilger was named president and CEO of Hachette Filipacchi in June, 1999. He bought the Kennedy family's half share in George, which gained circulation after the massive media blitz at the time of the tragic Kennedy plane crash. Increased circulation did not bring an increase in advertising and Hachette finally folded the magazine. Hachette now has 200 magazines in 34 markets, with profits of $82 million. Some of the profit comes from custom publishing magazines, each for a specific company, such as Trump *Style* for guests of Donald Trump's hotels and casinos.

Lagardère continued to explore new ventures. His efforts to develop an automobile failed with various models and various companies until Matra developed L'Espace, a minivan, produced by Renault in 1983 that has sold hundreds of thousands. The investment was costly and risky. In L'Espace's first month of production Renault sold only nine cars. It soon became popular and the new model, developed in 1996, is as ubiquitous as the old *deux-chevaux*. The money poured into its development has been returned many times over.

While Lagardère's horse farms have continued to produce winners, his efforts to produce a champion football team failed in spite of his and his wife Bethy's enthusiastic support. The Matra Racing football team was abandoned after costing a fortune.[11]

At the end of 1986, Lagardère created a firm called Arjil SA, the Ar for Arnaud and jil for Jean-Luc, with three banking partners. A spinoff from this was a small, wholly owned bank called Arjil Banque. Arjil SA has since been renamed Lagardère Capital.

An Internet press release in June, 1998 shows how the company has divided its interests into three departments under one head. Under Matra Haute Technologie are Marconi Space, BAe Dynamics, Systemes and Information, Nortel Communications and Datavision. The Matra division also includes Automobile and Transport International. The Hachette arm, under Medias, lists Hachette Livre, Hachette Fillipacchi Medias, Hachette Distribution Services, Europe 1 Communication and Grolier/Multimedia.

It was at Grolier that Lagardère's son Arnaud chose to try his wings. He settled in Danbury, Connecticut, in 1994, with his wife and children not far from the Grolier office. By closing out unprofitable groups he was able to wipe out Grolier's debt and open it to new ventures. He returned to Paris in 1998 as head of Lagardère Medias. He has been selling off non-core businesses there, among them a radio network, a billboard advertising company, a poster advertising group, and even Grolier, to focus on key activities in the audio-visual, press, and multi-media sectors.

The privatization of the French military-industrial complex begun by President Jacques Chirac several years ago has been a boon for the Lagardère Group. In February, 1999, the government agreed to merge the state-owned Aerospatiale group with Matra Hautes Technologies, creating the world's fifth-largest military and aerospace contractor and the second in Europe, behind only British Aerospace (BAe-Marconi). Lagardère purchased 33 per cent of the new company for $345 million in cash; the government kept 44 percent and around 20 percent was made available to private shareholders in June of 1999 and promptly oversubscribed. Lagardère is head of the supervisory board of the new company, which is titled Aérospatiale-Matra.

On October 14, 1999, Lagardère was appointed head of the new European Aeronautic Space and Defense Group (EAD). Daimler Chrysler Aerospace (Dasa) of Germany and Aerospatiale Matra merged to form the world's third largest aerospace company after Boeing and Lockheed-Martin. It will control Airbus Industrial as well as Arianespace S.A., the world's biggest commercial rocket-launching company, and Eurocopter, the world's largest helicopter company. The agreement was signed by Chancellor Gerhard Schroeder of Germany and Prime Minister Lionel Jospin of France at Strasbourg on the French-German border. The name and the official language of the business is English, the language used throughout space programs.

The appointment was a crowning achievement for Lagardère, who says he hopes to lure more partners. Spain's Construcciones Aeronautics SA (Casa) came aboard in December, 1999 and Italy and Britain may follow. The new group is owned 60 percent by a holding company split evenly between French and German interests; stock market investors will own the remaining 40 percent.[12]

On Dec. 19, 2000, Airbus Industrie announced the launch of a superjumbo jet. The 555- passenger airbus will be larger than Boeing's 747. Lagardère is co-chairman of EADS, which owns 80 percent of Airbus. He said, at the launching in Toulouse, that the competition with Boeing "is its top challenge." Airbus has been gaining steadily against Boeing and has more than 50 orders so far for the jumbo jet.[13]

A recent book, *Les Nouveau Rois de France*, by Herve Bentegeat, views with alarm the rise of dozens of little "lords" who have seized power in France and hold top administrative positions in politics, business and the media. He includes profiles of "La bande des quatre" to show how businessmen are taking over political life. One of the four is "Lagardère, the entrepreneur," who rose to power selling munitions. The book's subtitle "La Trahison des Elites" provides the premise that the political process is paralyzed by the new elite. Bentegeat says, "The new kings of France are shopkeepers changed with zeal into great bosses who control France."[14] The charge is familiar for U.S. citizens who believe corporate bosses rule America.

Like most media moguls, Lagardère has been involved in numerous lawsuits. In June, 1999, a Paris judge asked the city's criminal court to examine a case against Lagardère . The charge is that his personal holding company benefitted from illicit financing from Matra and Hachette. The case dates back to October, 1996 and has not yet been settled.

Lagardère is popular both at home and abroad. His decorations include the Cross of Officier de la Legion d'honneur and Commandeur de l'Ordre National du Merite. In 1979 he was named manager of the year by *Le Nouvel Economiste*. He has created La Fondation Hachette, which is under the aegis of the Fondation of France and aids hospitals that need help in communication skills.

Lagardère at 72 does not consider retirement but thinks ahead perhaps to when he is 75 and might let Arnaud and his top managers take over. The little firm of Matra had fewer than 1500 employees when he took the helm. At last count the Lagardère Groupe had 46,200 and space technology has opened up a whole new world for him to conquer.[15] Matra Marconi Space and Dasa plan a European Space travel group named Astrium which will deal with telecommunication satellites, research satellites and space travel infrastructure.

Vroom, vroom, vroom.

REINHARD MOHN AND FAMILY–
BERTELSMANN JUST GROWS AND GROWS

46

Beginning from scratch, Reinhard Mohn has built Bertelsmann A.G. into the third largest media empire in the world, behind only AOL-Time Warner and Disney. Bertelsmann grew from a small publishing house in a provincial German town into a global giant with more than 300 companies scattered over 52 countries. The businesses include book and music clubs, magazines, newspapers, television stations, book and music publishing houses, online services, multimedia productions and printing plants. Mohn and his family are worth $5.7 billion dollars, according to the July 3, 2000 issue of *Forbes*.[1]

How Mohn accomplished this feat is no secret. His philosophy is recorded in his book *Success Through Partnership*, published in the States in 1988 and revised in 1996.[2] He has maintained a tough stance on profits, demanding a 15 percent return on investments, insisting that only through a partnership of employees and management can the free enterprise system be saved.

Alvin Toffler, in his introduction to Mohn's book, quotes Mohn's concept that business should "create equal chances for personal development for everyone and guarantee a fair distribution of wealth," including "a share in company assets."[3] It's a far cry from the usual media moguls' emphasis on the bottom line, but it has worked for Bertelsmann.

Only the German employees may participate in the profit-sharing plan. Nearly half of Bertelsmann's earnings go into employee profit-sharing plans that involve non-voting participation notes, which give the holder a 15 percent annual dividend but no ownership in the company.[4] The certificates also provide a substantial payout when the employee retires.

Mohn's frugal life style, his eating lunch in the company cafeteria, riding a bike to work and walking or birding for pleasure, plus maintaining a Spartan office devoid of luxuries, conforms to his family's low key traditions and contrasts with the usual life style of the rich and famous. Even the parsimonious Lord Kenneth Thomson has an office full of fine paintings.

The family publishing house is in Gutersloh, a small provincial town in northern Germany with 100,000 inhabitants, most of whom work for Bertelsmann. Visitors may stay at the posh hotel, built by Mohn, eat in its excellent dining room, walk in Mohn Park, note the library built by Mohn, or check out the Mohndruck printing plant, latest incarnation of the family's humble print shop. Then there is Bertelsmann Distribution which also stocks non-Bertelsmann titles and ships 10,000 packages daily. It serves 5500 booksellers in Germany, delivering 90 percent of its orders within 48 hours. Sonopress, also in Gutersloh, produces compact disks for all of Europe, not only name brands such as RCA and Arista but also Rincordi, the Italian music house, original publisher of Verdi and Puccini, now owned by Bertelsmann.[5]

The business dates back to 1835 when Mohn's great grandfather, Carl Bertelsmann, published hymnals and religious tracts. There were no males in the third generation to continue the business, so Reinhard's grandfather, Johannes Mohn, who had married into the family, took it on. According to company histories, his son, Heinrich, published manuals for the army in World War II but fell into disfavor with the Nazis and the plant was closed down in 1944 for illegally importing paper from Finland. A few months later the plant was bombed to oblivion by the RAF.[6] However, two journalists writing in The *Nation*, said in fact Bertelsmann had close ties with the Hitler regime and published a wide range of Hitlerian propaganda and anti-Semitic works. According to de-Nazification files in the state archive, Heinrich was a passive member of the S.S. as well as a supporter of the Hitler Youth and a member of the National Socialist Flying Corps.

Bertelsmann appointed an independent group of scholars to examine its history during the Nazi era. In January, 2000, the scholars reported that the company had risen remarkably during the war to become the dominant publisher of reading material for German soldiers, but was closed by the Nazis when it was no longer considered important to the war effort. The commission will continue to study questions still unresolved, especially the role of Heinrich in the war effort.[7]

After the Simon Wiesenthal Center in Los Angeles complained about Barnesandnoble.com selling Hitler's *Mein Kampf* and other hate literature banned in Germany, Bertelsmann advised Barnes & Noble, in which it has a 50 percent interest, to stop selling Mein Kampf and other hate literature to anyone in Germany.[8]

Heinrich's son, fifth generation Reinhard Mohn, was drafted into the German Army and served under Rommel in Africa, where he was captured by the Allies, and then spent three years in a prisoner-of-war camp in Kansas. He came home with his belongings in a potato sack, and though he had been trained as an engineer, his father persuaded him to try to revive the family business.

Carts of used books had circulated in the Kansas prisoner-of-war camp. Realizing that most libraries had been destroyed in Allied air raids, Mohn began scavenging through bombed buildings and libraries for books to sell. In what *Global Dreams* calls a curious mix of serendipity and misunderstanding he had thought that the books came from Book of the Month Clubs. So as soon as he rebuilt the publishing plant he began to publish general interest books and started Germany's first book club, which by 1954 had a million members.[9] It is commonly said that Germans think of books as essential to a house as furniture.

He also added a record club and built a factory to cut records under the Ariola label. When the book and record clubs grew big enough to collide with anti-trust laws, he expanded them abroad. Today Bertelsmann has more than 25 million members in book and music clubs in 18 countries.[10] The French book club alone has five million members in France, Switzerland, Belgium and Canada; it is the largest book club in the world. More recently, Bertelsmann has set up a chain of mega-stores in France and other countries to sell music, video cassettes and multi-media as well as books.[11]

Mohn's 1969 purchase of a 25 percent interest in Gruner+Jahr has been increased to a 74.9 percent stake and includes three magazines of more than a million circulation each: *Stern*, a sophisticated women's magazine in Germany; *Femme Actuelle*, in France; and *Parents* magazine in the U.S. All told, Bertelsmann publishes more than 100 magazines and newspapers throughout Europe and the Western Hemisphere.[12] Its magazine division has teamed up with talk show host Rosie O'Donnell to remake its 125-year old women's magazine, *McCall's*, into a more lively product named *Rosie*. The division also bought *Fast Company*, a business magazine in December, 2000, from American media billionaire Morton Zukerman. It joins *Inc.*, a Boston-based business magazine bought earlier in the year, probably to challenge *Forbes* and *Fortune*.

An attempt to bring a version of *GEO*, Germany's popular geographic magazine, to the States failed after two years and $50 million. Although it sells half a million copies in France, it couldn't compete with the *National Geographic*. Another embarrassment was publication of Hitler's diaries in *Stern*, which proved to be a hoax.[13] These were mere blips in the magazine business, which contributes heavily to Bertelsmann profits.

Mohn retired from active management in 1981 at age 60 and appointed Mark Wossner as CEO. Wossner began Bertelsmann's invasion of the U.S. and the electronic media. He bought Doubleday Dell and merged it with Bantam; acquired RCA Records from General Electric and combined it with Arista to form BMG, the Bertelsmann Music Group, and leaped into European television in a major way.[14]

Doubleday took off with such best selling authors as John Grisham and Danielle Steele leading the way and BMG with Whitney Houston not far behind. Now two-thirds of the company's sales and profits come from *outside* Germany. Mohn's daughter, Brigitte, is an executive with Bantam in the New York office.[15] Two of his three sons are also in the company.

When Wossner reached the mandatory retirement age of 60 in October, 1998, Thomas Middelhoff was appointed CEO. He had come up through the ranks and before he took over had spent a year in the States. He is tall, good-looking with a ready laugh, and an easy-going informality. He persuaded the board to buy a five percent stake in America Online in April, 1995, for $50 million. Within five years it was worth $10 billion. When AOL merged with Time Warner, in January, 2000, Middlehoff resigned his seat on the AOL board and began selling off its stock to invest in other internet businesses. The stake is down to seven-tenths of a percent now.[16]

The Bertelsmann-AOL partnership continued to unravel after AOL's acquisition of Time Warner. AOL Europe, a 50-50 venture between Bertelsmann and AOL, dating back to 1995, was sold March 17, 2000, wholly to AOL. The sale included Bertelsmann's stake in AOL Australia. The price, between $7 billion and $8 billion, is for AOL shares or cash, to be paid on Jan. 31, 2002. Bertelsmann expects to use the money for content and e-commerce acquisitions. "We want to be No. 1 in e-commerce business," Middelhoff told the *New York Times*. "And from Bertelsmann's perspective, it's more important for us than to own a share in AOL."[17]

A shot heard round the world was Bertelsmann's purchase of the prestigious Random House publisher from Advance Publications, of the Newhouse family, in March, 1998. The sale was cleared by the Federal Trade Commission three months later, despite objections by The Authors Guild and the Association of Authors' representatives. It boosted Bertelsmann's share of the U.S. book market to 10 percent.[18] The deal was engineered by Middelhoff. By integrating Bantam Doubleday Dell into Random House, Middelhoff took control of a substantial portion of the American adult trade book market. "Since the deal had cultural as well as commercial implications a degree of wounded Anglophone pride was understandable," wrote Daniel Johnson in *The New Yorker*. "The destiny of American publishing may now lie in German hands," he said. "The history of publishing began in Germany; perhaps it will end there."[19]

In October, 1998, Middelhoff bought a half interest in BarnesandNoble.com which upset independent booksellers, who had hoped to work out a marketing program with Bertelsmann that would enable them to compete with the chains. It revived fears of monopoly power raised by the purchase of Random House in the spring. William Petrocelli, co-owner of Book Passage, an independent book store in Corte Madera, Calif., said , "The overriding issue is increasing concentration. I view it as a major threat to writers and readers, as well as to independent booksellers. It seems to me that as fewer and fewer people are making critical decisions along the chain of distribution for books, the more likely it is that diversity, quality and innovation will suffer."[20] When BarnesandNoble.com went public, Bertelsmann reduced its stake to 41 percent. Time Warner also owns 41 percent, and the remaining 18 percent is in the stock market.

Bertelsmann has created a string of electronic bookstores called BOL.com, with Web sites in various European countries as well as Hong Kong, Malaysia and Singapore. In April, 1999, the company joined with Seagram to create getmusic.com, a Web site that promotes artists from the two companies' labels and sells CD's on line. And in Germany, Bertelsmann created an electronic auction house called Andsold and acquired Pixelpark, a Web site designer, recently spun off in an IPO.[21]

The Bertelsmann Music Group, which has $6 billion in sales, is headquartered in a lavish New York Times Square office and operates in more than 27 countries under many labels, including RCA and Arista and features stars ranging from Whitney Houston and The Grateful Dead to James Galway and Arturo Toscanini. It also includes television, film, radio, interactive entertainment, direct marketing and home video. Middelhioff's desire to make BMG the world leader took a dramatic turn Dec. 31, 2000, when he announced an alliance with Napster, a company that makes software that allows users to share the MP3 libraries with each other, no matter where they are. Bertelsmann was one of five major music companies to sue Napster for copyright infringement but withdrew from the suit when Napster, with a $50 million investment from Bertelsmann, agreed to transform itself into a subscriber based business. The others all withdrew with the exception of Universal, which settled out of court.. Hailed by some as the most significant business move in years and by others as a step toward a total monopoly of entertainment, information and culture,. Middelhoff said, "Under terms of the agreement we will support Napster financially in the establishment of a legal business. In return we will receive an option for a stake in Napster with right to file-sharing technology, the Napster brand and Napster's customer data.[22] MP3 was released on the Internet in August, 1999, and became sensationally successful, especially among college students who quickly learned to download music from MP3's library and share with one another without any compensation for artists or composers.

Napster has been hit with a barrage of court cases. Members of the Recording Industry Association of America (RIAA) sued in December, 1999, claiming that it permitted swapping of copyrighted music that was tantamount to music piracy.. Several rock groups also sued, a Congressional committee headed by Orin Hatch heard arguments from both sides who discussed the future of entertainment with new technologies that could deliver not only music, but books, videos and other digital content directly to the consumer. After a federal district court issued an injunction against Napster halting the distribution of copyright material, another court stayed the injunction. The end is not in sight.

In April, 2001, Bertelsmann, Britain's EMI and AOL-Time Warner pledged to back Music-Net, an online platform for swapping, downloading and streamlining. Users will pay a monthly subscription fee to access music. It will attempt to offer consumers an easy way to get the highest quality music while protecting the intellectual property of the record companies and artists. It is scheduled to be launched in the fall of 2001 but is nowhere near a done deal.

Bertelsmann's BMG Direct, formerly RCA Record Club, offers thousands of titles to club members and has bought Nice Man Merchandising, a full service global merchandising company that provides promotional products for everything from Pearl Jam to Harley-Davidson for more than 7,000 retail accounts including Wal-Mart and Sears.[23]

In January, 1997, Bertelsmann AG completed a merger on a 50/50 basis of its broadcasting operation with the Luxembourgeoise de Telediffusion (CLT), combining Bertelsmann's Ufa television subsidiary with CLT to control 19 television stations and 23 radio stations in 10 European countries.[24] In January, 2000, the company completed a merger with Britain's Pearson TV to create a huge production group. Bertelsmann also has agreements with Rupert Murdoch's BskyB of England and Canal Plus of France.

Bertelsmann New Media, a Hamburg offshoot, launched Bertelsmann Interactive Studios in 1997 to produce interactive and broadband presentations for cable and satellite.[25]   Late in 1998, Bertelsmann bought a majority stake in Springer-Verlag, Germany's largest publisher of scientific journals and technical books with publishing houses all over the world and an electronic network called Link. Many of the companies are joint ventures and some have been spun off in IPO's. Bertelsmann's Ventures (BVG), with offices in New York, Santa Barbara, and Hamburg, Germany, is a company set up to invest in financing start-ups with support on management, recruitment and development. When and if the companies mature, Bertelsmann will have 10 to 30 percent of the new industry.

Doubleday Direct's Literary Guild and Time Inc.'s Book of the Month Club have formed a partnership and expect to increase growth, even though the Internet book companies are butting into their base. So many of the companies are inter-related that it is difficult to keep track.

In 1993 Mohn transferred 68.8 percent of the capital shares in Bertelsmann Corporation as non-voting shares to the Bertelsmann Foundation, which was created in 1977. The family retained 20.5 percent and an additional 10.7 percent is owned by the Bucerius Foundation, which traded Gruner+Jahr shares for a stake in Bertelsmann. Mohn controlled the one golden voting share in the company. "I am the annual shareholders' meeting," he once said.[26]

On Nov. 1, 1998, Mohn handed over the chairmanship of the Foundation to former CEO Mark Wossner, but he continues as a member of the board. On July 1, 1999, he transferred his voting rights to an administrative company, Bertelsmann Verwaltungagesellschaft (BV), composed of six main shareholders: Mark Wossner, who was made chairman of the Bertelsmann supervisory board but stepped down in May, 2000, after a disagreement with Mohn; CEO Middelhoff, a family member, another member of the supervisory board, another executive and an employee representative. Mohn is to be a shareholder in the administrative company until his death.[27] These moves not only saved hefty German inheritance taxes but made sure that the company will continue under the principles Mohn believes in.

In February, 2001, 79-year-old Mohn made a radical shift in policy by joining Belgian millionaire Albert Frere, who controls Groupe Bruxelles Lambert, in signing a contract handing each other a share of their huge fortunes according to a story by Michael Woodhead, of the *Sunday Times* (London). Mohn got 30 percent of RTL, Europe's biggest television company, which is second only to Hollywood as a movie maker (making his stake 67 percent). Frere got 25 percent of Bertelsmann which he will be allowed to sell on the stock market after three years, but does not give him any voting power. That could take the private company public, a dramatic change in management.[28]

Mohn and his wife, Liz, devote their energy now to the Bertelsmann Foundation. Like the MacArthur grants, the foundation does not accept applications or petitions but searches out projects that fit into the family ideals in areas such as education, medical research, solving social problems and cultural activities. Liz serves on the advisory board and is especially interested in the German Stroke Foundation which she founded and presides over.

As an example, the Foundation gave an award of DM300,000 to a Canadian School Board for the most innovative system in an international competition.

Grants have greatly enhanced the public school system of Oconee County, Georgia, whose students have won many awards in state and national contests and nearby Athens Academy, a college prep school which has also benefited from Foundation support. Of course, as a non-profit, the foundation is eligible for tax relief.[29]

Some analysts argue that the closely held corporation isn't aggressive enough to keep up with competition, but a German financial journalist says all Bertelsmann does is "grow and grow and grow."[30]

Media watchdogs in Germany worry that excessive media concentration may one day shut out minority voices and ultimately undermine democracy. "There is potential danger in their power even if it hasn't been abused," says Axel Zerdick, a professor at the Free University of Berlin.[31]

The company's 57,173 employees are well-paid and encouraged to participate in planning and development. The rapid growth requires a constant search for new managers for the many different companies Bertelsmann acquires. Prospective employees can not only look over job opportunities on the Internet; they may also fill out an application and apply for a job at http://www.Bertelsmann.com.

Many people may never have heard of Mohn or Bertelsmann because subsidiaries operate under their original names. For example, Prima Press, the French subsidiary of Bertelsmann AG, publishes 15 magazines in France.

The fifth generation of the family has built a world-wide media group of amazing diversity and strength. Whether this will carry into the millennium without Mohn's guidance remains to be seen. Meanwhile the growth of joint ventures and alliances, such as the integration of the large Ingram Distribution Company with Bertelsmann-Barnesandnoble.com, causes increasing concern.[32] Bertelsmann is, after all, the third largest media empire in the world.

THE LORDS ROTHERMERE–
FOUR GENERATIONS OF MEDIA MOGULS

47

Jonathan Harmsworth became the fourth Lord Rothermere and chairman of the family's $2 billion dollar media empire when his father, Vere Harold Esmond Harmsworth, the third Lord Rothermere, died in September, 1998. An only son and heir, Jonathan had been groomed from birth to take over. He was educated at Gordonstoun in Scotland, then sent to America. Since graduating from Duke University in 1991, he had been learning the ropes by managing various newspapers of the Daily Mail and General Trust (DMGT) group, then as assistant managing director of the London *Evening Standard* and as deputy chairman of Associated Newspapers. He was 30.

The strong management and editorial teams already in place made the transition an easy one. Jonathan, as the new chairman, announced that "the company had doubled earnings in the past two years but needed to look to other countries and other activities for expansion."[1] In addition to its newspaper group, it is involved in radio, teletext, magazines, exhibitions, conferences, training, computer software, video and book publishing. Operations are spread across Europe, North and South America, Asia and Australia.

The Rothermere family story goes back four generations, starting more than a century ago. Jonathan's great-great-uncle, Alfred Charles William Harmsworth, was the son of a barrister but not much of a student. He fell in love with journalism while editing a magazine for a small private day school and at 23 borrowed money to launch a penny weekly paper, the first of many such ventures. On May 4, 1896 at age 31, he founded the *Daily Mail* which was an instant success and was the beginning of popular journalism in Britain. The first day's sales totaled an astonishing 397,000 copies. The *Daily Mail* was aimed squarely at the middle class, with special features for women including recipes, household hints and society columns.

The appeal to women continues to this day: when President Bush fainted in Japan, the *Daily Mail* headline read, "Barbara's Moment of Anguish."[2] The Daily Mail and General Trust is capitalizing on this traditional appeal by setting up a web site for women. Its aim, according to Cathy Newman, of the *Financial Times*, is "to create a community for affluent and aspirational women."[3] The site was launched in September, 1999. The *Daily Mail* was also the first British newspaper to be financed primarily through advertising and its slogan was "a penny paper for a halfpenny." Although the paper cost more than a halfpenny to produce, the advertising enabled it to make handsome profits.[4] The short simple stories, scandal and sensationalism proved popular. Harmsworth's success lay not so much in educating his readers as in persuading them to buy newspapers. Today, circulation of the *Daily Mail* is 2.3 million.

Alfred Harmsworth was elevated to the peerage as Lord Northcliffe in 1906. He was active in bringing America into World War I and in fostering Anglo-American relations. At his death in 1922 he left bequests to several thousand employees. His funeral at Westminster Abbey was a civic event. He was greatly mourned. Because Lord Northcliffe had no children, his brother and business partner, Harold Harmsworth, inherited the estate.

Harold Harmsworth had a grammar school education and experience in the British merchant marine when he joined his brother's business at age 21. His business acumen combined with Lord Northcliffe's editorial talent made them successful. In addition to buying and running newspapers, he was interested in aviation and urged preparedness between the wars, paying for a prototype plane to help build Britain's air strength. He served as Air Minister for a short time. After World War I, the plight of Hungary was one of his passions and his support was so strong that the regent, Admiral Horthy, formally asked him to consider accepting the crown of Hungary. He declined. Among the DMGT assets are a newspaper and a printing company in Hungary. Harold became a peer of the realm in 1914, taking the title of Lord Rothermere. In the 1930's he met with Hitler and Mussolini in an effort to prevent war. As a result, some considered him to be an apologist for the dictators. When World War II broke out he retired to Bermuda and soon died there.[5]

New sources, such as the diaries of Rothermere's aide, Collin Brooks, reveal a deeper involvement. Roy Greenslade, who is writing a history of the British press, says Rothermere was one of the aristocracy who were pro-Hitler for a long period before the war. "It is a good reminder for those people who say there could never be fascism in Britain to find out how close we really came."[6]

Two of Harold's sons were killed in World War I. The remaining son, Esmond, became the second Lord Rothermere. His lavish living style and womanizing estranged his son, his wife and his employees. After a visit to Esmond's vast mansion in the Cotswolds, a *Daily Mail* editor said, "It was enough to make you a bloody communist."[7] He changed editors as often as he changed mistresses and the family empire was greatly diminished when Esmond retired in 1971 and his son Vere took over the business.

Vere Harold Esmond Harmsworth, the third Lord Rothermere, born in 1925, was educated at Eton and then at Kent School in Connecticut. After failing his commission in the Guards he horrified his aristocratic family by signing up in the

Army as a humble enlisted man and served four years during World War II, an experience that taught him a lot about the needs and desires of the common man.[8] After three years learning about the newsprint business at a Canadian paper mill, he joined Associated Newspapers in 1951, working in every department. Twenty years later he took control of the business and transformed the money-losing *Daily Mail* into a highly successful tabloid.

He built up the *Evening Standard* and created the *Mail on Sunday* in 1982. "A morning, an afternoon and a Sunday newspaper allows a degree of efficiency,"[9] he told an interviewer. Like Lord Northcliffe he took advantage of the latest printing developments and moved the antiquated Fleet Street plant to modern facilities, with efficient flexigraphic presses, at Harmsworth Quays. He developed an intuitive feel for the business and a liking for journalists, although employing them, he said, was like "keeping a hyena for a pet."[10] He hired David English, a feature editor on one of the papers to become editor of the *Daily Mail* and his lifelong partner. Rothermere was a formidable businessman and English was an extremely able editor. At his death only three months before Rothermere's, he had become the distinguished Sir David English, deputy chairman of Associated Newspapers.

The Daily Mail and General Trust group grew way beyond the three London papers under the joint control of Vere and David English. The Northcliffe Newspaper Group has two dozen regional papers in England plus the newspaper and printing company in Hungary. Euromoney Publications, another segment, provides information through magazines, books, electronic databases, training courses, seminars and conferences. The company owns close to 100 international magazines specializing in finance, aviation and law. DMG Information is an in- formation publisher with activities in education, careers, travel, insurance and medicine markets. Its products cover many formats: directories, guide books, magazines, electronic services and software, including CD-Roms, Teletext and online networks. It is expanding internationally especially in the USA.[11] The floundering company that Vere Harmsworth took over from his father has grown into one of the world's largest holding companies and remains in family hands.

The tall, ruddy aristocratic Vere had a passion for journalism and hoped to be remembered as someone "who had helped to bring back an appreciation that good journalism could succeed."[12]

Vere Rothermere first married Patricia Brooks, a former actress known as "Bubbles" for her "indefatigable love of parties." He remained fond of her despite what he described as her "tempestuous and exhausting nature," and found their family homes in Eaton Square, Sussex, France, Jamaica and New York increasingly impossible to live in. They remained friends and Pat was his consort on official occasions. He met Maiko Lee, a former model, in New York in 1978 and she became his constant companion and shared his flat on the Ile St. Louis in Paris. Rothermere developed an interest in Zen Buddhism and the couple lived part of each year in Kyoto. Pat died in 1991 and Rothermere married Lee a year later.[13]

Although he supported the Conservative Party all his life, Rothermere befriended Tony Blair and crossed over to Labor's benches in the House of Lords after Blair won the election. He said, "They (Labor) are carrying out so many policies I believe in."[14] The *Daily Mail* supported the Conservative Party in the 1997 election and the *Evening Standard* backed Labor.

When Lord Rothermere died suddenly of a heart attack in London in September, 1998, Lady Thatcher was moved to say, "He was one of the great figures in the British newspaper industry this century."[15]

One of his legacies is the American Institute at Oxford University, made possible by the generous support of the Harmsworth family. A pledge of one and one-half million pounds from the DMGT group has guaranteed the building designed by American architects. The Rothermere American Institute will be a research center for American studies. A state of the art library, supported also by the Annenberg Foundation and donations from and in memory of former Rhodes scholars, will be known as the Vere Harmsworth library.[16]

Sir David English said, "Vere was born with a silver spoon in his mouth but he was clever enough to turn it into gold — and to be loved by all who worked for him." It is uncertain whether this affection will pass on to Jonathan. He has always been interested in journalism, which is in his favor, but one journalist said, "Rothermere has always stuck up for us against the bean counters. None of us has ever seen Jonathan in the building so who knows how he feels."[17]

In the two years since his father's death, Jonathan has kept a low public profile but according to his associates he works hard in the business and has taken it in new directions. Associated Newspapers, a subsidiary of DMGT, in March, 1999, launched a new free newspaper, *Metro*, delivered to subway and mainline railway stations. Within a year, it became profitable and achieved a circulation of 350,000 a day. It has been expanded into four other cities and attracted a new readership, mostly younger people who like its lack of political bias — there is no op-ed page — and short stories. DMGT's Associated New Media division has four popular internet sites, including the www.charlottestreet.com site. especially for women. The chairman believes that information technology is the prime area for growth. His expansion into electronic media includes U.S. software company Risk Management Solutions and e data resources among others.

Jonathan has paid a reputed three million pounds for a 224-acre estate in Wiltshire which was once the country seat of the Dukes of Hamilton. He is building a stately home there for his wife and two children.

There was a bit of a stir when the New Zealand *Dominion* ran a story about another child, the result of a university alliance. Jonathan fell in love with one of his mother's assistants who followed him to the States and lived with him for a couple of years. His mother opposed marriage and when the young woman became pregnant she immediately left for her native New Zealand. He has supported the girl, now 13-years old, and has settled a trust on her.[18]

The new baron is worth $1.1 billion.[19] He has a hard act to follow but if genes make a difference he should be able to keep the presses rolling and the succession on line. His son is named Vere after his grandfather.

THE GAP BETWEEN THE RICH AND THE POOR

Multimillionaire Joe gives his wife a million and tells her to spend $10,000 a day, then come back for more. She's back in three months and 10 days.. Multibillionaire Bud gives his wife a billion, tells her to spend $10,000 a day, then come back for more. She doesn't live long enough to spend that billion; it would take 277 years.

Instead of $10,000 a day, the rank-and-file American worker, on the average, had to be content with his $51 *a day* in 1998. "Approximately 50 million Americans — 19 percent of the population — live below the national poverty line," according to a *Nation* editorial.[1] In 1998, "big league C.E.Os pocketed, on the average 419 times the earnings of the typical production worker," *New Yorker* writer John Cassidy reported, adding, "Michael Eisner, the chairman and C.E.O. and *primus inter parus* of nineties plutocrats, earned more than $575 million in 1998."[2] These figures highlight the dramatic difference between America's rich and the rest of society. Here we should also note that the three richest Americans, all profiled in this book, are Bill Gates with $63 billion, Paul Allen with $36 billion, and Warren Buffett with $28 billion. In 1999, they had "combined assets (that) were even more than the combined GNP of the 48 least developed nations."[3]

Bill Gates's wealth dropped by 15 *billion* the day after a federal judge ruled against Microsoft in March, 2000. But the drop in his stock's value didn't bother him as much as the ruling itself. He still enjoyed the largest fortune in the world. His co-founder, Paul Allen, who lost $4 billion that day, was still right up there with around $36 billion.

When the first Kerner Commission report was issued in the 1960s, the rich-poor gap was already quite wide. When it was updated in 1997, Fred R. Harris, a Commission member, said, "We have more poverty and a greater percentage of poor people than we did 30 years ago, while the wealth and income gaps have widened."[4] Indeed, reporting on a 1999 Congressional Budget Office study, the *New York Times* said, "the gap between rich and poor has grown into an economic chasm so wide that this year the richest 2.7 million Americans, the top one percent, will have as many after-tax dollars to spend as the bottom 100 million."[5] If we consider the rich and poor on an international scale, "Today the wealth of the world's 200 richest people is greater than the combined incomes of the poorest 41 percent of humanity."[6] A 1999 UN report showed that "over the last four years the world's 200 richest people have doubled their wealth to more than $1 trillion" and "in that same period the number of people living on less than a dollar a day has remained unchanged at 1.3 billion."[7] Our media moguls — all of them — are high on the lists of the country's -- and the world's -- richest.

The vast differences in wealth and income result in a wide range of contrasts in health, longevity, education, housing, travel, food, indeed everything that's important in life.

In matters of health, any one of our media billionaires can call on the services of as many medical specialists as he or she wants. When Microsoft co-founder Paul Allen developed a fever in Paris while on a business trip, he was not satisfied with the diagnosis of a French doctor, so he booked a flight on a supersonic Concord jetliner from Orly Airport to Seattle. There, a team of specialists found that he had Hodgkin's Disease, a form of lymph cancer. After two five-week courses of x-ray therapy, he resigned from Microsoft and took off for a year in Europe to think about what he wanted to do next. Today, the second richest man in the U.S., he is in good health, and heavily involved in a series of media companies.

A wealthy Allen can buy the latest medical treatment, no matter how costly, even if it isn't covered by health insurance, while many poor people — 44 million of them in the U.S. — can't afford even the most basic health coverage and so must rely on the federally-funded Medicaid program, if they can qualify. "In a number of studies, both international and domestic, rates of heart disease, cancer and longevity seem to be influenced for the worse by a skewed distribution of income and wealth."[8] The U.S. is among the few countries in the industrial world without universal health care.

A 1998 study at the University of Michigan found that those who are poor in the U.S. don't live nearly as long as those who are rich. The study by epidemiology professor John Lynch "found that the death rate is higher in areas with higher income inequality, and the higher the inequality, the higher the death rates."[9] A 1999 report on America's health by United for a Fair Economy found "21,000 children have stunted growth and 120,000 suffer from anemia because their families must decide between food and rent."[10] *The Economist* reported recently that "Almost one in five American children lives in poverty, a rate about twice as high as in the big economies of Western Europe."[11] In 1997, after the welfare reform law was passed, there were "an estimated 30 million hungry poor in America, of which 12 million were children" and "some 63 percent of the elderly are at moderate or high nutritional risk."[12] Among industrialized countries, the United States has the highest level of "human poverty — covering life expectancy, illiteracy and underemployment," according to a United Nations report in mid-2000.[13]

Ready access to medical care, good food and excellent housing all help the media billionaires stay active in their businesses well beyond normal retirement age. Kirk Kerkorian, who owns MGM Studios, just started a casino in Detroit and bought a second huge casino hotel in Las Vegas after he fathered a child at age 82. John Kluge, at 85, is still very much in charge at his

Metromedia conglomerate. So is Sumner Redstone, who, at age 76, runs the huge Viacom-Blockbuster-CBS megaconglomerate.

Most of the media billionaires completed college, some at schools like Harvard and Yale. And their children can make a choice of which universities to attend without looking at costs. Don Graham of the *Washington Post* empire went to Harvard and then to a special executive management program at Stanford. Rupert Murdoch went to Oxford, John Malone to Yale, Sumner Redstone to Harvard and Harvard Law School. Exceptions: Bill Gates dropped out of Harvard after the third year because he was involved in computers, and Ted Turner was kicked out of Brown for breaking the rules. Almost all of America's media billionaires had the college opportunity, and of course their children do. But for poor young Americans, and even many in the middle class, college is out of the question. This is especially true for ghetto-bound minorities, particularly Latinos, whose per capita income is even lower than that of blacks. Even at public colleges and universities, tuition and expenses have skyrocketed. "Tuition and fees have risen 94 percent since 1989, nearly triple the 32 percent increase in inflation," according to *Business Week* in 1994.[14] The article added, "Even as a good education has become the litmus test in the job market, the widening wage chasm has made it harder for lower-income people to get to college. Kids from the top quarter have no problem: 76 percent earn bachelor's degrees today, vs. 31 percent in 1980, but less than 4 percent of those in the bottom quarter families now finish college, vs. 6 percent then."[15] And since that 1994 report, tuition and living costs have risen steadily at both public and private colleges.

The income gap, growing at a time of unprecedented economic prosperity, is matched by a growing gap in living conditions. While almost all the media billionaires enjoy luxurious quarters, usually in several parts of the country, and often abroad, poor families have serious trouble getting a mortgage. Those who live in apartments often don't have enough money to buy adequate food and clothing after they pay the rent. Across the country, there are 700,000 homeless, who roam the streets during the day and sleep in doorways or under bridges unless they are lucky enough to find space in homeless shelters. In contrast, Anne Cox Chambers, worth $10 billion in 2000, has a villa in Provence, France, as well as the Rosewood Estate in Atlanta and a huge plantation in South Carolina. John Kluge's properties include the $250 million Morven Farm with its 50-room Albemarle House, a $30 million house in Palm Springs and a luxurious penthouse apartment in New York. Ted Turner is the largest landowner in the world, with homes on many of his properties scattered across the U.S.. Bill Gates's $75 million home in Medina, Washington, is actually five houses, "pavilions" connected by underground passageways, with the main house covering 40,000 square feet. David Geffen has a $47.5 million estate in Beverly Hills. Prince Alwaleed of Saudi Arabia lives in Riyahd in a palace, with five wings and more than 150 servants. The new palace is five times the size of his old one down the street, which has been set aside for his son. Exceptions: Warren Buffett and Sumner Redstone, both of whom live in simple homes in cities where they grew up.

But Buffett flies in a private plane, having once owned a jet which was so expensive he called it "The Indefensible." Like other billionaires, the media moguls all tend to fly in private planes; and become newsworthy only when they board a scheduled airliner. On the ground, of course, they travel in limousines, either private or rented.

Bill Gates's wealth in 1997 was $40 billion, the same year Congress passed and the President signed the new law to "end welfare as we know it;" the law made $54 billion in welfare cuts. "More than half those cuts were taken from food stamps on which 25 million poor Americans depended."[16] A year later, it was noted that Bill Gates's wealth (then $58 billion) was "greater than the (federal) budgets for welfare and food stamps combined."[17] And the U.S. Department of Agriculture told us in 1999 that almost 10 percent — one-tenth — of U. S. households "are going hungry or don't have access to adequate food."[18] Those who left welfare, according to Peter Edelman, former member of the Clinton administration, are, "on balance, worse off; a third to a half of them, depending on the state, haven't found jobs. Many others who have are still poor, their benefits cut."[19]

The media billionaires, both in the United States and abroad, are all white; only three are women — Anne Cox Chambers, her sister, Barbara Cox Anthony, and the late Katharine Graham — all three of whom inherited their media wealth. The "glass ceiling" prevents women from rising to the very top, no matter how good they are. And black Americans are also unable to reach up; their skin is the wrong color. Oprah Winfrey is the only black American in the *Forbes 400* with wealth well below a billion. "While the racial income gap is terribly wide, the racial wealth gap is even wider," reports *Shifting Fortunes*, a book about the wealth gap and its consequences.[20] It adds that "the median black household had a net worth of $7,400 in 1995 — about 12 percent of the $61,000 in median wealth for whites. Median black financial wealth (net worth minus home equity) was just $200 — a mere 1 percent of the $18,000 in median financial wealth for whites."[21]

Only two of the media billionaires have shown a willingness to give real chunks of their wealth to needy causes — Ted Turner and Bill Gates. Turner's billion dollar gift to the United Nations made headlines, as did the creation in 1999 of the Bill and Melinda Gates Foundation, with $17 billion to educate minority students and fight global poverty and health problems. By 2001, Gates Foundation funds totaled $25 billion. The others tend to give to their alma maters, as in John Kluge's gift of $125 million to Columbia University and George Lucas's $6 million to the University of Southern California. Some, like Steven Spielberg, make their gifts anonymously, so there is no way of knowing the amounts or the recipients.

While all the super-rich have far more than they need, they don't all engage in what Thorstein Veblen a century ago called "conspicuous consumption." Most of them are careful to look and act like ordinary members of the middle class. "Many of today's billionaires seem fantastically determined to appear middle class," writes a *Forbes* reporter, adding, "Bill Gates likes to be seen in his oversize sweater, Jeffrey Bezos sits at a ramshackle desk he made from an old door, and Warren Buffett always reminds us about his modest Omaha house."[22]

Of course, the multi-media billionaires are not the only ones responsible for the wide and widening gap between rich and poor. But that gap is not a topic frequently visited by the mogul-owned media, a panel of professional journalists agreed in

March, 2000. Panelist Paula Madison, vice president of News Channel 4 in New York, "laid responsibility on journalists for a lack of interest in poverty issues.[23]

The yawning gap between rich and poor at the beginning of the 21st century is very much like the gap brought by the Industrial Revolution a century ago. The people responded to that gap, and what it meant to their lives, with the Progressive movement, led by Teddy Roosevelt and Woodrow Wilson. That movement brought a better life for working families and a great enlargement of America's middle class. Another important product of the Progressive movement was the Sherman Anti-Trust Act, which led to breakup of the worst monopolies.

Is it time for a new Progressive movement? And if so, will it call for breakup of the super-giant media monopolies such as AOL-Time-Warner-Turner, Disney-ABC, Viacom-Blockbuster-CBS, and News Corporation's media properties in the U.S.? The Justice Department's use of the anti-trust laws at the end of the 20th century to try to break up the giant Microsoft empire may be a start.

THE MEDIA MOGULS GIVE US A VAST WASTELAND

The concentration of the media — all the media — in the hands of a tiny number of moguls is far from healthy for America's culture. For the media moguls and the CEOs who manage their properties, Wall Street is much more important than Main Street. Whether their companies are privately held or public, the moguls operate profit-driven megabusinesses, and they see lowest-common-denominator *entertainment* as most profitable.

A telling comment about corporate TV news was made by Michael Deaver, President Reagan's press secretary. He told TV newsman Bill Moyers, "You people think you're in the news business. You're in the entertainment business."[1] Again, the same thing can be said about newspapers, whose marketing experts have told editors to increase the feature stories, especially those about celebrities. Whether it's in print or on the air, the product is intended to be entertaining; information and education are secondary. The culture brought to us by the moguls is thus dominated by entertainment, which a *Fortune* article in 1998 called "one of the most influential industries in America — and one of the most profitable." Dan Rather, the CBS anchorman, commented in 1998 on what's happening to network news: "The Hollywoodization of the news is deep and abiding. We run stupid celebrity stories."[2] Reviewing a new book about *60 Minutes*, Neal Gabler concluded, "For networks and journalists alike, the money and the glory and the power are in the entertainment."[3] One media critic after another deplores the rapid rise of celebrity, lifestyle, violence and sex in all news media, but it continues. The sensational treatment of the Monica Lewinsky story, stretching over a year, would have been out of the question 20 years earlier. Washington reporters knew about the private lives of Eisenhower, Kennedy and Johnson, but none of it got into their newspapers or broadcasts.

When Clint Eastwood told a reporter that he would prefer not to make violent movies but they draw the biggest audiences, he was explaining part of the logic by which all the media -- especially TV and movies -- operate. Violence and sex get the highest ratings, which means they draw the most advertisers to TV and the biggest box office returns to theaters. Violent action is also cheapest to produce in both film

275

and TV. What's more, violence-packed movies and TV programs are most saleable to owners of *foreign* screens. Indeed, the violence-heavy TV series are more popular -- and profitable -- in Europe and Asia than in the United States. In Europe, some "live action" (meaning lots of violence and semi-nude stars), such as *Miami Vice* and *Xena, Warrior Princess,* bring high profits to their owners. A *Fortune* reporter called such programs "schlock products."[4] A *New York Times Magazine* article put it this way, "Much of what's on television, whatever its scale or country of origin, is garbage."[5]

FCC Chairman Reed Hundt confirmed in a 1996 speech the "strong connection between television watching and aggressions," citing a cable TV industry-funded study which found "substantial risks of harmful effects from viewing violence throughout the television environment."[6] When 15-year-old Ronny Zamora shot and killed the 82-year-old woman who lived next door to him in Florida, his lawyer pleaded "not guilty by reason of the boy's having watched too much television," adding that television had "dangerously inured" the boy to violence.[7] The jury convicted Zamora of murder.

Children of both elementary and high school age now try to imitate the kinds of wrestling they see on TV. "In the World Wrestling Federation shows *Smackdown!* and *Raw*, the plots include bikini-clad women partaking in kidnapping, simulated sex, and pudding wrestling."[8] Even the commercials contain violence. "By the end of 1997, the use of graphic violence — always an attention-getter — was growing more common in TV ads aimed at children and youth," says media scholar Robert McChesney.[9] When CBS bosses realized that *Nash Bridges* and *Walker, Texas Ranger* — both violence loaded — were getting good ratings, they added *Martial Law,* featuring a Hong Kong actor who specializes in kung fu, the brutal art of mangling opponents with fists and feet. A 1998 study, conducted by the University of Santa Barbara's Center for Communications and Social Policy, found that for three years in a row "violent TV shows accounted for 60 percent of TV programming, and that the amount of violence has increased each year."[10] The 1997-98 rash of school shootings -- and killings -- in Colorado, Arkansas, Tennessee, Pennsylvania and Oregon were examples of how teenagers with guns can duplicate the kinds of "live action" they see on TV and in film. In 1997, a 16-year-old in Chippewa Falls, Wisconsin, went to prison for 45 years after confessing that he had stabbed his girlfriend's parents while wearing a black robe and mask. He said he was imitating the attacker in the slasher movie, *Scream 2.*[11]

Even animated movies like *Aladdin* and *The Lion King* have become more violent in the 1990s, "exposing young children to 'significant' amounts of mayhem," according to a new study in the *Journal of the American Medical Association.*[12]

After the 1998 school shootings, President Clinton ordered a federal inquiry into the marketing of violent entertainment. The inquiry report, released by the Federal Trade Commission in September, 2000, was a sweeping indictment. "The entertainment industry routinely markets to young people violent movies, video games and music, ignoring its own guidelines for age-sensitive material," the FTC said.[13] The report cited use of a broad range of advertising and marketing to reach young people with products rated for adults. Columnist Ellen Goodman summarized the report, "After combing the industry's own incriminating papers, they (the FTC officials) concluded that the entertainment folks are violating their own rating system."[14]

"The level of violence on commercial television remains invulnerable to change, yet the data show that nonviolent programs have 33 percent more viewers than violent ones," Ben Bagdikian reported in *The Media Monopoly*[15] And he added, "A *Times* Mirror poll in 1993 showed that 53 percent of Americans want less violence and 80 percent agreed that TV violence is harmful to society." Indeed, a Stanford University study found that "aggressive tendencies fostered in children by violent television shows and video games can be tempered if they cut back their viewing and playing."[16]

On local news, the rule that "if it bleeds, it leads" still holds; local news editors look for shootings, holdups, fires, car chases and collisions -- none of which need explanation or analysis -- for much of their evening and late night broadcasts. Here they ignore findings of a study by the National Institute of Public Health that TV drama and TV news both instill feelings of insecurity, especially among women and minorities.[17] They also brush aside the comment of Ralph Nader, "Policies on street crime regularly make the evening news; policies on corporate crime don't. Welfare reform proposals are always newsworthy, corporate welfare reform rarely."[18]

Sex is also pervasive on TV. In 1998, a *New York Times* reporter concluded that "mainstream television this season is flaunting the most vulgar and explicit sex, language and behavior that it has ever sent into American homes."[19] "The Center for Population Options . . . determined that the typical teenager sees nearly 14,000 sexual encounters on television every year; moreover, a study by the conservative Media Research Council found that portrayals of premarital sex outnumber portrayals of sex within marriage by eight to one."[20] Early in 2001, the Fox Network launched *Temptation Island*, on which four unmarried couples travel to an island to see if they can withstand getting seduced by models of both sexes. "Stripped to its essentials, a *San Francisco Chronicle* editorial said, "the show is about as subtle as peeping through a bedroom window. But, hey, if sex sells, forbidden sex figures to put the demand curve into kinky positions."[21] During the 1999-2000 season 75 percent of major network prime-time shows carried sexual content.

The use of profanity and crude language on TV programs has become more and more common since the giant media mergers began. The Center for Media and Public Affairs studied movies, TV shows and music videos and found that "prime time network shows averaged one scene with a profanity every six minutes during the 1998-99 season" and "Fox had an average of 20 such scenes an hour, almost twice the overall average."[22] The Fox Network is owned by Rupert Murdoch.

The fact that violence and sex are so prevalent and profitable has not escaped writers of popular novels. Violence and anti-social themes have increased dramatically in the last quarter-century. The authors, of course, hope to sell their plots to movie or TV producers.

It can't be argued that all readers and viewers prefer violence and sex over other kinds of content. Such programs as *Cheers, Mister Rogers' Neighborhood* and *the Mary Tyler Moore Show* drew huge audiences over long periods. Documentaries such as Ken Burns' *Jazz* and *Civil War* also get consistently high ratings. "In its early years, mass television was essentially nonviolent," Ben Bagdikian writes, adding, "It carried far more pleasant, unaggressive children's programs; it lacked today's endless staccato of commercials, and it was almost entirely family oriented."[23] The TV and movie producers are not necessarily giving audiences what they want but what is most profitable. The saturation of "crud," including violence and sex, has shared with competition from cable as a major factor in the steep decline of prime time audiences for all the Big Three -- CBS, NBC and ABC — in the last decade. For some of the same reasons, readership of daily newspapers has declined in the last 20 years, especially among women and children

The social scientists aren't the only ones now criticizing media content; journalists are. A long *Columbia Journalism Review* piece in 1998 was titled "Money Lust: How Pressure for Profit is Perverting Journalism." Author Neil Hickey contended that "mainstream print and TV news outlets purvey more 'life-style' stories, trivia, scandal, celebrity gossip, sensational crime, sex in high places, and tabloidism at the expense of serious news," adding that "editors shrink from tough coverage of major advertisers lest they jeopardize ad revenue."[24]

Concern about advertisers has become central to most decisions made by managers in all media — TV, radio, cable, newspapers and magazines. The ads in newspapers and commercials on TV, radio and cable all have the same purpose: to get the reader or viewer to buy more and more, even of products they don't need. For a single one-hour episode of the hospital drama ER, its makers and cast divided up $13 million during 1999. That made the cost of a 30-second commercial $565,000, higher even than the cost of commercials on *Seinfeld*, the long-running program about nothing, during its last year before syndication. Between 60 and 70 percent of the space in daily papers is given to advertisements, and at least eight minutes of every half hour TV program are devoted to commercials. "Television networks now broadcast 6,000 commercials a week; the number has risen 50 percent (from 1983 to 1995)."[25] There's now evidence that the more the viewer watches TV, the more he or she spends. It seems that "TV inflates our sense of what's normal" even though "lifestyles depicted on television are far different from (those of) the average American's."[26]

In her book *Deadly Persuasion*, Jean Kilbourne contends that advertising in all media contributes to a "toxic cultural environment," poisons human relations and debases women by preying on their need to form relationships.[27] Scholar Michael Kammen, in his book on American culture, says "Because ads are supervasive, aggressive, repetitive, and intrusive, they are much more difficult to ignore than they were 30 years ago."[28]

Many of the TV commercials are aimed specifically at children. Most frequent are commercials for food products and fast food restaurants.[29] Moreover, the story content of children's programs often contains promotion of specific products, especially on the Disney Channel. "A show like News Corp's *The Simpsons* has tie-ins with four major firms, including Pepsi-Cola and Subway sandwiches."[30]

However, some of the companies that pay for the commercials have recently shown concern about the content of prime-time TV programs. Leading them is

Andrea Alstrup, who is in charge of $600 million a year of Johnson & Johnson commercials. Speaking to ad executives in 1998, she vigorously attacked the sex, violence and vulgarity on prime-time TV. She cited the NBC sitcom *Friends* as "embarrassing, outrageous, unacceptable."[31] And she announced that some 10 companies, including Proctor & Gamble, Coca Cola and her own Johnson & Johnson, were starting Family Friendly Programming Forum to pressure networks "to run mature-themed shows later in the evening." One result is *Gilmore Girls*, on the WB network, which has Family Forum support. Meantime, a grass-roots organization, Parents Television Council, has begun to campaign for more prime-time family shows.

During the very limited public discussion of the 1996 Telecommunications Act, President Clinton worked out an agreement with the TV industry calling for three hours a week of educational programs for children. It was left to the networks to decide the meaning of "educational" and even to decide when the programs would be scheduled. "CBS simply informed all of the children's shows that they were now 'educational' shows." [32] Most networks and local stations tend to confine their "children's hours" to Saturday mornings. Many of the programs are cartoons, which are "violence filled, crudely rendered and heavily loaded with commercials," media scholar Leo Bogart comments.[33] A 1999 study by the Annenberg Public Policy Center at the University of Pennsylvania found that "28 percent of children's television programs contained four or more acts of violence, that 45 percent contained 'problematic language' and that only a third of shows classified as 'educational' by the FCC were in fact 'highly educational'." The study "concluded that there's little of value in children's television."[34]

"TV has no agenda, except to be profitable," writes Richard M. Cohen, former editor at CBS News, in an essay titled "The Corporate Takeover of News."[35] Cohen's comment can be made about newspapers as well. In his book, *When MBAs Rule the Newsroom*, journalist Doug Underwood wrote that the "Reagan-Bush years have seen a return to the days of quashed stories about corporate wrongdoing, deference to corporate interests in the community, and boosteristic accounts of business activity."[36] Similarly, Dean Orville Schell of the Journalism School at University of California, Berkeley, says, "Today there are fewer countervailing forces to the imperatives of the bottom line and the marketplace."[37]

One result of the merger frenzy in the 1980s and 1990s, according to *New York Times* editor Gene Roberts, is that "talk at the high level of newspapers is of increasing profits, increasing corporate pressure, increasing responsibility to shareholders."[38] Roberts added that many newspapers have "cut back on quality of product and level of service." The emphasis on marketing can also be seen in television. As Cohen says, "TV news is supportive of establishments," adding "corporate ownership of the networks and local stations is destroying the integrity of news."[39]

In network and newspaper editorial rooms, reporters and editors insist that there is never any censorship. Almost all of them believe that to be true, not realizing there is self-censorship that takes place almost unconsciously. If the interests of the company or one of its officials might be jeopardized, the story or the quote doesn't get used. But sometimes the censorship is conscious, as in the case of the CBS cancellation of a *60 Minutes* segment on tobacco and the ABC investigative piece on the same subject. CBS ultimately aired an edited version of the segment. ABC aired its program, and when sued by the tobacco industry paid millions in legal fees and apologized on the air repeatedly. The *60 Minutes* story was dramatized in the 1999 movie, *The Insider.*

In January, 2000, *60 Minutes* carried an aggressive investigative story about Westinghouse's inhumane management of its Savannah River plutonium plant, but by then Westinghouse no longer owned the plant, nor did it any longer own CBS, having sold the network in September, 1999 to Sumner Redstone's Viacom.

In fact, censorship is practiced widely. "As a News Corporation executive put it in 1998 when two New Corp. reporters were fired for doing a critical investigation of Monsanto Chemical Company, 'We paid $3 billion for these TV stations. We will decide what the news is. The news is what we tell you it is'."[40]

Since 1976, Project Censored, headquartered at Sonoma State University in California, has annually published *Censored: The News That Didn't Make the News,* listing 25 stories that got little or no coverage in mainstream media the previous year. The 1999 edition listed, among others, "Chemical Corporations Profit Off Breast Cancer," "Catholic Hospital Mergers Threaten Reproductive Rights for Women," "U.S. Nuclear Program Subverts UN's Comprehensive Test Ban Treaty," and "Private Prison Explosion Becomes Big Business." The 25 stories had all appeared in alternative media, such as *The Nation* and *The Progressive,* but not in the mainstream media.

Censorship is also practiced by book publishers. *The Nation* magazine devoted a whole issue to "The Crushing Power of Big Publishing." The lead article commented that "the giants have shrunk the culture actively -- by dumping or red-lighting (any book) that offers revelations irksome to themselves."[41] Author Marc Crispin Miller offered as examples Marc Eliot's *Walt Disney: Hollywood's Dark Prince,* aborted suddenly by Bantam, and *Katharine the Great,* Deborah Davis's life of Katharine Graham, pulped by Harcourt Brace Jovanovich after Ben Bradlee of the *Washington Post* sent a letter threatening a lawsuit.

Most readers and viewers are aware of bias in the news media controlled by the moguls. More than three-quarters of the public (78%) believe bias exists and that powerful people can get stories into the newspapers — or keep them out.[42] The study, conducted by the American Association of Newspaper Editors, also found that about the same number (74%) believe TV news puts more emphasis on personalities than on issues. More and more, the same comment can be made about the country's newspapers, which dropped their budgets for news-gathering from 15 percent in the 1980's to nine percent in the mid-90's. Most of the CEOs, like the one who took over the Chandler empire based in Los Angeles, found they could fill the news space with fewer reporters, assigning those left to less time-consuming stories. That meant the number of investigative stories, which had skyrocketed after Watergate in the 70's, dropped dramatically; investigative stories are costly and time-consuming..

The media mergers of the 1980s and 1990s left many readers and viewers distrustful. A *Newsweek* poll in 1998 found 35 percent of respondents saying the mergers had not "improved the quality or accuracy of news reporting" but "made it worse."[43] Only 14 percent found that the mergers had "improved the quality and accuracy" of the news.

The failure of the broadcast industry to reflect the America's ethnic diversity was underscored in the fall of 1999 when the NAACP launched a campaign to end the "whites only" content of network television. The campaign scored its first victory in January 2000 when NBC signed an agreement with the NAACP to increase the number of minorities before the camera. Note: the "age of TV" began in 1950, exactly 50 years earlier. Since the NBC-NAACP agreement, the number of minorities actors has increased, but most of the minority cast members play minor roles.

Under the direction of profit-hungry moguls, the media today -- newspapers, television, cable, magazines, movies -- are pushing down the quality of our culture on all fronts. More and more, Americans are led to believe that celebrities are important, that they live in a dangerous and violent world, that theirs is a tabloid culture, and that they must buy products even if they don't need them.

The news media's fixation on celebrity and other kinds of soft news is at the expense of foreign news and serious stories about what's happening in the country and its thousands of communities. The Project for Excellence in Journalism surveyed over a 20-year period thousands of stories on the Big Three network news, on news magazine covers and on front pages of major papers. It found that "celebrity, scandal, gossip and other 'human interest' stories increased from 15 percent in 1977 to an astonishing 43 percent in 1997."[44]

A summary of what the media moguls are doing to the culture appeared in a *New Yorker* 1996 article titled "Buried Alive: Our Children and the Avalanche of Crud." "The tone of our popular culture has coarsened in the last couple of decades," writer David Denby commented. "Everyone has said so, and everyone is right. The boasting polygamists on trash TV, the rap lyrics, the rancorous and openly racist talk radio shows -- these are just the most obvious examples."[45]

Much is made of the increasing variety of communications outlets available to us as the result of satellites, cable, the fourth, fifth and sixth networks, and the computer Internet. But with the exception of the Internet, these are all dominated by the same media monopolies that the billionaire moguls own and control. The merger of America Online (AOL) with Time Warner early in 2000 was not likely to change the *content* of offerings by the new giant, only the methods of delivery. Steve Case of AOL and Gerald Levin of Time Warner are still focused on the bottom line; their stocks are still on Wall Street. The sex and violence will continue on TV, cable, and now on personal computers; the over-emphasis on celebrities and lifestyle will still dominate all media; news needed for democracy will be suppressed. And because the multi media moguls have such a fixation on the bottom line, they will not allow good taste to overcome greed.

As Newton Minow retired from the Federal Communications Commission 40 years ago, he called the programming of the TV industry "a vast wasteland." Minow repeated the "wasteland" comment ten years ago. Today, aside from an occasional oasis of good taste, it's a *vaster* wasteland, and it will continue to degrade and coarsen our culture until the present concentration of media conglomerates is broken up.[46]

CONCLUSION–WHAT CAN WE DO?

What is logical and good ought to be expressed even if it appears unachievable at the moment.

–Ben Bagdikian

Can the multi-media moguls with their outrageous fortunes be made more accountable to the public their empires are supposed to serve? Can we hope for media that will improve our culture, rather than abuse and degrade it? A growing number of Americans believe we can — and must. They are represented by such organizations as the Cultural Environment Movement, Fairness and Accuracy in Reporting (FAIR), Ralph Nader's Consumer Alert, the Institute for Public Accuracy, United for a Fair Economy, Rev. Jesse Jackson's Rainbow/PUSH Coalition, People for Better Television, and Citizens for Independent Public Broadcasting.

We must agree from the start that it will take *political action* to persuade Congress and the various government agencies to do what is clearly needed. And we must remember that the big media maintain a permanent, powerful lobby in Washington. Since neither major party -- Democratic or Republican -- is likely to join such a revolt, we must work with the smaller ones. That means the Green Party, New Party, Labor Party, Democratic Socialists of America, and Americans for Democratic Action. What is needed is a political movement, a left wing movement which rallies thousands and ultimately millions for major changes .

Such a movement will need its own lobbyists in Washington to push for reform legislation and to monitor the federal agencies involved in media, especially the Federal Commission and the Federal Trade Commission. It will take awhile, if we recall that while the Sherman Antitrust Act was passed in 1890, Rockefeller's monopolistic Standard Oil Company of Indiana wasn't broken up by the Supreme Court until 1911.

There's lots to do if real changes are to be made. Bu we must realize that even on the Internet, the media giants are staking out turf, as evidenced by the merger of America Online with media conglomerate Time-Warner-Turner. The Internet also plays host to problems. Harvard law professor Lawrence Tribe contends that with the Internet, "there's no filter, there's no cross-examination, there's no assurance of accuracy . . . we're in danger of assuming that we're seeing the real thing just because we have such instant access."[1] Still, the invasion of the corporate media biggies is demonstrated that by 1998, "more than three-quarters of the 31 most visited news and entertainment websites were affiliated with large media firms, and the rest were connected to outfits like AOL and Microsoft," according to *Broadcasting & Cable*, which adds, "With their deep pockets, the media giants are aggressive investors in startup Internet companies."[2] And in *The Global Media*, Herman and McChesney tell "how quickly the media and communication giants have taken charge of the new technologies and set them on an explicitly commercial course."[3] No reforms have been suggested or tried on the Internet, even though it continues to grow rapidly.

The media reformers are in agreement on their goals, although they vary in the emphasis they place on each one. We have five major proposals.

First, the Telecommunications Act of 1996 must be repealed. That law opened the doors to a frenzy of mergers and buyouts, which still continues. For example, it allowed Lowry Mays to expand his Clear Channel Communications empire to 1200 radio stations spread across the country. It consolidated the stranglehold on broadcast media by Sumner Redstone's Viacom-Blockbuster-Paramount-CBS, Rupert Murdoch's News Corporation-Fox, and Gerald Levin's Time-Warner-Turner, now Steve Case's AOL-Time-Warner-Turner. At the 1997 Media and Democracy Congress, Communications Professor Nolan Bowie of Temple University, called the 1996 act "the biggest corporate giveaway in the history of the world."[4]

Second, an even more direct assault on the behemoths would be a new anti-trust law, such as the one proposed by Communications Professor Robert W. McChesney, a law "to break up such media conglomerates as Time Warner, News Corporation, and Disney, so that their book publishing, TV show production, movie production, TV stations, TV networks, amusement parks, retail chain stores, cable TV channels, cable networks and so on all become independent firms."[5] McChesney didn't include Viacom-Blockbuster-CBS in his list, but it belongs there.

Ralph Nader comments, "We all need to start talking about the power that the people have to use existing anti-trust and broadcast regulations -- as well as new laws and new technologies -- to break up monopolies and open up a true, wide-ranging democratic dialogue in the country."[6]

Third, reform and refinance the public broadcasting system, both television and radio. Most important here is the need for huge increases in public funding, from the present pitiful $260 million a year to at least $10 billion a year. That kind of hike would put U. S. public broadcasting on a par with counterparts in Japan, England and other industrialized countries. And that kind of funding should be accompanied by the total elimination of all commercials on public TV and public radio. We need to remember two important facts: 1) that the airwaves belong to the public, and 2) that in the early days of both radio and TV, there was no commercial advertising. Incidentally, a by-product of a strong, truly non-commercial public TV could be growth of independent film-makers, outside the orbit of the Hollywood companies.

Fourth, increase the number of *public service* announcements required on all commercial TV and radio stations. From the start, the broadcast station owners have gotten their licenses free. They -- and we -- should look upon broadcasting as both a privilege and a responsibility. Incidentally, media critic Dennis W. Mazzocco proposes *charging* the broadcasters for their use of the public airwaves. He points out that all media operators are eligible for "huge federal and state tax deductions for program costs as well as the interest on the debt to buy even more properties."[7] And Mazzocco calls attention to the 1991 proposal of Lawrence Grossman, former president of both NBC News and PBS, that "all commercial stations pay a 1 percent or 2 percent spectrum tax to help finance public broadcasting."[8] Like many others, Mazzocco believes that "Congress should bring back the Fairness Doctrine, which the FCC threw out in 1987, requiring all broadcasters and cable operators to present a balanced presentation of controversial public issues."[9] If the Doctrine came back, right-wing Rush Limbaugh would be balanced by liberal Jim Hightower.

Another good idea would be to set strict limits on the content of advertising on both children's programs and news programs. Just as important, set limits on the number and length of commercials on *all* programs. Also, require by law that all commercial TV and radio stations give a specified amount of free time to *all* candidates for Congress and the Presidency during the six weeks before elections. And on a year-round basis, every commercial station, both TV and radio, should devote at least an hour every day to public service.

Fifth, create a National Media Council, organized like the National News Council, which monitored press coverage from 1973 to 1975. Such a council, with both public and media representatives, would not be limited to monitoring the press; it would also focus on radio, television, and cable. It would investigate complaints coming from individuals and organizations concerning practices, programs, even omissions. An example might be the current drive to limit pornography on the Internet and the over-use of violence in movies and on television. A National Media Council could work to curb these dangerous trends. In effect, the National Media Council would be a watchdog, working to correct any kind of media abuse or mistake.

Can we win these changes? To win even one of them won't be easy. We can be encouraged by the comment of Herman and McChesney that "the system may be far more vulnerable and subject to change than appears to be the case at present."[10] To make even one major change will require a powerful movement made up of people who are determined to bring us the kind of media environment we need and deserve. But if we remind ourselves of the Progressive movement's accomplishments a century ago, we know it can be done.

NOTES

INTRODUCTION
1. "Piecing Together a TV Power," by Michael Burgi, *Mediaweek*, Oct.27, 1997, pp.4 and 5.
2. *We the Media*, edited by Don Hazen and Julie Winokur, The New Press, 1997, p.63.
3. *Rich Media, Poor Democracy*, by Robert W. McChesney, University of Illinois Press, 1999, p.64.
4. "A Lobby the Media Won't Touch," by Arthur E. Rowse, *Washington Monthly*, May, 1998, p.9.
5. "The Man Who Counts the Killings," by Scott Stossel, *Atlantic Monthly*, May, 1997, p.99.
6. *Defining Vision: The Battle for the Future of TV*, by Joel Brinkley, Harcourt Brace, 1997, p.375
7 "Why Media Mergers Matter," by Rifka Rosenwein, *Brill's Content*, Dec.1999/Jan.2000, p.94.

CHAPTER 1
1. "Will Gates Crush Newspapers," by Neil Henry, *Columbia Journalism Review*, Nov/Dec 1997, p. 28
2. "Making Microsoft Safe for Capitalism," by James Gleick, *New York Times Magazine* Nov. 5, 1995, p. 5.
3. *Conglomerates and the Media,* by Eric Barnouw, The New Press, 1997, p. 136.
4. "All Over the Map," by Nathan Vardi, *Nation*, Dec. 25, 2000, p. 102.
5. "How Gates Keeps the Magic Going," by Brenton Schlender, *Nation*, June 18, 1990, pp. 83-84.
6. "The George S. Patton of Software," by Jeffrey Young, *Forbes*, Jan. 27, 1997, p. 86.
7. *Gates: How Microsoft's Mogul Reinvented an Industry — and Made Himself the Richest Man in America*, by Stephen Mannes and Paul Andrews, Simon & Schuster, 1994, p. 212.
8. *The Road Ahead*, by Bill Gates, Viking Penguin, 1995, p. 91.
9. *Gates: How Microsoft's Mogul Reinvented an Industry — and Made Himself the Richest Man in America*, p. 447.
10. "Making Microsoft Safe for Capitalism," p. 53.
11. "Investor's Edge: Profiting From New Economy; World Lately Seems to be Catching Up to Paul Allen's Vision," by Edward Silver, *Los Angeles Times*, Sept. 20, 1999, p.C5.
12. "Final Offer," by Ken Auletta, *New Yorker*, . Jan. 15, 2001, p. 42.
13. Ibid. p. 46.
14. "Bill Gates, Health Crusader," by John Donnelly, *(Boston Globe) Monterey County Herald*, Dec. 24, 2000, p. A1.

CHAPTER 2
1. *Buffett: The Making of an American Capitalist*, by Roger Lowenstein, Random House, 1995, p. 25.
2. "I Don't Have To Work With People I Don't Like," by Robert Lenzer, *Forbes 400*, Oct. 18, l993, p. 43.
3. "The Not-So-Silent Partner: Meet Charlie Munger," by Robert Lenzer, *Forbes 400*, Oct. 18, 1993, pp. 78-85.
4. "Warren Buffett's 'annus horribilis'," by J.M.P., *U.S. News & World Report.*, Jan. 17, 2000, p. 57.
5. "Warren Buffett Takes Blame for Low Performance," by Charles V. Zehren, *San Francisco Examiner & Chronicle*, Mar. 12, 2000, p. B16.
6. Daily Briefing," *Atlanta Constitution*, Dec. 21, 2000, p. 2E.
7. *The Warren Buffet Way*, by Robert Hagstrom, John Wiley & Sons, 1994, pp. 22-23.
8. Ibid., pp. 22-23.
9. *Of Permanent Value: The Story of Warren Buffett*, by Andrew Kilpatrick, AKPE, 1994, p. 98.
10. "Jet Setting Becomes Time Travel," by Andrew Clark, *The Guardian*, Mar. 28, 2001, p.24.
11. "Taking After His Father, Sort Of," by David Barboza, *New York Times*, Sept. 3, 2000, p. BU2.
12. *Warren Buffett Speaks: Wit and Wisdom From the World's Greatest Investor*, by Janet Lowe, John Wiley & Sons, p. 47

CHAPTER 3

1. "America's Best Export," *Forbes*, Oct. 21, 1991, p. 88.
2. "The Making of a Media Giant, by Adam Bryant, *Newsweek*, Sept. 20, 1999, p. 36.
3. "The New Establishment," *Vanity Fair*, Oct., 2000, p. 270.
4.. "Viacom: Redstone's Remarkable Ride to the Top," by Marc Gunther, *Fortune*, Apr. 26, 1999, p. 132.
5. *Current Biography Yearbook*, January, 1996, p. 39.
6. "Fort Sumner," by Judith Newman, *Vanity Fair*, Nov. 1999, p. 252.
7. "Late Bloomer," by Robert Lenzer and Marla Matzer, *Forbes*, Oct. 17, 1994, p. 44.
8. "Sumner's Gemstone," by Brett Pulley and Andrew Tanzer, *Forbes*, Feb. 21, 2000, p. 107,
9. Ibid., p. 44.
10. *We The Media*," edited by Don Hazen and Julie Winokur, The New Press, 1997, p. 102.
11. "Study Blames MTV for Video Violence," by John Carman, *San Francisco Chronicle*, May 15, 1997, pp. E1,4.
12. "Controversial Rapper Takes Top Honors at MTV Awards," by Associated Press, *Monterey County Herald*, Sept. 8, 2000, p. A10.
13. "South Park: The Rude Tube," by Paula Howard, *Newsweek*, Mar. 23, 1998, pp. 57-62.
14. "All in the Family to Carry Warning," Associated Press, *San Francisco Chronicle*, Oct.
15, 1998.
15. "Can Viacom's Reporters Cover Viacom's Interests?" by Mark Crispin Miller, *Columbia Journalism Review*, Nov/Dec. 1999, p.50.
16. "The New Establishment," *Vanity Fair*, Oct. 1999, p. 202.
17. "Cosby Condemns Stereotypes on TV," by Lynn Elber, *San Francisco Chronicle*, Mar. 24, 1999, p. E3.
18. "MTV Goes Big Time," by Joel Selvin, *San Francisco Chronicle*, Nov. 5, 2000, Datebook, p. 50.
19. "The Big Picture: How Thrills Pay the Bills at Paramount," by Patrick Goldstein, *Los Angeles Times*, Apr. 10, 2001, Calendar, p. F1.
20. "BET: The King of Black Mediocrity," by Frank McKissick, *The Progressive*, Jan. 2001, p. 34.
21. "Can Viacom's Reporters Cover Viacom's Interests?" by Mark Crispin Miller, *Columbia Journalism Review*, Nov/Dec. 1999, p. 50.
22. "The Vindication of Sumner Redstone," by Robert Langner and Peter Newcomb, *Forbes*, June 15, 1998, p. 52.
23. "A Deal Too Far for Sumner's Wife," by Christopher Parkes, *Financial Times*, Sept. 21, 1999.
24. "Fort Sumner," by Judith Newman, *Vanity Fair*, Oct. 4, 1999, p. 43.
25. "Milestone, *Time*, Oct. 4, 1999, p. 43.
26. "Last Stand," by Elizabeth Lesly and Ronald Grover, *Business Week*, Mar. 3, 1997, p. 68.
27. "Pay Per Views," by Ken Auletta, *New Yorker*, June 5, 1995, p.54.
28. "Team Gore," *Nation*, Aug. 21/28, 2000.
29. "Last Stand," by Elizabeth Lesly and Ronald Grover, *Business Week*, Mar 3., 1997, p. 68

CHAPTER 4

1. *Forbes*, Oct. 16, 1995, p. 117.
2, "Trying to Make Atlanta Papers World Class," by Bill Cutler, *Columbia Journalism Review*, Mar/Apr, 1988, p. 40.
3.*Paper Tigers, the Latest, Greatest Newspaper Tycoons*, by Nicholas Coleridge, Birch Lane Press, 1994, p. 196.
4. Ibid., p. 182.
5. "Missing the Story at the Statehouse," by Charles Layton and Mary Walton, *American Journalism Review*, July/Aug, 1998, p. 53.

6. *Media Circus*, by Howard Kurtz, Times Books, 1994, p. 383.

7. Ibid., p.191.

8. Ibid., p. 191.

9. "First Lady of Atlanta," by Lloyd Grove, *Vanity Fair*, Aug. 1988, p. 139.

10. Ibid., p. 179.

11. *Paper Tigers, the Latest, Greatest Newspaper Tycoons*, p. 184.

CHAPTER 5

1. "Metromania," by Christopher Palmeri, *Forbes*, Feb. 26, 1996, p. 95.

2. "Repeat Performance," by John Gorham, *Forbes*, May 15, 2001, p. 60.

3.. "Rich, 82, and Starting Over," by John Landler, *New York Times*, Jan 5, 1997.

4. "Metromedia to Buy AboveNet," by Bloomberg News, *New York Times*, June 24, 1999, p. C3

5. "Fiber-optics Company in Deal," by Bloomberg News, *San Diego Union-Tribune*, Oct. 11, 2000, p. C9.

6. "Building a New Empire in Thin Air," by Mark Landler, *New York Times*, Jan. 5, 1997.

7. "Streetwalker: Clever Kluge," by Thomas Jaffe, Stephane Fitch, Brandon Copple, and Matthew Schifrin, *Forbes*, June 6, 1999, p. 392.

CHAPTER 6

1. "Turner Funds Effort to Cut Nuclear Arms," *Monterey County Herald*, Jan. 6, 2001, p. A2.

2. "Ted Turner, Man of the Year," *Time*, Jan. 6, 1992, p. 36.

3. *Citizen Turner: the Wild Rise of an American Tycoon*, by Robert Goldberg and Gerald Jay Goldberg, Harcourt, Brace & Co., 1995, p. 121.

4. "The Taming of Ted Turner," by Priscilla Painton, *Time*, Jan. 6, 1992, pp. 36-37.

5. "Raiding the Global Village," by Ken Auletta, *New Yorker*, Aug. 2, 1993, pp. 25-30.

6. *"It Ain't as Easy as it Looks,"* by Porter Bibb, Brown Publishers Inc., 1993, p. 313.

7. *Citizen Turner*, p. 420.

8. "Ted's Buffalo Need to Roam," *Newsweek*, July 5, 1999, p. 6.

9. "Turncoat Ted," by Mary Summers, *Forbes*, July 26, 1999, p. 52.

10. Jerry's Deal," by Connie Bruck, *New Yorker*, Feb. 19, 1996, p. 69.

11. "A Tank is Rolling Through CNN Before *Time*-Warner-AOL Merger," by Jim Rutenberg, *New York Times*, Dec. 4, 2000.

12. *Citizen Turner*, p.420.

CHAPTER 7

1. *Murdoch*, by William Shawcross, Simon & Schuster, 1992, p. 95.

2. Ibid., p. 116.

3. *Columbia Journalism Review*, July/Aug, 1982.

4. *Barefaced Cheek: The Apotheosis of Rupert Murdoch*, by Michael Leapman, Hodder & Stoughton, 1983, p. 253.

5. *Megamedia: How Corporations Dominate Mass Media, Distort Competition and Endanger Media*, by Dean Alger, Rowman & Littlefield, 1998, p. 1.

6. "Fox's Action Gets Down and Dirty," by John Carman, *San Francisco Chronicle*, Feb. 2, 2000, p. A21.

7. "Women Are Looking for Mr. Big Bucks," by Cynthia Tucker, *San Francisco Chronicle*, Feb. 2, 2000, p. A21.

8. "Man Bites Dog," by Peter Kafka, *Forbes*, Nov. 29, 1999, p. 120.

9. "Murdoch's Fox News; They Distort, They Decide," by Daphne Eviatar, *Nation*, Mar. 12, 2001, p. 12.

10. "Rupert's Misses," *The Economist*, July 3, 1999, p.62.
11. "Murdoch Tries to Sweeten Bid for DirecTV," by David Lieberman, *USA Today*, Dec. 7, 2000, p. 1B.
12. "Murdoch Executive Calls Press Coverage of China Too Harsh," by Bill Carter, *New York Times*, Mar. 26, 2001, p. C8.
13. "Rupert Does the Cyberhustle," by Richard Siklos, *Business Week*, July 12, 1999, p. 88.
14. "Murdoch is Betting Heavily on a Global Vision," by Geraldine Fabrikant, *New York Times*, July 29, 1996, p.C6.
15. "His Biggest Takeover - How Murdoch Bought Washington," by Ken Silverstein, *The Nation*, June 8, 1998, p. 29.
16. "The Rules According to Rupert," by Marc Gunther, *Fortune*, Oct. 26, 1999, p. 104.
17. "The Making of James Murdoch," by Lisa Urquhart, *Financial Times*, May 31, 2000.
18. "The Sun Hasn't Set — Yet," by David Usborne, *The Independent*, Mar. 11, 2001, p. 24.
19. "Murdoch's New Life," by William Shawcross, *Vanity Fair*, Oct., 1999, p. 324.
20. "Who's Afraid of Rupert Murdoch?" Frontline, PBS, Sept. 8, 1997.
21. "Rupert Murdoch Assessment," by David Plotz, *Slate*, MSNBC, May 24, 1997, p. 1.
22. "Murdoch's New Life," by William Shawcross, *Vanity Fair*, Oct. 1999, p. 270.
23. "*Citizen Newhouse,*" by Carol Felsenthal, Seven Stories Press, 1998, p. 463.
24. *The Highwaymen,* by Ken Auletta, Random House, 1997, p. 266.
25. "Murdoch's New Life," by William Shawcross, *Vanity Fair*, Oct., 1999, p. 272,

CHAPTER 8
1. "Two Birds of a Feather," by Mark Miller, *Newsweek*, Aug. 14, 2000, p. 62.
2. "Hearst Heir Challenges Secrecy of Estate," by Mark Simon, *San Francisco Chronicle*, Apr. 15, 1999, p. A17.
3. "5 Hearst Heirs Get $100G Mad Money," by Helen Peterson, *New York Daily News*, Feb. 28, 2001, p. 17.
4. *Forbes 400*, Oct. 22, 1990, p. 172.
5. *Citizen Hearst,* by W. A. Swanberg, Charles Scribner's Sons, 1951, p. 484.
6. *The Powers That Be,* by David Halberstam, Laurel, 1979, p. 396.
7. *The Chief: The Life of William Randolph Hearst,* by David Nasaw, Houghton Mifflin Company, 2000, p. 594.
8. *Citizen Hearst,* pp. 524-525.
9. *The Hearst: Father and Son,* by Jack Casserly, Roberts Rinehart, 1991, p. 353.

CHAPTER 9
1. "Big Deal in Las Vegas," by Sally Denton and Roger Morris, *Columbia Journalism Review*, Nov/Dec, 2000, p. 49.
2. "Kerkorian: Feed My Lion," *Business Week*, Aug. 31, 1998, p. 38.
3. "MGM Lion Looks for Roar," by David Germain, *San Francisco Chronicle*, Nov. 25, 1999, p. C15.
4. "German Bank Backs Daimler/Chrysler," by Hans Greimel, *San Francisco Chronicle*, Nov. 29, 2000, p. B7.
5. "MGM Looking for Hannibal Boost," by Phyllis Furman, *New York Daily News*, Feb. 14, 2001, p. 28.
6. "The Wizard of MGM," by Brett Pulley, *Forbes*, May 28, 2001, p. 124.
7. "Third Try at the Club," by David McClintick, *Forbes*, Dec. 15, 1997, p. 219.
8. *Current Biography Yearbook*, 1996," p. 269.
9. "Third Try at the Club," by David McClintick, *Forbes*, Dec. 15, 1997, p. 237.

CHAPTER 10
1. *Newspaperman: S. I. Newhouse and the Business of News,* Tichnor & Fields, 1983, p. 252.
2. Ibid., p. 180.
3. Ibid., p. 217.
4. Ibid., p. 201.
5. *Newhouse: All the Glitter, Power and Glory of America's Richest Media Empire and the Secretive Man Behind It,* by Thomas Meier, St. Martin's Press, 1994, pp 3-4.
6. Ibid., p. 6.
7. *Citizrn Newhouse: Portrait of a Media Merchant,* by Carol Felsenthal, Seven Stories Press, 1998, p. 195.
8. "Tina's *New Yorker,*" by Eric Utne, *Columbia Journalism Review,* Jan/Feb 2000, pp. 33 and 36.
9. *Newhouse,* p. 351.
10. Ibid., p. 352.
11. "The Newhouse Way," by Brent Cunningham, *Columbia Journalism Review,* Jan/Feb 2000, p. 23.
12. "Newhouse," p. 366.
13. "Wired: Under Conde Nast, Magazine has Boosted its Fortune by focusing on 'New Economy,' by Dan Fost, *San Francisco Chronicle,* June 7, 1999, p. E1.
14. *Citizen Newhouse: Portrait of a Media Merchant,* p. 408.
15. Ibid., p. 435.
16. "The Biggest Private *Fortune,*" by Carol Loomis, *Fortune,* Aug. 17, 1987, p. 64.
17. Ibid., p. 64.
18. *Citizrn Newhouse: Portrait of a Media Merchant,* p. 444.

CHAPTER 11
1. "The New Establishment 2000," *Vanity Fair,* Oct. 2000, p. 296.
2. "A New Guy Can Do it Better," by Richard L. Stern and Jason Zweig, *Forbes,* Nov. 25, 1991, p. 122.
3. "Media Giant Looks for New Ways to Grow," by Felicity Barringer and Geraldine Fabricant, *New York Times,* Mar. 21, 1999.
4. Ibid., p. 48.
5. "A New Guy Can Do it Better," p. 124.
6. "Still Blooming," by Stephen S. Johnson, *Forbes,* Feb. 13, 1995, p. 14.
7. "Street Fighter," by Thomas Carroll, *Time,* Oct. 5, 1992, p. 73.
8. *Current Biography Yearbook ,* 1996, p. 29.
9. "Mayor Bloomberg?" by Alex Williams, *New York,* Mar. 2, 1998, p. 13.
10. "The Buzz," *New York Daily News,* July 15, 2000, p. 6.
11. "Bloomberg Chief Looks Ready to Run," by Paul D. Colford, *New York Daily News,* Dec. 12, 2000, p. 70.
12. "Volume Down at Bloomberg," by Brian Dumaine, *Fortune,* Mar 6, 1995, p. 34.
13. "The New Establishment 2000, *Vanity Fair,* Oct. 2000, p. 296.
14. "Hackers Caught in Bloomberg e-sting," *Sunday Times* (London), Aug. 20, 2000,
15. "Street Fighter," by Thomas Carroll, *Time,* Oct. 5, 1992, p. 73.

CHAPTER 12
1. *Paper Losses,* by Bryan Gruley, Grove Press, 1993, p. 17.
2. *About E. W. Scripps, Introduction to Selected Disquisitions of E. W. Scripps,* by Oliver Knight, University of Wisconsin Press, 1966, p. 19.
3. *The Astonishing Mr. Scripps,* by Vance H. Trimble, Iowa State University, 1992, p. 76.

4. *About E. W. Scripps,* p. 46.
5. Ibid., p. 47.
6. Ibid., p. 70.
7. Ibid., p. 72.
8. *Paper Losses,* by Bryan Gruley, Grove Press, 1993, p. 18.
9. *The Press and America,* by Edwin Emery and Michael Emery, Prentice-Hall, 1978, p. 259.
10. *Scripps: The Divided Dynasty,* by Jack Casserly, Donald I. Fine, 1993, p. 3.
11. *A Handbook of Sscripps-Howard,* by John H. Sorrells, E. W. Scripps Co., 1948, p. 53.
12. *The Astonishing Mr. Scripps,* p. 54.
13. *Scripps: The Divided Dynasty,* p. 43.
14. *Journalism History,* Summer, 1995.
15. *Makers of Modern Journalism,* by Kenneth Stewart and John Tebbel, Prentice-Hall, 1952, p. 209.
16. *Scripps: The Divided Dynasty,* p. xv.
17. "Peace Comes to Denver," by Alan Prendergast, *Columbia Journalism Review,* July/Aug, 2000, p. 16.
18. *Scripps-Howard News,* Jan/Feb, 2000, p. 2.

CHAPTER 13
1. "Times Mirror Agrees to Merger With Tribune Co.," by David Shaw and Sallie Hofmeister, *Los Angeles Times,* Mar. 13, 2000, p. A1.
2. "Tribune-Times Merger, the Chandler Dynasty Steps Aside," by David Shaw, *Los Angeles Times,* Mar 14, 2000, p. A11.
3. "Slimming Down," by Kathryn S. Wenner, *American Journalism Review,* Dec. 2000, p. 39.
4. "Blowing Up the Wall," by Alicia C. Shepard, *American Journalism Review,* Dec. 1997, p. 20.
5. Ibid., p. 20.
6. "L.A. Times ad deal labeled a 'fiasco'," by Scott Winokur, *San Francisco Examiner,* Nov. 28, 1999, p. D3.
7. "Ex-Publisher Assails Paper in Los Angeles," by Felicity Barringer, *New York Times,* Nov. 5, 1999.
8. "*The Press: Inside America's Most Powerful Newspaper Empires,*" by Ellis Cose, William Morrow, 1989, p. 132.
9. *Current Biography Yearbook,* p. 87.
10. "Absolutely No Sense of Humor," by Ken Hughes, *American Journalism Review,* Apr. 1997, p. 14.
11. *The Media Monopoly,* by Ben Bagdikian, Beacon Press, 1997, p. 116.
12. *The Press,* p. 148.
13. "Look Out, the Boss is Back," by Joshua Hammer, *Newsweek,* Nov. 15, 1999, p. 76.
14. "The Chandlers," by Bob Waters, e-mail comment, Dec. 6, 1999.
15. "Choppy Waters for the Press," by Ken Garcia, *San Francisco Chronicle,* Nov. 10, 1999, p. A18.

CHAPETR 14
1. *The Mansion on the Hill,* by Fred Goodman, Times Books, p. 141
2. Ibid., p. 142.
3. Ibid., p. 252.
4. *The Operator: David Geffen Builds, Buys and Sells the New Hollywood,* by Tom King, Random House, 2000, p. 276.
5. Ibid., p. 491.

6. "It's All Over Now," by Charles Kaiser, *New York Times Book Review* Mar. 2, 1997.
7. *Current Biography Yearbook*, 1992, p. 226.
8. "The Richest Man in Hollywood," by Lisa Gubernick and Peter Newcomb, *Forbes*, Dec. 24, 1990, p. 94.
9. *The Mansion on the Hill*, p. 372.
10. "Media: DreamWorks in Tighter Focus: DreamWorks Scales Back Its Grand Vision," by Geraldine Fabrikant and Rick Lyman, *New York Times*, Sept. 26, 2000, p. C-1.
11. "Private Spiielberg," by Kim Masters, *Time*, Apr. 14, 1999, p. 64.
12. "For a Few Dollars More," by Jeffrey St. Clair and Alexxander Cockburn, *In These Times*, Nov. 19, 1996, p. 16,
13. "Hollywood's King Cashes Out," by Peter Boyer, *Vanity Fair*, Mar. 1991, p. 105.
14. *The Mansion on the Hill*, p. 354.
15. Ibid., p. 159.
16. "David vs. Goliath," by Paul Rosenfeld, *Vanity Fair*, Mar. 1991, p. 162.
17. *The Operator*, pp. 587-588.
18. "David Geffen's Ruthless Rise to the Top," by David Weigand *San Francisco Chronicle*, Mar. 8, 2000, p. E6.
19 "Moon Struck," *People*, Mar. 5, 2000, p. 146.
20. "The Richest Man in Hollywood," p. 98.

CHAPTER 15
1. "Vivendi Chief Bets on His Ability to Create Media Empire," by Edmund L. Andrews, *New York Times*, June 15, 2000, p. C4.
2. "The New Establishment 2000," *Vanity Fair*, Oct. 2000, p. 320
3. "Grand Vision for Viviendi-Seagram; Executive Sees Product of $30 Billion Merger as Internet Titan," by Christopher Stern, *Washington Post*, June 21, 2000, p. E1.
4. "An Emperor Without Clothes," by Robert La Franco, *Forbes* Nov. 2, 1998 p. 30.
5. "Rising Son," by Ken Auletta, *New Yorker*, June 6, 1994, p. 59.
6. Ibid., p. 63.
7. "Universal Seems to Have Magic Marketing Touch," by Patrick Goldstein, *San Francisco Chronicle*, Dec. 24, 2000, Datebook, p. 24.
8. "MCA Blamed for Selling Lewd Rock Songs," by Bob Dart, *San Francisco Chronicle*, Nov. 11, 1996, p. 3.
9. Ibid., p. E3.
10. "Deal Time at Seagram," by Anthony Blanco, *Business Week*, June 26, 2000, p. 68.

CHAPTER 16
1. *Skywalking: The Life and Times of George Lucas*, by Dale Pollock, Harmony Books, 1983, p. 29.
2. "Why Is the Force Still With Us?" by John Seabrook, *New Yorker*, Jan 6, 1997, p. 40.
3. "A Galaxy of Myth, Money and Kids," by Orville Schell, *New York Times*, Mar. 21, 1999, p. 1A.
4. *Mythmaker: The Life and Work of George Lucas*, by John Baxter, Avon Books, Inc., 1999, p. 209.
5. Ibid., p. 119.
6. "The Magician," by Randall Lne, *Forbes*, Mar. 11, 1996, p. 123.
7. Ibid., p. 126.
8. "Lucas Tries to Avoid Star Wars Hype," by Associated Press, *New York Times*, May 9, 1999,   9. "Catholics in Mexico Angry With New 'Star Wars' Film," by Dan Trotta, *San Francisco Chronicle*, July 14, 1999.
10. "Shuffling Through the Star Wars," by Brent Staples, *New York Times*, June 20, 1999,

11. "Fu Manchu on Naboo," by John Leo, *U.S. News & World Report*, July 12, 1999, p. 13.

12. "The Magician," p. 123.

13. "Forward Into the Past," by Richard Zoglin, *Time*, Mar. 12, 19992, p. 68.

14. "Why Is the Force Still With Us?" p. 53.

15. "Lucasfilm Reveals Big Prsidio Plan," by Eric Brazil, *San Francisco Examiner*, June 18, 2000, p. B1.

16. Ibid., p. B1.

17. "A Galaxy of Myths, Money and Kids," p. 27.

18. "The Dark Side of a Hit," by David Ansen, *Newsweek*, Jan. 20, 1997, p. 56.

19. "*Skywalking: The Life and Films of George Lucas*," p. 271.

20. "Why Is the Force Still With Us?" p. 50.

21. "*Skywalking: The Life and Films of George Lucas*," p. 130/

CHAPTER 17

1. "Muchas Gracias, Congress," by Kerry A. Dolan, *Forbes*, Oct. 7, 1996, p. 46.

2. "Univision: TV Success Story That Will Last?" by Elizabeth Jensen and Kevin Baxter, *Los Angeles Times*, July 13, 1999, p. A1.

3. "Univision's Perenchio Hablas Success," by Cynthia Littleton and Andrew Paxman, *Variety*, , May 24, 1999, p. 5.

4. "Univision vs. Telemundo," by David Tobenkin, *Broadcasting & Cable*, Oct. 7, 1997, p.42.

5. "Spanish Word-of-Mouth sells 'Ciudad' Tickets," by Lorenza Munoz, *Los Angeles Times*, Nov. 16, 1999, p.F3.

6. "Revamped Univision Newscast Bows Tonight," by Dana Calvo, *Los Angeles Times*, Oct. 25, 1999, p. F10.

7. "Numero Uno Gets Bigger," by Frank McCoy, *U.S. News & World Report*, Dec. 18, 2000, p.48.

8. "Univision Says it Will Buy Stations From USA Networks," by Associated Press, *New York Times*, Dec, 8, 2000, p.C3.

9. "L.A. Financier Buys Univision, *San Francisco Chronicle*, Dec. 21, 1992, p.B2.

10. "Univision Adds Site to Bridge the Divide," by Lee Romney, *Los Angeles Times*, June 29, 2000, p. C1.

11. "The Fight for Hispanic Viewers," by Andrew Pollack, *New York Times*, Jan. 19, 1998, p.1

12. "Univision Peers Into Cyberspace," by Ronald Grover, *Business Week*, Jan. 17, 2000, p.74.

CHAPTER 18

1. "John Malone: Flying Solo," by Ken Auletta, *New Yorker*, Feb. 7, 1994, p. 2.

2. "John Malone Prepares for a New Life as Pa Bell," by Eben Shapiro, *Wall Street Journal*, June 25, 1998, p.B1.

3. "What Others Are Saying About John Malone," *Rocky Mountain News*, Dec. 12, 1995, and *Extra*, Feb. 1, 1995, p.1.

4. "John Malone" TV's New Uncrowned King?" by Ronald Grover and Richard Siklos, *Business Week*, Oct. 5, 1998, p.122.

5. "John Malone Prepares for a New Life as Pa Bell," by Eben Shapiro, *Wall Street Journal*, June 25, 1998, p.B1.

6. "John C. Malone," 1995 *Current Biography Yearbook*, p. 388.

7. "Hardwired," by Jennet Conant, *Esquire*, June, 1993, p.88.

8. "Want This Stock? It's Up 91,000%," by Christopher Knowlton, *Fortune*, July 31, 1989, p. 100.

9. *The Billionaire Shell Game: How Cable Baron John Malone and Assorted Corporate Titans Invented a Future Nobody Wanted*, by L. J. Davis, Doubleday, 1998, p. 4.

10. Ibid., p. 174.

11. John C. Malone, 1995 *Current Biography Yearbook*, p. 391.

12. "Taking Liberty," by Neil Weinberg, *Forbes*, Oct. 18, 1999, p.130.

13. Ibid., p.104.

14. *Extra*, Feb. 12, 1994, p. 1.

15. "Malone!" by John Accola, *Rocky Mountain News*, Dec. 12, 1994, p. 40A.

16. "The Call of the Wired," by Allan Sloan, *Newsweek*, July 6, 1998, p. 44.

17. "Tenacious Tycoon," by Mark Lindner and Geraldine Frabricant, *New York Times*, Sept. 5, 1995.

18. "The New Establishment 2000," *Vanity Fair*, Oct. 2000, p. 290.

19. "How the AT&T Deal Will Help John Malone Get Into Your Home," by Ken Auletta, *New Yorker*, July 13, 1998, p. 25.

Chapter 19

1. "Short Circuit: McGraw Hill's Push Into Electronic Data Fails to Bolster Profits," by Johnnie L. Roberts, *Wall Street Journal*, Feb. 6, 1990, p. 1.

2. Ibid., p. 1.

3. "Family Defends Its Dynasty," by Leslie Wayne, *New York Times*, July 24, 1988, Section 3, p. 6.

4. *Endless Frontiers: The Story of McGraw-Hill*, by Roger Burlingame, McGraw-Hill Book Co., 1959, p. 236.

5. *Fortune Magazine*, Aug. 1, 1988, p. 16.

6. "Remarks," by Harold McGraw III at 1997 annual shareholders meeting Apr. 10, 1997.

7. "Management by Concept," by Suzanne L. Oliver, *Forbes*, Nov. 26, 1990, p.38.

8. "What's With McGraw-Hill?" by Sandra Ward, *Barron's*, Oct. 21, 1996, p. 5.

9. "Ado in Textbooks — Controversy Widens," by Greg Lucas, *San Francisco Chronicle*, June 26, 1999, p. A1.

10. "Brand Names in Texts Rile PTA," by Deborah Tedford, *Houston Chronicle*, Mar. 23, 1999, p.A1.

11. "Errors Testing CTB McGraw-Hill's Mettle," by Martha Mendoza, *Monterey County Herald*, Sept. 8, 1999, p.A1.

12. "Online Learning Curve," by Mark Tran, *The Guardian*, No. 30, Guardian Online Pages, p.8.

CHAPTER 20

1. *Steven Spielberg: A Biography*, by Joseph McBride, Simon & Schuster, 1999, p. 16.

2. Ibid., p. 62.

3. "I Dream for a Living," by Richard Corliss, *Time*, July 15, 1985, pp. 54-59.

4. *Steven Spielberg: A Biography*, p. 414,

5. "*Jurassic Park* Sequel Serves Up Crunchy Thrills But Isn't Thrilling," by Mark LaSalle, *San Francisco Chronicle*, May 27, 1997, p.C1..

6. "Seriously Spielberg," by Stephen Schiff, *New Yorker*, Mar 2, 1994, p. 106.

7. *Steven Spielberg: A Biography*, p. 16.

8. Ibid., p. 108.

9. "American Dreamers," by Andrew Gumbel, *The London Independent*, May 5, 1999, p. 3.

CHAPTER 21

1. "Endangered Species," by James V. Risser, *American Journalism Review*, June 1998, p. 30.

2. "The Worst Newspaper in America," by Bruce Selcraig, *Columbia Journalism Review*, Jan/Feb, 1999, pp. 46-51.

3. "Another Changing Face," by Shelly Hickman, *Oklahoma Gazette*, Jan. 19, 2000, p. 15.

4. "The Most Important Relationship," by Brent Cunningham, *Columbia Journalism Review*, May/June,, 2000, p.32.

5. "Another Changing Face," p. 15.

6. "Entertainment Empire Built on Bold Moves," by Richard A. Oppel Jr., *Dallas Morning News* Mar.14, 1993, p. 21.

7. "Country and Western Europe," by Richard A. Oppel, *Dallas Morning News*, March 14, 1903, p.H1.

8. "Lord of Oklahoma," by Bill Turque, *Dallas Morning News*, Dec. 8, 1984.

9. Even Troy, *Oklahoma Observer*, telephone interview, Feb. 19, 1998

10. "His Father's Son," by Toni Mack, *Forbes*, March 24, 1987, p. 105.

11. "Lord of Oklahoma."

12. "The Worst Newspaper in America," p. 48.

Chaper 22

1. "Pat McGovern Has Built a Computer News Empire," by John Yemma, *Boston Globe*, Apr. 9, 2000, p.A1.

2. "Cliffnotes Aims to Revise Reputation," by Laurence Chollet, *Arizona Republic*, Oct. 29, 2000, p. 15.

3. "Pat McGovern Has Built a Computer News Empire," by John Yemma, *Boston Globe*, Apr. 9, 2000, p. A1.

4. Ibid., p. A1.

5. "Industry Standard, N.Y.Times Digital Job Cuts," by Vanessa Hua, *San Francisco Chronicle*, Jan. 9, 2001, p.C2.

6. "Publisher Builds Strategy on Diversification," by Glenn Rifkin, *New York Times*, Apr. 21, 1997.

7. "Pat McGovern Has Built a Computer News Empire," by John Yemma, *Boston Globe*, Apr. 9, 2000, p. A1.

8. "Who's Spoiled?" by Brigid McMenamin, *Forbes*, June 12, 2000, p. 272.

9. Ibid., p.210.

10. "MIT Thinking Big, Thanks to $350M Gift," by Tim McLaughlin, *Boston Herald*, Feb. 29, 2000, p.001.

11. "IDG Books Fills Appetite With Deal for Hungry Minds," by Benny Evangelista, *San Francisco Chronicle*, Aug. 11, 2000, p.B2.

CHAPTER 23

1. "The Biggest Media Mogul You Never Heard Of," by Stephanie Anderson Forest and Richard Siklos, *Business Week*, Oct. 18, 1999, p.56.

2. "Clear Channel in $3 Billion Deal to Acquire SFX Entertainment," by Stuart Elliott, *New York Times*, Mar.1, 2000, p. C1.

3. "Clear Channel Tunes in to Rock," by Christopher Parkes, *Financial Times*, Mar. 1, 2000.

4. "Tamales? Cars? Coke?" by Peter Newcomb, *Forbes*, Jan. 27, 1997, p.64.

5. "Texas Size: Clear Channel Builds a Broadcast Dynasty," by Elizabeth A. Rathbun, *Broadcasting & Cable*, July, 5, 1993, p.21.

6. "Consolidation Becomes Key to Improved Program Profits," by Jordanna E. Burger, *Monterey County Herald*, Oct. 4, 1999, p. E1.

7. "Sending Strong Signals: Timing Tunes Clear Channel's Growth," by Ida Picker, *Houston Chronicle*, Dec. 15, 1999, p.1.

8. "The Biggest Media Mogul You Never Heard Of," by Stephanie Anderson Forest and

Richard Siklos, *Business Week*, Oct. 18, 1999, p.56.

9. "Sending Strong Signals: Timing Tunes Clear Channel's Growth," by Ida Picker, *Houston Chronicle*, Dec. 15, 1999, p.1.
10. "What? A Quiet Texas Billionaire?" by Robert Bryce, *New York Times*, Mar. 19, 2000, Section 3, p. 2.
11. "Stay Tuned for More of the Same," by Ken Auletta, *New Yorker*, Nov. 8, 1999, p.29.
12. "Out With the New, In With the Old," by Laura Rich, *Industry Standard*, Dec. 11, 2000.
13. "Wise Investment," (Editorial), *Broadcasting & Cable*, Feb.22, 1999, p. 26.
14. "Fund Set Up to Aid Diversity Among Broadcast Owners," by Associated Press, *New York Times*, Nov.4, 1999, p.C2.
15. "Sending Strong Signals: Timing Tunes Clear Channel's Growth," by Ida Picker, *Houston Chronicle*, Dec. 15, 1999, p. 1.
16. "What? A Quiet Texas Billionaire?" by Robert Bryce, *New York Times*, Mar.19, 2000, Section 3, p,.2.
17. "Lowry Mays," *Forbes 400* (in *Forbes*), Oct. 11, 1999, p. 242.

CHAPTER 24

1. "The Weather Channel," by Brian Knowlton, *International Herald-Tribune*, Sept. 30, 1999.
2. "The Weather Channel: Hot Enough for Ya?" by Marc Gunther, *Fortune*, Oct. 25, 1999, p.48.
3. "The Weather Channel's High Profit Center," by Geraldine Fabricant, *New York Times*, Mar.11, 1999, pC9.
4. "Weather Channel Pinning Hopes for International Growth on Net," by Matt Klempner, *Atlanta Journal & Constitution*, Nov. 2, 2000, Business, p.3E.
5. "Super-source Software Goes Public," *Economist*, June 12, 1999.
6. "Red Hat in Stock Deal for Cygnus Solutions," by Tom Foreminski, *Financial Times*, Nov. 16, 1999, p.37.
7. "Virginian Reaps Wealth From Durham, N.C.-based Software Company's Stock," by Bob Rayner, *Richmond Times-Dispatch*, Dec. 18, 1999.
8. Ibid.
9. "Buying Net Stocks? Read This First," by Geoffrey Colvin, *Fortune*, Jan 24, 2000,p.150.

CHAPTER 25

1. "Hubbard's DBS Dream: 10 Years in the Making," *Broadcasting*, June 10, 1991, p.36.
2. "The Hubbards: Trailblazers in Radio, TV and DBS," by Sean Scully, *Broadcasting & Cable*, Dec. 6, 1993, p.34.
3. "The Hubbards: Broadcasting in the Space Age," by Cathy Madison, Twin Cities Business Monthly, Apr. 1994.
4. "Hubbard's DBS Dream," *Broadcasting*, June 10, 1991, p.36.
5. Telephone interview with Stanley Hubbard, June 13, 2000.
6. "Countdown to DBS," by Sean Scully, *Broadcasting & Cable*, Dec. 6, 1993, p.34.
7. "Turning DBS Into a Reality," *Broadcasting & Cable*, Mar. 31, 1997, p.89.
8. "Stanley Eugene Hubbard," *Broadcasting*, Apr. 13, 1992, p.74.
9. "Once a Laughingstock, Direct-Broadcast TV Gives Cable a Scare," *Wall Street Journal*, Nov. 7, 1996, p. 1.

CHAPTER 26

1. "The On Line Roller Coaster," *Business Week*, Apr. 11, 1994, p. 40.

2. "A Two-Man Network," by Joshua Cooper Ramo, *Time*, Jan.24, 2000, p.47.

3. *Current Biography, 1996*, p. 79.

4. "Definitely Upper Case," by Jim Jones and Gary Marx, *San Francisco Examiner*, Jan.23, 2000, p.B5.

5. "A Two-Man Network," by Joshua Cooper Ramo, *Time*, Jan.24, 2000, p. 49.

6. "Bertelsmann Plans Acquisition Strategy," by Bernard Benoit and James Harding, *Financial Times*, Mar.18, 2000.

7. "The Internet is Mr. Case's Neighborhood," by Marc Gunther, *Fortune*, Mar.30, l998, p.70

8. "Happily Ever After?" by Daniel Okrent, *Time*, Jan.24, 2000, p.41.

9. Ibid., p. 43.

10. "What Keeps AOL on Top," by Stephen H. Wildstrom, *Business Week*, Jan 24, 2000, p.25.

11. "AOL/Time Warner : Media Group Wins Premium in Marriage," by Peter Thai Larsen, Andrew Edgecliffe Johnson and Gary Silverman, *Financial Times*, Jan. 11, 2000.

12. "Hunting the Big Bucks," by Allan Sloan, *Newsweek*, Jan. 24, 2000, p. 28.

13. "The New Establishment 2000," *Vanity Fair*, Oct. 2000, p. 270.

14. "AOL-Time Warner Merger Foes Warn of 'Chokehold' on the Internet," by Marilyn Geewax, *Atlanta Journal & Constitution*, July 28, 2000, p. F1.

15. "Does Deal Signal Lessening of Media Independence?" by Felicity Barringer, *New York Times*, Jan.11, 2000.

16. "Communication Breakdown: AOL *Time* Warner Threatens the Public Interest," by Joel Bleifuss, *In These Times*, Feb. 21, 2000, p. 3.

17. "Time Warner, Earthlink Deal," by Kalpana Srinivasan, *Monterey County Herald*, Nov. 21, 2000, p. E1.

18. "Not So Subtle Engine Drives AOL Profit Forecasts," by Saul Hansell, *New York Times*, Jan 31, 2000.

19. "The Little People vs. America Online, by Michael S. Malone, *Forbes* ASAP, Feb. 19, 2001, pp.59-72.

20. "The Internet is Mr. Case's Neighborhood," by Marc Gunther, *Fortune*, Mar 30, 1998, p.70.

21. "He's Not Your Typical CEO, But Steve Case Knows His Cards," by Kevin Maney, *USA Today*, Jan. 12, 2000, p. 38.

22. "Building a Case," by Neil Munro, *The National Journal*, July 31, 1999, p. 2218.

Chapetr 27

1. "He's Proving His Critics Wrong," *Forbes*, July 23, 1990, p.20.

2. Ibid., p. 20.

3. "*U.S.News* Owner Says He's Not Going Anywhere," by David Lieberman, *USA Today*, Apr.27, 2000, 1B.

4. *Citizen Newhouse: Portrait of a Media Merchant*," by Carol Felsenthal, Seven Stories Press, 1998, p. 463.

5. "Topless Tabloids of Gotham," by Hendrik Hertzberg, *New Yorker*, Feb. 22, 1999, p.127.

6. "*U.S.News* Owner Says He's Not Going Anywhere," by David Lieberman, *USA Today*, Apr.27, 2000, p.Bl.

7. Ibid., p.B1.

8. "Mortimer Zuckerman," *1990 Current Biography*, p.641.

9. "Citizen Mort," by Jeanie Kasindorf, *New York*, Oct. 5, 1992, p. 46.

10. "The Me in Media," by Michael Wolff, *New York*, Dec.7, 1998, p.22.

11. "Companies & Finance Europe," by Christopher Grimes, *Financial Times*, Dec. 20, 2000, p.32.

12. Ibid., p. 32.

13. "Sweetheart, Get Me Rewrite," by Richard Siklos, *Business Week*, Nov. 30, 1998, p. 110.
14. "The Importance of Being Mort," by Devin Leonard, *Fortune*, Nov. 13, 2000, p.164.
15. "Zuckerman Unbound," by Robert Schmidt, *Brill's Content*, Sept. 2000, p.135.

CHAPTER 28

1. *Katharine the Great*, by Deborah Davis, Harcourt Brace Jovanovich, 1979.
2. "A Place Called Pamelot" (cq) by John Corry, *The American Spectator*, Apr. 1997, p.51.
3. *Personal History*, by Katharine Graham, Alfred A. Knopf, 1997, p. 138.
4. *In the Shadow of Power*, by Chalmers Roberts, Seven Locks Press, 1989, p. 369.
5. The Imperial Post: The Meyers, the Grahams and the Paper That Rules Washington, by Tom Kelly, William Morrow & Co., 1983, p. 115.
6. *Personal History*, p. 246.
7. *Katharine the Great*, p. 160.
8. *Paper Tigers: The Latest, Greatest Newspaper Tycoons*, by Nicholas Coleridge, Carol Publishing Co., 1993, p.82.
9. "Citizen Kay," by David Remnick, *New Yorker*, Jan. 20, 1997, p. 65.
10. Ibid., p.68.
11. *Personal History*, p.458.
12. Ibid., p.459.
13. Ibid., p.465.
14. Ibid., p.502.
15. Ibid., p. 506.
16. "The Union-Busting Post," by John Hanrahan, *The Progressive*, Feb., 1989, pp.18-25.
17 Ibid., p. 19.
18. *The Powers That Be*, by David Halberstam, Dell Publishing Co., 1979, p. 995.
19. "The National Business Hall of Fame,"*Fortune*, Apr.15, 1993, p. 110.
20. *Power, Privilege, and the Post*, by Carol Felsenthal, Sven Stories Press, 1993, p. 443.
21. Ibid., p. 426.
22. "Katharine the Great," by Sally Quinn, *Vanity Fair*, Feb., 1997, p.120.
23. "The New Generation at the Newspaper Giants," by Ellis Cose, *Gannett Center Journal*, Winter 1989, p.114.
24. *Citizen Kay*, p. 65.
25. *Citizen Kay*, p. 21.
26. *Power, Privilege, and the Post*, by Carol Felsenthal, Seven Stories Press, 1993, p. 417.
27. *Voluntary Slavery: My Authentic Negro Experience*, by Jill Nelson, The Noble Press, 1993.
28. "Class, Not Race," by Amy Waldman, *Washington Monthly*, Nov. 1995, pp.22-30.
29. Ibid., p. 23.
30. "The New Establishment," *Vanity Fair*, Oct. 1997, p.142.
31. *The Washington Post: The First 100 Years*, by Chalmers Roberts, Houghton Mifflin, 1977, and *In the Shadow of Power: The Story of the Washington Post*, by Chalmers Roberts, Seven Locks Press, 1989.
32. *Paper Tigers*, p. 103.
33. *The Imperial Post: The Grahams and the Paper That Rules Washington*, by Tom Kelly, William Morrow & Co., 1983, p. 303.

CHAPTER 29

1. Telephone interview with Bishop, Apr. 7, 1997.
2. Telephone Interview with Johnson August 19, 1998.
3. "The Post-Dispatch Has Become Unbalanced," by Ed Bishop, *St. Louis Journalism*

Review, Dec/Jan 2000, p. 4.

4. "The End of the Line," by Alicia Shepard, *American Journalism Review*, July/Aug 2000, pp. 45-51.

5. *New York Times*, Apr.1, 1955, p.27.

6. Interview with William Woo in Palo Alto, Calif., Apr. 20, l997.

7. Telephone interview with Bishop Apr.7, 1997.

8. "Then and Now: The State of the American Newspaper," by Carl Sessions Stepp, *American Journalism Review*, Sept. 1999, p. 68.

9. "Post Names New Editor," by Ed Bishop, *St. Louis Journalism Review*, Dec. 2000/Jan.2001, p.20.

CHAPTER 30

1. *Walt Disney: Hollywood's Dark Prince*, by Marc Elliot, Carol Publishing Group, 1993, p. 271.

2. "Disney Family Firm Invests in Scandinavian Company," *Los Angeles Times*, July 11, 2000, p.B3.

3. *Walt Disney: Hollywood's Dark Prince,* p.274.

4. Ibid., p.276.

5. Ibid., p.278.

6. "Nephew Fulfills Walt's Wish," by Jeff Strickler, *Minneapolis Star-Tribune*, Dec. 31, 1999, p.24.

7. *Ovitz: The Inside Story of Hollywood's Most Controversial Power Broker,* by Robert Slater, McGraw-Hill, 1997, p.305.

8. "The Eisner School of Business," by Frank Rose, *Fortune*, July 6, 1998, p. 29.

9. "Future Perfect," by David Remnick, *New Yorker*, Oct. 20, 1997, p. 221.

10. "Disney Executive Reacts to SBC Boycott," *Christian Century*, Dec.10, 1997, p.1150.

11. "Disney's 'Condor' Draws Ire of Arab-Americans," by Josh Cetwynd, *San Francisco Chronicle*, Oct. 20, 1997.

12. "Only PBS Offers Quality Shows for Kids," by Marcia Meier, *San Francisco Chronicle*, Aug. 13, 1996.

13. *Mother Jones*, May/June 1998, p. 34.

14. "Future Perfect," by David Remnick, *New Yorker*, Oct. 20, 1997, p. 221.

15. "Revision Returns *Fantasia* to Walt Disney's Original Idea," by Stephen Schaefer, *Boston Herald*, June 15, 2000, p.O-57.

CHAPTER 31

1. "The World's Richest People," *Forbes*, July 8, 2001, p.110.

2. "An Arabian Warren Buffett," by Scott MacLeod, *Time*, Dec.1, 1997, p.62.

3. Ibid., p. 66.

4. "Buffett of Arabia? Well, Maybe," by Douglas Jehl, *New York Times*, Mar 28, 1999, Sec.3, p.12.

5. "Alwaleed's Kingdom, The mystery of the world's second-richest businessman," *Economist*, Feb.27, 1999, pp.67+.

6. "Buffett of Arabia? Well, Maybe," p. 12.

7. Ibid., p.12.

8. "Not Since Babel Has Such a Tower Risen from the Sand," by Mitchell Pacelle, *Wall Street Journal*, Dec. 18, 1997, pp.A1 and 14.

9. "Saudi Prince to Invest in a Satellite Venture," *New York Times*, Dec. 26, 1997, p. D6

10, "Jacko's Adventures in Arabian Magic Kingdom," by Scott MacLeod, *Time*, Dec. 1, 1997, p.66.

11. "The Saudi Mogul Who Sees Lights in the Darkness: Prince Alwaleed," by Heather Formby, *Financial Mail*, Jan. 29, 1999, p.44.

12. "Farming Toshka is no Pipe Dream for Saudi Prince," *Middle East Times* archive.
13. "Alwaleed, Investor With a Global Vision," by Abdul Wahed Al-Fayez, *Riyadh Daily*, May 2, 1999.
14. "Saudi Prince Raises Profile as Succession Looms," by Vernon Silver, *International Herald Tribune*, Oct. 5, 1999, p.A1.
15. "Tech is King; Now Meet the Prince," by Andy Serwer, *Fortune*, Dec. 6, 1999, P. 108.
16. Ibid., p.122.

CHAPTER 32
1. "The Amazing Mr. Kuok," *Forbes*, July 28, 1997, p. 99.
2. "The World's Richest People," *Forbes*, July 9, 2001, p. 112.
3. "Robert Kuok," *Current Biography Yearbook*, 1998, p. 36.
4. "The Amazing Mr. Kuok," p.94.
5. *Far Eastern Economic Review*, Feb.7, 1991, p.48+.
6. "Robert Kuok," Current Biograohy Yearbook, 1998, p. 36.
7. "The Amazing Mr. Kuok," p. 91.
8. "Kuok the Kingpin," by Jonathan Friedland, *Far Eastern Economic Review*, Feb.7, 1991, p.47.
9. "Robert Kuok," *Current Biography Yearbook, 1998*, p. 37.
10. "Over to You," by Bruce Gilley, *Far Eastern Economic Review*, Mar.19, 1998, pp. 12, 13.
11. Ibid., p. 12.
12. "Hong Kong: The Future of Press Freedom," by Elliott Cohen, *Columbia Journalism Review*, May/June 1997, p.49.
13. "Hong Kong: Media Jitters Over Press Freedom as Handover Nears," by Yojanna Sharma, *Internet Press Service,* Apr. 17, 1997.
14. Internet web page.
15. "Hong Kong Media Abuzz Over Rights," by Tyler Marshall, *Los Angeles Times*, Dec.8, 2000, Part A, Part 1, p. 5.
16. "Malaysia News," by Eddie Toh, *Singapore Business Times*, Mar.28, 2001, p. 13.
17. "Over to You," by Bruce Gilley, *Far Eastern Economic Review*, Mar.19, 1998, pp. 13, 14.

CHAPTER 33
1. "The World's Working Rich," *Forbes*, July 3, 2000, p.188.
2. *Sony: The Private Life*, by John Nathan, Houghton Mifflin, 1999, p. 87.
3. *Global Dreams: Imperial Corporations and the New World Order,* by Richard J. Barnet and John Cavanagh, Simon & Schuster, 1994, p. 1+.
4. "The World's Working Rich," p. 190.
5. *Global Dreams,* p. 42.
6. Ibid., pp.46-49.
7. *Made in Japan,* by Akio Morita, *New York*, NAL, pp. 111-117.
8. *Global Dreams,* p.52.
9. *Made in Japan,* p. 143.
10. Ibid., p. 183.
11. *Global Dreams,* pp.55-56.
12. *Hit and Run: How Jon Peters and Peter Guber Took Sony for a Ride in Hollywood,* by Nancy Griffin and Kim Masters, Simon & Schuster, 1996.
13. *Current Biography,* Mar. 1997, p. 28.
14. *Business Week*, Oct. 11, 1999, p. 118.
15. *Sony: The Private Life*, p.87.

CHAPTER 34

1. "The World's Working Rich," *Forbes*, July 5, 1999, p. 162.
2. "Giving Paper Chase," by Christopher Helman, *Forbes*, Mar. 20, 2000, p. 53.
3. "The World's Richest People," *Forbes*, July 9, 2001, p. 112.
4. "Success Began at Berkeley," by David Armstrong, *San Francisco Examiner*, Nov. 12, 1995, p.D1+.
5. "Japanese Style Entrepreneurship:An Interview with Softbank's CEO, Masayoshi Son," by Alan M. Webber, *Harvard Business Review*, Jan/Feb, 1992, p. 94.
6. Ibid., p. 99.
7. "Emperor of the Internet," by Frank Gibney, Jr., *Time*, Dec. 6, 1999, p. 70+
8. *Bloomberg News, news.cnet.com,* May 9, 2000.
9. "Softbank in Finnish Deal," by Lucy Killgren, *Financial Times on line*, Apr. 24, 2000.
10. "World Bank, Softbank Unite to Bridge Global Digital Divide," by Joseph Kahn, *San Francisco Chronicle*, Feb. 14, 2001, p. E1.
11. "Nasdaq Japan Faces Storm," by Jonathan Watts, *The Guardian*, June 19, 2000, p. 21
12. Ziff-Davis Publishing Division Sells for $780 million," by James Mosher for *Bloomberg News, San Francisco Chronicle*, Dec. 7, 1999., pp. D1 and 4.
13. "Japan's Top Technology Investor Takes a Hit.," by Edward W/ Desmond, *Fortune*, Sept.8, 1997, p.150+.
14. "Softbank Seeks Japan Bank," *San Francisco Chronicle*, Feb. 25, 2000, p.B1.
15. "Softbank Family," http//www.sbholdings.com, Mar.8,2000.
16. "The Last True Believer," by Bruce Bremner and Irene Kunii, *Business Week*, Jan.22, 2001, p.EB22.

CHAPTER 35

1. "The World's Richest People, *Forbes*, July 9, 2001, p. 116.
2. "Fairfax Hunting," *Economist*, May 30, 1998, p. 63.
3. "Rival Media Scions Plot Growth in Asia-Pacific," by Geoffrey Lee Martin, *Advertising Age*, Sept.19, 1996, p.46.
4. "Packer Sets Resignation from Media Firm," *Facts on File*, Mar.28, 1996, p. 209.
5. "Time to Raid the Piggy Bank," *Economist*, Mar.28,1992, p. 77.
6. "A Summer of Scandals in the Land Down Under," by Jane Perlez, *New York Times*, Jan.5, 1985, p. 2.
7. "The World's Working Rich," *Forbes*, July 5, 1999, p.160.
8. "Gambling Fever Hits Australia," *Associated Press*, by Rohan Sullivan, Mar.8, 1998.
9. "Packer Abandons Casino Deal," *Facts on File*, May 8, 1997, p.328.
10. Media Magnate Was Among Heidi Fleiss' Customers," by John Horn, *Associated Press*, July 14, 1995.
11. "How Has Packer's World Series Cricket Changed the Game?" by Sambo, *CLI Interactive Magazine*, May 27, 1997, pp.1 and 2.
12. "Gaucho Polo," *Economist*, June 22, 1995, p. 84.
13. "Friend or Foe?" By Faith Keenan and Jacqueline Rees, *Far Eastern Review*, Sept. 11, 1995, p.77.
14. Softix internet press release, 1996.
15. "Aussie Moguls Hit the Road," Christie Eliezer, *Billboard*, June 15, 1996, p.55.
16. "Gates Open to Australia," *CNN Digital Jam*," June 20, 1997.
17. "At the Courthouse," Philip Fox internet release, Feb.21, 1997.
18. "Packer Heads Australis Rescue," *Facts on File*, May 9, 1996, pp.327-328.
19. "Foxtel and Pay TV Interests in Australia," News Corp. Internet news release, June 20, 1997.

20. "The World's Working Rich," *Forbes*, July 6, 1998, p. 196.
21. "Baby Packer Goes Public," by J. G. Estiot, *Mediawatch* internet article quoting *The Age*, Sept. 23, 1997.
22. "Former Prime Minister Criticizes Howard," *Facts on File*, Oct.14, 1999, p.748.

CHAPTER 36
1. "The World's Working Rich," *Forbes*, July 6, 1998, p. 235
2. "Izzy's Dream," by Jennifer Wells, *McLean's*, Feb. 18, 1996, pp. 40+
3. Canadian Corporate News, Internet, Feb. 1, 1000.
4. "Izzy's Dream," p. 4l.
5. "Bargain-basement broadcaster," by Josse Aguay, *Forbes*. Nov. 3, 1997, p. 360.
6. "Ease TV Restrictions: Asper," *The Gazette* (Montreal) May 18, 1999.
7. "TV Titan sues movie mogul over speech," by Antonia Zerbisias, *Toronto Star*, Feb. 4, 1999.
8. "CTRC protection has helped Global sail to profits," by Matthew Fraser, *National Post*, Feb. 2, 1999.
9. "Special Report on Global Ontaario's 25th Anniversary," by Cheryl Binning,, Brunico Communications, Inc., Jan. 25, 1999.
10. "Izzy's Dream," pp. 43-44.
11. "Izzy looks beyond the small screen," by Michael Hanlon, *Toronto Star*, Nov. 26, 1999.
12 "Growing Up Yiddish in Minnedosa," by Haroon Siddiqui, *Toronto Star*, Jan. 24, 1999.
13. Canadian Corporate News, Feb. 1, 1999.

CHAPTER 37
1. "How West Was Won," by John E. Morris, *The American Lawyer*, Sept., 1996, p.74.
2. Ibid., p.74.
3. Ibid., p.81.
4. "The World's Richest People," *Forbes*, July 9, 2001, p.110.
5. *Current Biography Yearbook, 1960*, pp. 431-432.
6. *The Thomson Empire, The First Fifty Years,* by Susan Goldenberg, 1984, p.55.
7. *The Titans,* by Peter C. Newman, Penguin Group, 1998, p.58.
8. "Newspapers in a ReDeal Across Canada," by Clyde H. Farnsworth, *New York Times*, May 12, 1996, Business, pp.C1 and C5.
9. *Current Biography Yearbook, 1960,* pp.431-432.
10. *The Thomson Empire*, p.52.
11. *Current Biography Yearbook, 1989,* p.591.
12. *Murdoch,* by William Shawcross, Touchstone, 1994, p.275.
13. *Facts on File*, May 5, 1982, p.367B.
14. *Facts on File*, July 6, 1983, p.93.
15. "Lord of Cyberspace," *Business Week*, Mar.11, 1996, p.36.
16. "In Lord Thomson's Realm," by William Prochnau, *American Journalism Review*, Oct.1998, p. 58.
17. "Newspaper Owners Do the Shuffle," by William Glaberson, *New York Times*, Feb.19,1996, p.C4.
18. "Split Screen," by Nathan Vardi, *Forbes*, Dec. 11, 2000, p.114.
19. *The Thomson Empire*, p.130.
20. "BCE and Thomson to Form $2.7bn Canadian media giant," by Ken Wam, *Financial Times on the web*, Sept. 16, 2000.

CHAPTER 38
1. "The World's Richest People," *Forbes*, July 9, 2001, p. 114.
2. *Advertising Age*, July 23, 1998.
3. "Mexico's Telecommunications Mogul Expanding His Empire," by Jeffrey Silverstein, *San Francisco Chronicle*, Dec.28, 1992, p.B1.
4. Ibid., p.B8.
5. Obituaries, *Variety*, Apr.21-17, p.13.
6. "Sex, Drugs and Dinero," by Edward A. Robinson, *Fortune*, Nov.10, 1997, pp.163-165.
7. "Two Mexican Networks in Pitched Battle for Markets," by James Smith, *Los Angeles Times*, Aug. 23, 1998, p.D13.
8. "Sex, Drugs and Dinero," pp.163-165.
9. "Showtime for Televisa," *Business Week*, Sept. 1, 1997, p.50.
10. "Televisa is in Deal that Cuts Pressure on its Chairman," by Jonathan Friedland, *Wall Street Journal*, Oct.23, 1998, p.13.
11. "Televisa Family Feud Risk," by Andrea Mandel-Campbell, *Financial Times*, May 12, 1999.
12. "El Tigre turns Televisa over to his young cub," by Andrew Paxman, *Variety*, Mar.10-16, 1997, pp.33+.
13. *New York Times*, Sept. 22, 1998, p.C6.
14. *Facts on File*, Sept. 20, 1998, p.740 E1.
15. *Video Age International*, June-July, 1998.
16, "Billionaire's Death Means Changing of the Guard for Mexican Media." by Dudley Althaus, The *Houston Chronicle*, Apr. 18, 1999.
17. *Video Age International*, June-July, 1998.
18. Ibid., Apr.1998.
19. "Two Mexican Networks in Pitched Bttle for Markets," by James Smith, *Los Angeles Times*, Aug. 23, 1998, p.D13..

CHAPTER 39
1. "The World's Richest People," *Forbes*. July 9, 2001, p. 120.
2. "Brazil: A Mogul's Muscle," by Sandra H. Necchi, *Columbia Journalism Review*, Nov-Dec, 1989, p. 6.
3. "Brazil's Power of the Press," by Julia Preston, *Washington Post*, Dec. 9, 1992, p. C1.
4. "The World's Working Rich," *Forbes*, July 5, 1999, p. 202.
5. "Independent Film &Video in Brazil," by Patricia Aufderheide, *MacArthur Report*, July, 1996.
6. "Cover Story," by Dom Serafini, *Video Age International*, Vol. 18, No. 1, Jan. 1998.
7. " Rede Globo Dominates Brazil's Prime Time, Ad Revenues," by Lauren Wentz, *Advertising Age*, Sept. 28, 1998, p. 22.
8. "In the Company of Giants," by Mac Margolis, *Media Studies Journal*, Spring/Summer, 1996, p. 151.
9. "Brazil's TV Titans," *Forbes*, by Kerry A. Dolan with Alexandra Kirkman, July 3, 2000., p. 234.
10, "Brazil's Power of the Press," p. C2.
11. " One Man's Political Views Color Brazil's TV Eye," by Alan Riding, *New York Times*, Jan 12, 1987, p. A4.
13. "Brazil's TV Titans," p. 235.
14. *World Reporter*, Internet news release, April 22, 1999.
15. Ibid., July 9, 1998.
16. *Gazeta Mercantil on line*, March 12, 1998.

CHAPTER 40

1. "The Global Power Elite," *Forbes*, July 28, 1997, p. 160.
2. "Where Have All the Oligarchs Gone?" by Paul Klebnikov, *Forbes*, July 3, 2000, P.226.
3. "Godfather of the Kremlin?" *Forbes*, Dec. 30, 1996, p.91+.
4. *Kommersant-Daily*, July 21, 1993, quoted in *Godfather of the Kremlin*, by Paul Klebnikov, Harcourt, Inc., 2000, p.12.
5. "Logovaz," *Radio Free Europe*, January, 1998.
6. "Godfather of the Kremlin?" *Forbes*, Dec. 30, 1996, p.95.
7. "The Day They Raided Aeroflot," by Paul Klebnikov, *Forbes*, Mar.22, 1999, pp.106+
8. Ibid., p.110.
9. Ibid., p.110.
10. "Moscow Tries to Pluck a Thorn in its Side," by Paul Quinn, *Time*, Feb.15, 1999, p.16.
11. "Conflagration in Russia," by Paul Klebnikov, *Forbes*, Nov.1, 1999, p.96.
12. "The Black Box," by David Remnick, *New Yorker*, Mar.27, 2000, p.48.
13. Ibid., p.48.
14. Ibid., p.49.
15. Ibid., p.50.
16. Network Giveaway is Set to Thwart Kremlin," by Michael Wines, *New York Times on the Web.*, Sept. 8, 2000.
17. "Tycoon Hits Out at His Kremlin Monster," by Amelia Gentleman, *The Guradian*, Dec.21, 2000, p.15.
18. "New Russian Governors," by Agence France-Presse, *New York Times*, Dec.26, 2000, Sec.A, p.17.
19. "I Was Wrong to Help Elect Putin, Says Bitter Kingmaker," by Steve Crawshaw, *The Independent* (London), Nov.28, 2000, p.16.
20. *Godfather of the Kremlin*, p.326.

CHAPTER 41

1. "Media Mogul Set to Return as Italy's Premier," by Frances D'Emilio, *San Francisco Chronicle*, May 15, 2001, p.A9.
2. "The World's Richest People," *Forbes*, July 9, 2001, p.110.
3. "Arrivederci Berlusconi," by Joan Bachrach, *Vanity Fair*, Jan. 1995, p.108.
4. "Cleared on Technicality," *San Francisco Chronicle*, Oct.27, 1999, p.A13.
5. "Italy"s Billion Dollar Populist," by William Drozdiak, *Washington Post National Weekly*, Apr.4-10, 1994, p.16.
6. "Ciampi Wins Swift Confirmation as Italy's President, *Boston Globe*, May 14,1999, p.A13.
7. "Big Brother," by Martin Jacques, *London Sunday Times*, Apr.3, 1994, Section 4, p.1.
8. *1994 Current Biography Yearbook*, pp.49-50.
9. Ibid., p.49-50.
10. *The New Italian Republic From the Fall of the Berlin Wall to Berlusconi*, edited by Stephen Gundle and Simon Parker, Routledge Press, 1996, p.217.
11. "Candidate With Checkered Past Holds the Aces," by Tom Hundley, *Chicago Tribune*, May 11, 2001, Section 1, p.4.
12. "Italian Print to be Spun Off," by Paul Betts, *Financial Times*, June 25, 1999, p.28.
13. *Financial Times* Global Archive, Aug.3, 1999.
14. "Company Town; Investors to Provide Kirch Money to Expand," by Carol Williams, *Los Angeles Times*, Mar.23, 1999, Part C, p.12.
15. "Fininvest to Focus on European Media Sector," by Paul Betts, *Financial Times*, Apr.21, 1999, p.31.
16. "Arrivederci Berlusconi," p. 109.

CHAPTER 42

1. "The World's Richest People," *Forbes*, July 9, 2001, p.116.
2. *1995 Current Biography Yearbook*, p.60.
3. Ibid., p.60.
4. "Many Times a Virgin," by Bonnie Angelo, *Time*, Jun24, 1996, p.52.
5. "Born-Again Virgin," by Julie Baumgold, *Esquire*, Aug. 1996, p.132.
6. *Richard Branson: Virgin King*, by Tim Jackson, Prima Publishing Co., Rocklin, California, 1996, pp.26+.
7. *Losing My Virginity*, by Richard Branson, Random House, 1998, p. 50.
8. *Richard Branson, Virgin King*, pp.26+
9. "Necker Island," by Chris Caswell, *Millionaire Magazine*, pp. 34+
10. *1995 Current Biography Yearbook*, p. 68.
11. "Virgin Jets to Lure Concorde Class," by David Parsley, *Sunday Times (London)*, Business Section, Mar.25, 2001.
12. "Singapore to Buy 49% of Virgin," by Bruce Stanley, *San Francisco Chronicle*, Dec.21, 1999, p.D2.
13. "Eight Little Virgins," *Economist*," Jan.11, 1997, p.63.
14. "Encore," *Forbes*, Dec. 2, 1996, p.228.
15. "Virgin-Bechtel Group Picked for Rail Project," *New York Times*, Mar.1, 1996, p.D3.
16. *Richard Branson, Virgin King*, p.19.
17. Ibid., p.418.
18. "Companies & Finance UK," by Martin Dickson, *Financial Times*, Dec. 30, 2000, p.13.
19. *Losing My Virginity*, p.357.
20. "Richard Branson," by David Sheff, *Forbes ASAP.*, Feb. 24, 1997, p. 102.

CHAPTER 43

1. "The World's Richest People," *Forbes*, July 9, 2001, p.112.
2. "The German Front," by David Margolick, *Vanity Fair*, June 9, 1998, p.136.
3. "Publishers Began With Book Club," by John Tagliabue, *New York Times*, July 4, 1986, p.D1.
4. "The German Front," p.132.
5. "They All Know More About Publishing Than I Do," by Herbert R. Lottman, *Publishers Weekly*, Dec.4, 1995, pp.40-41.
6. "Holtzbrinck's New Word on U.S. Publishing," by Doreen Carvajal, *New York Times*, Sept. 11, 1997, pp.D1-4.
7. "The German Front," p.132+.
8. Ibid., p.139.
9. Ibid., p.136.
10. Ibid., p.142+.
11. *Publishers Weekly*, June 15, 1998, p.16.
12. "Dow Jones in Link With Germans as Rivalry Grows in Europe," by Edmond L. Andrews, *New York Times*, June 6, 1999.

CHAPTER 44

1. "Germany's Kirch Opens Gates to Investors in Drive to Grow," by William Boston, *Wall Street Journal*, Jan.5, 1999, p.A17.
2. "A Jump Up the Television Ratings," by Judy Thompson, *Financial Times*, July 19, 1996, p.13.
3. "The Global Power Elite," *Forbes*, July 28, 1997, p.150.
4. "KIRCH; Media Empire Inspires Awe and Fear," by Mary Williams Walsh, *Los Angeles Times*, Sept. 1, 1996, p.A12.

5. "Unitel: Making Music for the Eyes and Ears," Kirch Online press release, 1997.
6. "The World's Working Rich," *Forbes*, July 6, 1998, p.222.
7. "Kirch Group Secures Grip on German TV," by John Schmid, *International Herald Tribune*, June 29, 2000.
8. "Germany's Enigmatic Media Mogul," by David Brierly, *The European*, Sept. 21-27, 1995.
9. "Germany's Media-Meister Cuts it Close," by Cacilie Rohwedder, *Wall Street Journal*, July 18, 1997, p.A12.
10. "Kirch Group Chief is Subject of Tax Probe," *Bloomberg News*, Aug. 26, 1997.
11. "KIRCH: Media Empire Inspires Awe and Fear,"0 p.A12.
12. "Mogul's Sleigh Ride of Power Has Hit Quite a Few Bumps," by Mary Williams Walsh, *Los Angeles Times*, Apr.10, 1997, pp.D1 & 4.
13. *World Reporter*, Mar. 27, 2000.
14. "German Firms Set TV Pacts," *Wall Street Journal*, July 3, 1997, p.A8.
15. "German Effort on Digital TV Moves Ahead," by Edmund L. Andrews, *New York Times*, July 3, 1997, p.D4.
16. Kirch Online Press Release.
17. "German Effort on Digital TV Moves Ahead," by Edmund L. Andrews, *New York Times*, July 3, 1997, p. D4.
18. *Development of Multimedia in Germany*, Telecommunications Research Group, University of Bremen, Aug.1, 1997, pp.3 and 5.
19. "Kirch Group at Forty," by Miriam Hils and Michael Williams, *Variety*, Jan.13-19, 1997, p.121.
20. "Kohl Admits He Accepted Free Flights," by Roger Cohen, *New York Times*, Jan.27, 2000, p.A11.
21. "Ich Bin Ein Mogul," by David Fondiller, *Forbes*, Dec. 19, 1994, p.102.
22. "The World's Richest People," *Forbes*, July 9, 2001, p. 110.

CHAPTER 45
1. *1993 Current Biography Yearbook*, p.332.
2. *L'Acrobate*, by Vincent Nouzille and Alexandra Schwartzbrod, Editions Du Seuil, Paris, 1998. P.123.
3. *1993 Current Biography Yearbook*, p.332.
4. "Matra Maintaining Its Independence," *Wall Street Journal*, Mar.1, 1983, p.29.
5. *L'Acrobate*, p.164.
6. Ibid., p.57+
7. Ibid., p.243.
8. Ibid., pp.104-105.
9. "Lagardère Invades America," by Edward J. Epstein, *Vanity Fair*, Nov. 1988, p.224.
10. "A Media King With Much to Prove," by Roger Cohen, *New York Times*, Feb.1, 1993, pp.D1 and D8
11. *L'Acrobate*, p.122.
12. "Daimler and Aérospaciale to Merge Their Aerospace Businesses," by Edmund L. Andrews, *New York Times*, Oct.15, 1999.
13. "555 Seat A380 is Launched by Airbus," by Associated Press, *St. Louis Post-Dispatch*, Dec. 20, 2000, p.C13.
14. *Les Nouveaux Rois de France*, by Herve Bentegeat, Editions Ramsay, Paris, 1998.
15. *Forbes*, July 27, 1998, p.130.

CHAPTER 46
1. "The World's Richest People," *Forbes*, July 9, 2001, p.112.
2. *Success Through Partnership*, by Reinhard Mohn, Doubleday, 1996.

3. Ibid., p.xv.
4. "Bertelsmann Sticks to its Traditional Ways," by Cacilie Rohwedder, *Wall Street Journal*, Jan.15, 1997, p.A4.
5. "Beyond Books at Bertelsmann," *Publishers Weekly*, Jan.23, 1995, p.17.
6. *Global Dreams*, by Richard Barnet and John Cavanagh, Simon & Schuster, 1994, p.70+.
7. "Commission Disputes That Bertelsmann Was Nazi Foe," by Doreen Carvajal, *New York Times*, Jan.18, 2000, p.B1.
8. *New York Times on the Web*, by Reuters, Aug.10, 1999.
9. *Global Dreams*, p.73.
10. Ibid., p.73.
11. *Publishers Weekly*, July 8, 1996, p.12.
12. *Global Dreams*, p.74.
13. *Nation*, June 12, 1989, p.810.
14. "Bertelsmann's New Media Man," by Marc Gunther, *Fortune*, Nov. 23, 1998, p.180.
15. "The International 500," *Forbes*, July 15, 1996, p.212.
16. "Bertelsmann Sells AOL Shares," by Bridge News, *New York Times*, Aug. 25, 1999.
17. "Leading Bertelsmann's Race to the Future," by Doreen Carvajal, *New York Times*, Jan. 30, 2000, Sec.3, p.2.
18. "FTC Clears Purchase of Random House by Bertelsmann AG," *Wall Street Journal*, June 1, 1998, Sec.3, p.2.
19, "Springtime for Bertelsmann," by Daniel Johnson, *New Yorker*, Apr.27 & May 4, 1998, p.104.
20. "A Marriage Maelstrom Industrywide, as the High-Technology Plot Thickens," by Doreen Carvajal, *New York Times* on the Web, Jan.4, 1999.
21. "Leading Bertelsmann's Race to the Future," by Thomas Middelhoff, Online memo, Dec.31, 2000.
22. "The Napster Wedding," by Thomas Middelhoff, online memo, Dec. 31, 2000.
23. BMG Entertainment news release, Feb. 24, 1997.
24. *Facts on File*, Feb. 13, 1997, p.94.
25. *Publishers Weekly*, Jan. 20, 1997, p.269.
26. *Global Dreams*, p.68.
27. *Wall Street Journal*, Jan. 15, 1997, p.44.
28. "German Giants Lose Their Taste for Secrecy," by Michael Woodhead, *Sunday Times* (London) Feb.11, 2001.
29. Bertelsmann press release.
30. "Media Giant Continues to Grow Without Mega-Deals," *Los Angeles Times*, Nov. 19, 1995, pp. D1, D2.
31. Ibid.
32. "A Marriage Maelstrom Industrywide, as the High Technology Plot Thickens," by Doreen Tarvajal, *New York Times* on the Web, Jan.4, 1999.

CHAPTER 47
1. Chairman's statement, 1999 DMGT internet news release
2. *Forbes*, Feb.17, 1992, p.50.
3. "DMGT Internet Portal for Women," by Cathy Newman, *Financial Times*, Internet release, June 11, 1999.
4. *Encyclopedia Britannica,* Vol. 15, 15th Edition, p.241.
5. *Collier's Encyclopedia*, 1993, vol. 11, p. 658.
6. "Diaries Reveal Hitler's Fleet Street Favorites," by Vanessa Thorpe, *The Observer*, Aug.1, 1999.
7. "The Reluctant Press Lord," by Geoffrey Goodman, *New Statesman and National Publishing Company*, May 8, 1998, p.48.

8. "The Sage of Fleet Street," by Peter Fuhrman, *Forbes*, Feb.17, 1992, p.50.
9. *Daily Telegraph* (London), Sept. 3, 1998, p.35.
10. Ibid.
11. DMGT 1999 Internet news release.
12. *The Independent* (London), Sept. 3, 1998, p.11.
13. Obituary of Lord Rothermere, *Daily Telegraph* (London), Sept.3, 1998, p.35.
14. "Blair Bags a Press Baron as Rothermere Switches," *The Independent* (London), May 23, 1997, p.1.
15. "Rothermere, the Last Press Baron, is Dead," *The Independent*, (London), Sept. 3, 1998, p.11.
16. Oxford University network news release.
17. "Lord Rothermere's Young Heir Who Was Groomed to be Political Baron," by Alison Boshoff, *Daily Telegraph* (London), Sept.3, 1998, p.10.
18. "Aristocrat 'has secret Kiwi love child'," *The Dominion*, New Zealand, Dec. 4, 1999, p.1.
19. "The World's Richest People," *Forbes*, July 9, 2001, p. 124.

THE GAP BETWEEN THE RICH AND THE POOR
1. "Underground Economy," editorial, The *Nation*, Jan.12/19, 1998, p.3.
2. "Wall Street Follies," by John Cassidy, *New Yorker*, Sept.12, 1999, p.32.
3. "Battle in Seattle," by Robert L. Borosage, The *Nation*, Dec.6, 1999, p.20.
4. "Income Inequality," by Mary H. Cooper, *Congressional Quarterly Researcher*, Apr.17, 1998, p.339.
5. "Gap Between Rich and Poor Substantially Wider," by David Cay Johnston, *New York Times*, Sept. 5, 1999, p.14.
6. "Ten Myths About Globalization," by Sarah Anderson and John Cavanagh, The *Nation*, Dec.6, 1999, p.14.
7. "Income Inequalities Reach 'Grotesque' Gap, UN Says," by Charlotte Denny and Victoria Brittain, *Houston Chronicle*, July 13m 1999, p.A11.
8. "The Rich Get Richer," by James Lardner, *U.S.News & World Report*, Feb.21, 2000, p.43.
9. Ibid.
10. "The Poor Get Poorer, the Rich Get SUVs," by Stephanie Salter, *San Francisco Examiner*, Apr.11, 1999.
11. "Out of Sight, Out of Mind," *The Economist*, May 20, 2000, p.27.
12. "Hungry and Poor in a Rich *Nation*," by Anurahda Mittal, *San Francisco Chronicle*, Nov. 25, 1998.
13. "United States First Among Industrialized Nations in 'Human Poverty'," by Geir Moulson, *Monterey County Herald*, June 30, 2000, p.A7.
14. "Inequality: How the Gap Between Rich and Poor Hurts the Economy," *Business Week*, Aug. 15, 1994.
15. Ibid.
16. "Hungry and Poor in a Rich Nation," by Anurahda Mittal, *San Francisco Chronicle*, Nov. 25, 1998.
17. "Gap Between Rich and Poor is Wider Than Ever," by Martin McLaughlin, *World Socialist Web*, June 23, 1998.
18. "10% of U.S. Households Found to Face Hunger," Associated Press, *San Francisco Chronicle*, Oct.16, 1999, p.A10.
19. "To Have and Have Less," by David Gergen, *U.S. News & World Report*, July 26, 1999, p.64.
20. "Shifting Fortunes: The Perils of the Growing American Wealth Gap, by Chuck Collins, Betsy Leonder-Wright and Holly Sklar, *United for a Fair Economy*, 1999, p.55.
21. Ibid., p.55.

22. "The Billionaire Next Door," by Dinesh D'Souza, *Forbes*, Oct. 11, 1999, p.50.
23. "Panel: Poor Are Ignored, Stereotyped in Media," *Quill Magazine*, May 2000, p.33.

THE MEDIA MOGULS GIVE US A VAST WASTELAND

1. *Conglomerates and the Media*, by Richard M. Cohen, The New Press, 1997, p.33.
2. "Dan Rather on Fear, Money, and the News," *Brill's Content*, Oct., 1998, p.117.
3. "The *60 Minutes* Man," Neal Gabler, *Brill's Content*, May, 2001, p.111.
4. "Universal Appeal of Schlock," by Henry Goldblatt, *Fortune*, May 12, 1997, p.32.
5. "The Whole World Isn't Watching," by A.O.Scott, *New York Times Magazine*, Jan 30, 2000, p.12.
6. "The Man Who Counts the Killings," by Scott Stossel, *Atlantic Monthly*, May, 1997, p. 37.
7. Ibid., p.36.
8. "Pro Wrestlers on TV Imitated by Children," by Beth Dailey, *San Francisco Chronicle*, Jan. 19, 2000, p.A9.
9. *Rich Media, Poor Democracy* ,by Robert W. McChesney, University of Illinois Press,1999, p.46.
10. "Researchers Shocked to find — TV Violence," by Christopher Stern, *Variety*, Apr.20-26, 1998, p. 24.
11. *Television and Behavior: Ten Years of Progress and Implementation in the Eighties*, by D. Pearl, L.Bouthelet, and J. Lazar, (eds.) National Institute of Mental Health, 1982.
12. "Harvard Study Reveals Violence in G-Rated Movies Has Increased," by Paul Farhi, *Monterey County Herald*, May 24, 2000, p.A7.
13. "Violence Sold to Youth, Says Federal Report," by Kalpana Srinivasan, *San Francisco Chronicle*, Sept. 11, 2000, p.A1.
14. "Hollywood Takes a Whipping and Loves It," by Ellen Goodman, *San Francisco Chronicle*, Sept. 14, 2000, p.A23.
15. *The Media Monopoly*, by Ben Bagdikian, Beacon Press, 1997, p.243.
16. "Kids Less Violent After Cutting Back on TV," by Ulysses Torassa, *San Francisco Chronicle*, Jan.5, 2001, p.1.
17. "The Man Who Counts the Killings," by Scott Stossel, *Atlantic Monthly*, May, 1997, p.92.
18. "My Untold Story," by Ralph Nader, *Brill's Content*, Feb. 2001, p. 154.
19. "TV Stretches Limits of Tastes: Social Change and the 20th Century," by Laurie Mifflin, *New York Times*, Apr. 6, 1999, p.A1.
20. "The Man Who Counts the Killings," by Scott Stossel," *Atlantic Monthly*, May, 1997, p.92.
21. "Vast Wasteland Strikes Again," *San Francisco Chronicle*, Jan.4, 2001, p.A24.
22. "Fox Leads TV in Profane Scenes," by Associated Press, *San Francisco Chronicle*, Dec. 16. 1999, p.B5.
23. *The Media Monopoly*, by Ben Bagdikian, Beacon Press, 1997, p.244.
24. "Money Lust: How Pressure for Profit is Perverting Journalism," by Neil Hickey, *Columbia Journalism Review*, July/Aug, 1998, p. 29.
25. *Toxic Sludge is Good for You: Lies, Damn Lies and the Public Relations Industry,* by John Stauber and Sheldon Rampton, Common Courage Press, 1995, p.291.
26. "Keeping Up With the Trumps," by Juliet B. Schor, *Washington Monthly*, July/Aug. 1998, p. 35.
27. "Former Model Examines Evils of Ads," by Greg Farrell *USA Today*, Jan.31, 2000, p.6B.
28. *American Culture, American Tastes: Social Change and the 20th Century,* by Michael Kammen, Alfred A. Knopf, p.192.
29. "As the Dial Turns," by Douglas Gomrey, *Wilson Quarterly*, Autumn, 1993, p.42.6.
30. *Rich Media, Poor Democracy*, by Robert W. McChesney, University of Illinois Press, 1999, p. 38.

31. "Nice TV," by Jim Edwards, *Brill's Content*, Mar. 2001, p.90
32. Ibid., p.71.
33. *Commercial Culture, The Media System and the Public Interest,* by Leo Bogart, Oxford University Press, 1995, p. 169.
34. "Who Said TV Wasn't Educational?" by Nick Gillespie, *New York Times*. July 11, 1999.
35. "The Corporate Takeover of News," by Richard M. Cohen, in *Conglomerates and the Media,* The New Press, 1997, p.33.
36. *When MBAs Rule the Newsroom,* by Doug Underwood, Columbia University Press, 1993, p.132.
37. "The Journalism Dean Searches for Intelligent Life in the Media," by Russell Schoch, *California Monthly,* Nov.1998, p.25.
38. "Conglomerates and Newspapers," by Gene Roberts, in *Conglomerates and the Media,* p.65.
39. Ibid., p.33.
40. *Extra! Update,* June, 1998, p.1.
41. "The Crushing Power of Big Publishing," by Marc Crispin Million, The *Nation,* Mar.17, 1997, pp.11-18.
42. "Study Sees Papers as Biased," by Susan Sward, *San Francisco Chronicle*, Dec. 16, 1998.
43. "The Media's Credibility Gap," *Newsweek*, July 20, 1998, p.25.
44. "Money Lust: How Pressure for Profit is Perverting Journalism," by Neil Hickey, *Columbia Journalism Review*, July/Aug., 1998, p.33.
45. "Buried Alive: Our Children and the Avalanche of Crud," by David Denby, *New Yorker*, July 15, 1996, p.57.
46. *Commercial Culture, The Media System and the Public Interest,* by Leo Bogart, Oxford University Press, 1995, p. 136.

CONCLUSION – WHAT CAN WE DO

1. "Net Comes of Age," by Christopher Matthews, *Quill Magazine,* Dec. 1998, p.16.
2. *Broadcasting & Cable,* June 22, 1998.
3. *The Global Media: The New Missionaries of Global Capitalism,* by Edward S. Herman and Robert W. McChesney, Cassell, 1997, p.195.
4. "Democratizing the Media," by Ronnie Dugger, *Nation Magazine,* Nov. 24, 1997, p.6.
5. *Rich Media, Poor Democracy,* by Robert W. McChesney, University of Illinois Press, 1999, p.312.
6. *It's the Media, Stupid,* by John Nichols and Robert W. McChesney, Seven Stories Press, 2000, p.12.
7. *Networks of Power,* by Dennis W. Mazzocco, South End Press, 1994, p.158.
8. Ibid., p.163.
9. Ibid., p. 162.
10. *The Global Media: The New Missionaries of Global Capitalism,* by Edward S. Herman and Robert W. McChesney, Cassell, 1997, p. 205.

PHOTO BY WEI H. CHANG

ABOUT THE AUTHORS

Chicago-born **Rod Holmgren** has been a journalist since he won a high school essay contest in 1931. While a senior at Northwestern University's Medill School of Journalism, he produced all the university's radio programs. He won the Harrington Memorial Award as the outstanding student in his journalism class.

He was news editor for WOI, Iowa State College's radio station, and KSO, the Des Moines Register station, and then joined the staff of the "Air Edition of the Chicago Sun." During World War II, he was a regional director of the Domestic Radio Bueau, Office of War Information. After the war, he was "Labor's Own Commentator" on WCFL, the Chicago Federation of Labor station.

In the 1950s, he edited *The Union,* an international labor paper based in Denver. After obtaining an MA in journalism at the University of California, Berkeley, he taught journalism at Monterey Peninsula College for 20 years. In his first sabbatical year, 1966-67, he was a Fulbright Lecturer in Journalism at Kabul University in Afghanistan. In 1972, he joined William Norton in producing *The Mass Media Book,* published by Prentice-Hall.

Since retirement in 1979, he has taught in Beijing, China, three times — in 1982-83 at the Graduate Institute of Journalism, in 1986 at Beijing Broadcasting Institute, and again in 1991 at BBI.

From 1993 to 1995, he lectured on the American media for the Elderhostel program, "Arts and Humanities Seminars," in San Francisco. He currently lives in Carmel, California.

Alma Oberst Holmgren grew up in Owensboro, Ky., before moving to Indiana to work on The Evansville Press. She worked in various capacities from editorial secretary to Amusements and Promotion Editor for Scripps-Howard, now E. W. Scripps, for 21 years in Evansville and San Francisco.

She was administrative assistant to the editor and book editor of The San Francisco News, then with the News-Call-Bulletin until it was sold wholly to Hearst. She returned to college for a master's in Journalism at U.C.Berkeley and taught Journalism at Contra Costa College in San Pablo, CA for 16 years. She was named Journalism Teacher of the Year by the California Newspaper Publishers Association in 1997. During the summers she continued graduate study at the University of Valencia, the Sorbonne and Stanford.

After retirement, she wrote a weekly travel and food column for the West County Times for six years and edited newsletters for the California State Friends of the Library, the East Bay chapter of the Native Plant Society, the Monterey Peninsula's New Forum and founded Symphony Notes, a monthly newsletter for the Volunteer Council of the San Francisco Symphony.

Honors include a summer as a Wall Street Journal seminarian at the University of Minnesota and participation at a Wilton Park Conference at Wiston House in England.